Translator : Jay Chung

Editor : Kevin P. Croall

Production Artist : Mei Chun Cheng

US Cover Design : Mei Chun Cheng

Production Manager : Janice Chang

Art Director : Yuki Chung

Marketing : Shawn Sanders

President : Robin Kuo

Publisher
ComicsOne Corporation
48531 Warm Springs Blvd., Suite 408
Fremont, CA 94539
www.ComicsOne.com

First Edition: October 2004
ISBN 1-58899-331-0

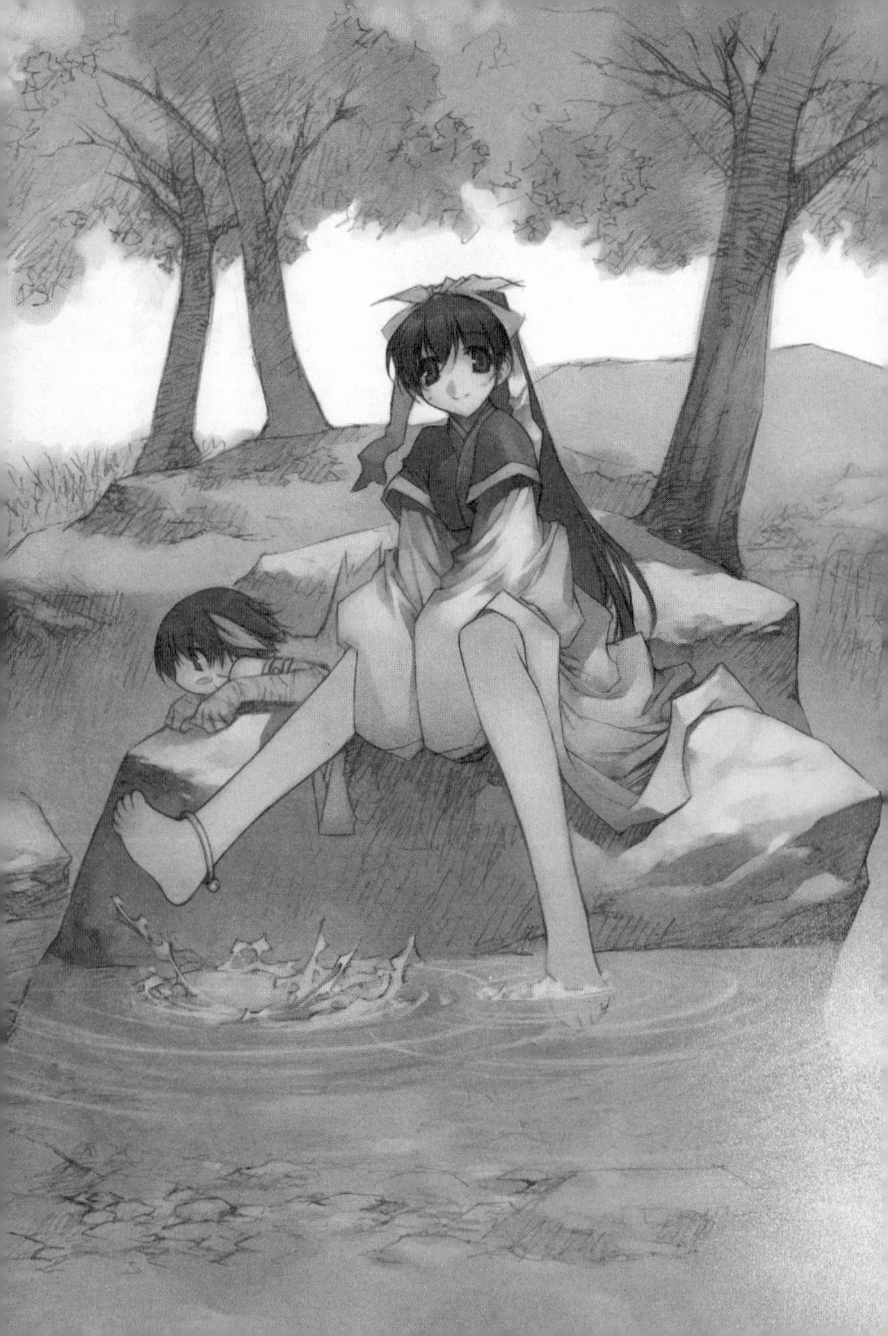

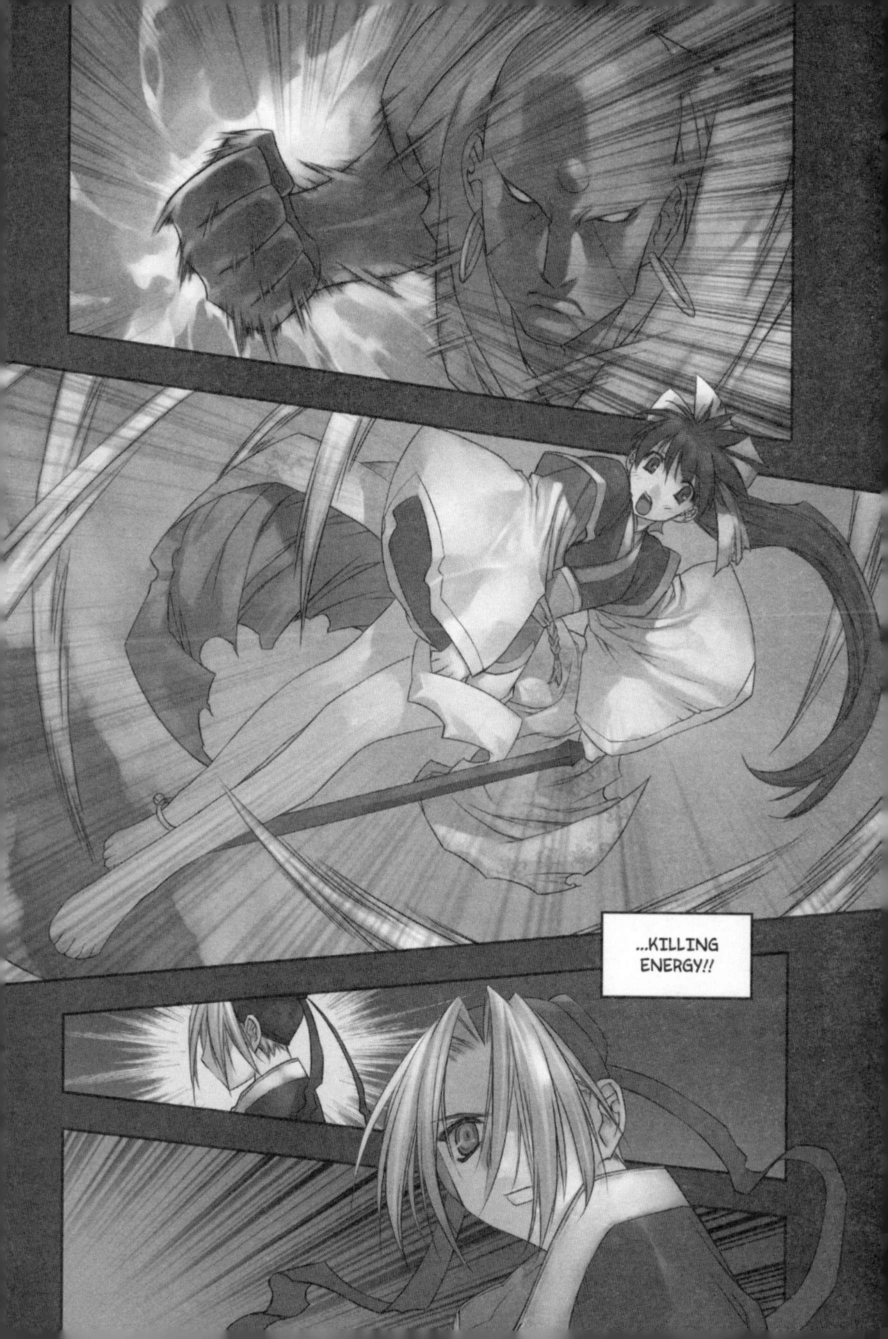
...KILLING ENERGY!!

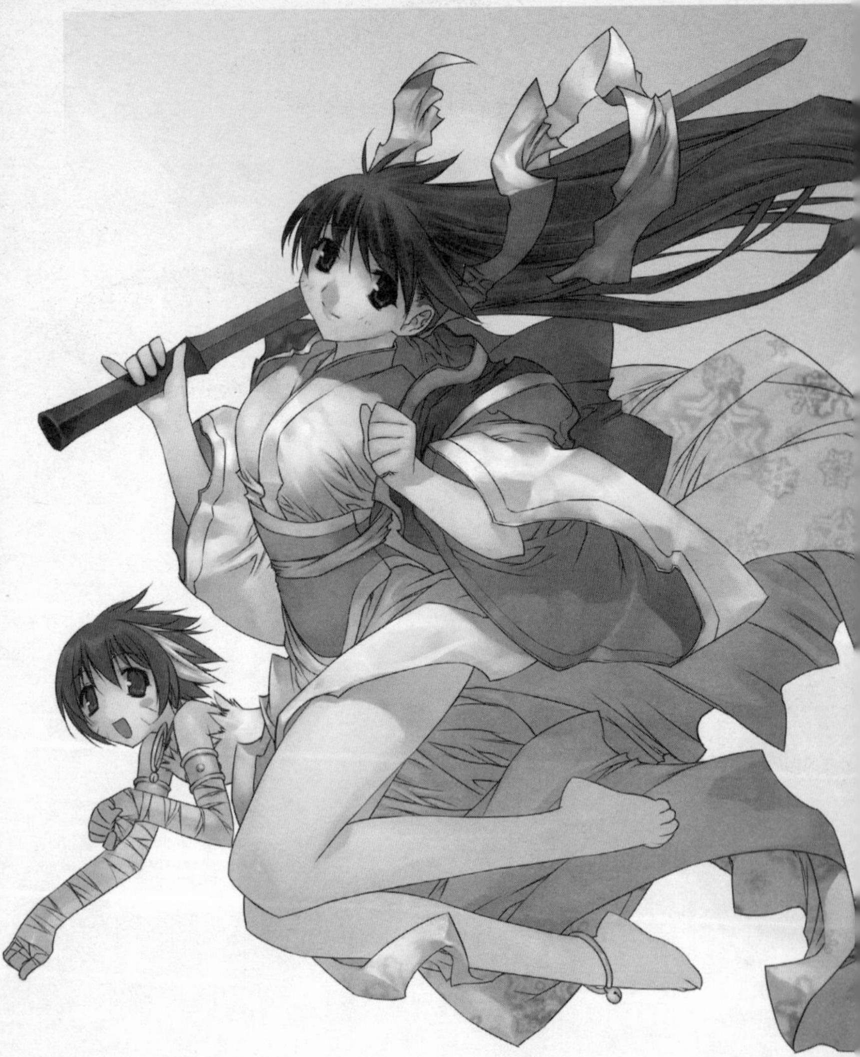

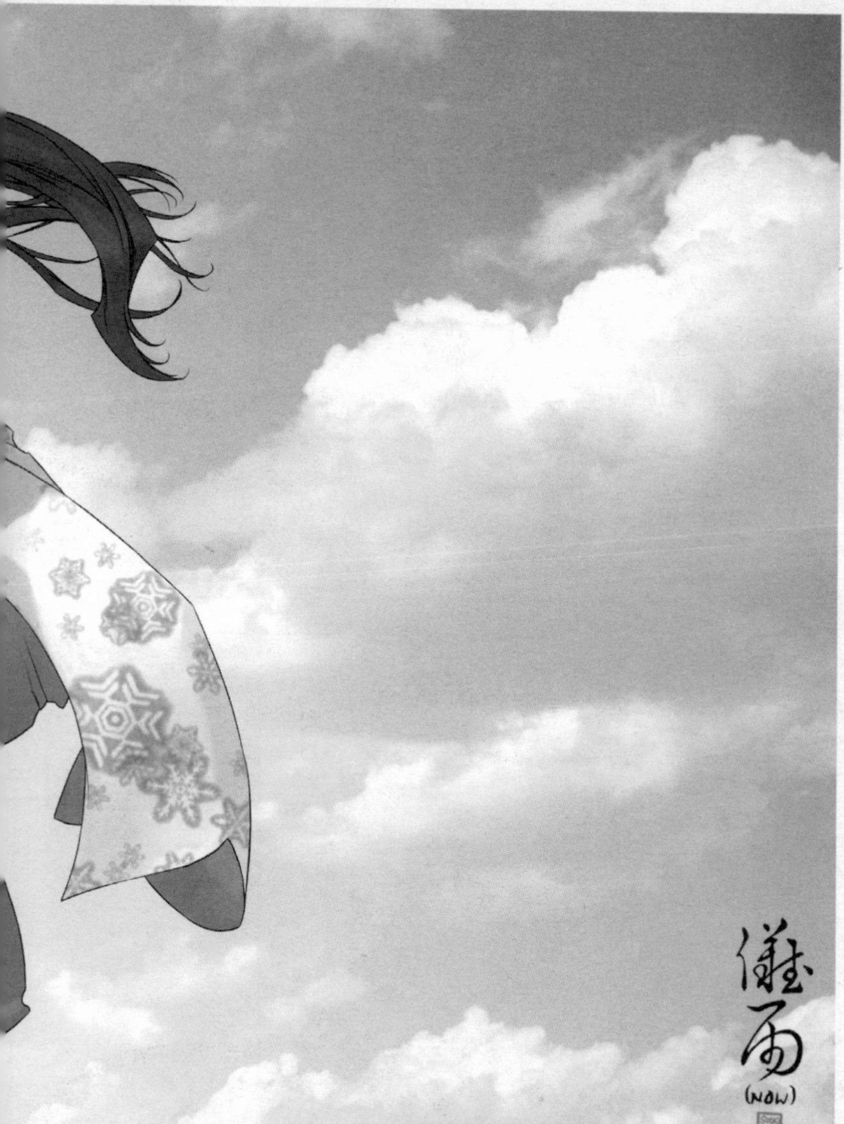
(NOW)

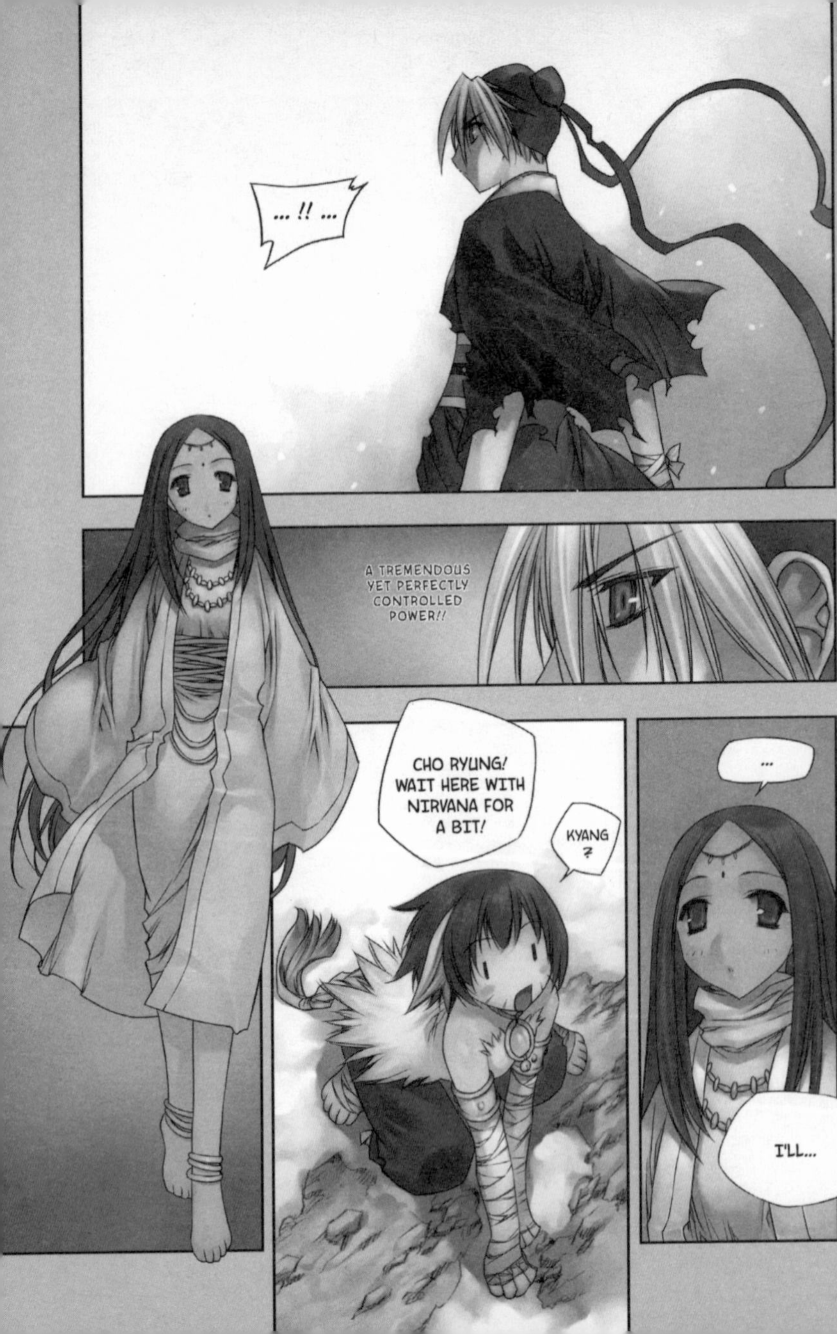

... !! ...
A TREMENDOUS YET PERFECTLY CONTROLLED POWER!!
...
CHO RYUNG! WAIT HERE WITH NIRVANA FOR A BIT!
KYANG ?
I'LL...

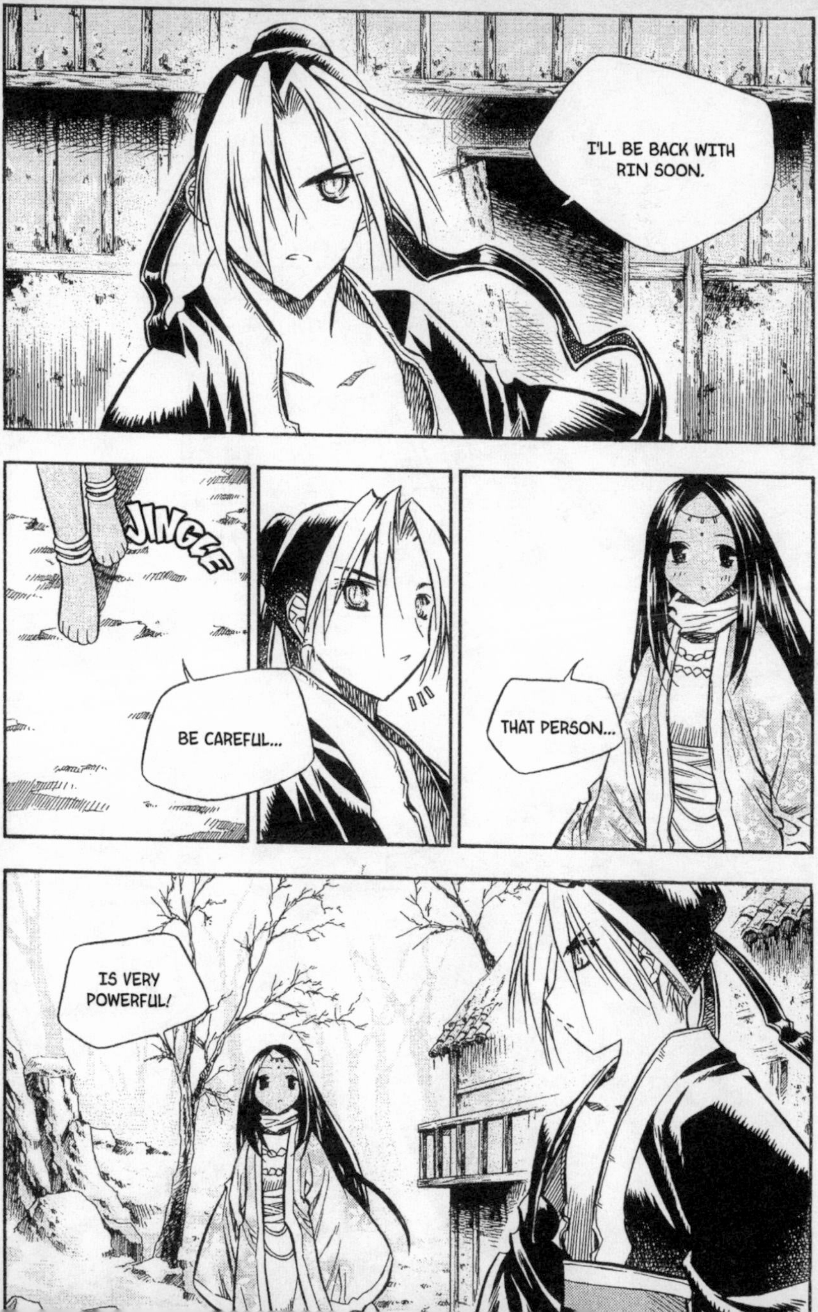
I'LL BE BACK WITH RIN SOON.
JINGLE
BE CAREFUL...
THAT PERSON...
IS VERY POWERFUL!

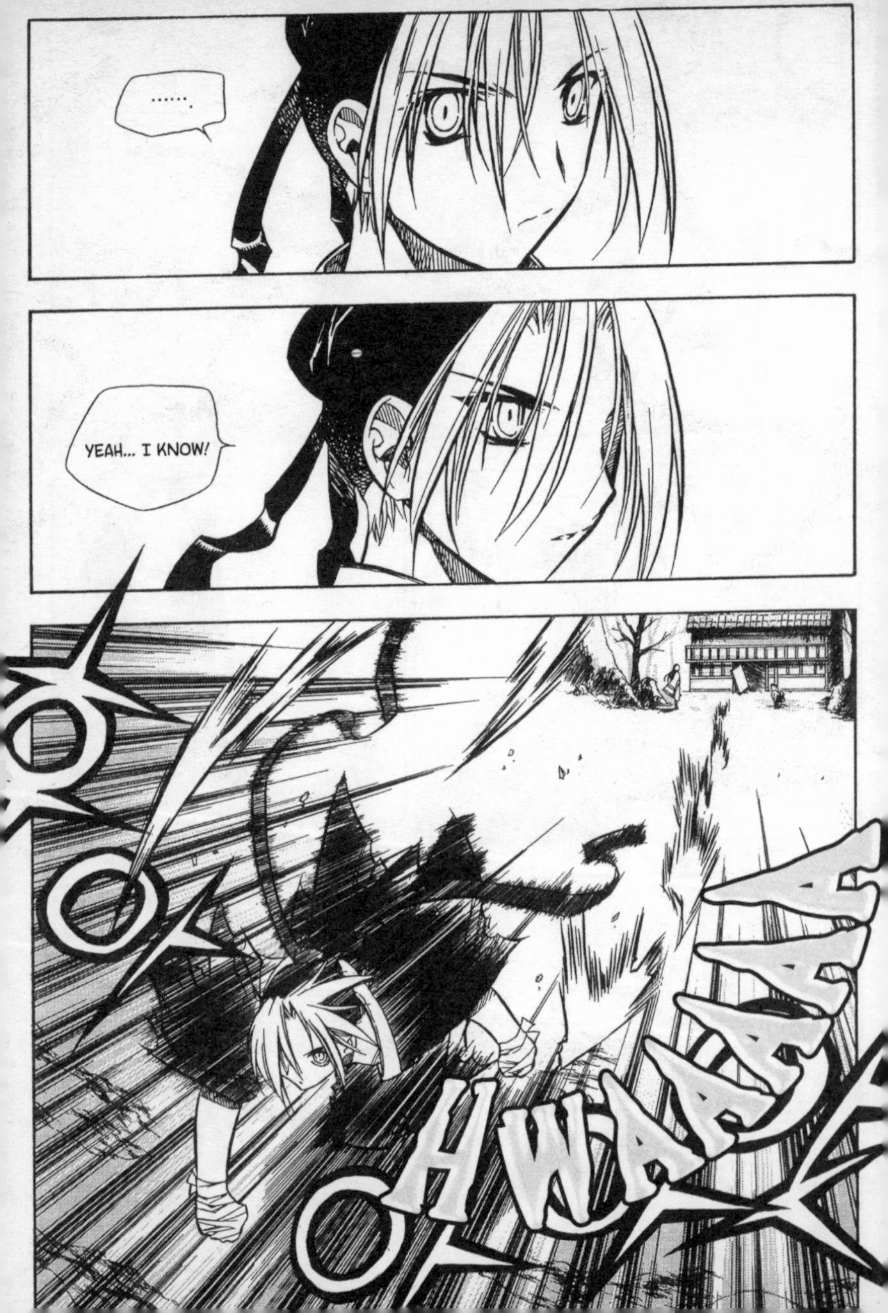
....
YEAH... I KNOW!
HWAAAAA

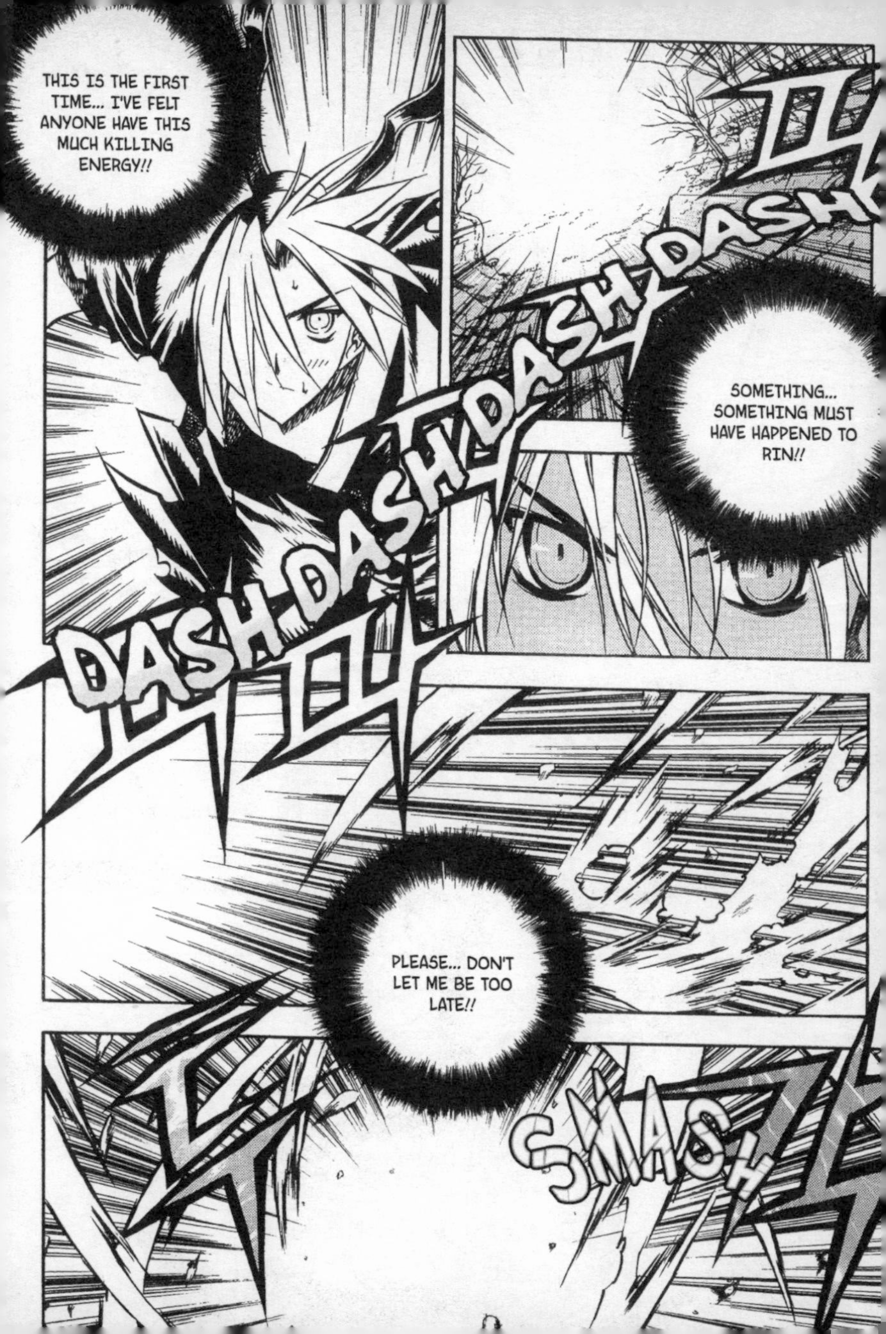
THIS IS THE FIRST TIME... I'VE FELT ANYONE HAVE THIS MUCH KILLING ENERGY!!
DASH DASH DASH DASH DASH
SOMETHING... SOMETHING MUST HAVE HAPPENED TO RIN!!
PLEASE... DON'T LET ME BE TOO LATE!!
SMASH

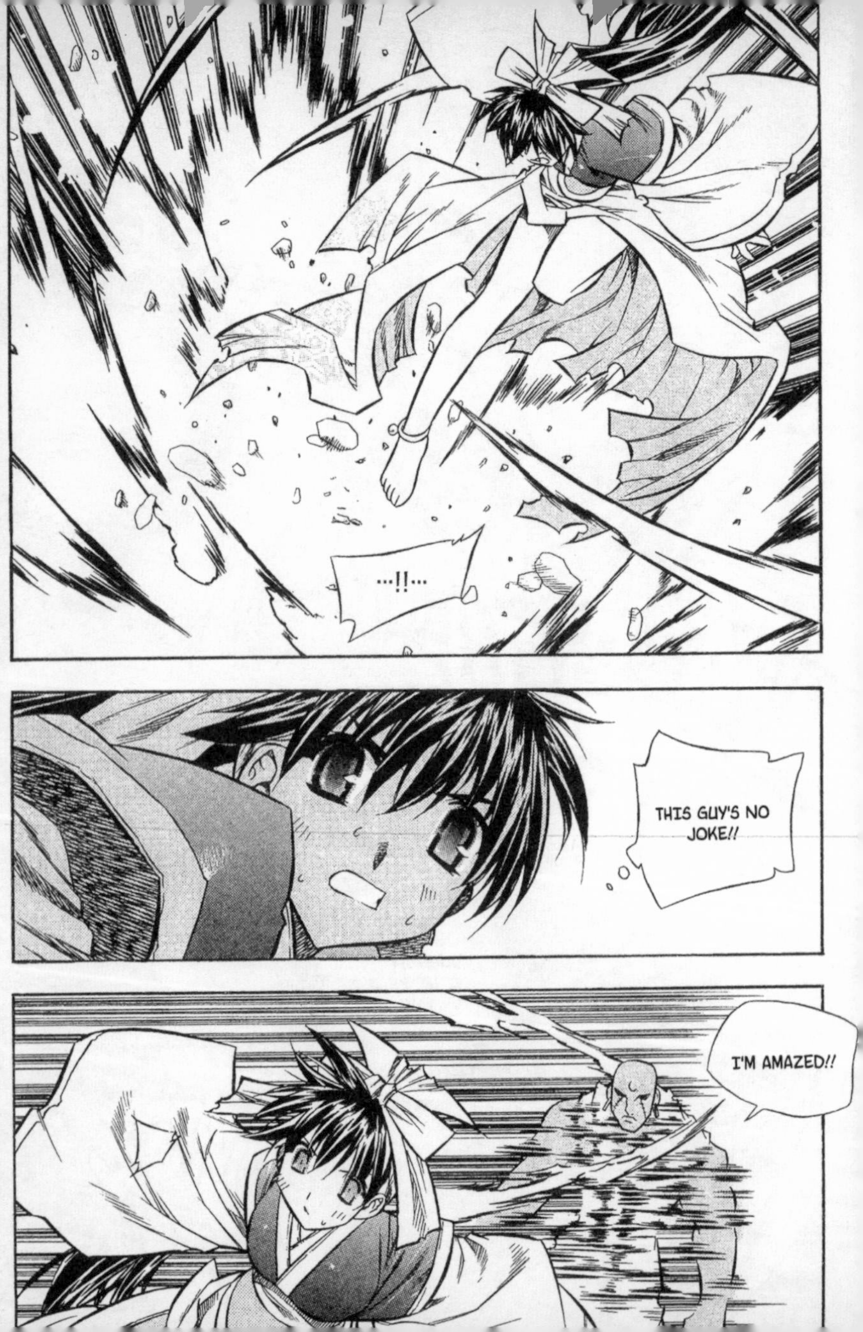
...!!...
THIS GUY'S NO JOKE!!
I'M AMAZED!!

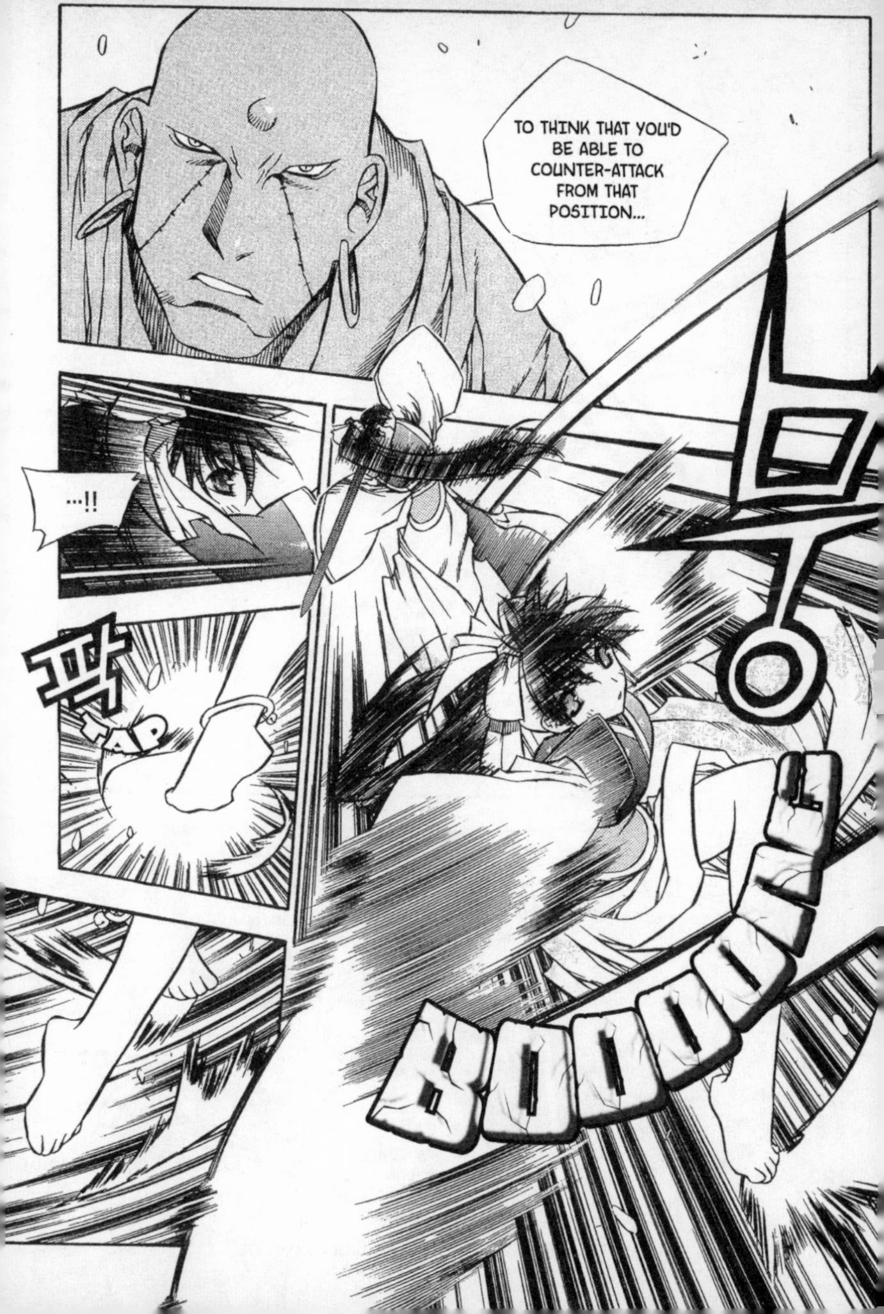
TO THINK THAT YOU'D BE ABLE TO COUNTER-ATTACK FROM THAT POSITION...
...!!
TAP

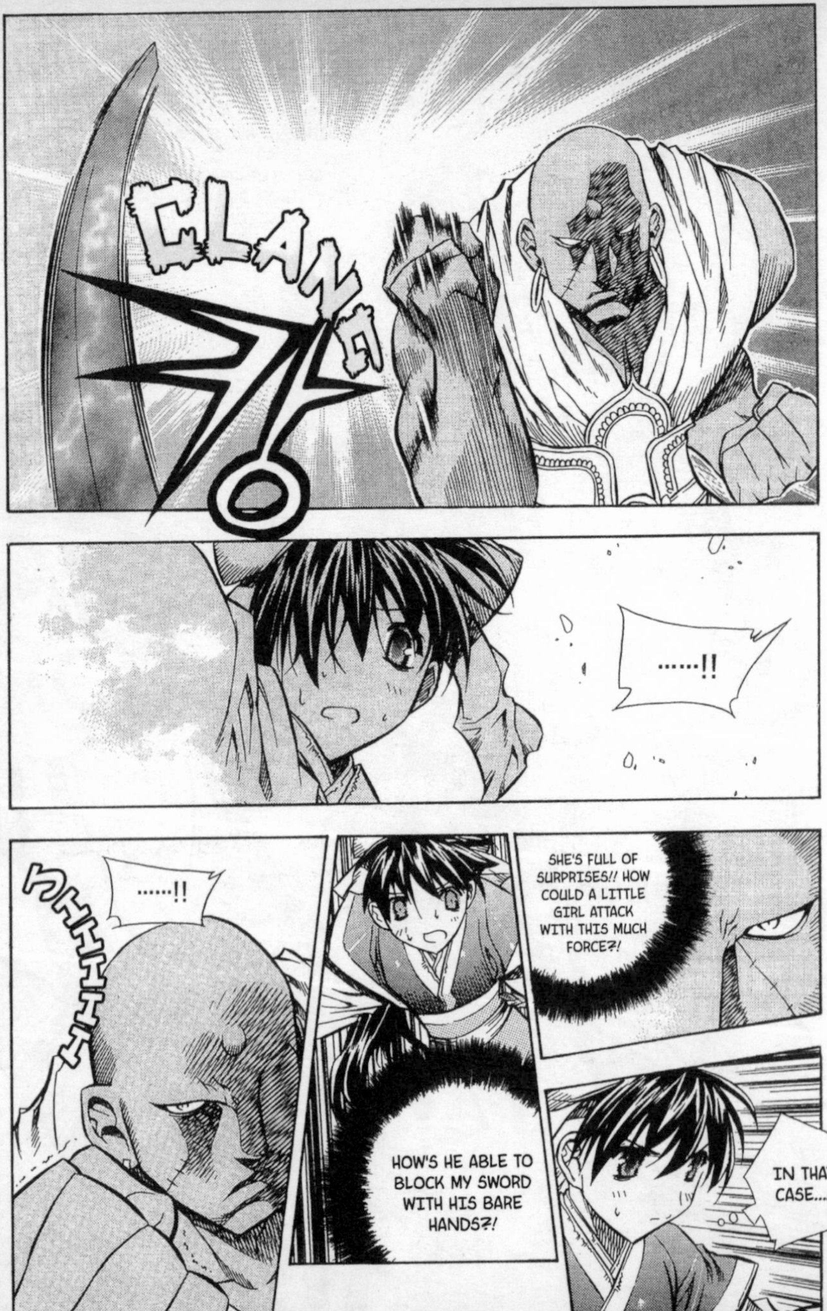
CLANG
......!!
SHE'S FULL OF SURPRISES!! HOW COULD A LITTLE GIRL ATTACK WITH THIS MUCH FORCE?!
IN THAT CASE...!
HOW'S HE ABLE TO BLOCK MY SWORD WITH HIS BARE HANDS?!
......!!

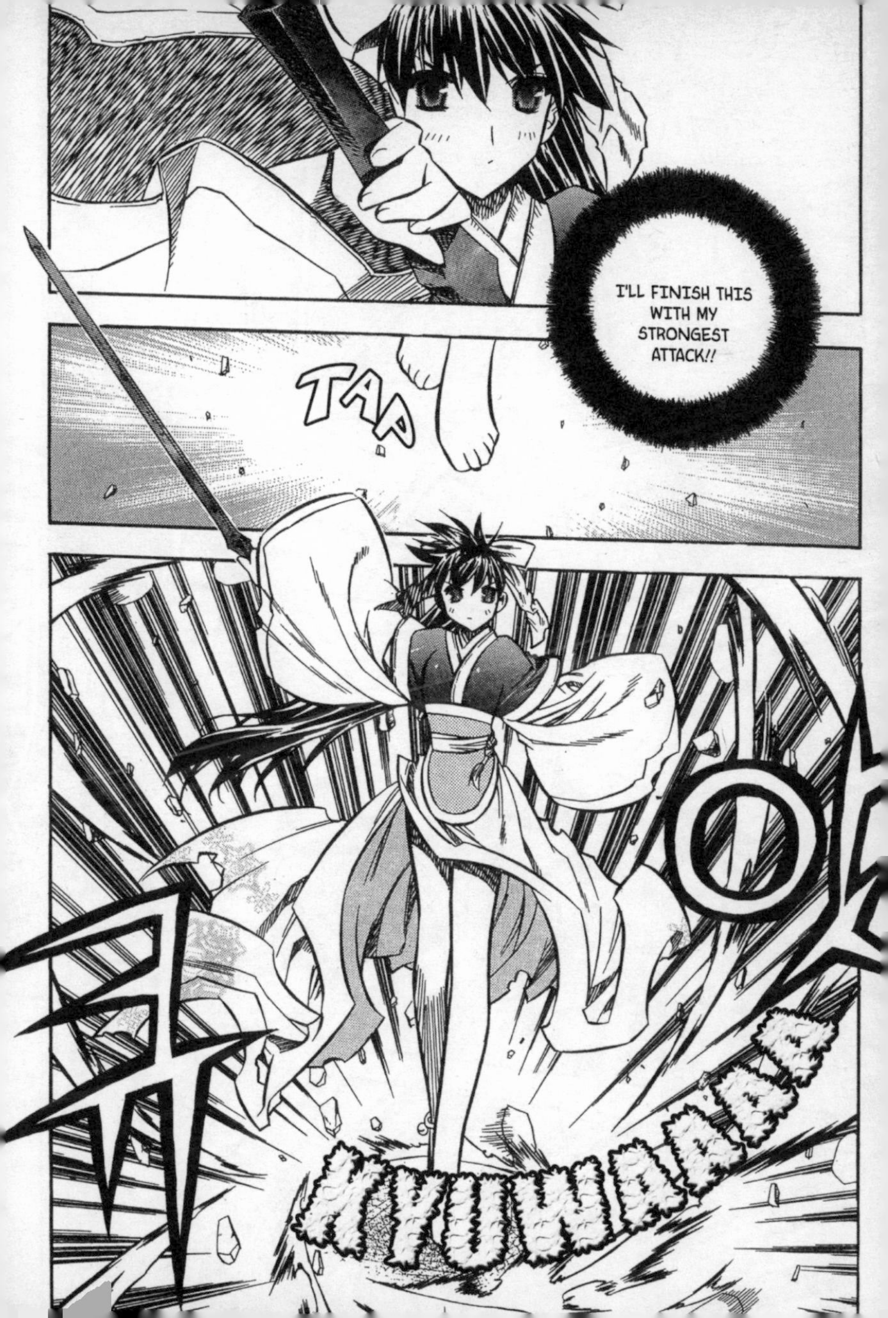
I'LL FINISH THIS WITH MY STRONGEST ATTACK!!
TAP

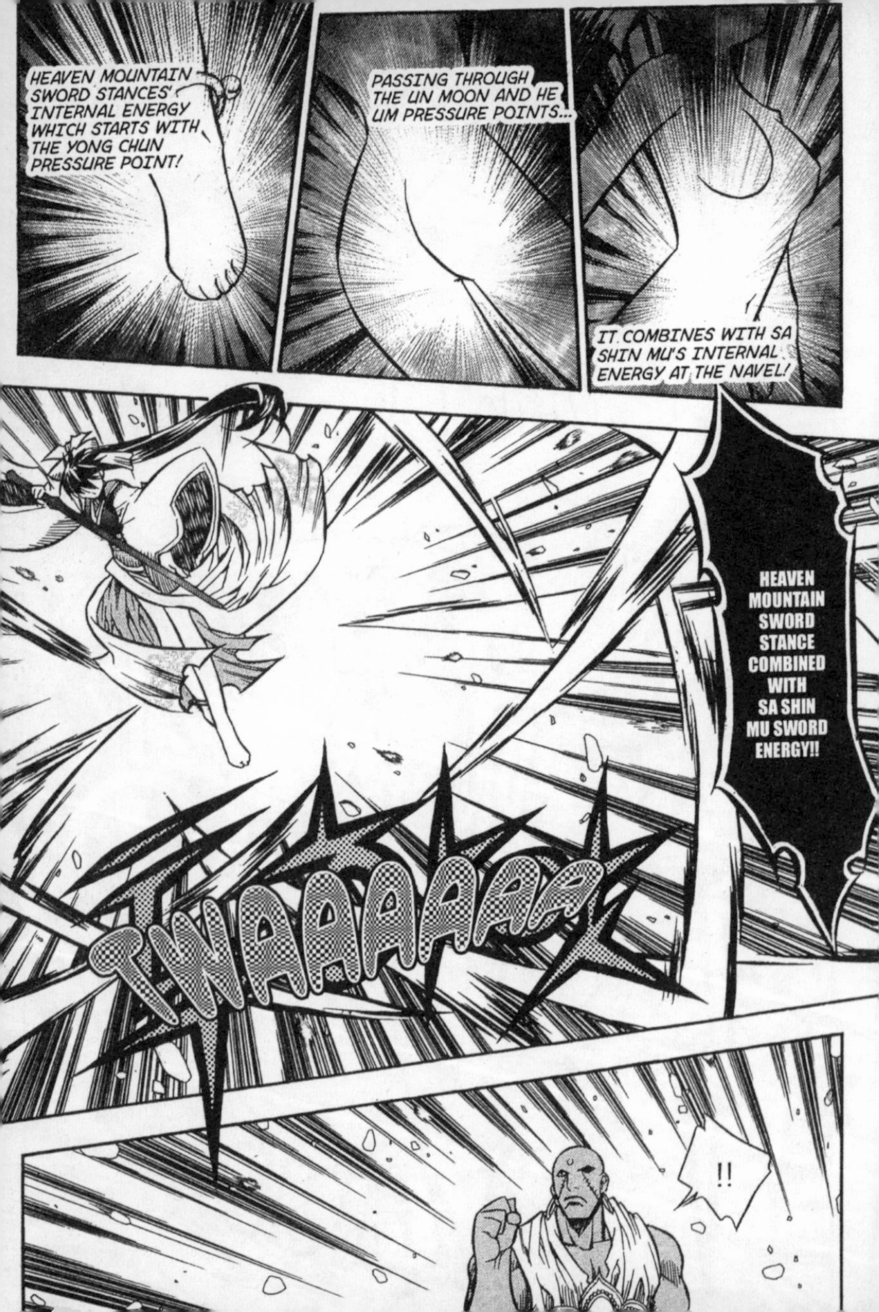
HEAVEN MOUNTAIN SWORD STANCES' INTERNAL ENERGY WHICH STARTS WITH THE YONG CHUN PRESSURE POINT!
PASSING THROUGH THE UN MOON AND HE UM PRESSURE POINTS...
IT COMBINES WITH SA SHIN MU'S INTERNAL ENERGY AT THE NAVEL!
HEAVEN MOUNTAIN SWORD STANCE COMBINED WITH SA SHIN MU SWORD ENERGY!!
TWAAAAAAA
!!

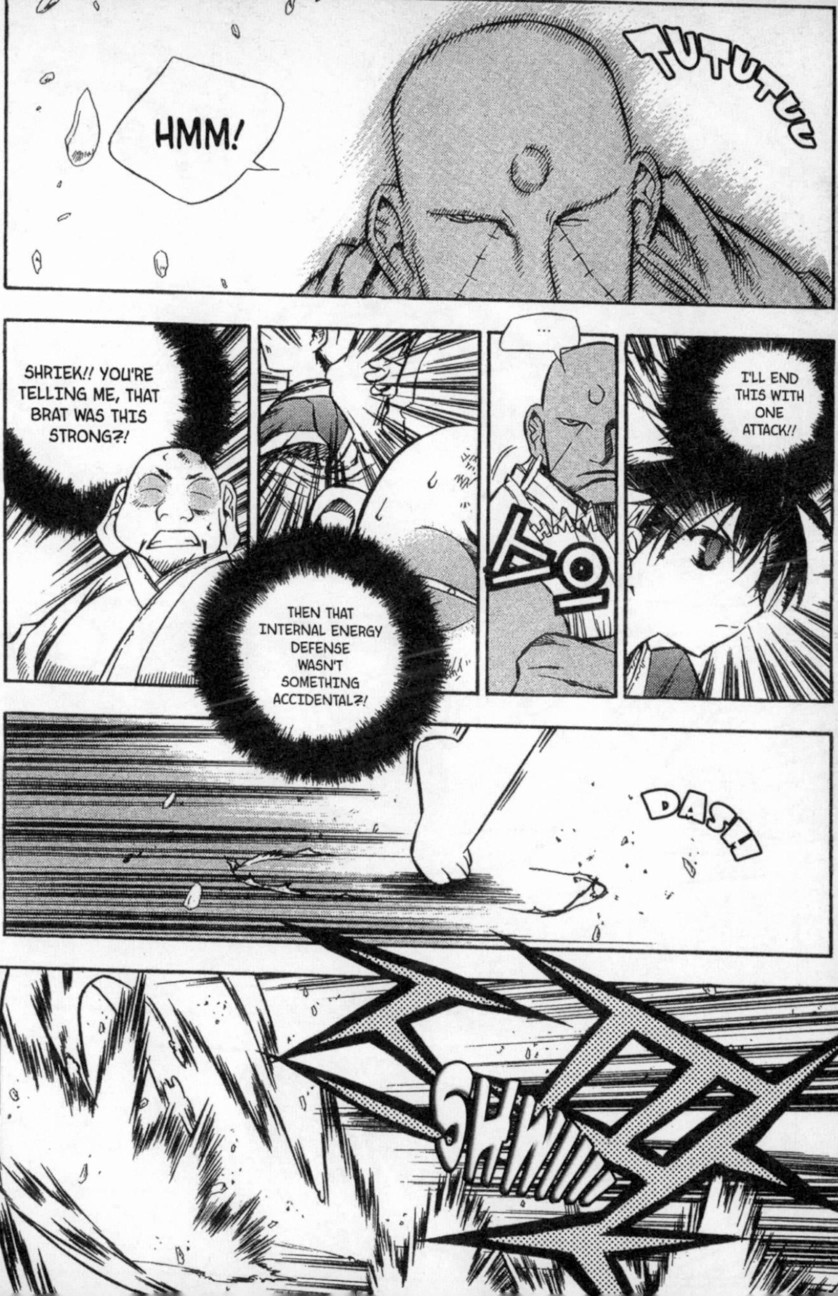
HMM!
TUTUTUU
SHRIEK!! YOU'RE TELLING ME, THAT BRAT WAS THIS STRONG?!
THEN THAT INTERNAL ENERGY DEFENSE WASN'T SOMETHING ACCIDENTAL?!
...
I'LL END THIS WITH ONE ATTACK!!
DASH
SHWIII

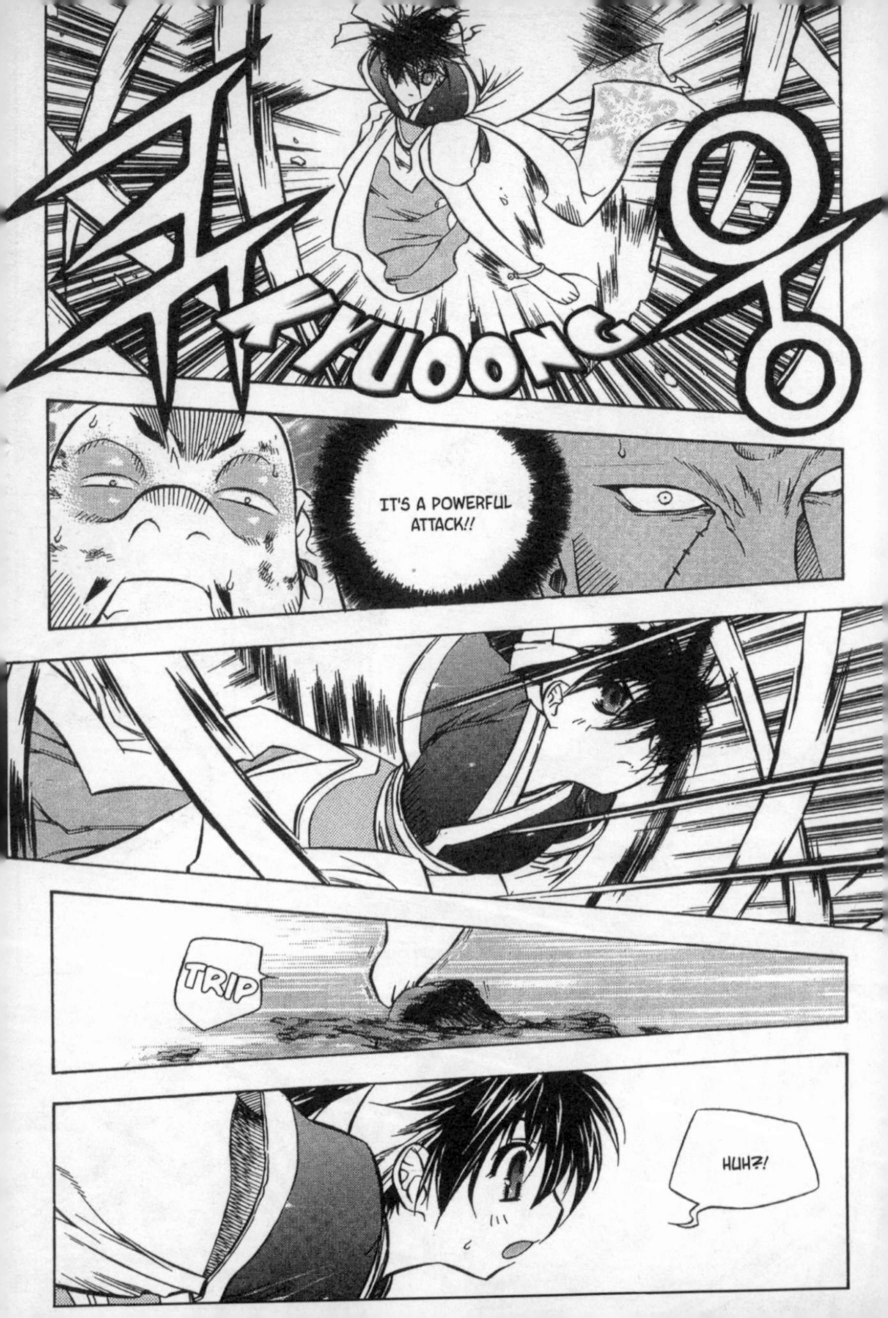
KYUOONG
IT'S A POWERFUL ATTACK!!
TRIP
HUH?!

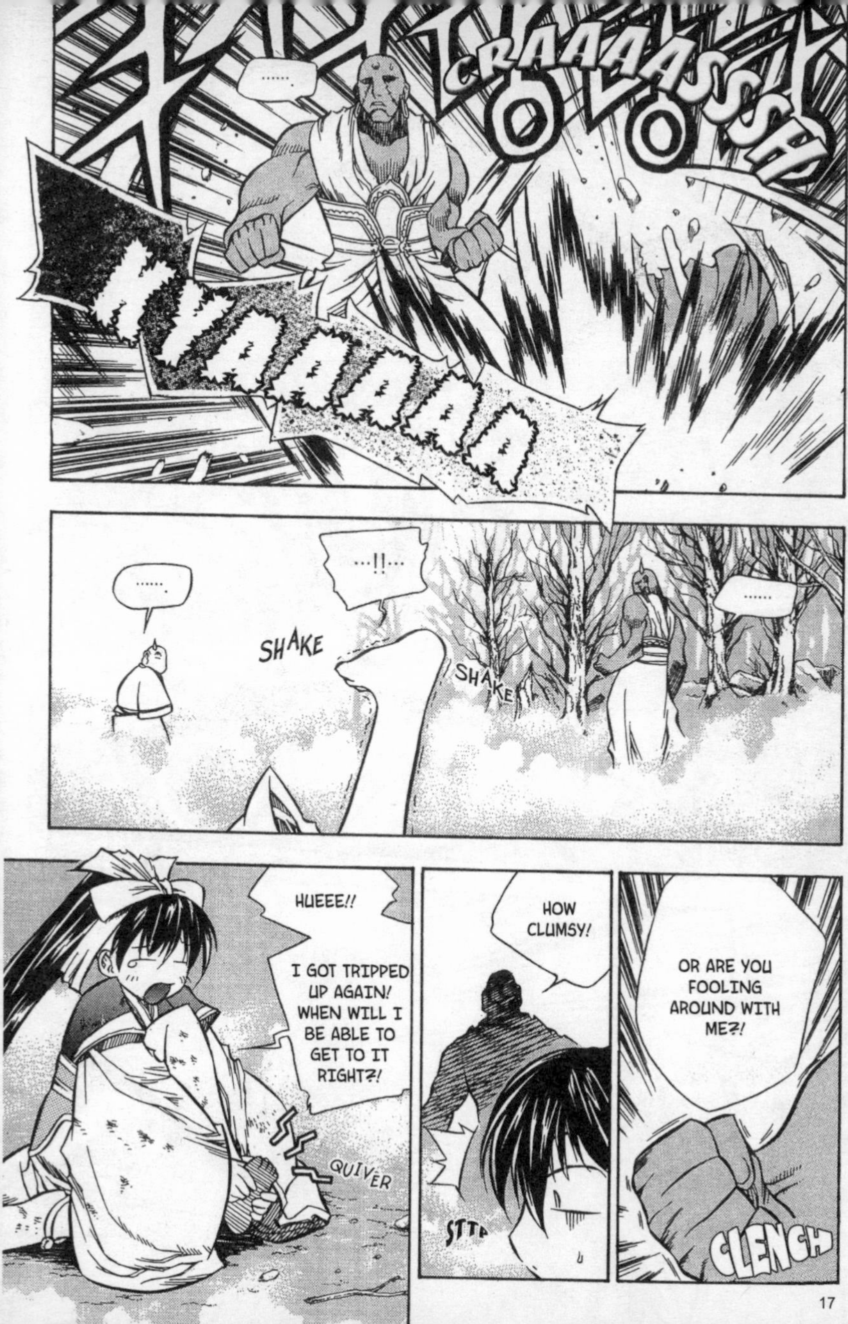

CRAAAASSH
....
......
...!!...
SHAKE
SHAKE
....
OR ARE YOU FOOLING AROUND WITH ME?!
CLENCH
HOW CLUMSY!
HUEEE!!
I GOT TRIPPED UP AGAIN! WHEN WILL I BE ABLE TO GET TO IT RIGHT?!
QUIVER

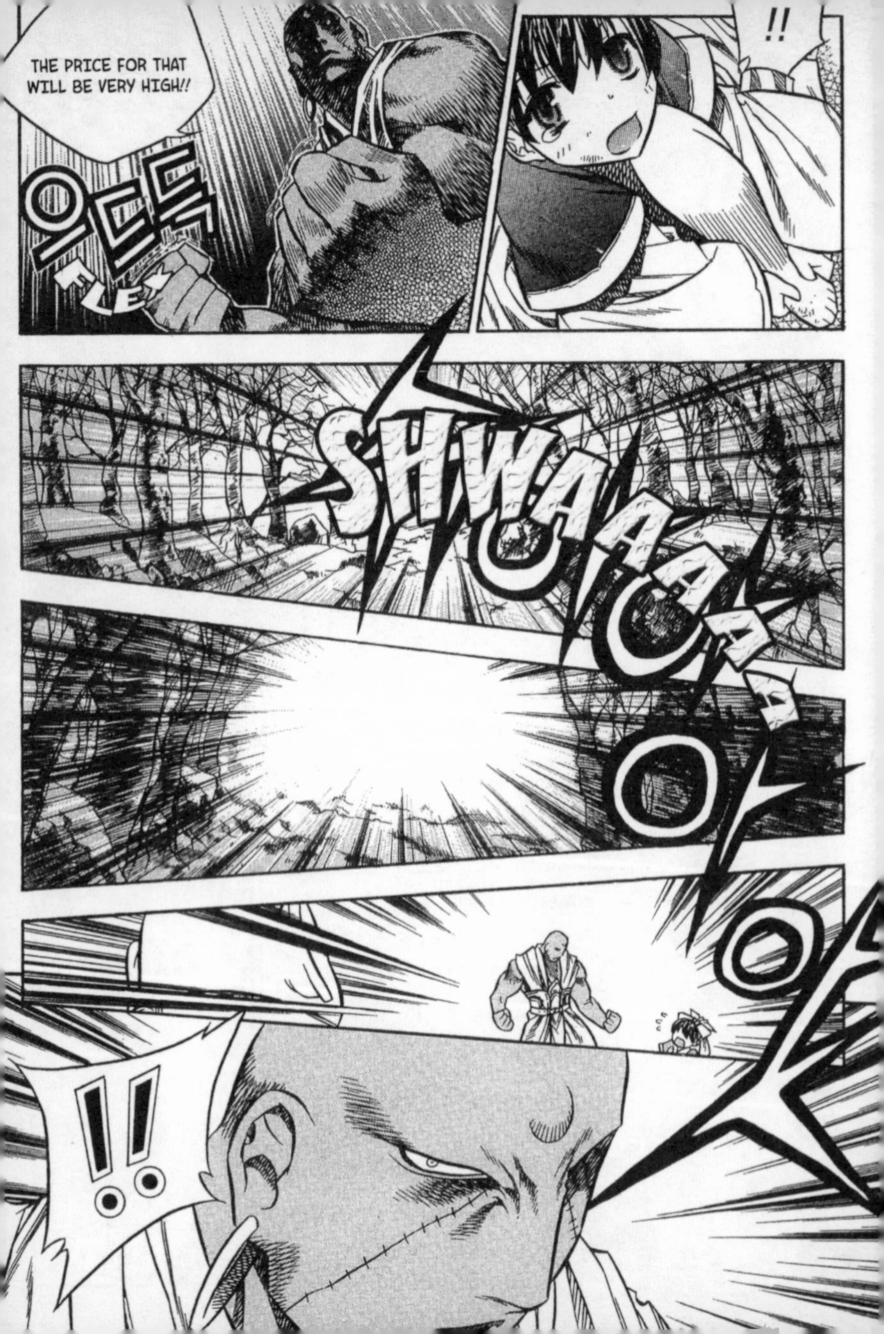
!!
THE PRICE FOR THAT WILL BE VERY HIGH!!
FLEX
SHWAAAAOOO
!!

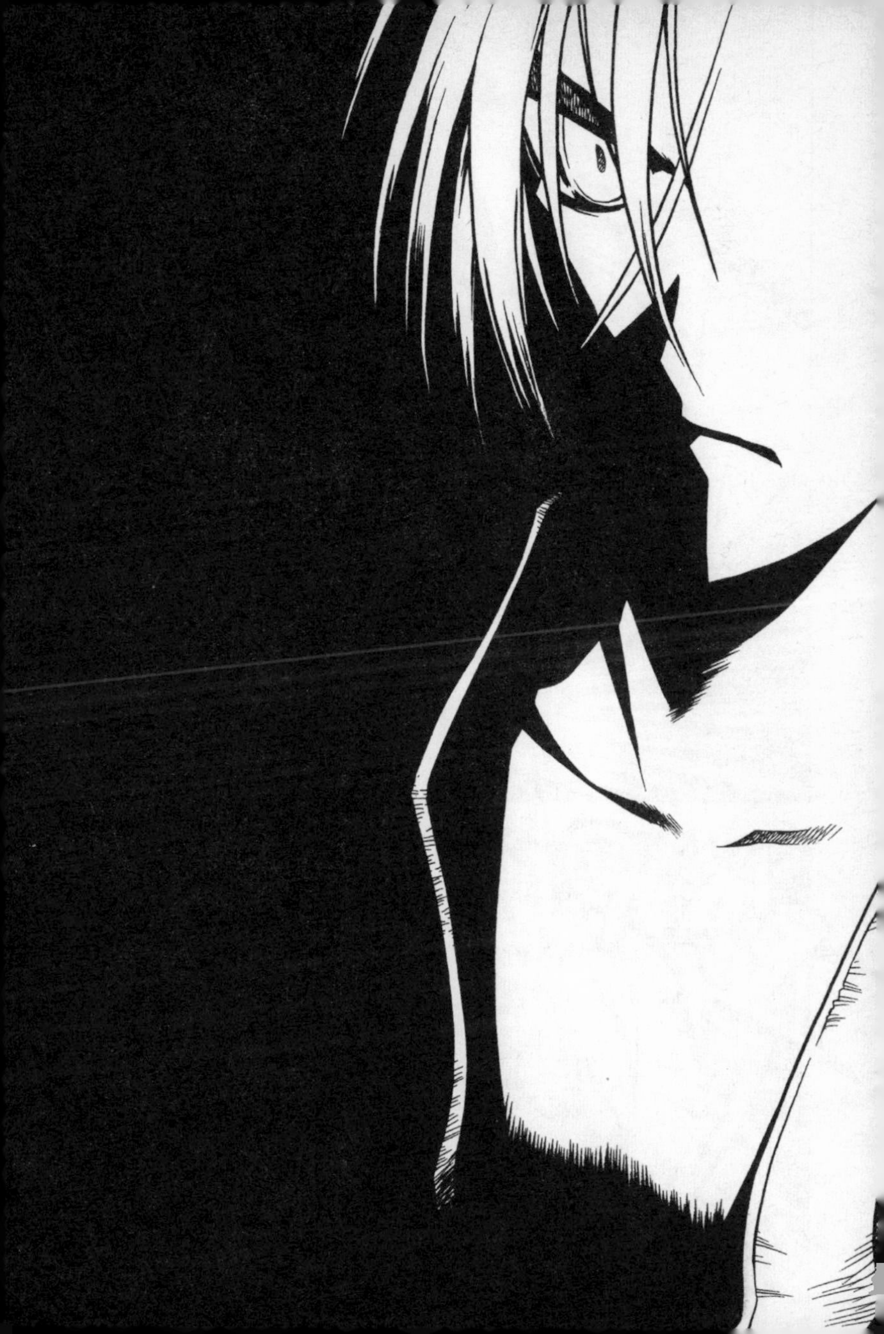

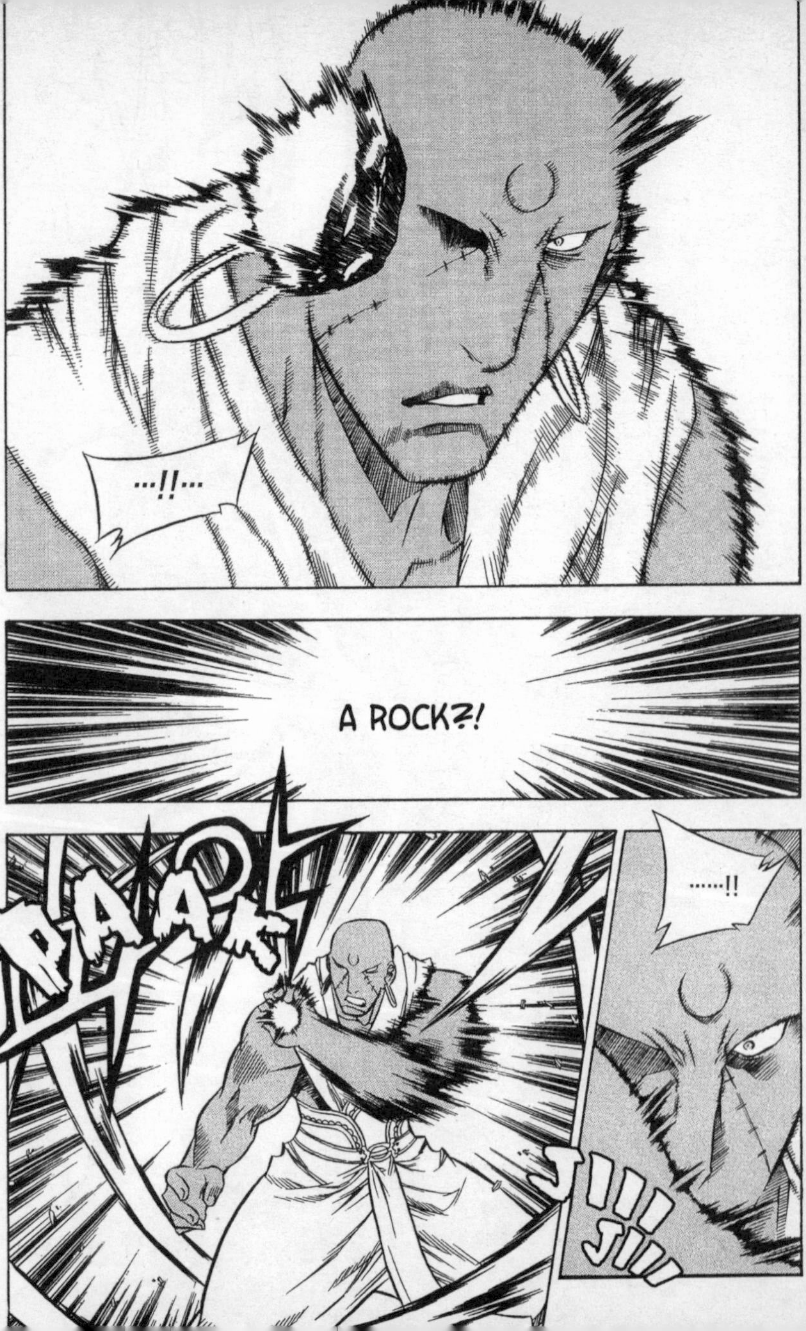

...!!...
A ROCK?!
......!!
PAAK
JIII JIII

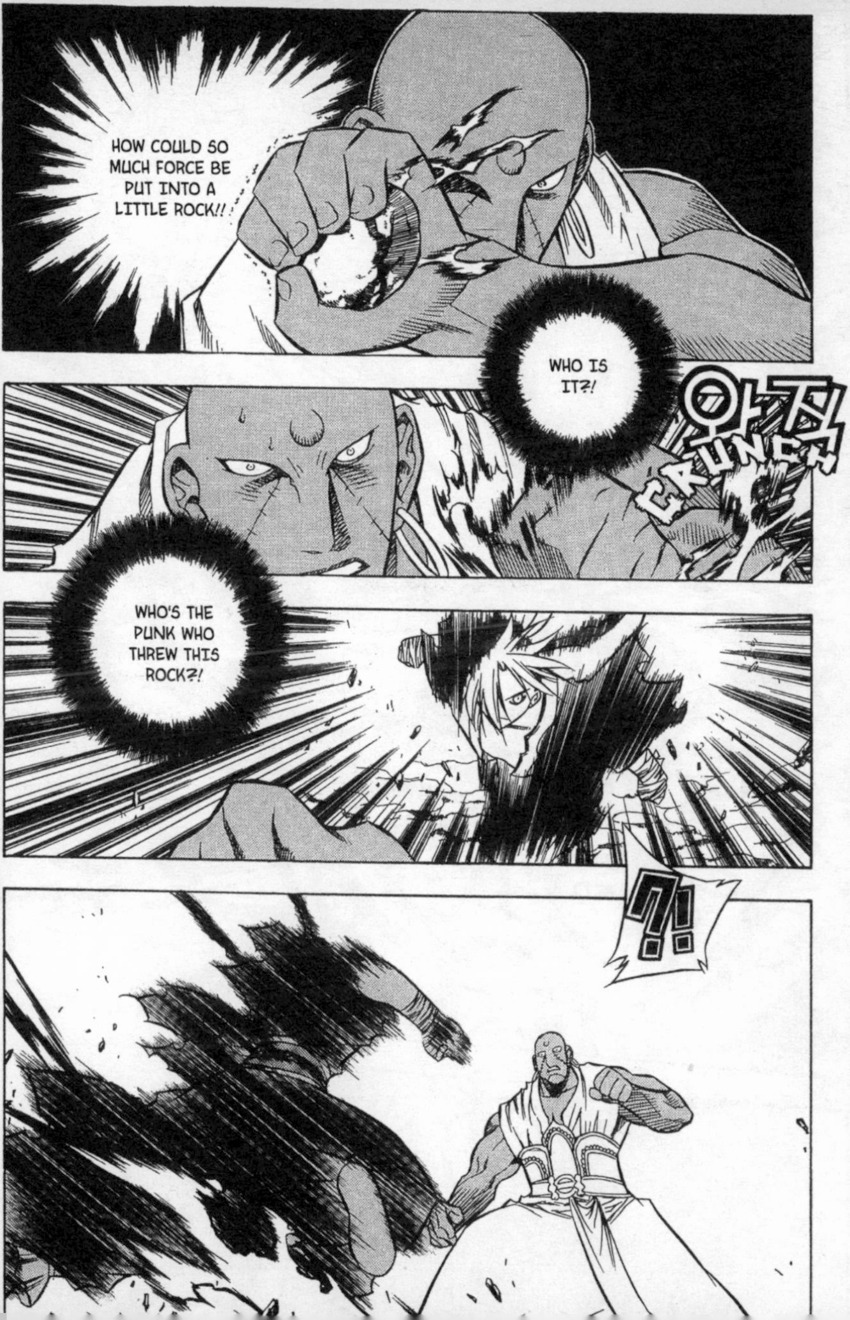
HOW COULD SO MUCH FORCE BE PUT INTO A LITTLE ROCK!!
WHO IS IT?!
CRUNCH
WHO'S THE PUNK WHO THREW THIS ROCK?!
?!

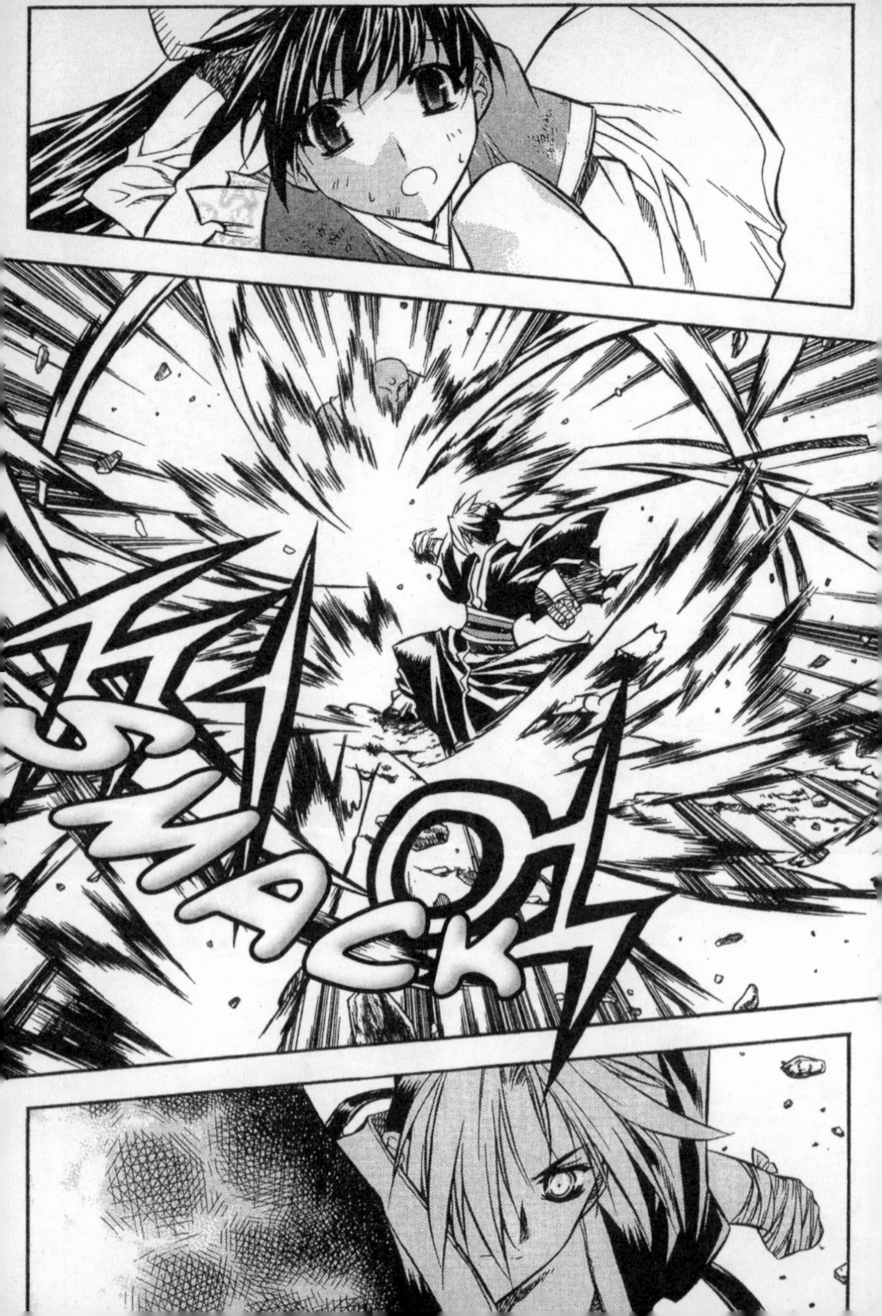
SMACK

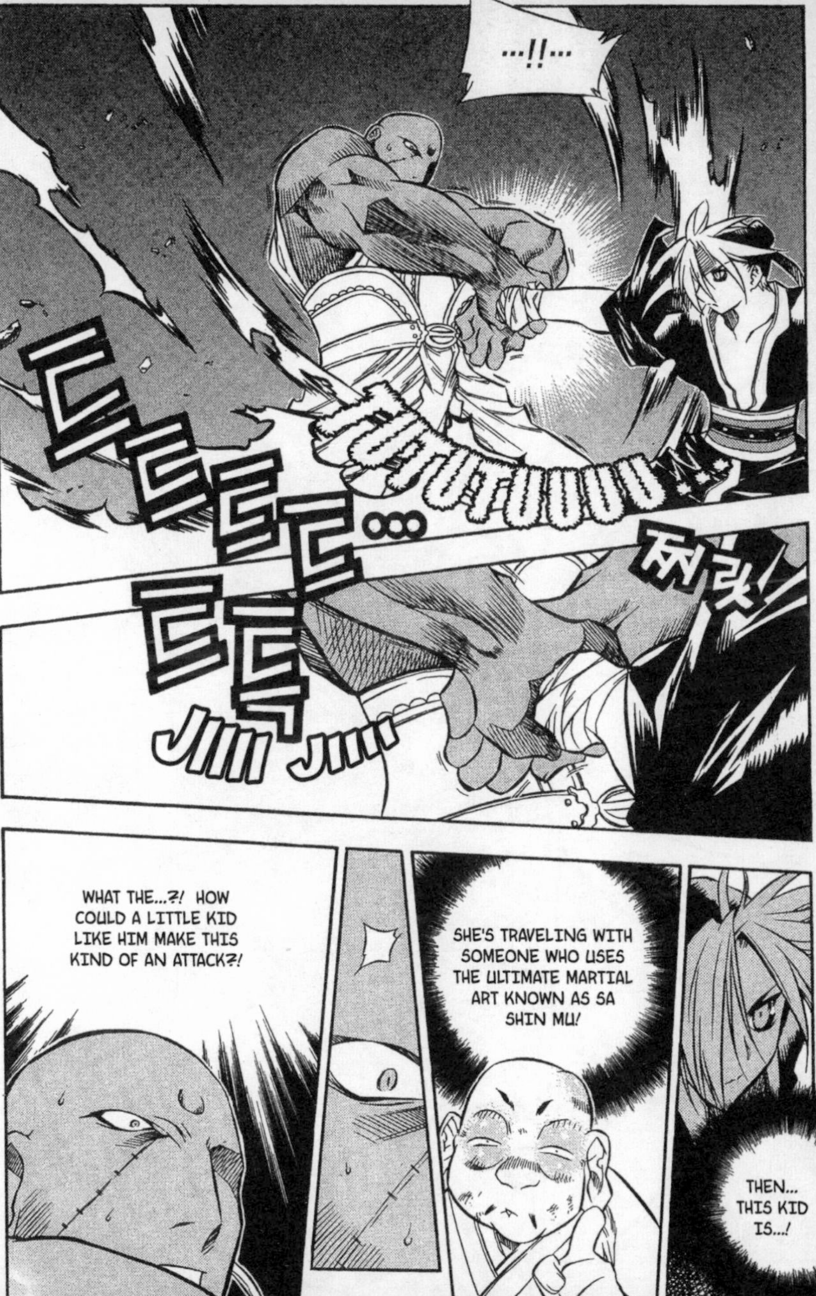
...!!...
TUTUTUUUUU..!!
JIII JIIII
THEN... THIS KID IS...!
SHE'S TRAVELING WITH SOMEONE WHO USES THE ULTIMATE MARTIAL ART KNOWN AS SA SHIN MU!
WHAT THE...?! HOW COULD A LITTLE KID LIKE HIM MAKE THIS KIND OF AN ATTACK?!

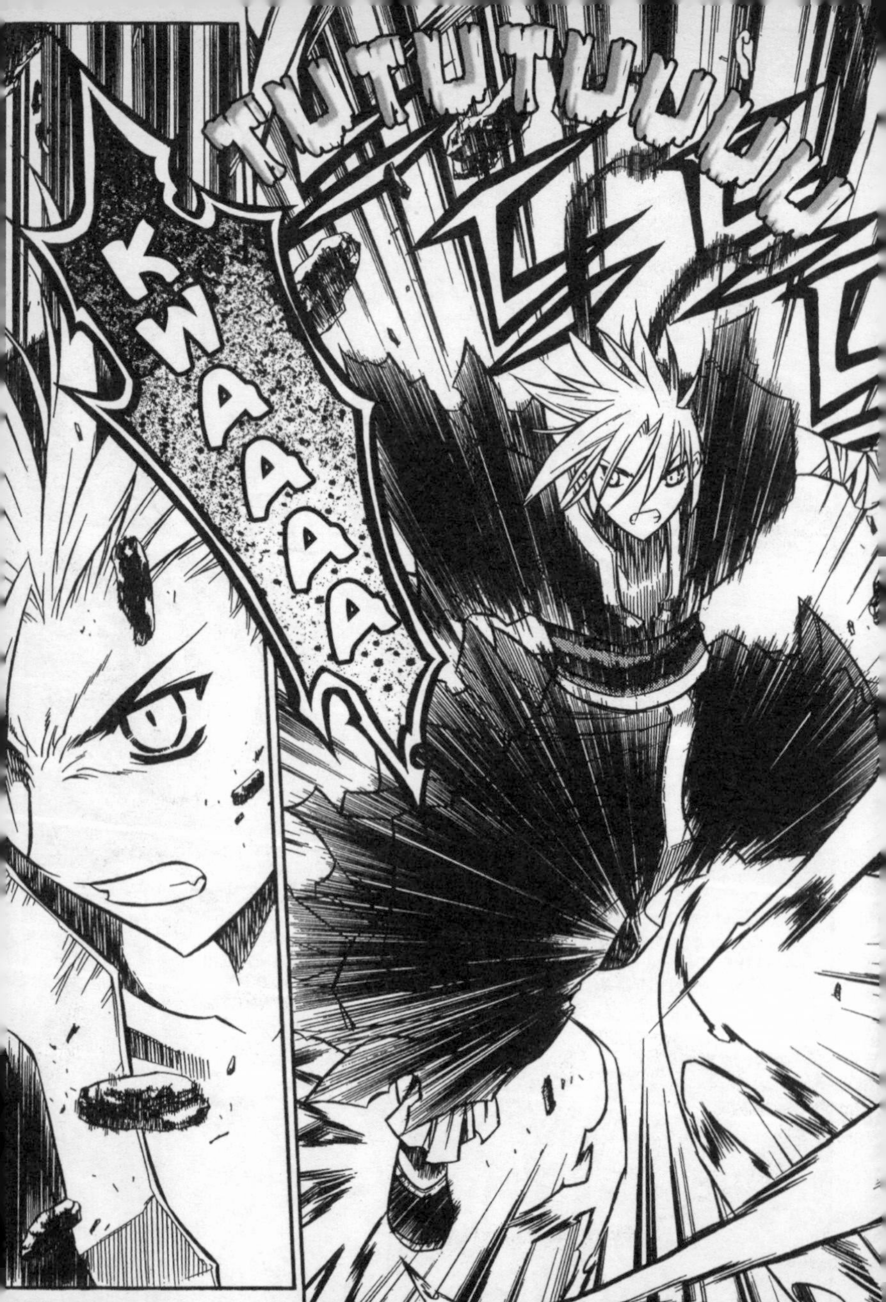
TUTUTUTUUUUU
KWAAAA

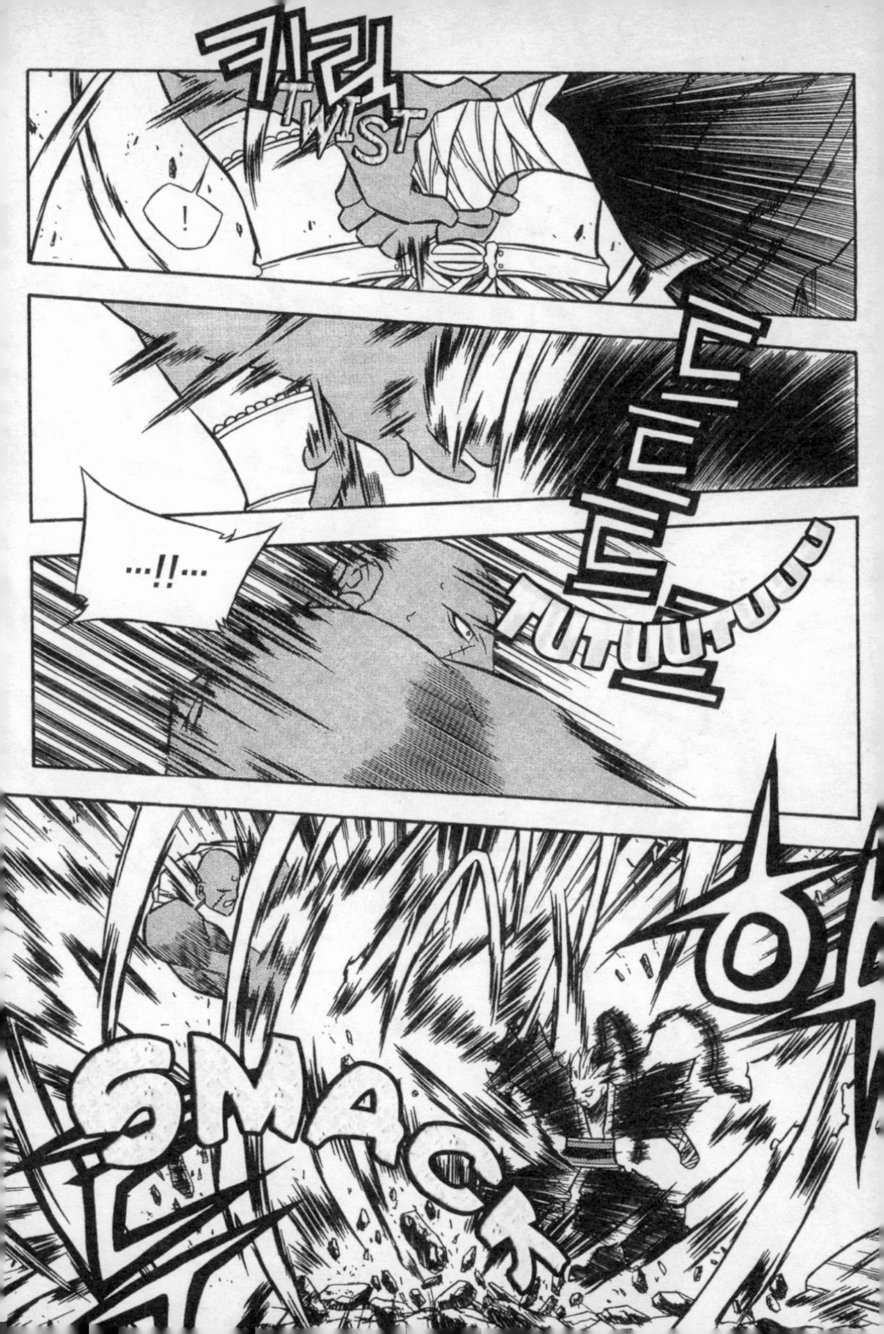
TWIST
!
...!!...
TUTUUTUUU
SMACK

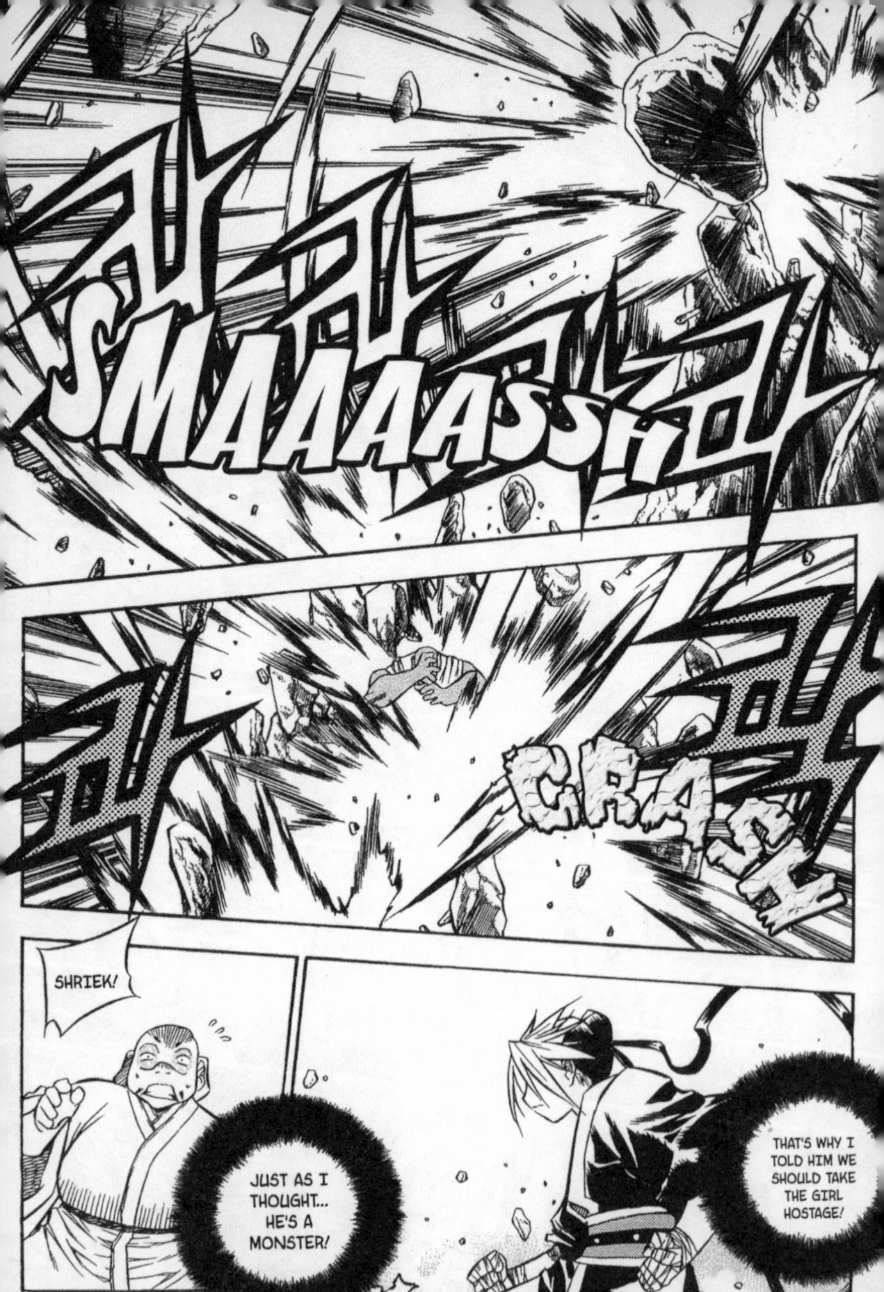
SMAAASH!
CRASH
SHRIEK!
JUST AS I THOUGHT... HE'S A MONSTER!
THAT'S WHY I TOLD HIM WE SHOULD TAKE THE GIRL HOSTAGE!

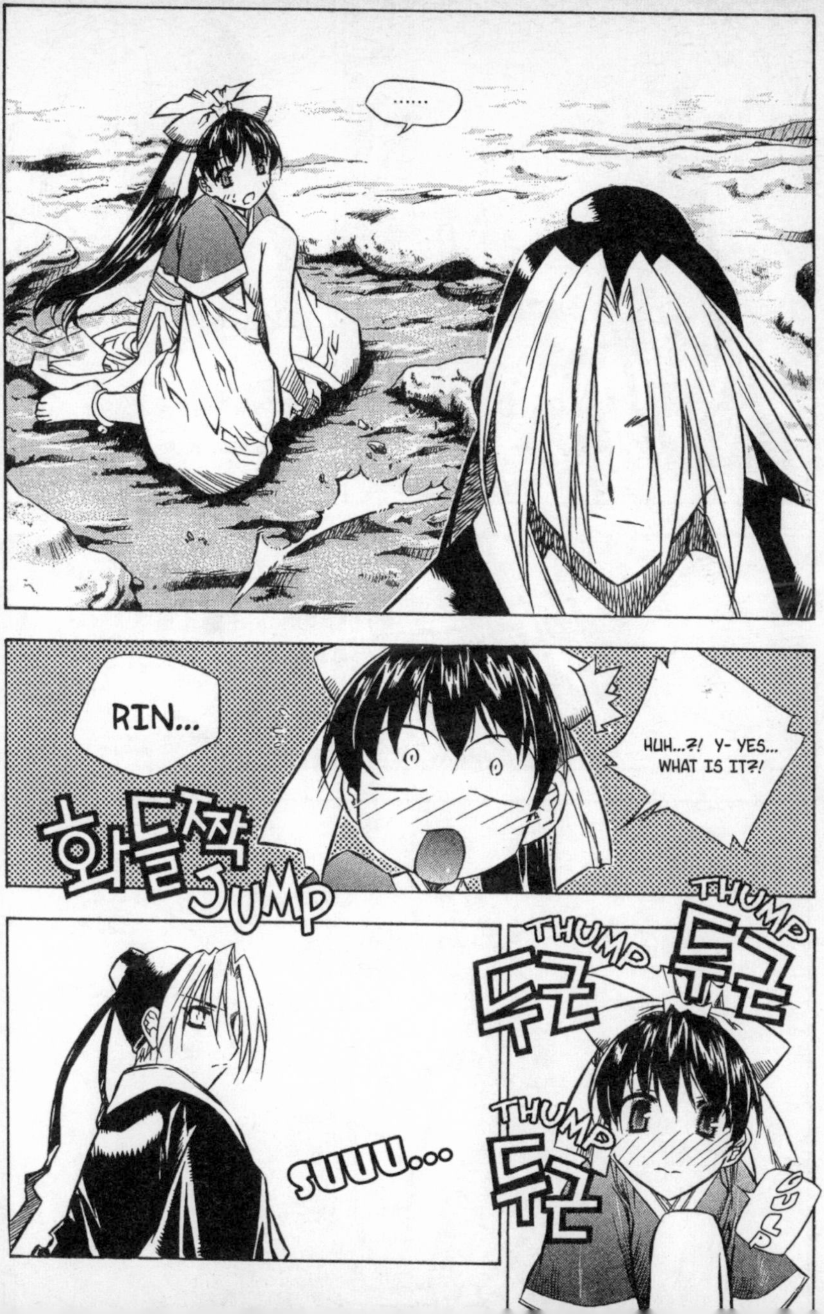
......
RIN...
화들짝
JUMP
HUH...?! Y- YES... WHAT IS IT?!
SUUU...
THUMP
두근
THUMP
두근
THUMP
두근
GULP

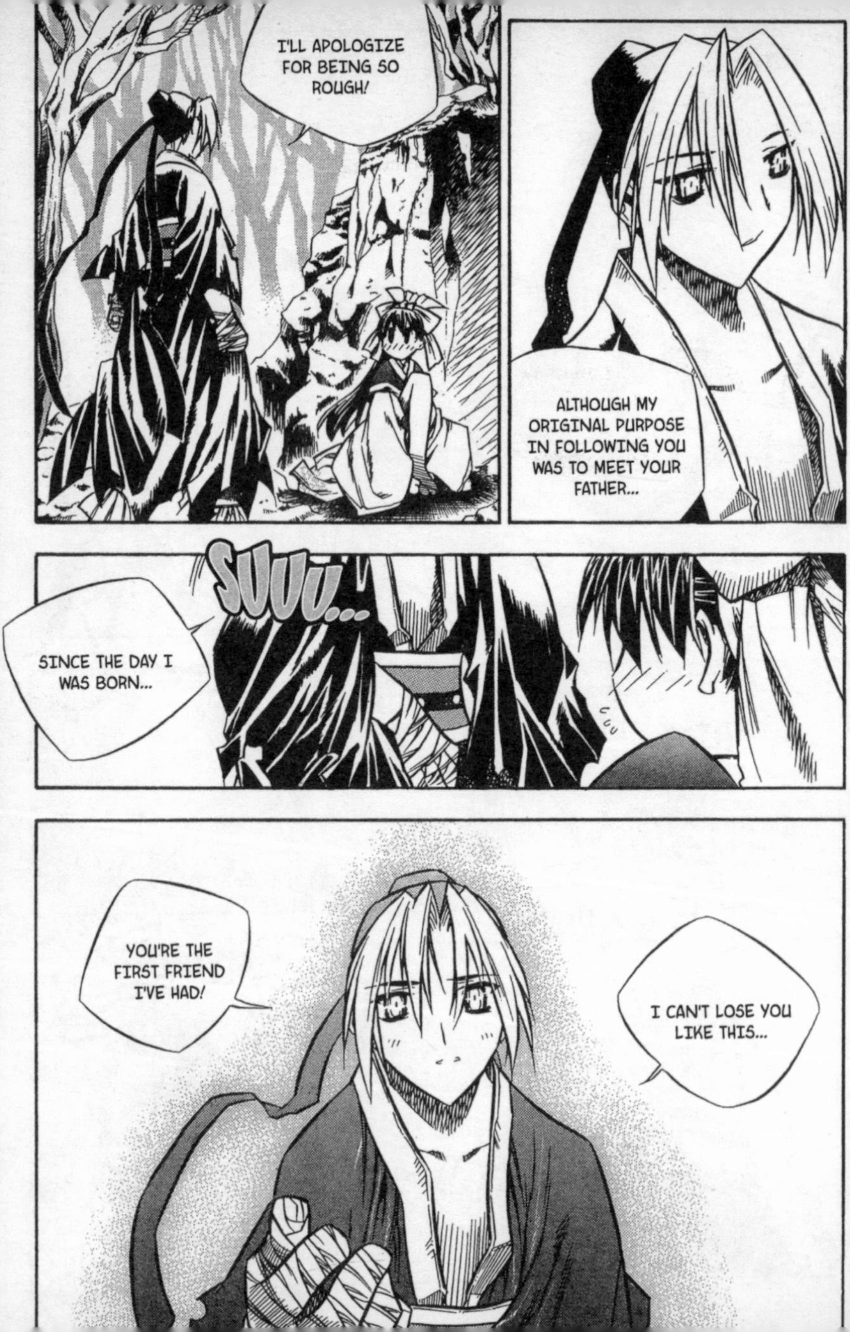
I'LL APOLOGIZE FOR BEING SO ROUGH!
ALTHOUGH MY ORIGINAL PURPOSE IN FOLLOWING YOU WAS TO MEET YOUR FATHER...
SUUU...
SINCE THE DAY I WAS BORN...
YOU'RE THE FIRST FRIEND I'VE HAD!
I CAN'T LOSE YOU LIKE THIS...

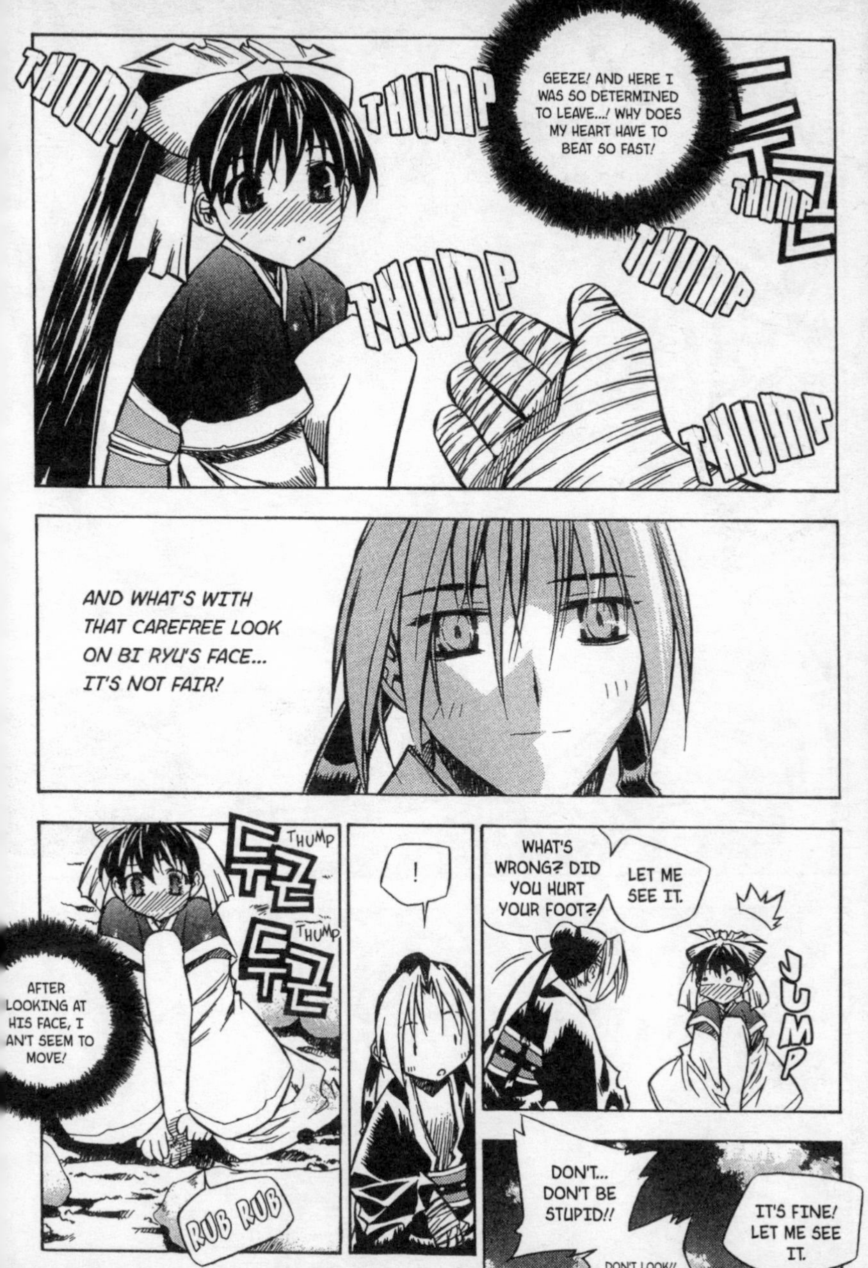
GEEZE! AND HERE I WAS SO DETERMINED TO LEAVE...! WHY DOES MY HEART HAVE TO BEAT SO FAST!
THUMP
THUMP
THUMP
THUMP
THUMP
THUMP
AND WHAT'S WITH THAT CAREFREE LOOK ON BI RYU'S FACE... IT'S NOT FAIR!
WHAT'S WRONG? DID YOU HURT YOUR FOOT?
LET ME SEE IT.
JUMP
!
THUMP
THUMP
AFTER LOOKING AT HIS FACE, I AN'T SEEM TO MOVE!
RUB RUB
IT'S FINE! LET ME SEE IT.
DON'T... DON'T BE STUPID!!
DON'T LOOK!!

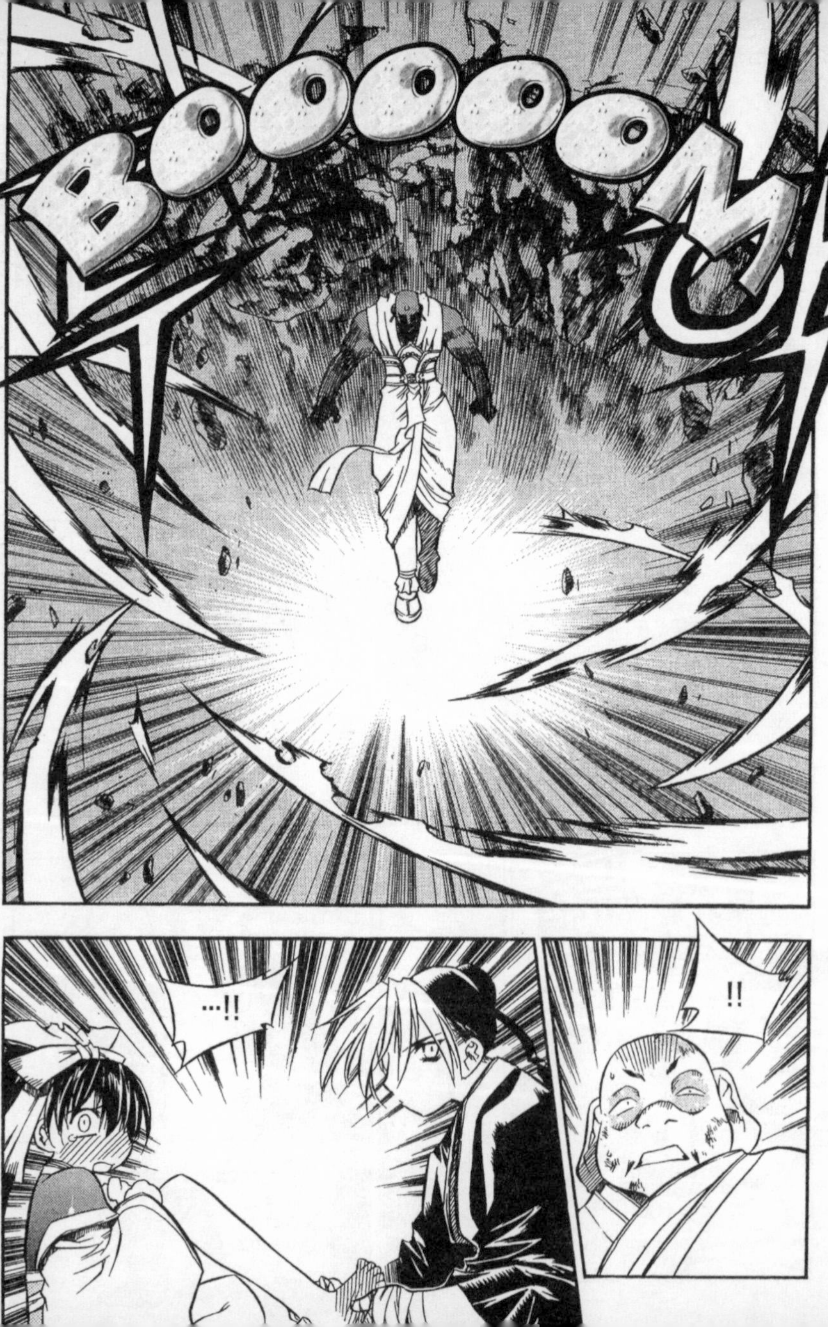
BOOOOOOM
!!
...!!

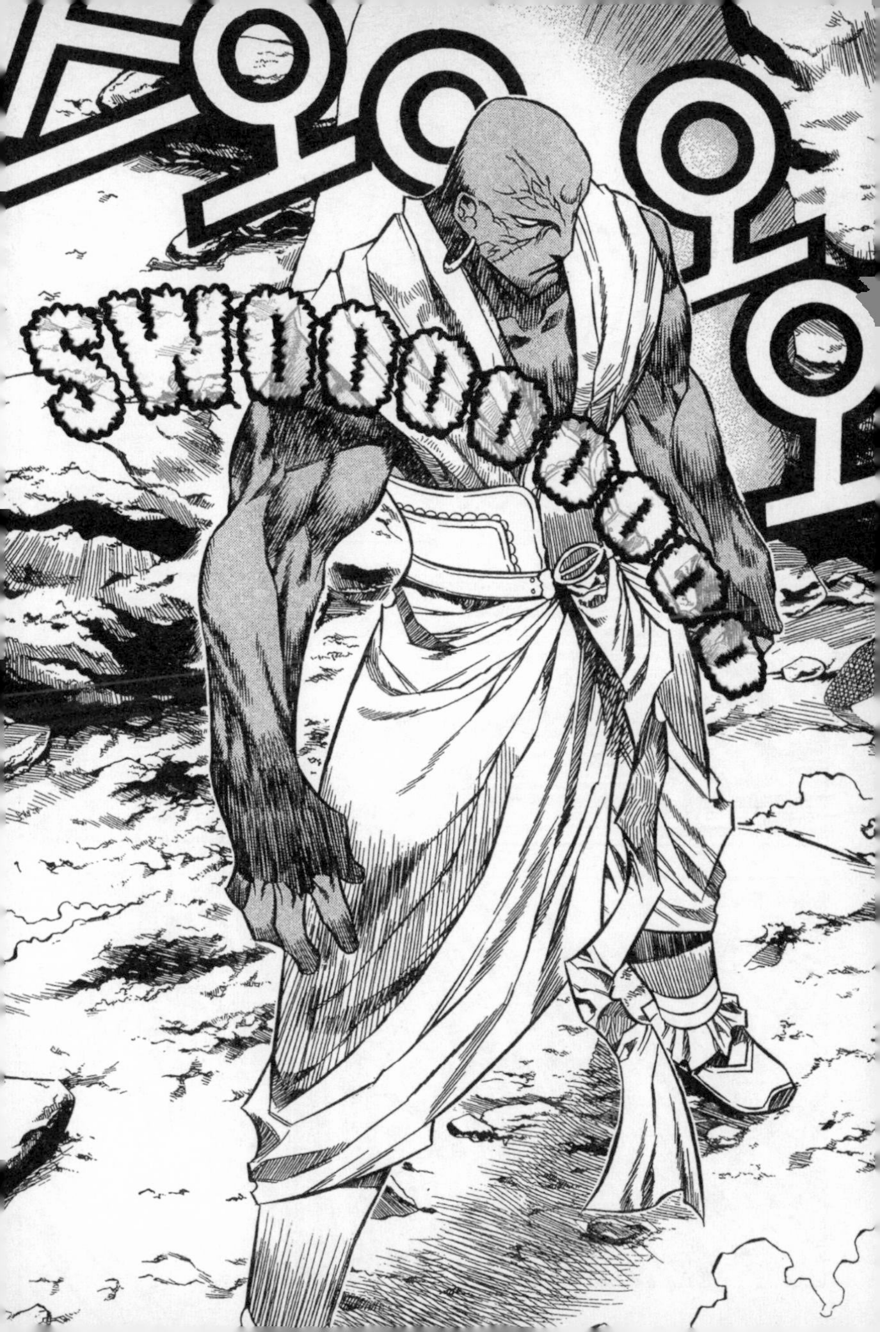
SHOOOOOOOO

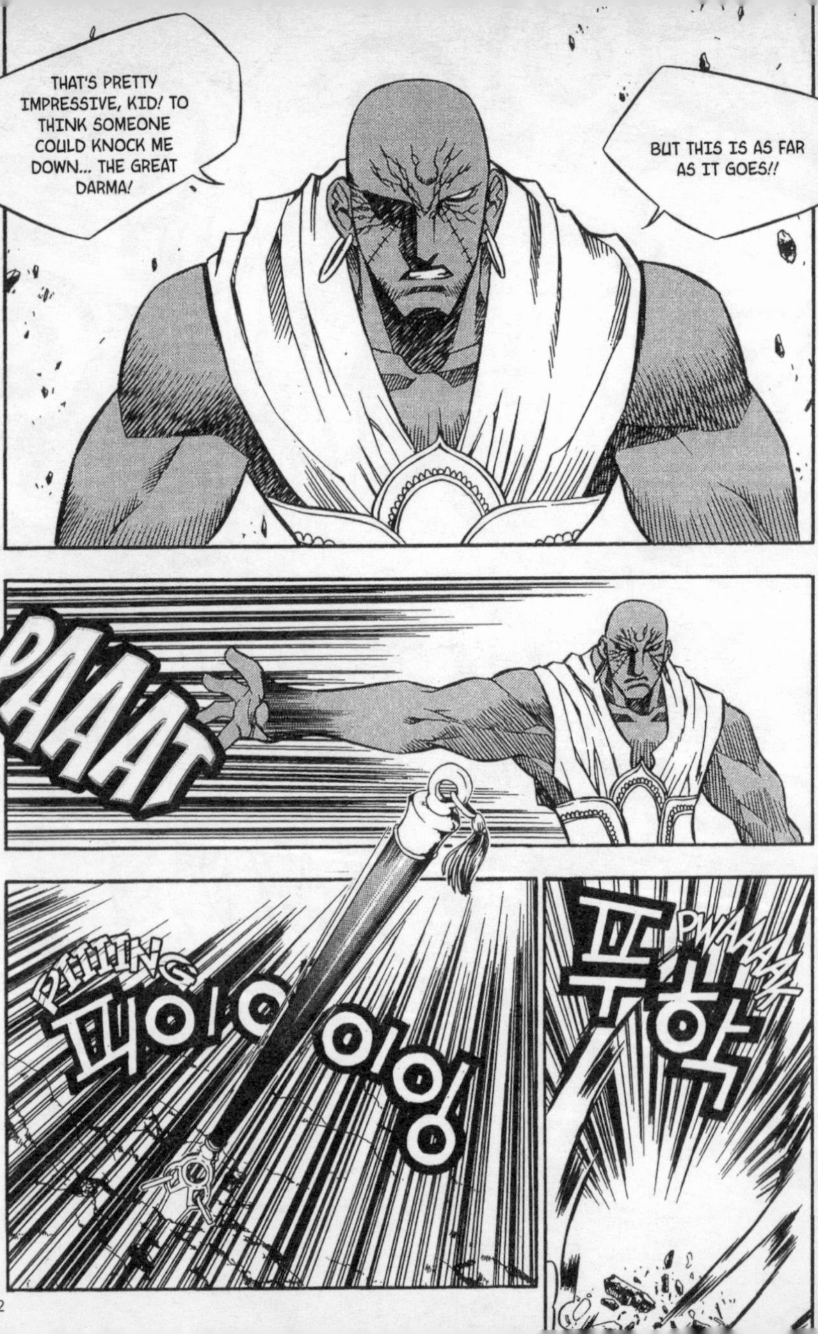
THAT'S PRETTY IMPRESSIVE, KID! TO THINK SOMEONE COULD KNOCK ME DOWN... THE GREAT DARMA!
BUT THIS IS AS FAR AS IT GOES!!
PAAAT
PTIIING
PWAAAAK

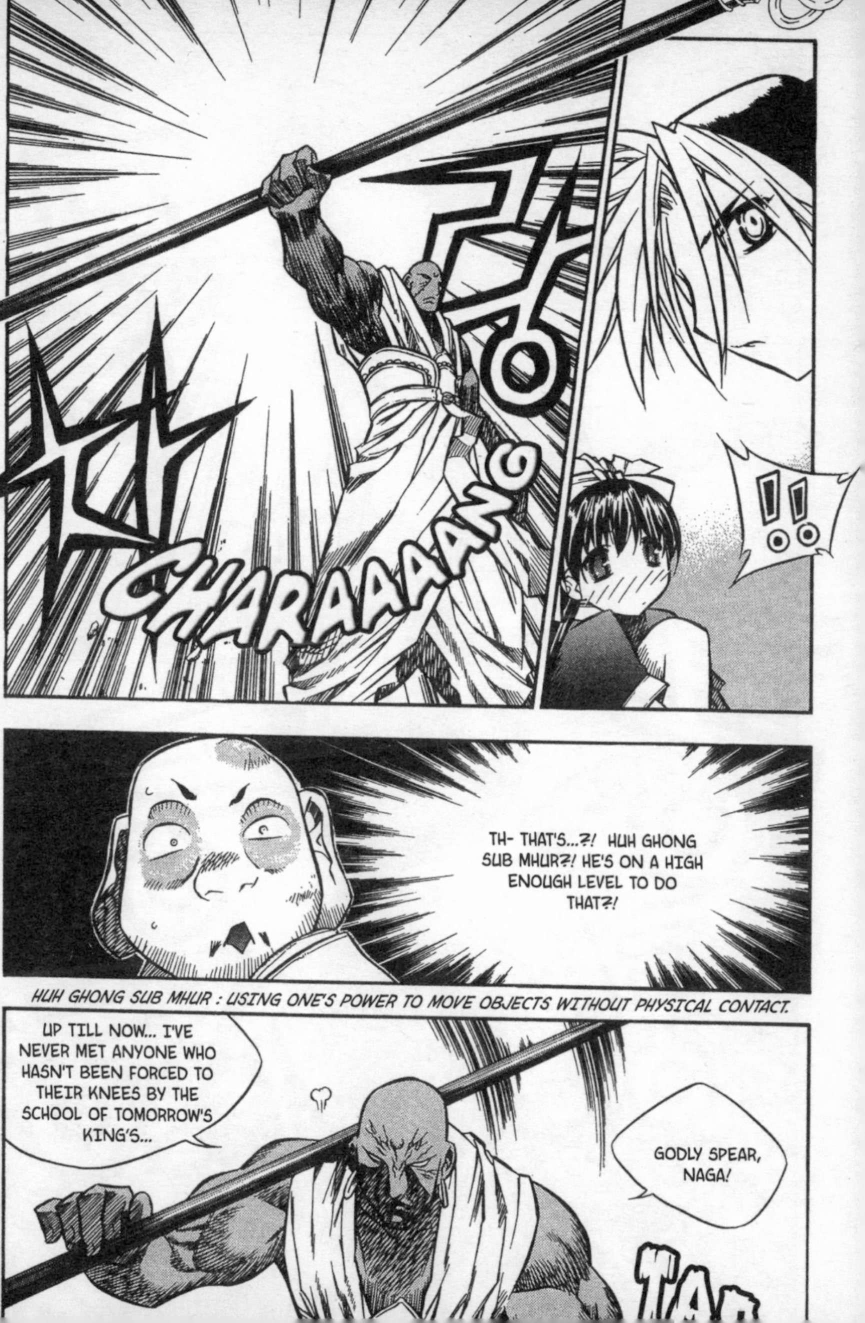
!!
CHARAAAANG
TH- THAT'S...?! HUH GHONG SUB MHUR?! HE'S ON A HIGH ENOUGH LEVEL TO DO THAT?!
HUH GHONG SUB MHUR : USING ONE'S POWER TO MOVE OBJECTS WITHOUT PHYSICAL CONTACT.
GODLY SPEAR, NAGA!
UP TILL NOW... I'VE NEVER MET ANYONE WHO HASN'T BEEN FORCED TO THEIR KNEES BY THE SCHOOL OF TOMORROW'S KING'S...

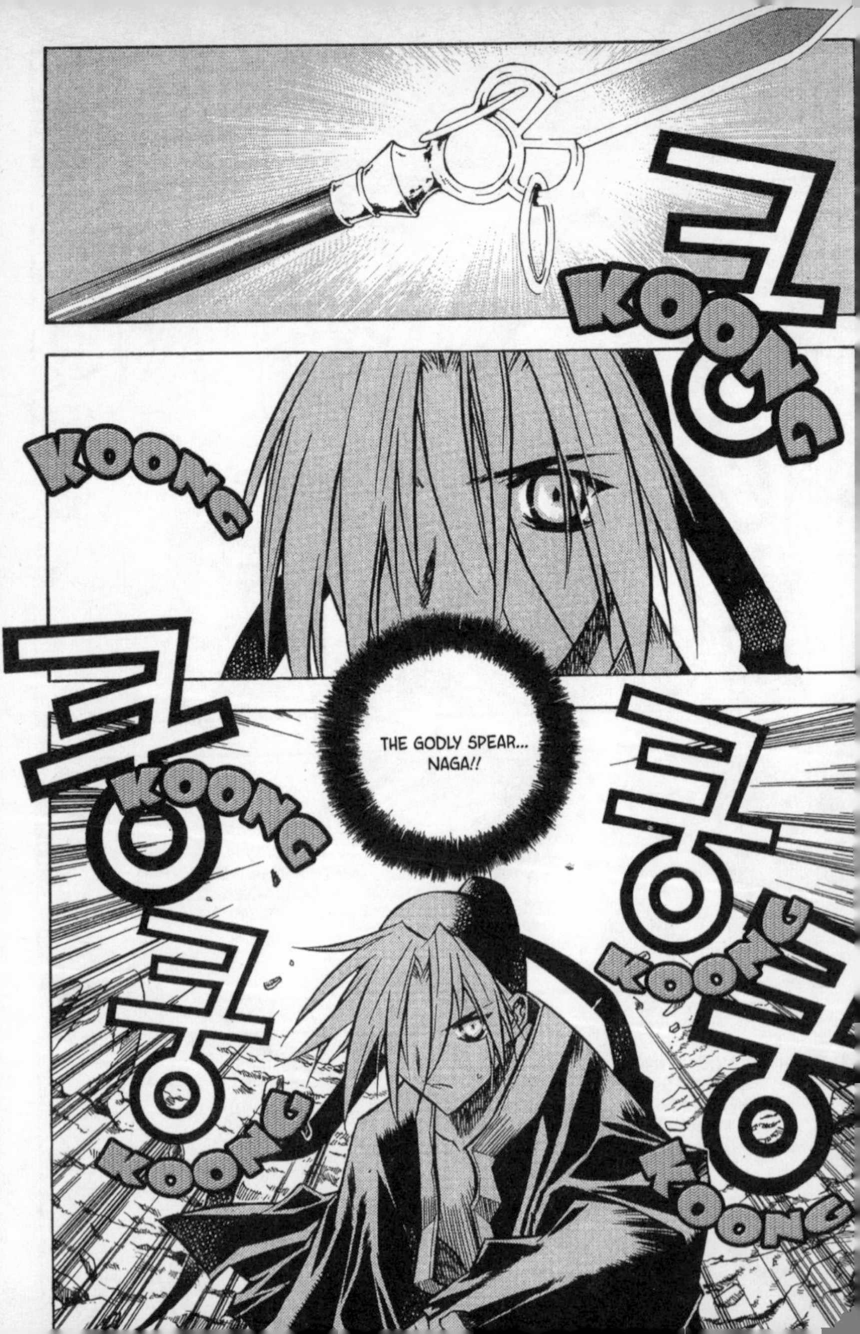
KOONG
KOONG
THE GODLY SPEAR... NAGA!!
KOONG
KOONG
KOONG
KOONG
KOONG

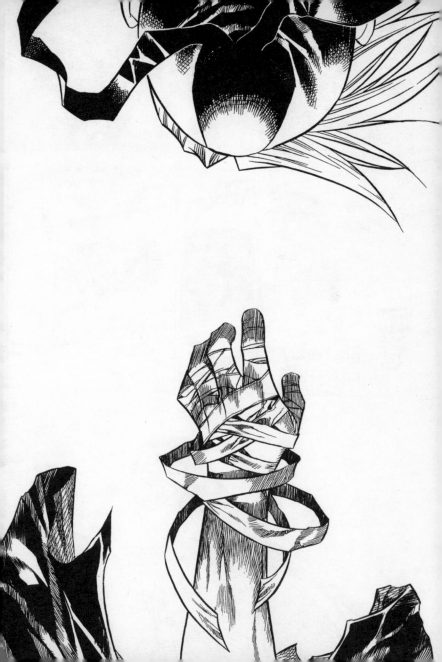

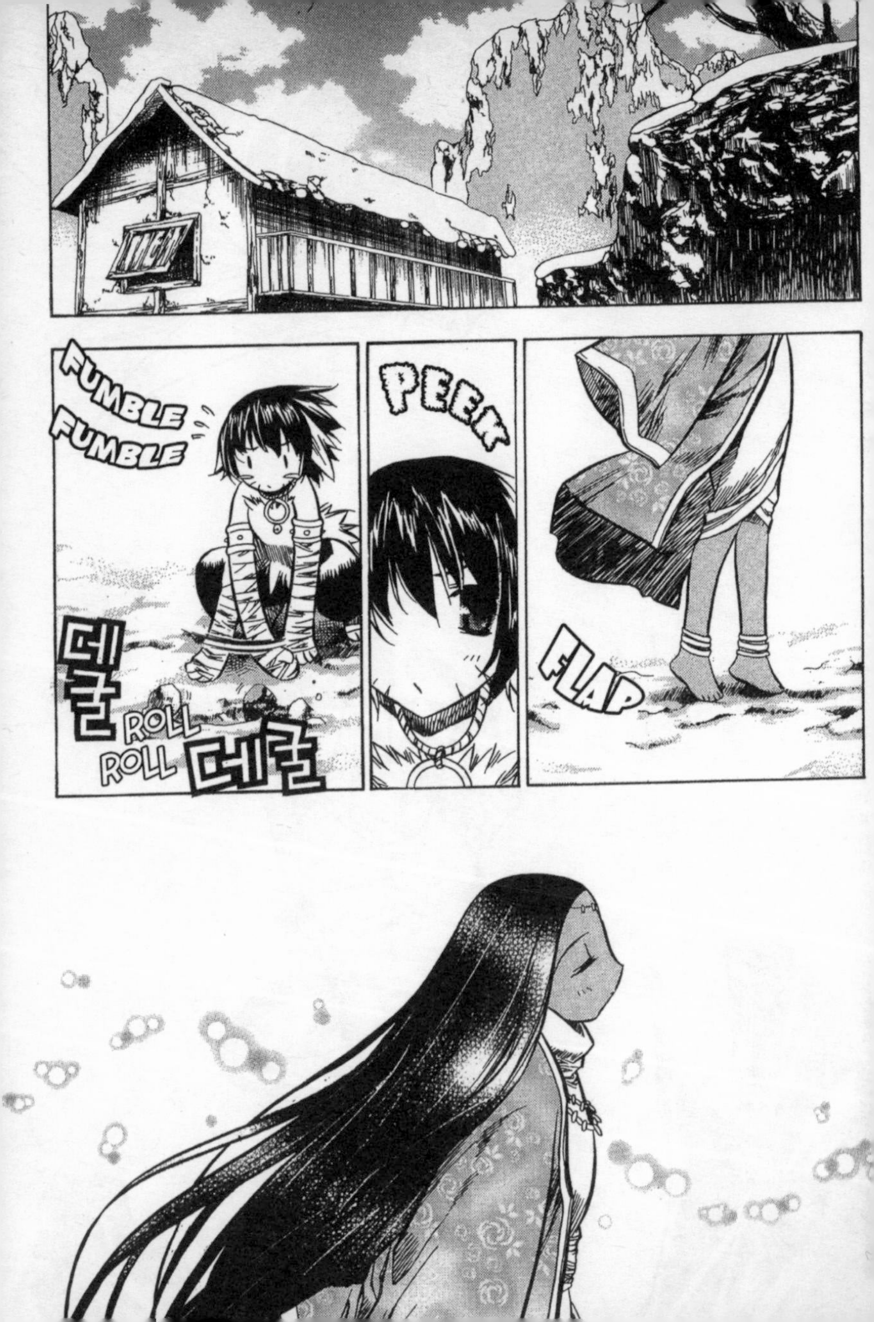
FUMBLE
FUMBLE
데굴
ROLL
ROLL
데굴
PEEK
FLAP

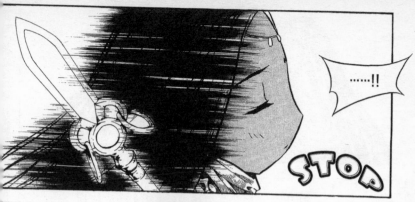

......!!

STOP

THIS FEELING OF A TREMENDOUSLY SHARP KILLING ENERGY... SOMETHING ONLY A DRAGON OF THE SCHOOL OF TOMORROW'S KING WOULD HAVE...

IT'S DANGEROUS...

KYANG?

?

?

THE DRAGON'S CLAW IS TOO DANGEROUS OF A WEAPON...

GOODNESS! WHAT'S ALL THIS? IT'S A COMPLETE DISASTER AREA IN HERE!!

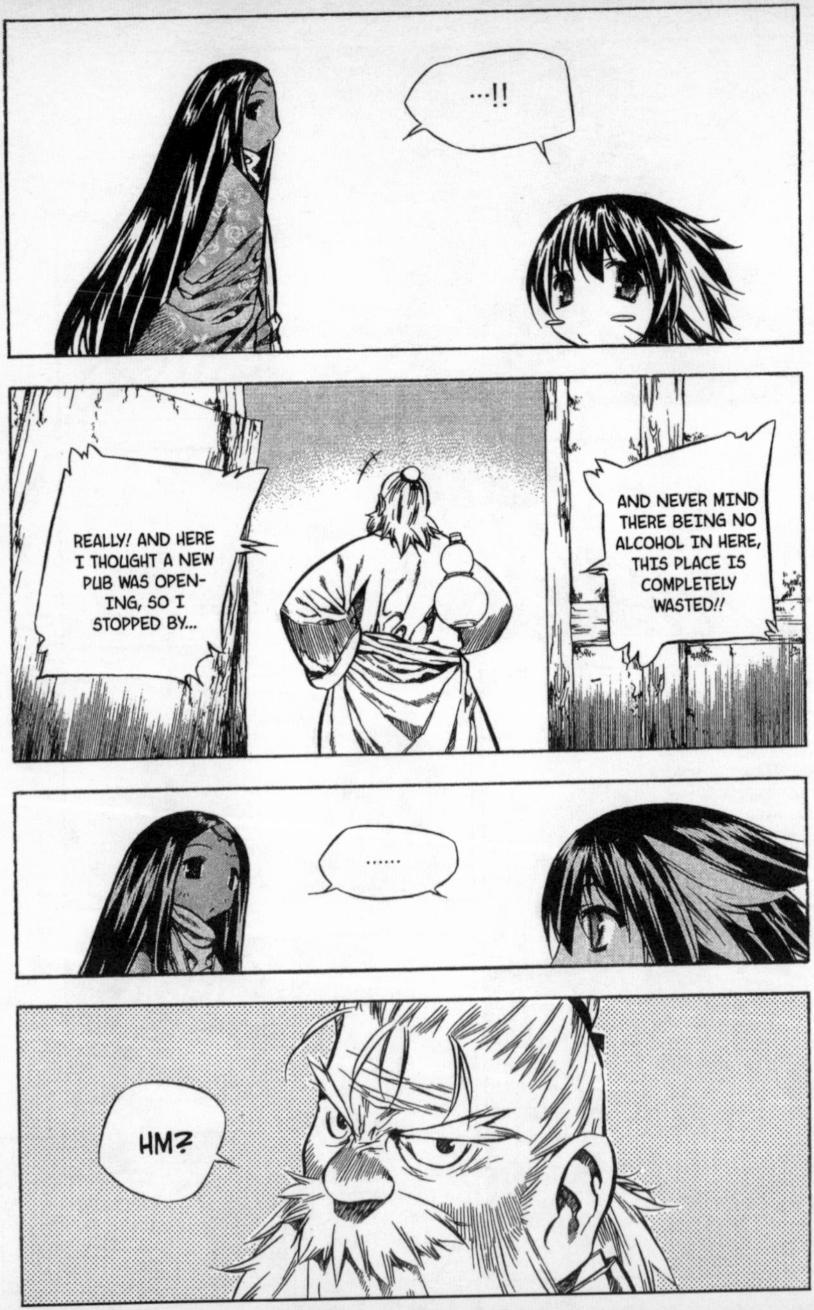

...!!
REALLY! AND HERE I THOUGHT A NEW PUB WAS OPEN-ING, SO I STOPPED BY...
AND NEVER MIND THERE BEING NO ALCOHOL IN HERE, THIS PLACE IS COMPLETELY WASTED!!
......
HM?

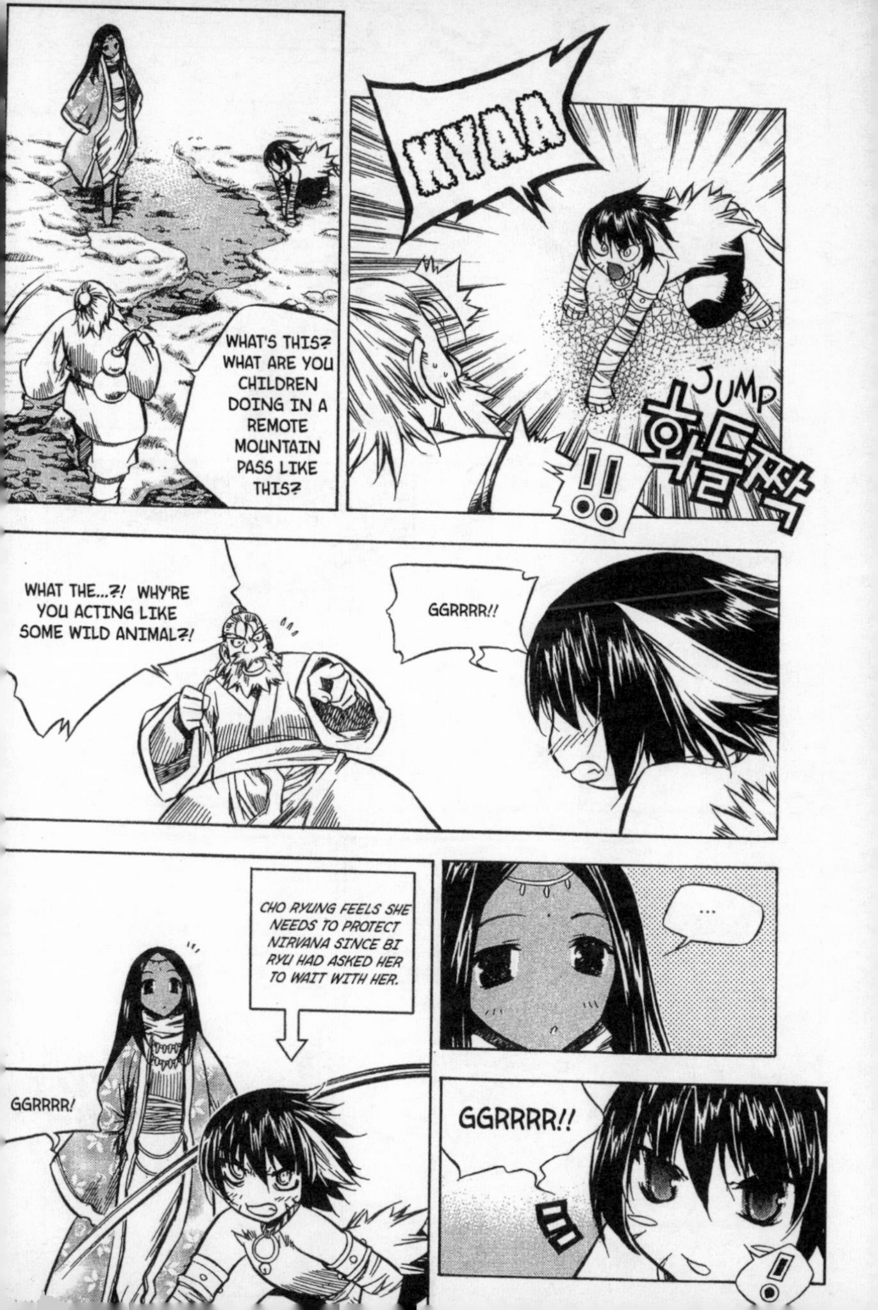
WHAT'S THIS?
WHAT ARE YOU CHILDREN DOING IN A REMOTE MOUNTAIN PASS LIKE THIS?
KYAA
JUMP
화들짝
!!
WHAT THE...?! WHY'RE YOU ACTING LIKE SOME WILD ANIMAL?!
GGRRRR!!
CHO RYUNG FEELS SHE NEEDS TO PROTECT NIRVANA SINCE BI RYU HAD ASKED HER TO WAIT WITH HER.
...
GGRRRR!
GGRRRR!!
!

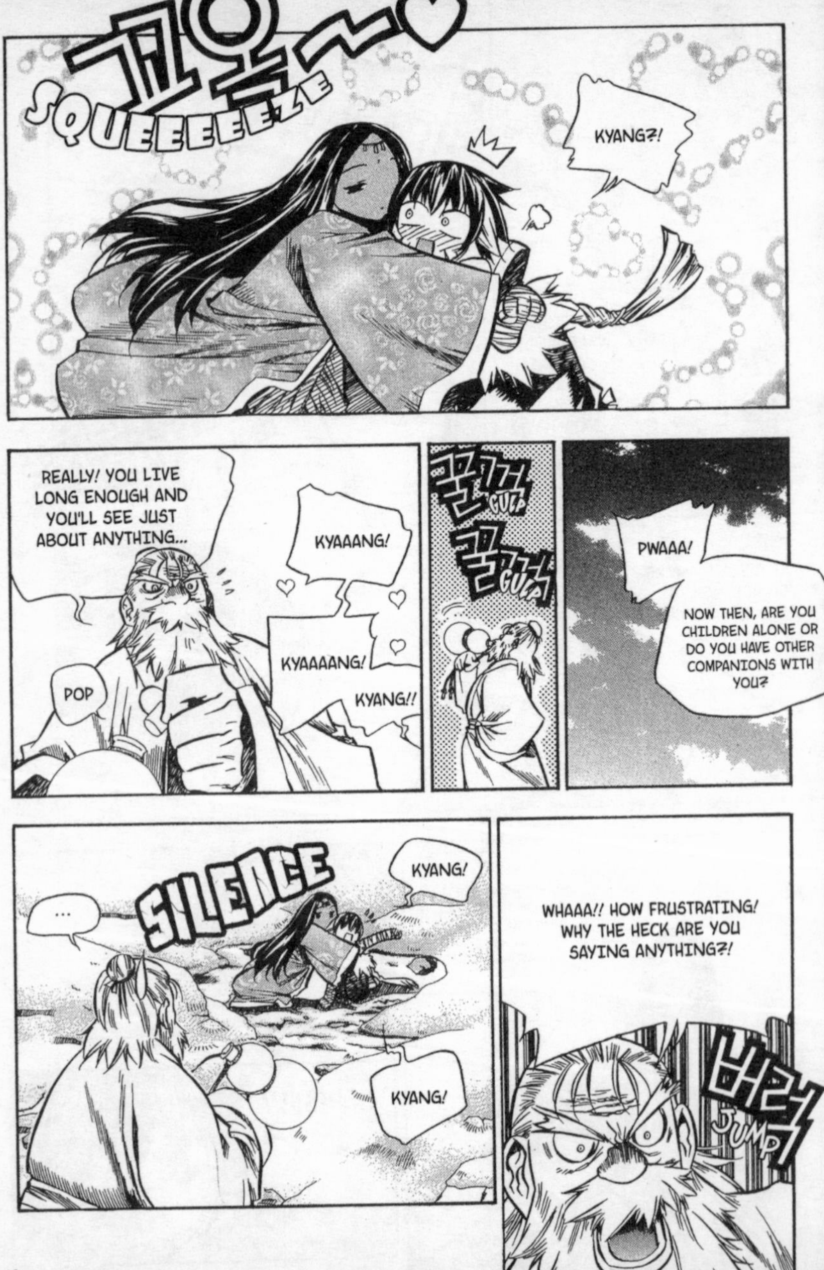
SQUEEEEEEZE
KYANG?!
REALLY! YOU LIVE LONG ENOUGH AND YOU'LL SEE JUST ABOUT ANYTHING...
KYAAANG!
KYAAAANG!
KYANG!!
POP
GULP
GULP
PWAAA!
NOW THEN, ARE YOU CHILDREN ALONE OR DO YOU HAVE OTHER COMPANIONS WITH YOU?
SILENCE
KYANG!
...
KYANG!
WHAAA!! HOW FRUSTRATING! WHY THE HECK ARE YOU SAYING ANYTHING?!
JUMP

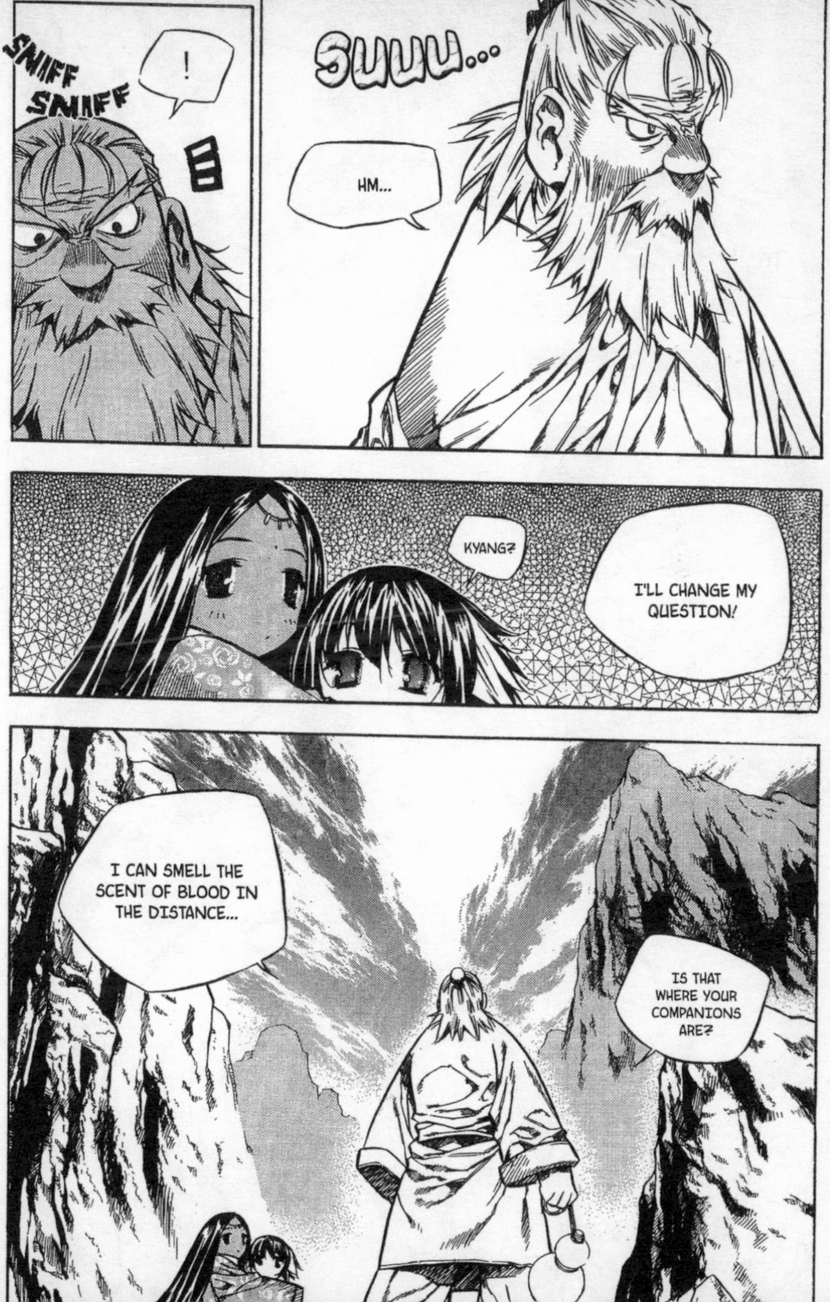
SUUU...
HM...
SNIFF SNIFF
!
I'LL CHANGE MY QUESTION!
KYANG?
I CAN SMELL THE SCENT OF BLOOD IN THE DISTANCE...
IS THAT WHERE YOUR COMPANIONS ARE?

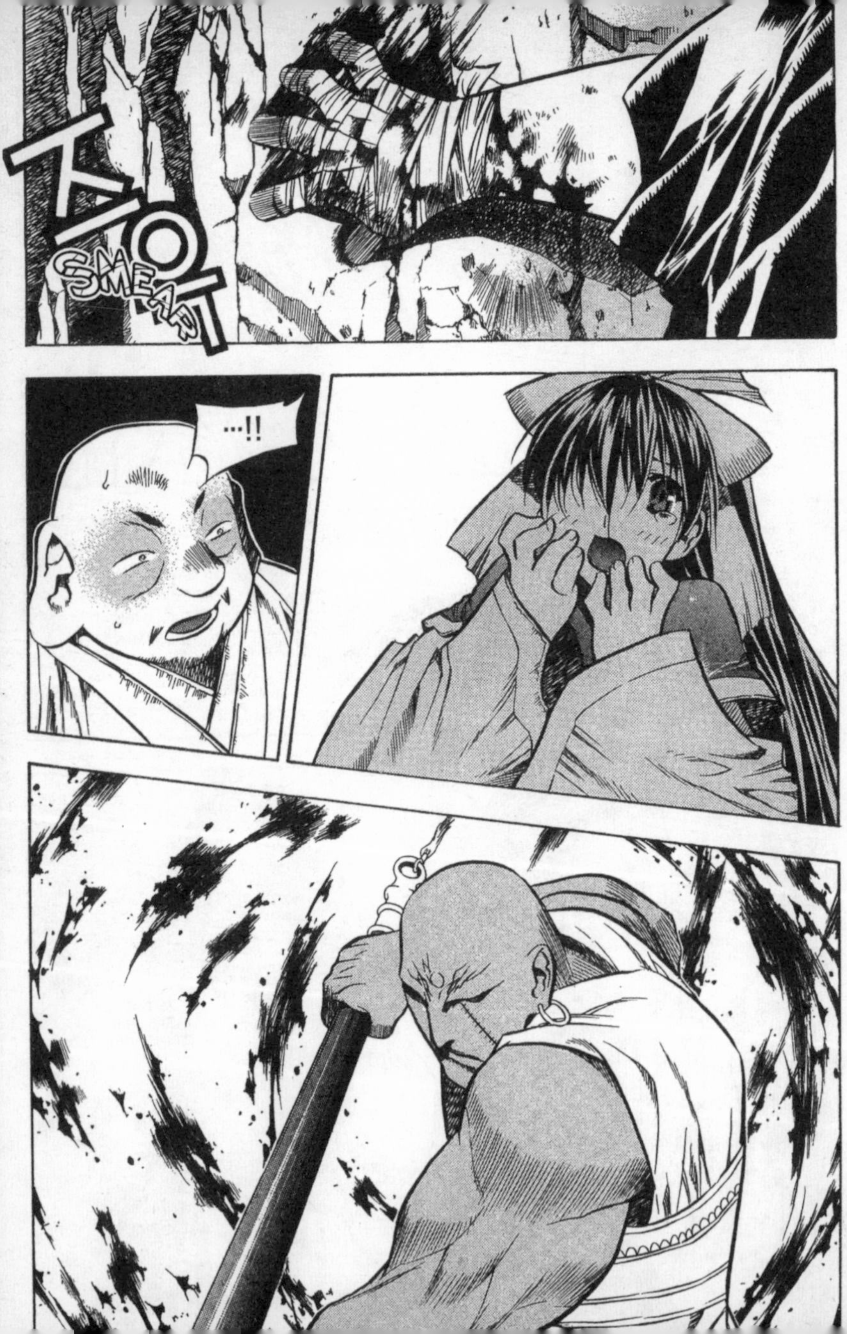

KLOT
SMEAR
...!!

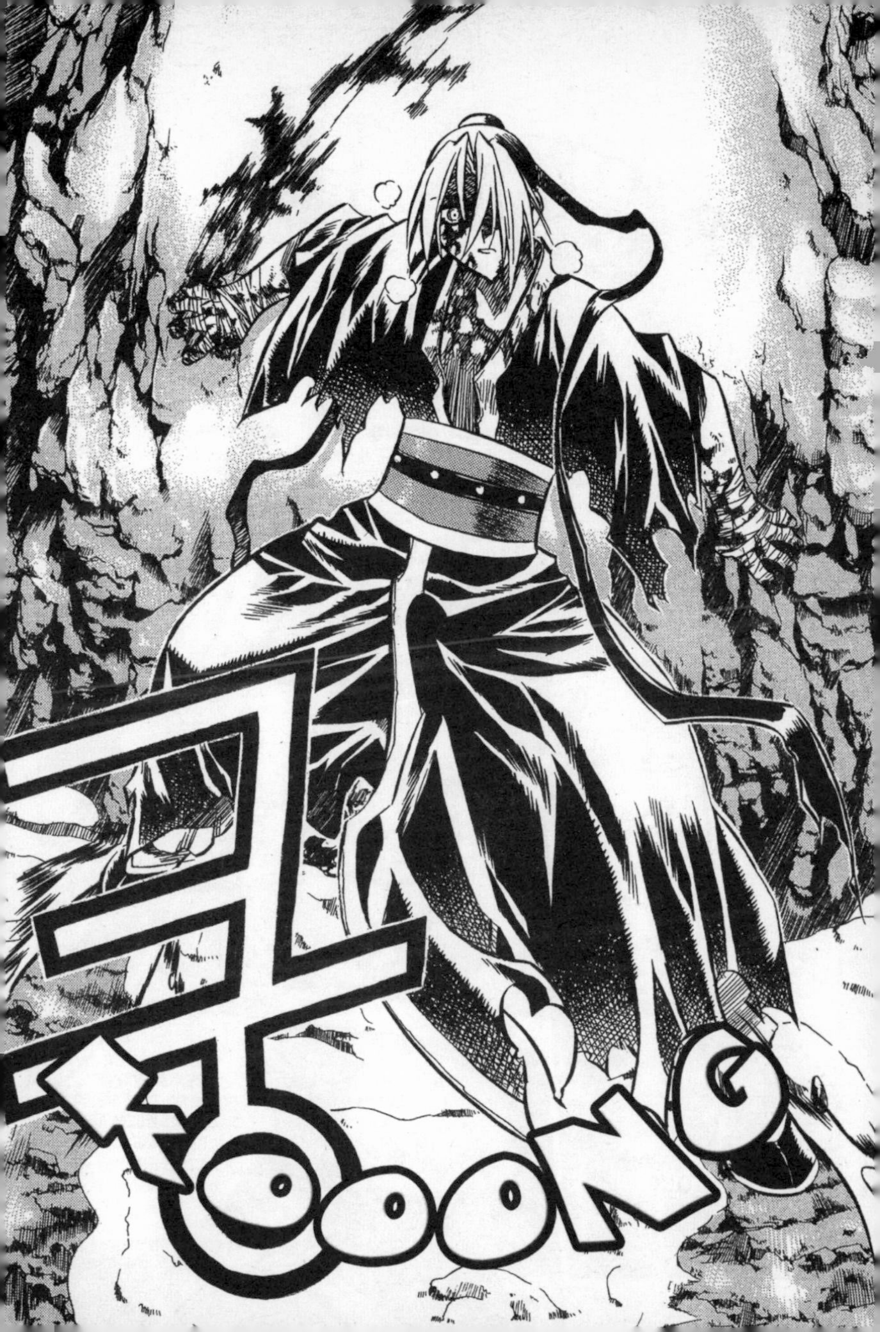
KOOONG

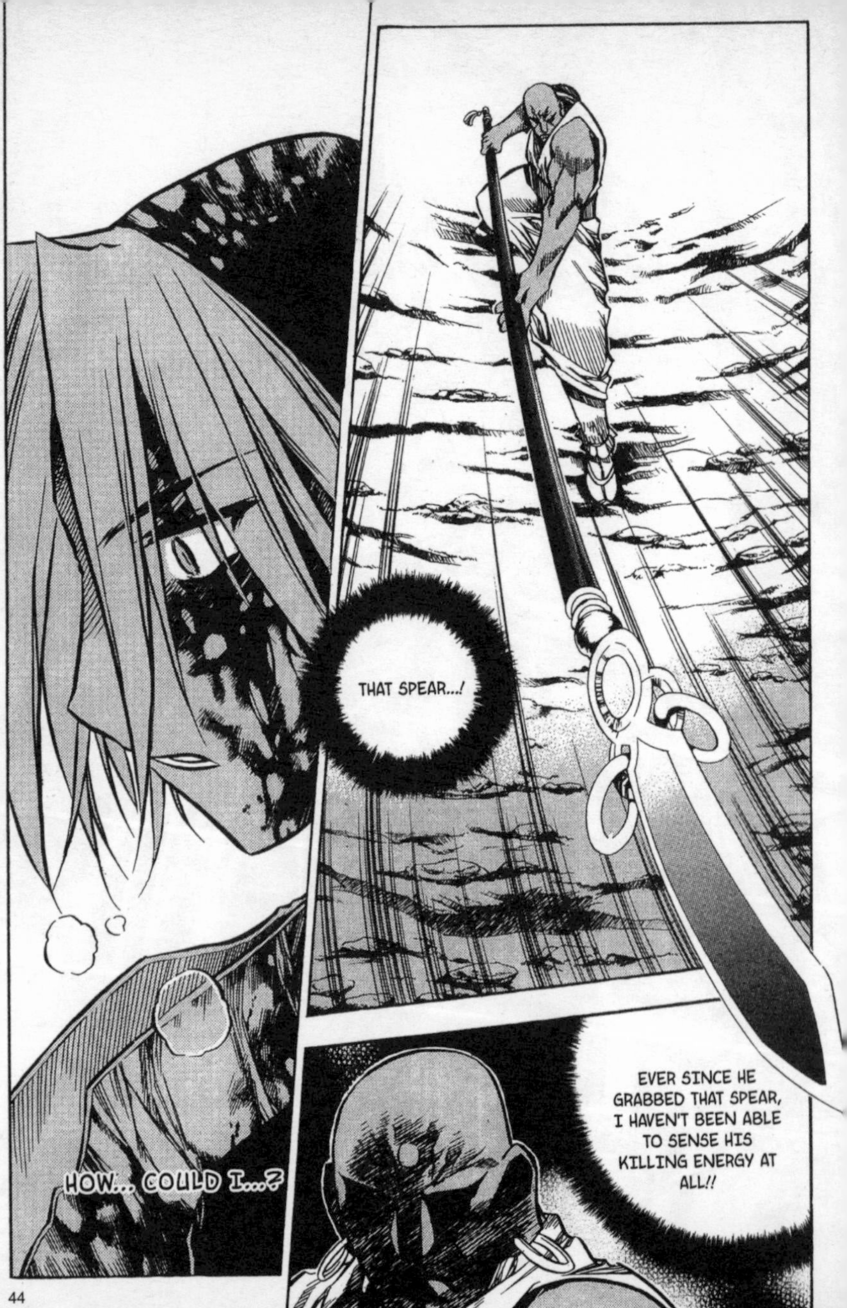
THAT SPEAR...!
EVER SINCE HE GRABBED THAT SPEAR, I HAVEN'T BEEN ABLE TO SENSE HIS KILLING ENERGY AT ALL!!
HOW... COULD I...?

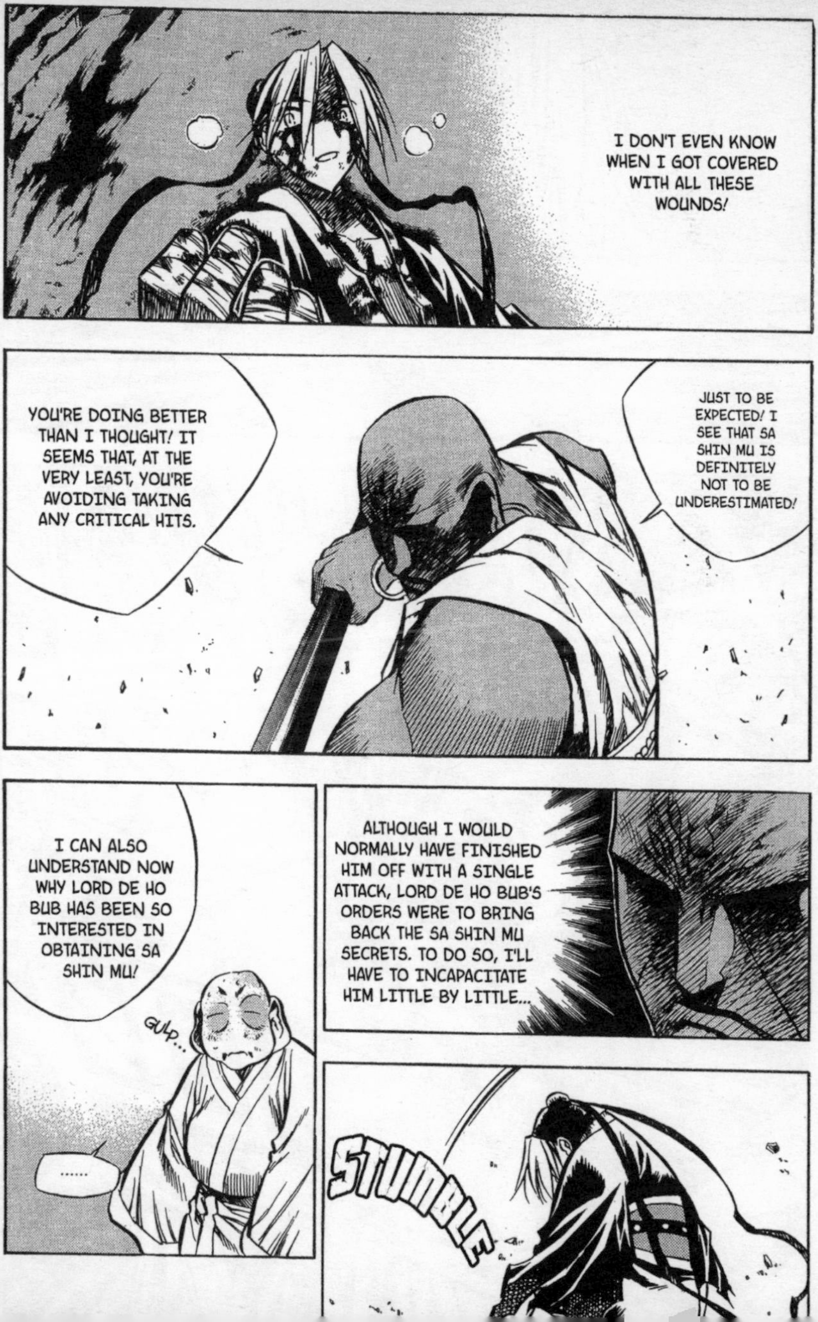
I DON'T EVEN KNOW WHEN I GOT COVERED WITH ALL THESE WOUNDS!
YOU'RE DOING BETTER THAN I THOUGHT! IT SEEMS THAT, AT THE VERY LEAST, YOU'RE AVOIDING TAKING ANY CRITICAL HITS.
JUST TO BE EXPECTED! I SEE THAT SA SHIN MU IS DEFINITELY NOT TO BE UNDERESTIMATED!
I CAN ALSO UNDERSTAND NOW WHY LORD DE HO BUB HAS BEEN SO INTERESTED IN OBTAINING SA SHIN MU!
GULP...
......
ALTHOUGH I WOULD NORMALLY HAVE FINISHED HIM OFF WITH A SINGLE ATTACK, LORD DE HO BUB'S ORDERS WERE TO BRING BACK THE SA SHIN MU SECRETS. TO DO SO, I'LL HAVE TO INCAPACITATE HIM LITTLE BY LITTLE...
STUMBLE

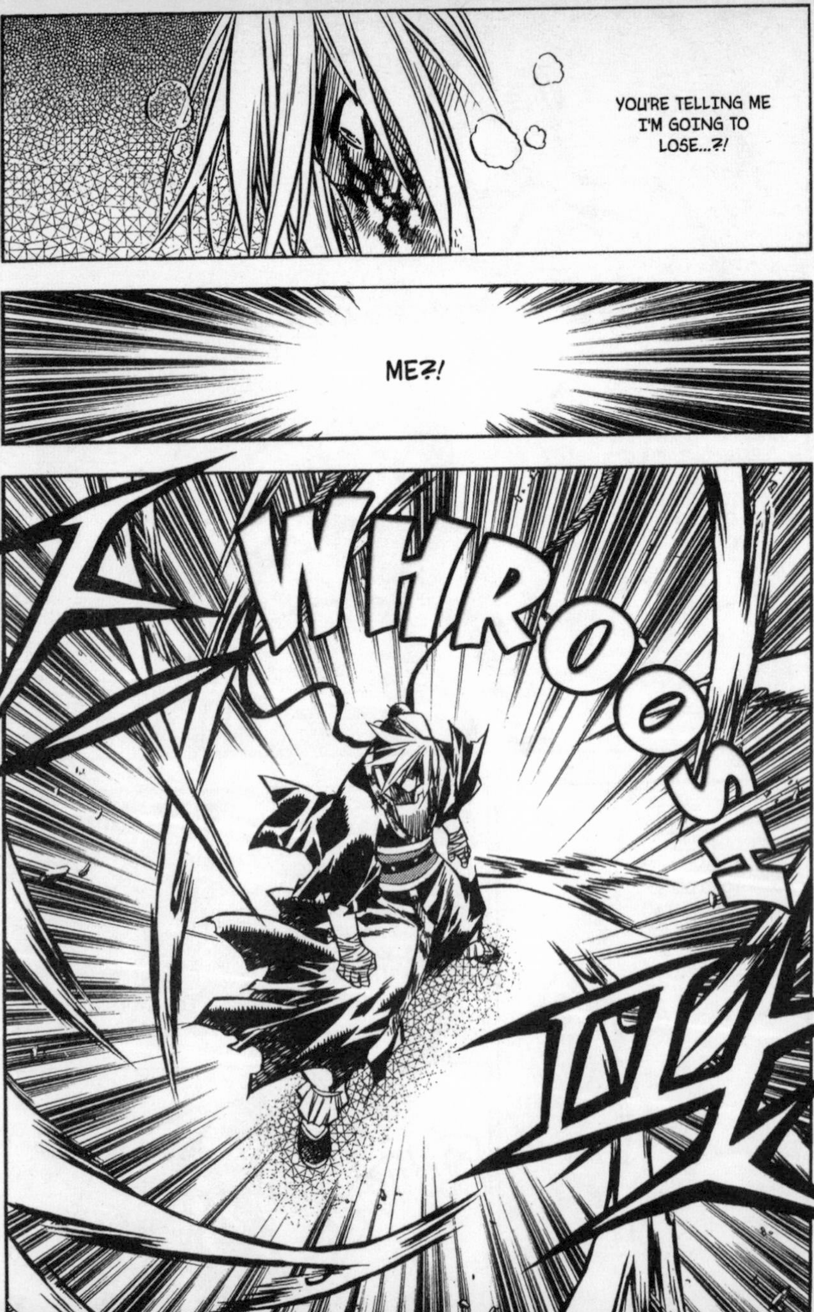
YOU'RE TELLING ME I'M GOING TO LOSE...?!
ME?!
WHROOSH

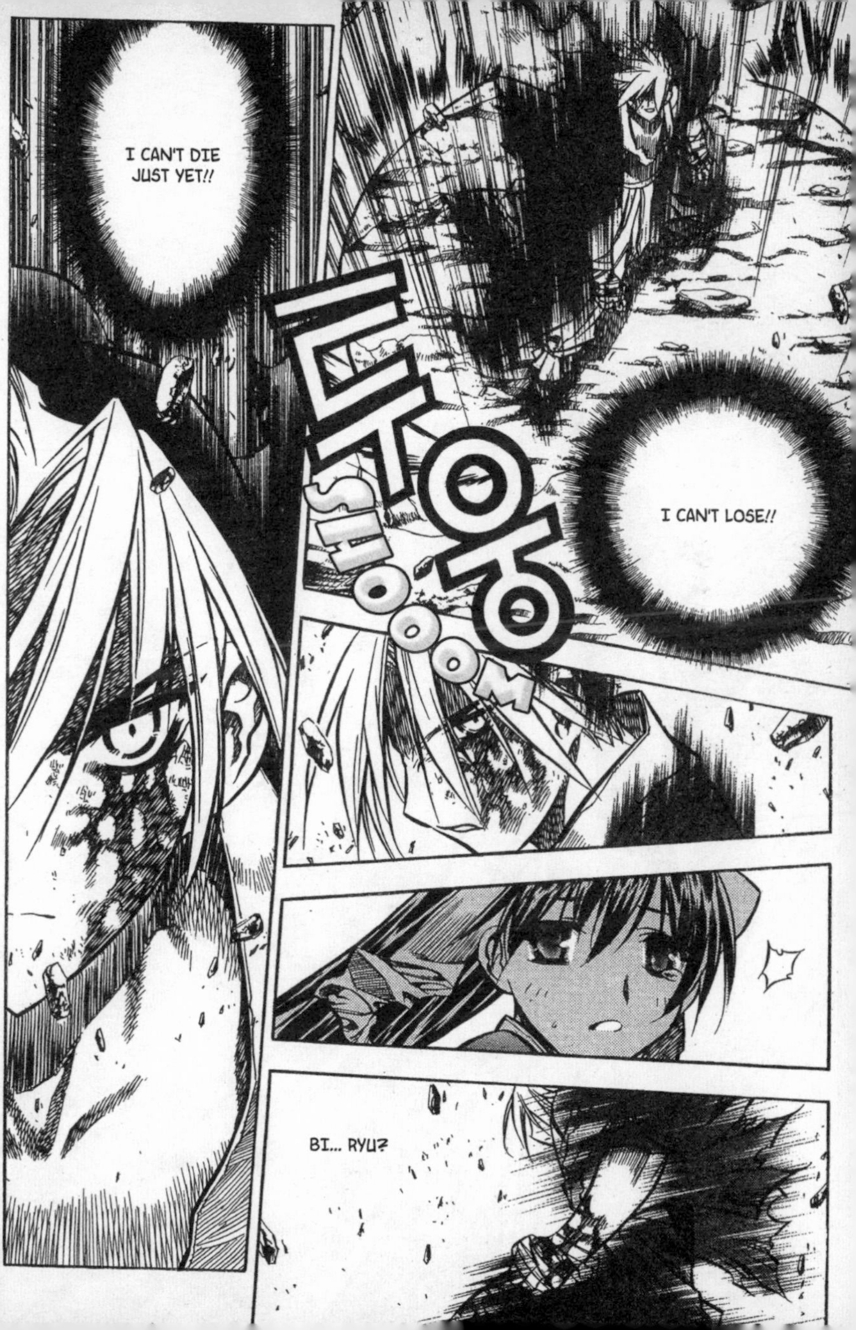
I CAN'T DIE JUST YET!!
I CAN'T LOSE!!
SHOOOOM
BI... RYU?

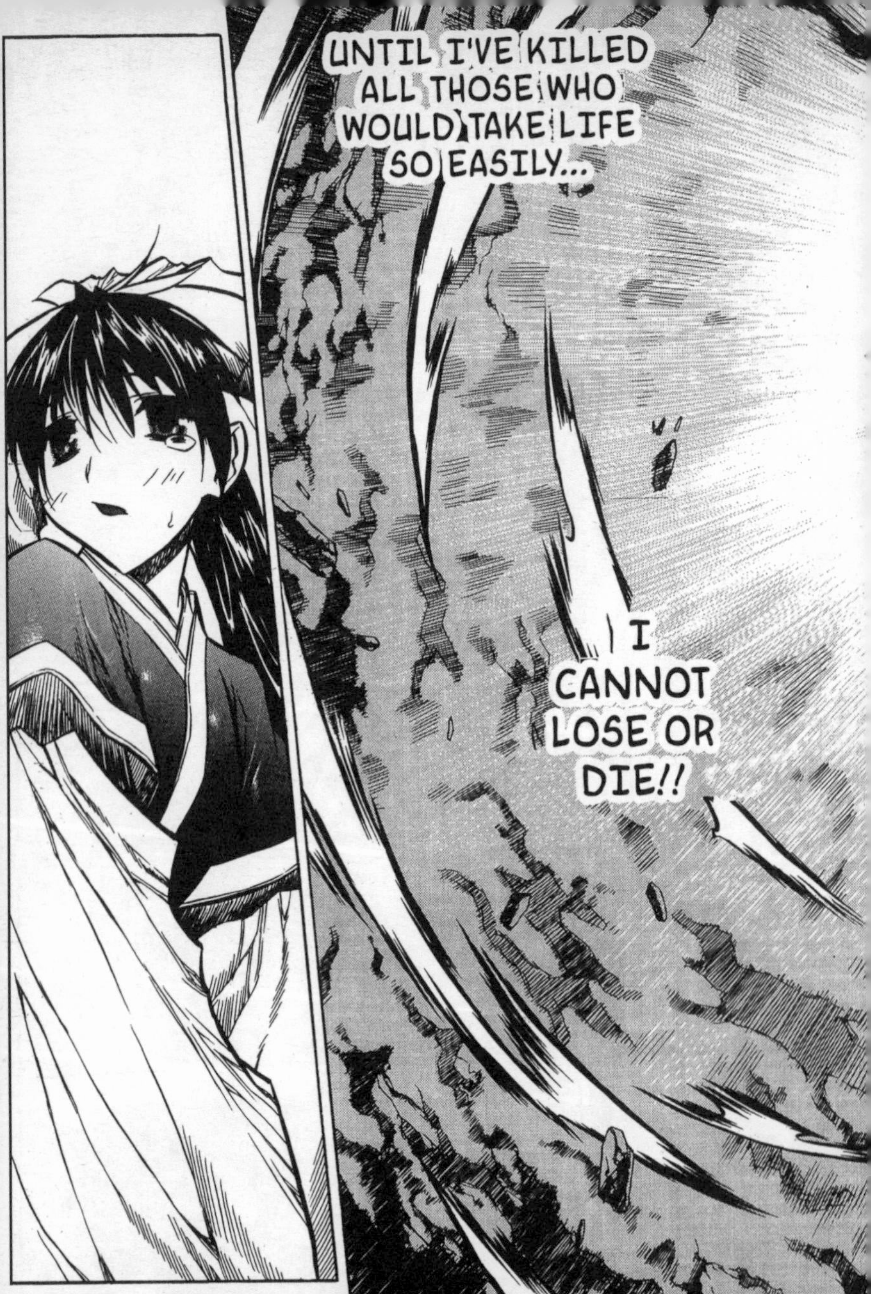
UNTIL I'VE KILLED ALL THOSE WHO WOULD TAKE LIFE SO EASILY...
I CANNOT LOSE OR DIE!!

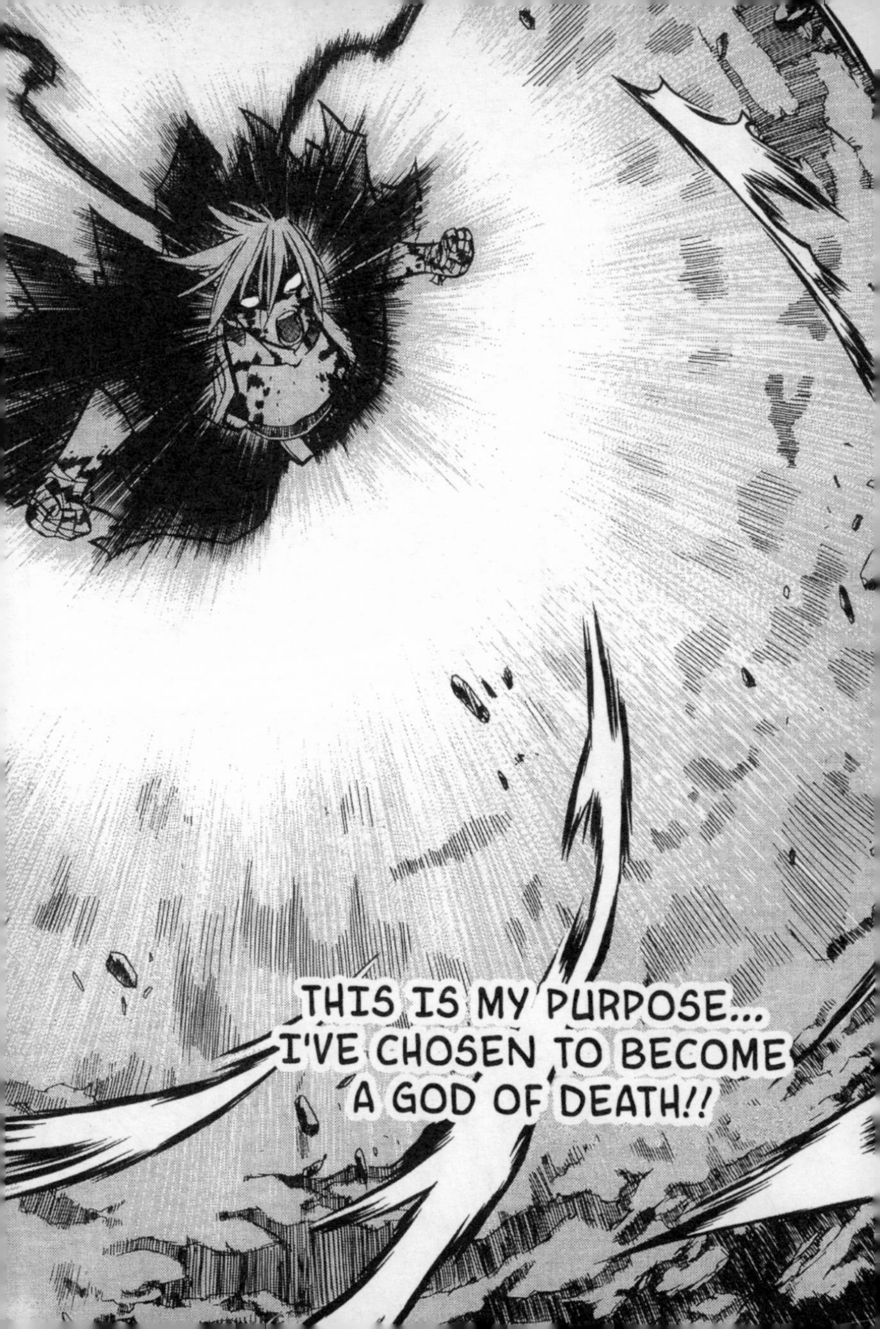
THIS IS MY PURPOSE... I'VE CHOSEN TO BECOME A GOD OF DEATH!!

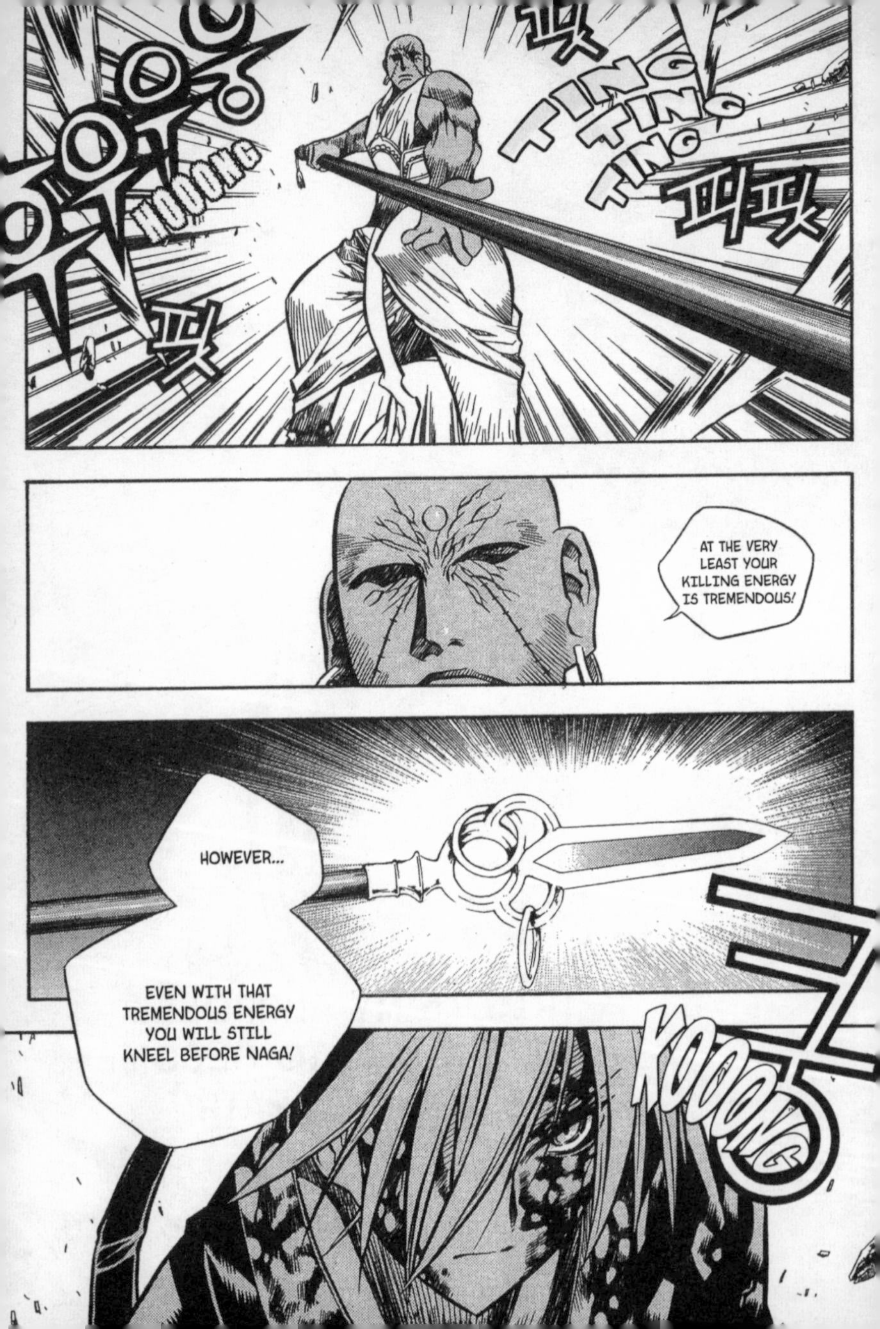

KOOOONG
TING TING TING
AT THE VERY LEAST YOUR KILLING ENERGY IS TREMENDOUS!
HOWEVER...
EVEN WITH THAT TREMENDOUS ENERGY YOU WILL STILL KNEEL BEFORE NAGA!
KOOOONG

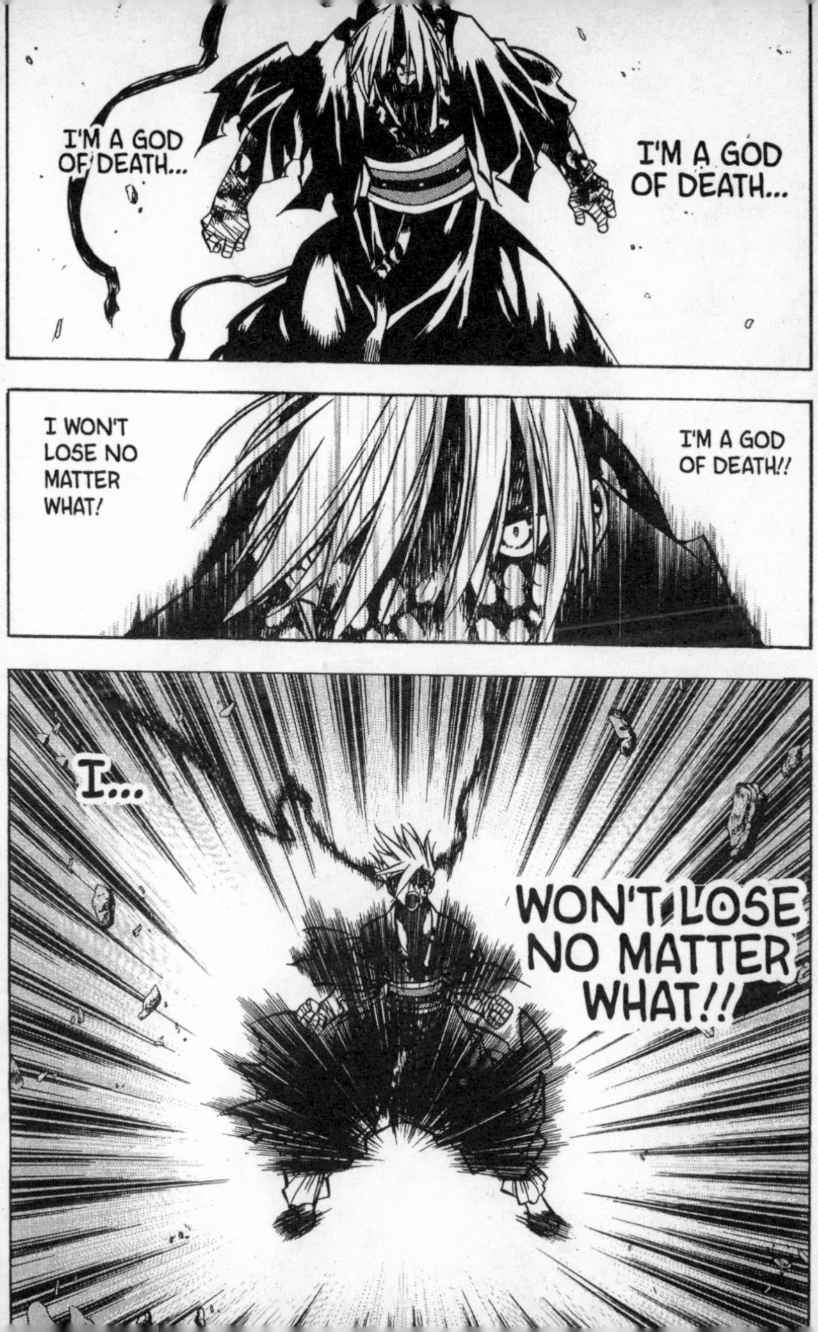
I'M A GOD OF DEATH...
I'M A GOD OF DEATH...
I'M A GOD OF DEATH!!
I WON'T LOSE NO MATTER WHAT!
I...
WON'T LOSE NO MATTER WHAT!!

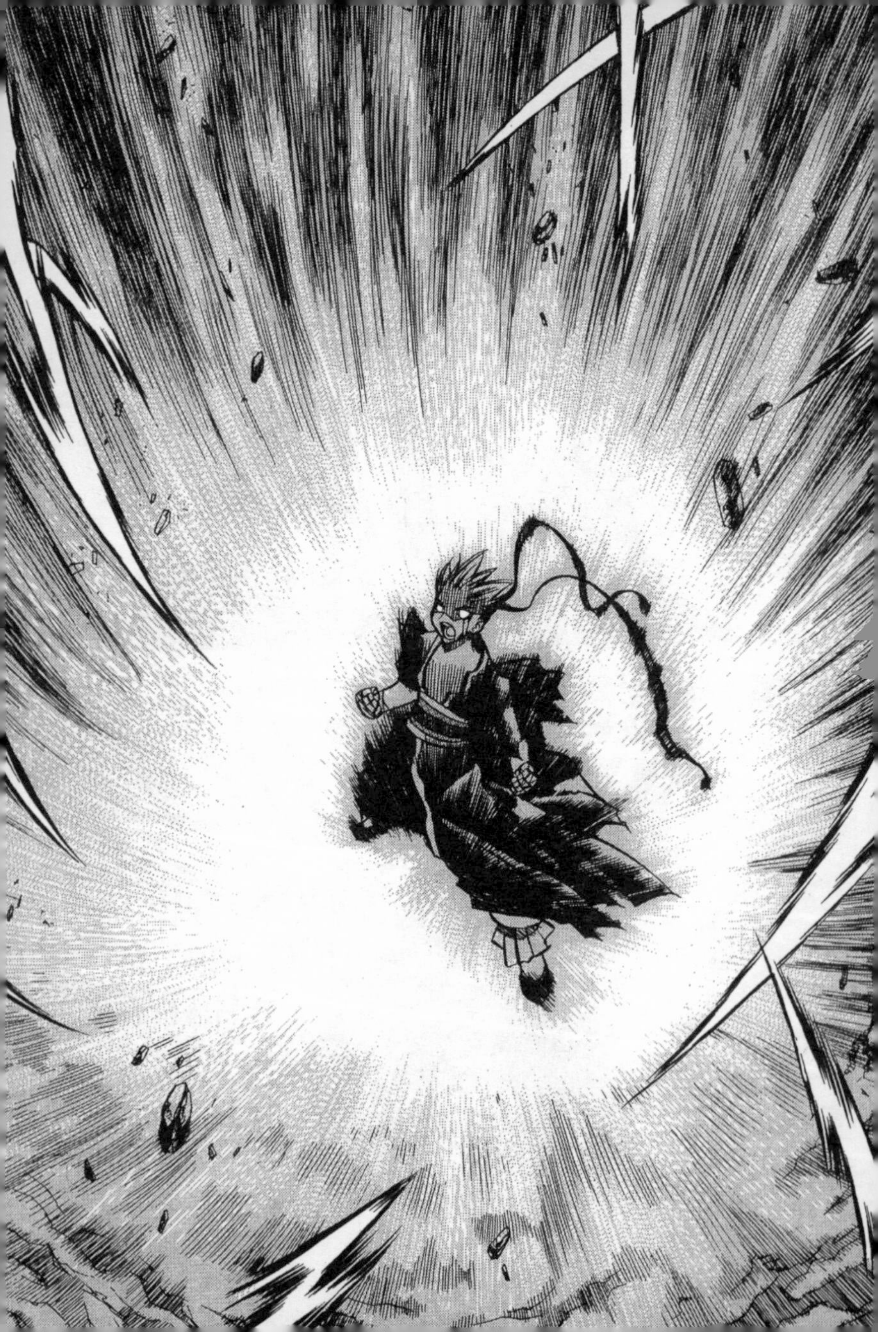

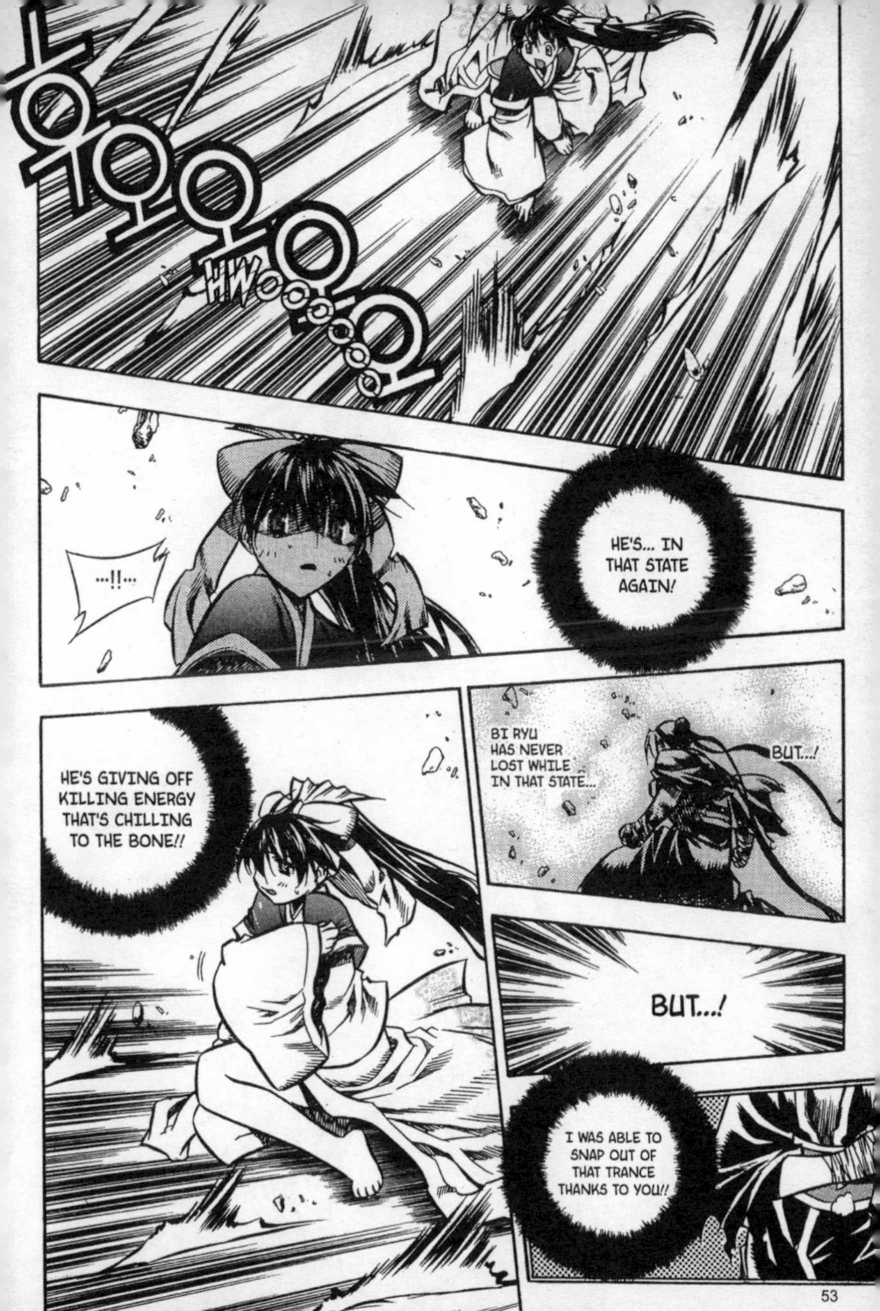
HWOOOOOOO
...!!...
HE'S... IN THAT STATE AGAIN!
HE'S GIVING OFF KILLING ENERGY THAT'S CHILLING TO THE BONE!!
BI RYU HAS NEVER LOST WHILE IN THAT STATE...
BUT...!
BUT...!
I WAS ABLE TO SNAP OUT OF THAT TRANCE THANKS TO YOU!!

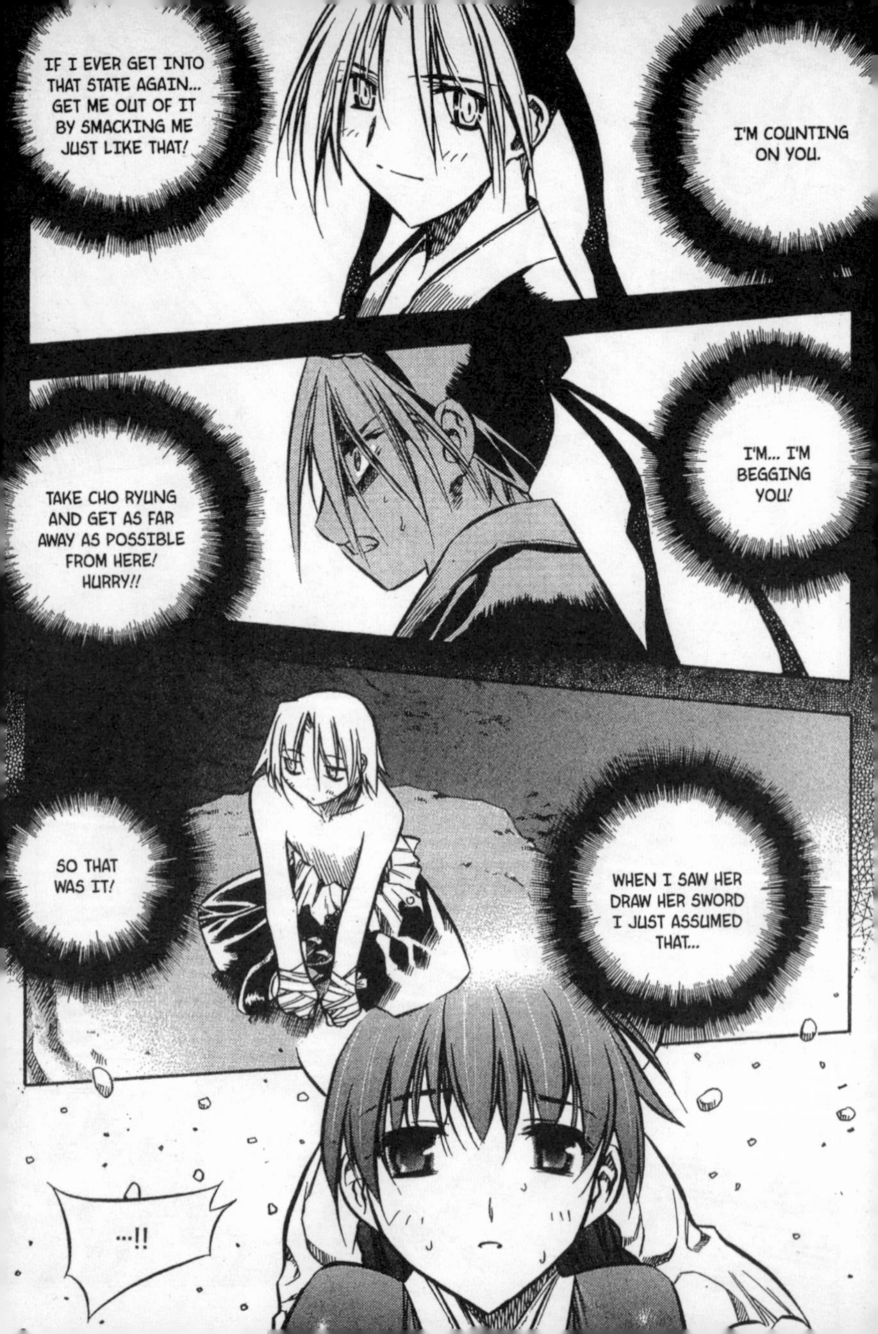
IF I EVER GET INTO THAT STATE AGAIN... GET ME OUT OF IT BY SMACKING ME JUST LIKE THAT!
I'M COUNTING ON YOU.
TAKE CHO RYUNG AND GET AS FAR AWAY AS POSSIBLE FROM HERE! HURRY!!
I'M... I'M BEGGING YOU!
SO THAT WAS IT!
WHEN I SAW HER DRAW HER SWORD I JUST ASSUMED THAT...
...!!

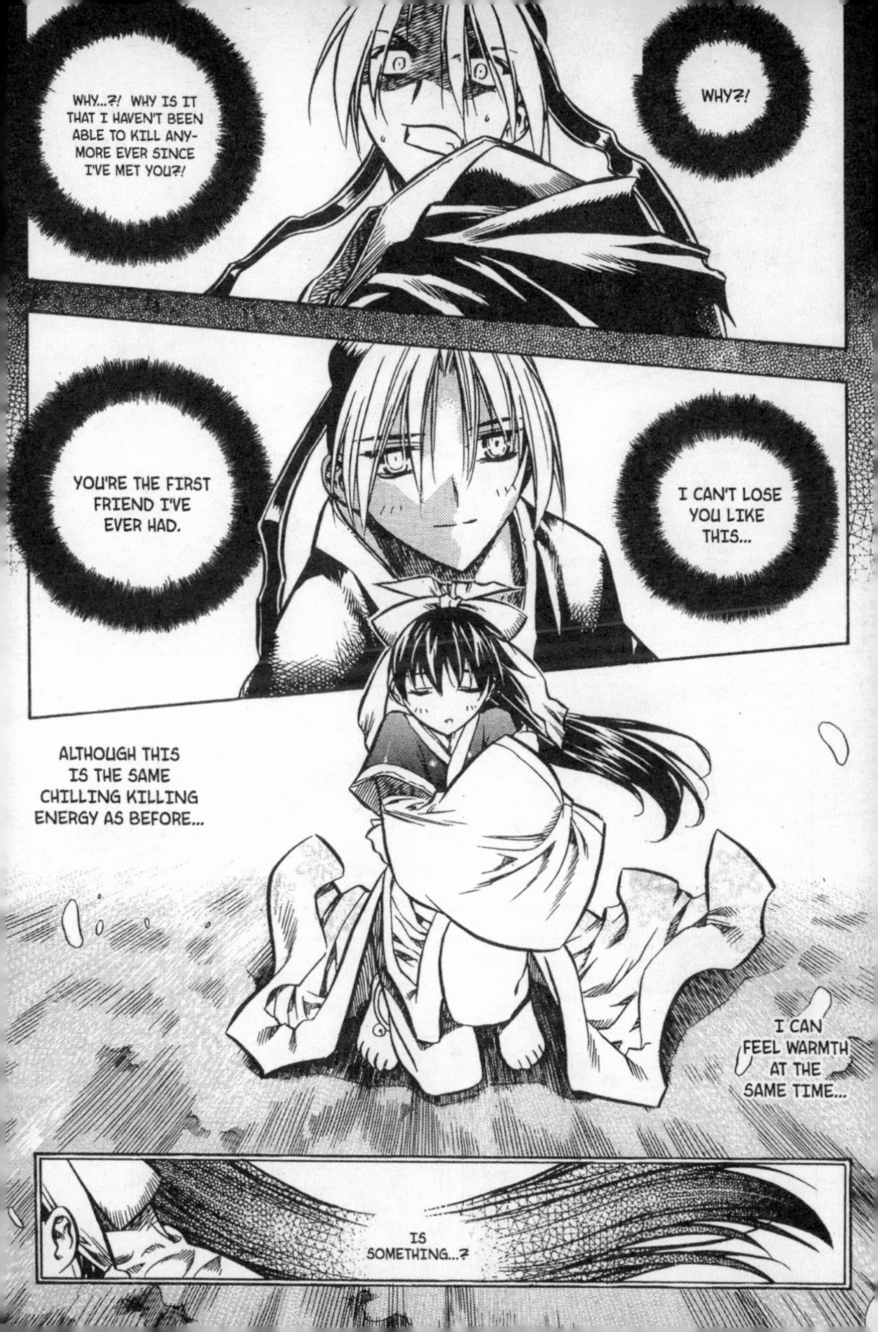

WHY?!
WHY...?! WHY IS IT THAT I HAVEN'T BEEN ABLE TO KILL ANY-MORE EVER SINCE I'VE MET YOU?!
I CAN'T LOSE YOU LIKE THIS...
YOU'RE THE FIRST FRIEND I'VE EVER HAD.
ALTHOUGH THIS IS THE SAME CHILLING KILLING ENERGY AS BEFORE...
I CAN FEEL WARMTH AT THE SAME TIME...
IS SOMETHING...?

CHANGING
WITHIN BI RYU?!

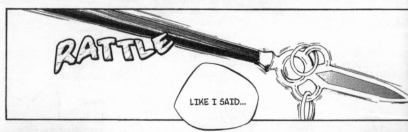

RATTLE

LIKE I SAID...

REGARDLESS OF HOW
MUCH KILLING
ENERGY YOU MAY
HAVE...

IT'S ALL USELESS
IN FRONT OF
NAGA!!

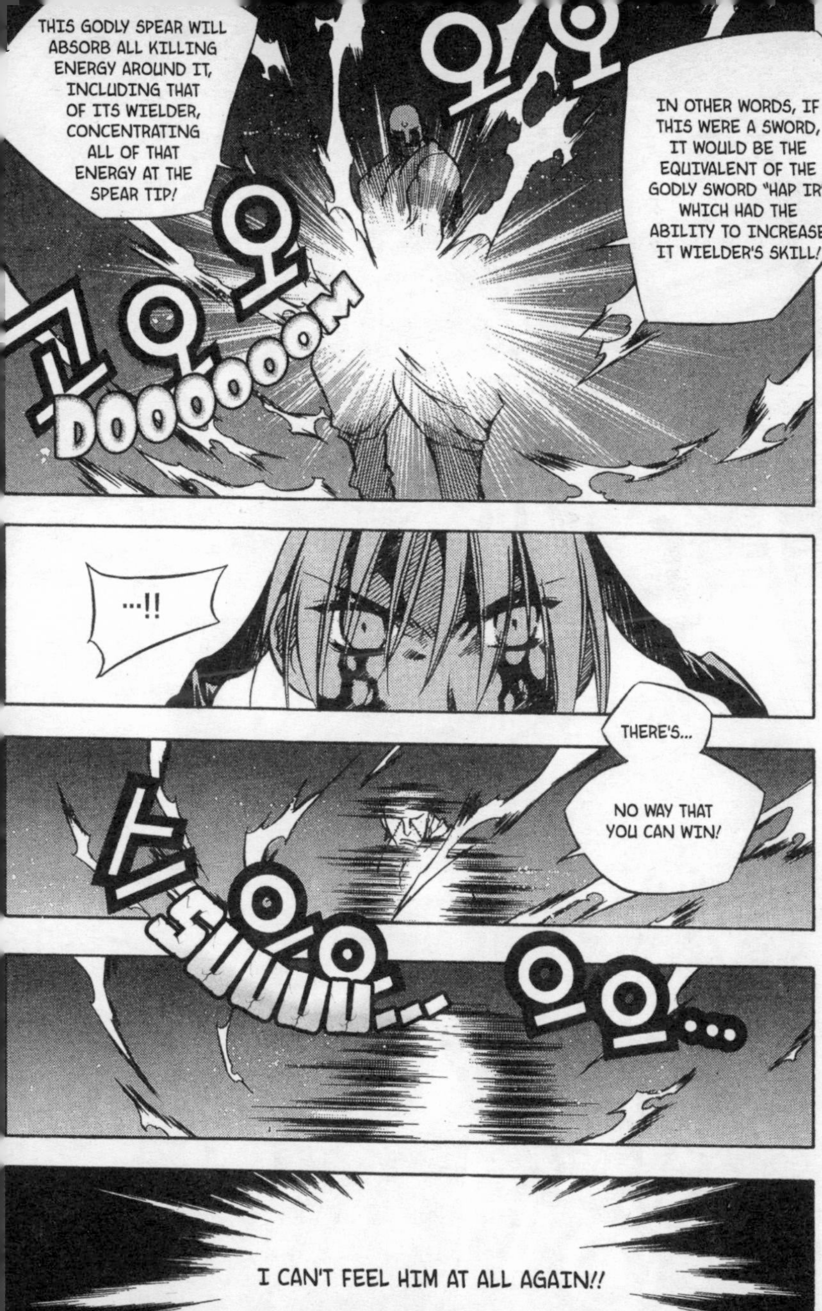
THIS GODLY SPEAR WILL ABSORB ALL KILLING ENERGY AROUND IT, INCLUDING THAT OF ITS WIELDER, CONCENTRATING ALL OF THAT ENERGY AT THE SPEAR TIP!
IN OTHER WORDS, IF THIS WERE A SWORD, IT WOULD BE THE EQUIVALENT OF THE GODLY SWORD "HAP IR" WHICH HAD THE ABILITY TO INCREASE IT WIELDER'S SKILL!
DOOOOOOM
...!!
THERE'S...
NO WAY THAT YOU CAN WIN!
SUUUU...
I CAN'T FEEL HIM AT ALL AGAIN!!

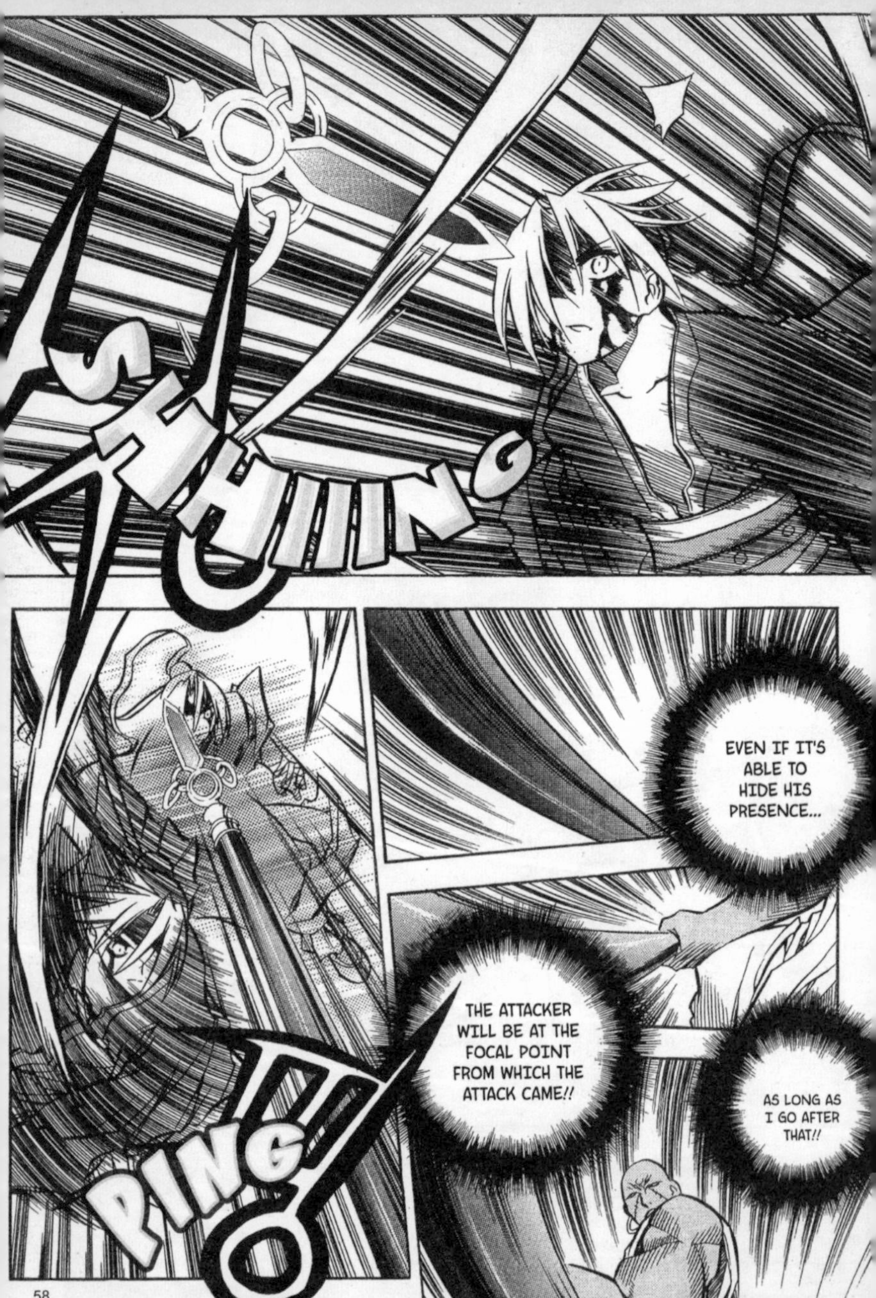
SHIIING
EVEN IF IT'S ABLE TO HIDE HIS PRESENCE...
THE ATTACKER WILL BE AT THE FOCAL POINT FROM WHICH THE ATTACK CAME!!
AS LONG AS I GO AFTER THAT!!
PING!!

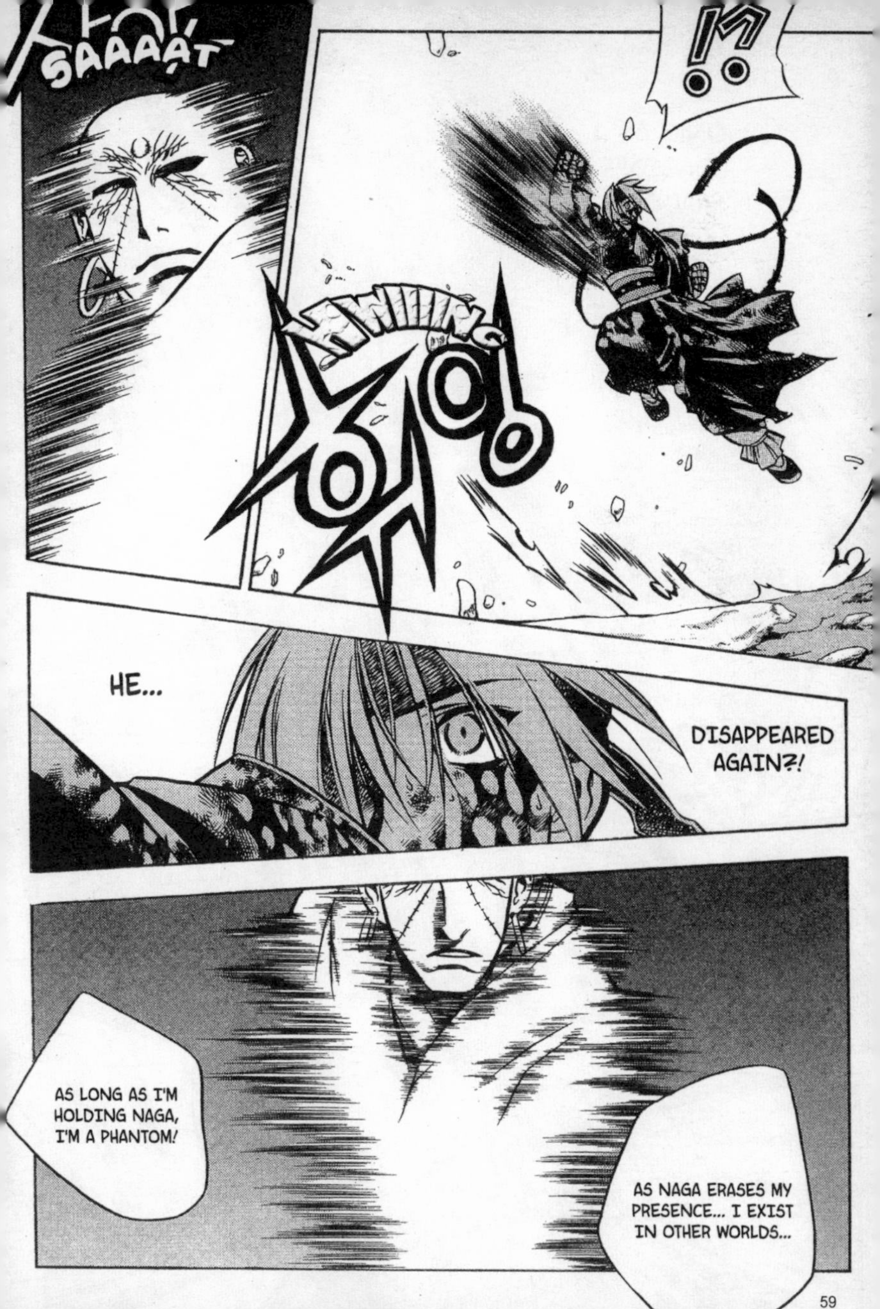

SAAAAT
!?
WHHNG
HE...
DISAPPEARED AGAIN?!
AS LONG AS I'M HOLDING NAGA, I'M A PHANTOM!
AS NAGA ERASES MY PRESENCE... I EXIST IN OTHER WORLDS...

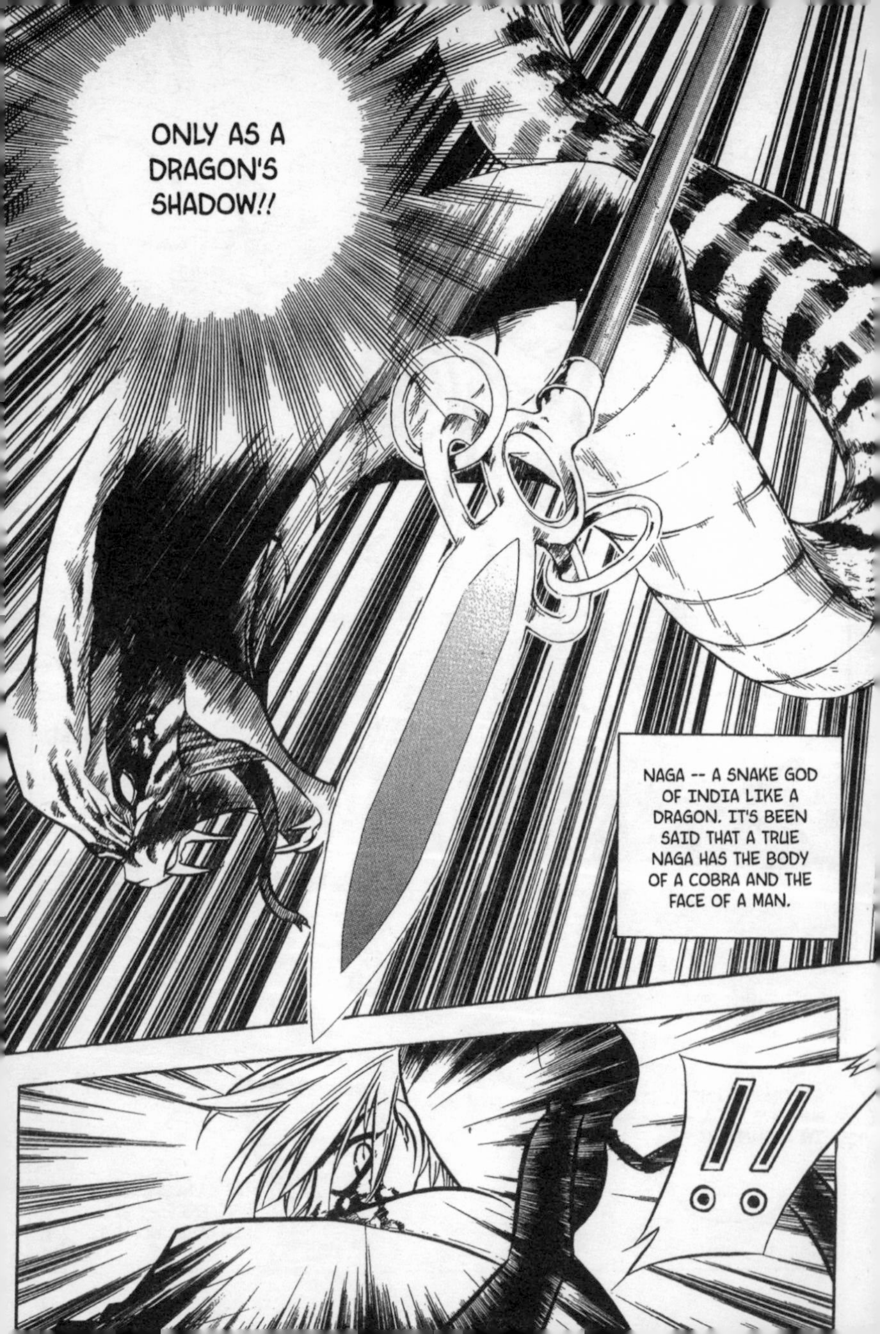
ONLY AS A DRAGON'S SHADOW!!
NAGA -- A SNAKE GOD OF INDIA LIKE A DRAGON. IT'S BEEN SAID THAT A TRUE NAGA HAS THE BODY OF A COBRA AND THE FACE OF A MAN.
!!

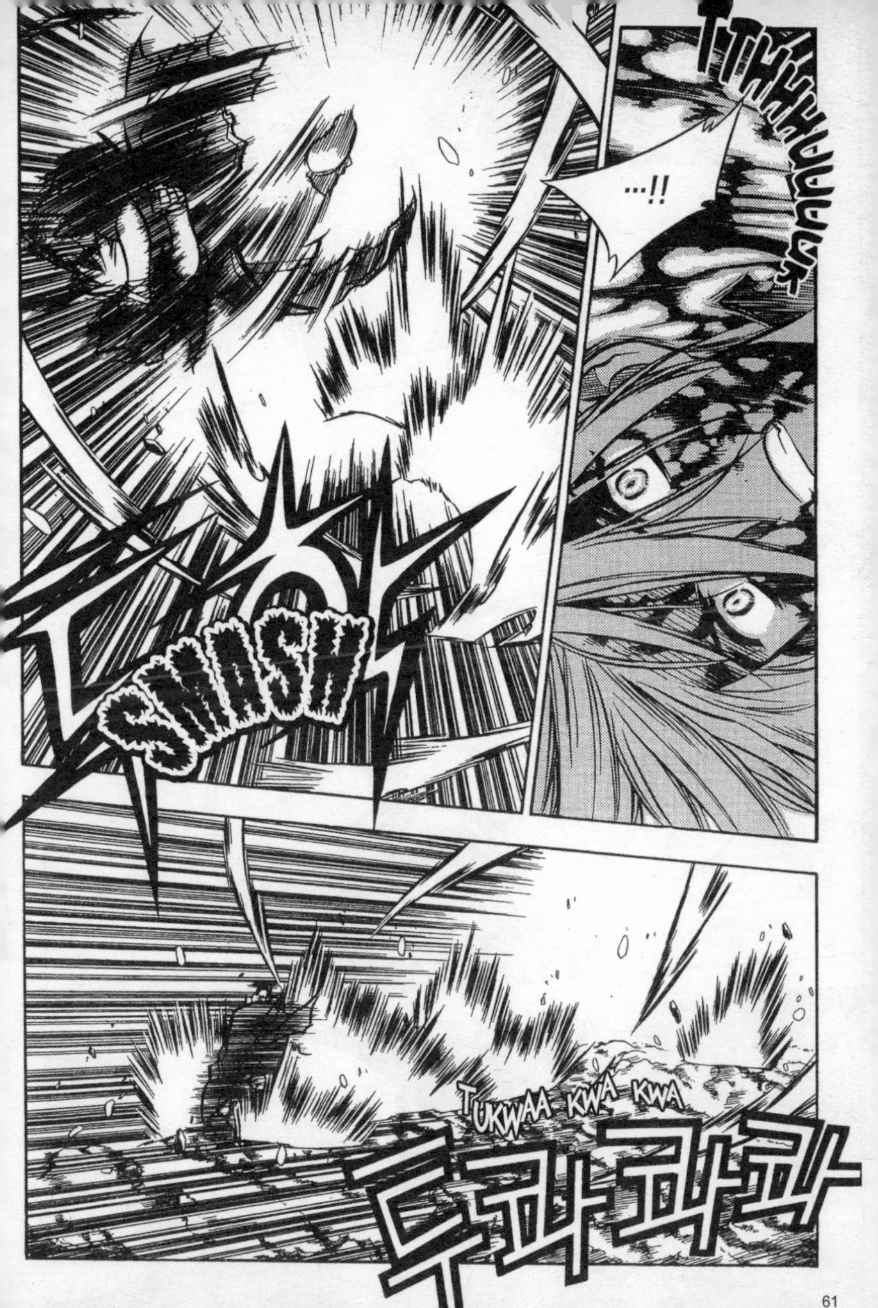
TTHHUUUUK
...!!
SMASH
TUKWAA KWA KWA

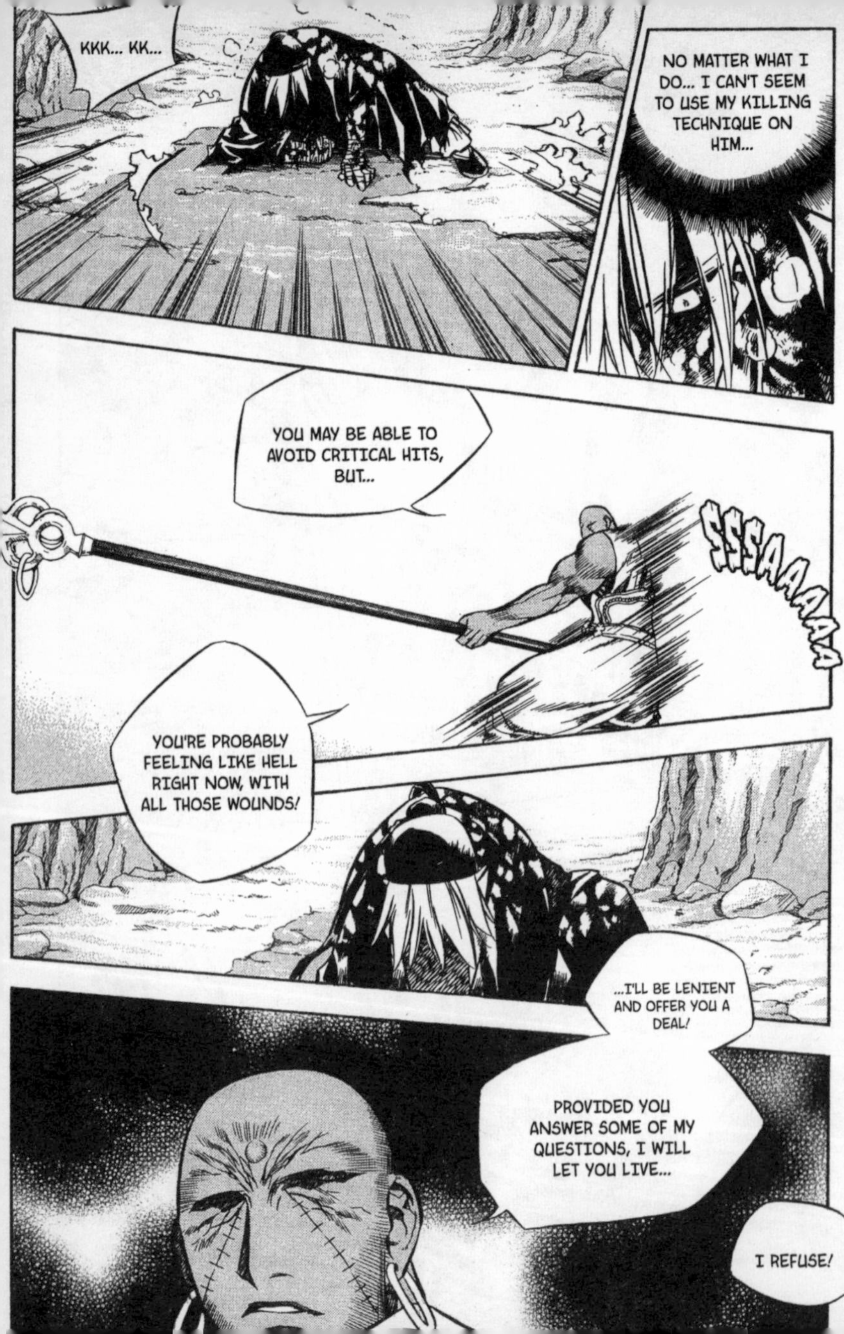
KKK... KK...
NO MATTER WHAT I DO... I CAN'T SEEM TO USE MY KILLING TECHNIQUE ON HIM...
YOU MAY BE ABLE TO AVOID CRITICAL HITS, BUT...
SSSAAAAAA
YOU'RE PROBABLY FEELING LIKE HELL RIGHT NOW, WITH ALL THOSE WOUNDS!
...I'LL BE LENIENT AND OFFER YOU A DEAL!
PROVIDED YOU ANSWER SOME OF MY QUESTIONS, I WILL LET YOU LIVE...
I REFUSE!

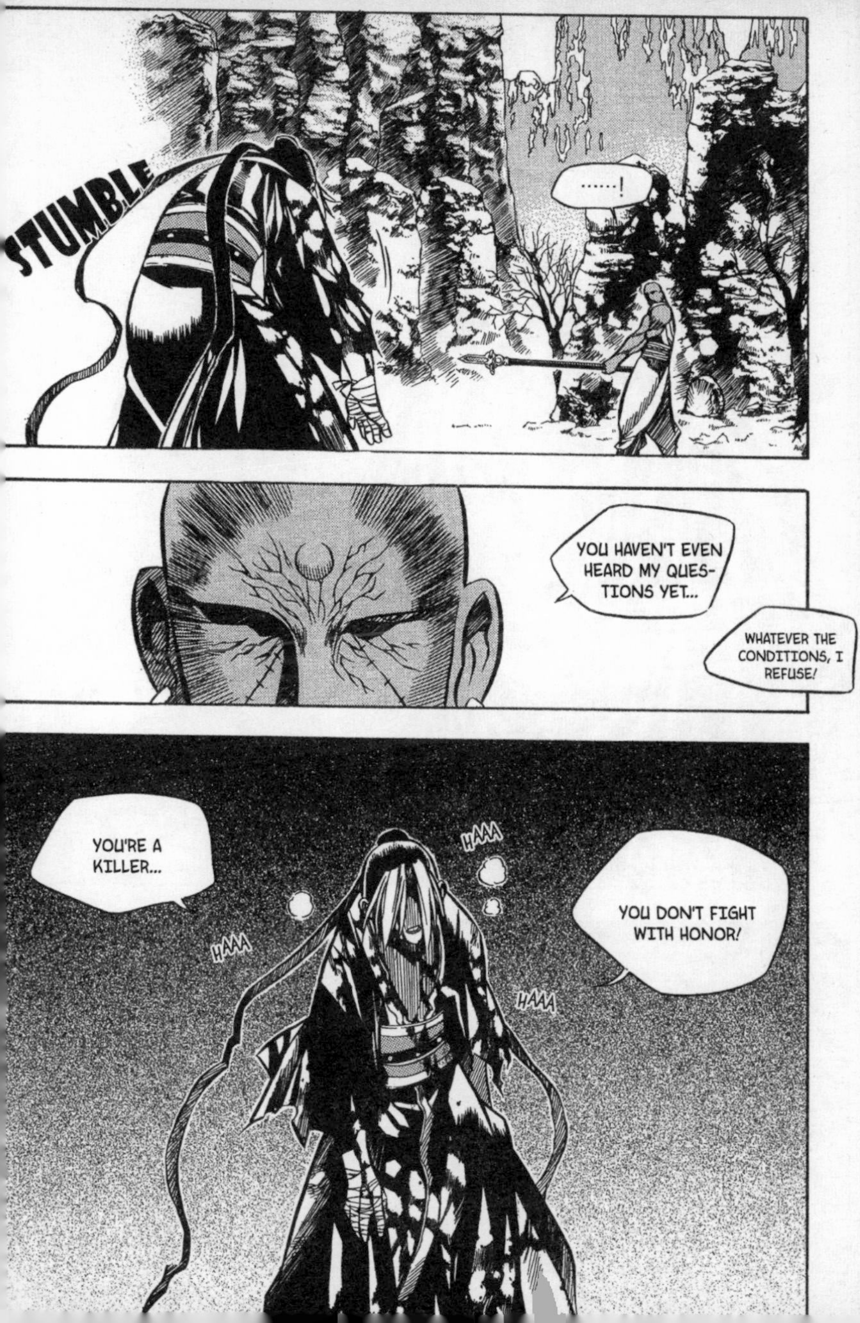
STUMBLE
......!
YOU HAVEN'T EVEN HEARD MY QUES-TIONS YET...
WHATEVER THE CONDITIONS, I REFUSE!
YOU'RE A KILLER...
HAAA
YOU DON'T FIGHT WITH HONOR!
HAAA
HAAA

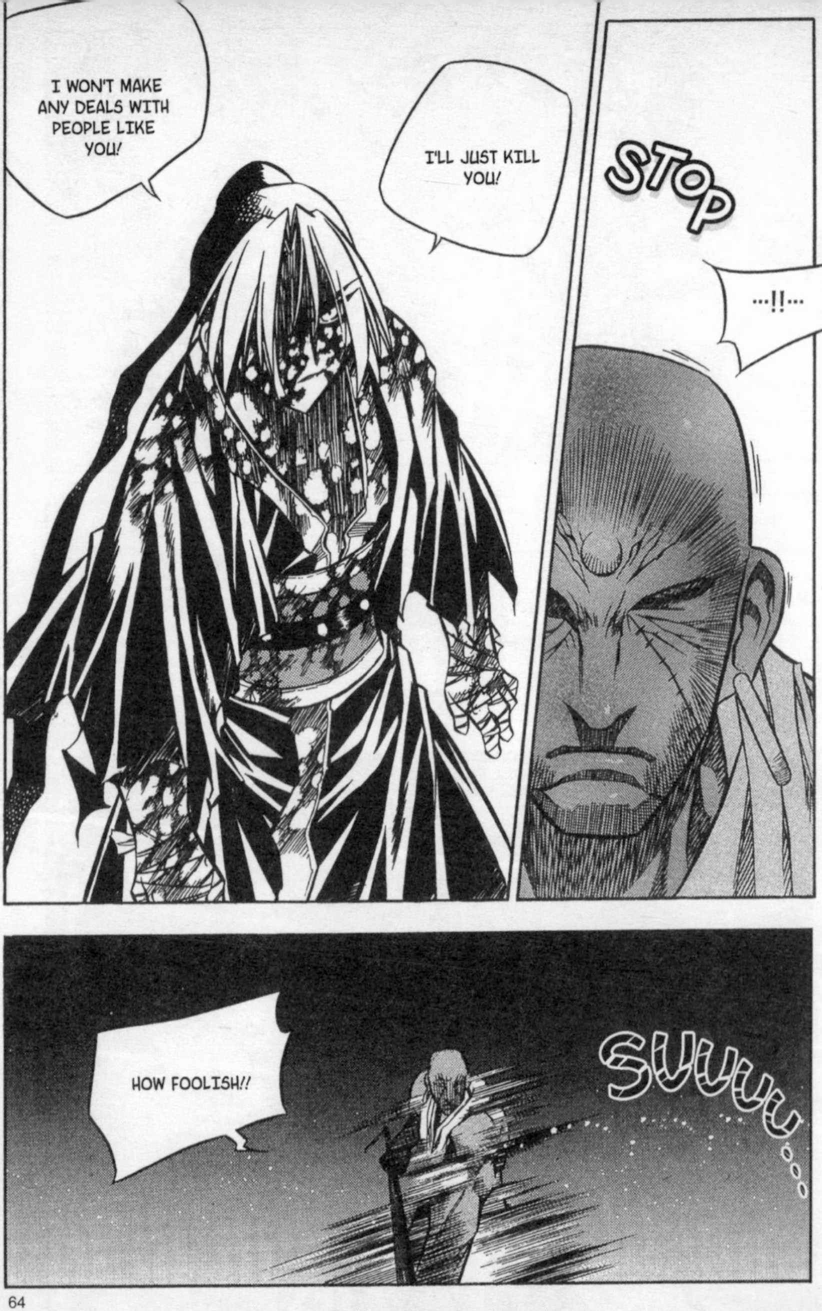
I WON'T MAKE ANY DEALS WITH PEOPLE LIKE YOU!
I'LL JUST KILL YOU!
STOP
...!!...
HOW FOOLISH!!
SUUUU...

HAAA

I WONDER... IF MY KILLING TECHNIQUES WON'T WORK ANYMORE...

IS THIS...

THE RESULT OF...

CHOOSING A FRIEND OVER KILLING? DON'T WORRY! IT ISN'T YOUR FAULT...

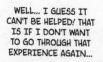

WELL... I GUESS IT CAN'T BE HELPED! THAT IS IF I DON'T WANT TO GO THROUGH THAT EXPERIENCE AGAIN...

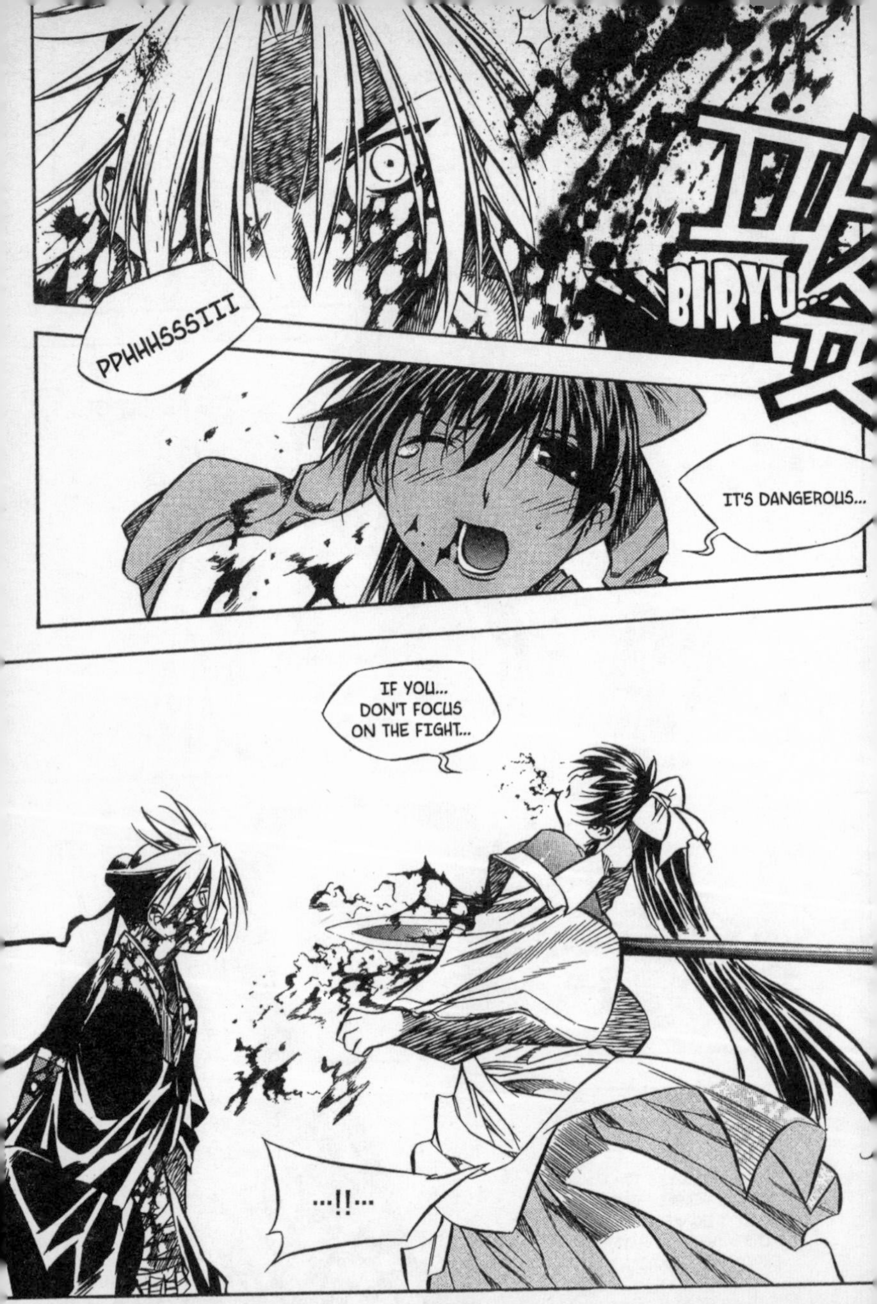
BIRYU...
PPHHHSSSIII
IT'S DANGEROUS...
IF YOU...
DON'T FOCUS
ON THE FIGHT...
...!!...

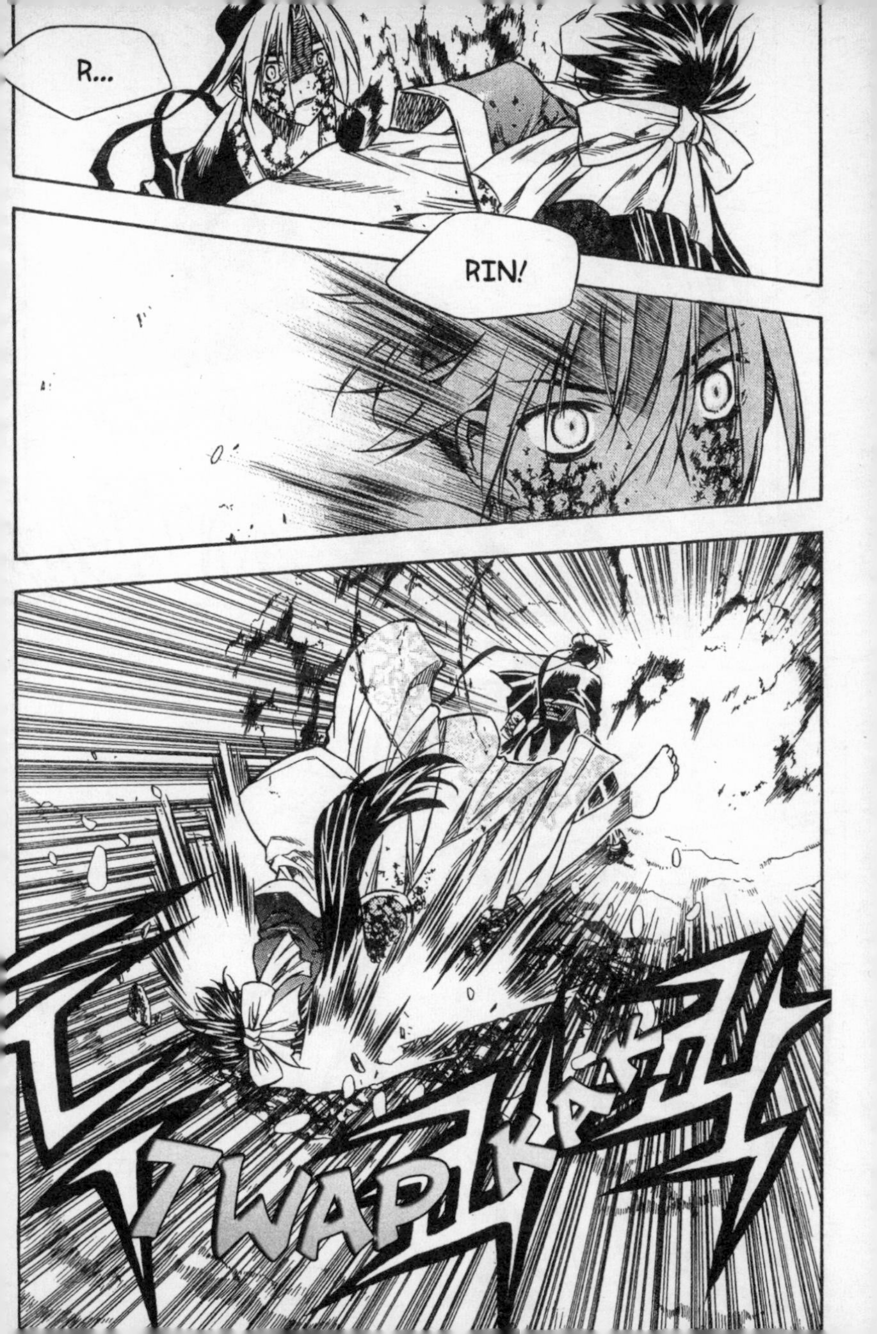
R...
RIN!
TWAPKESH

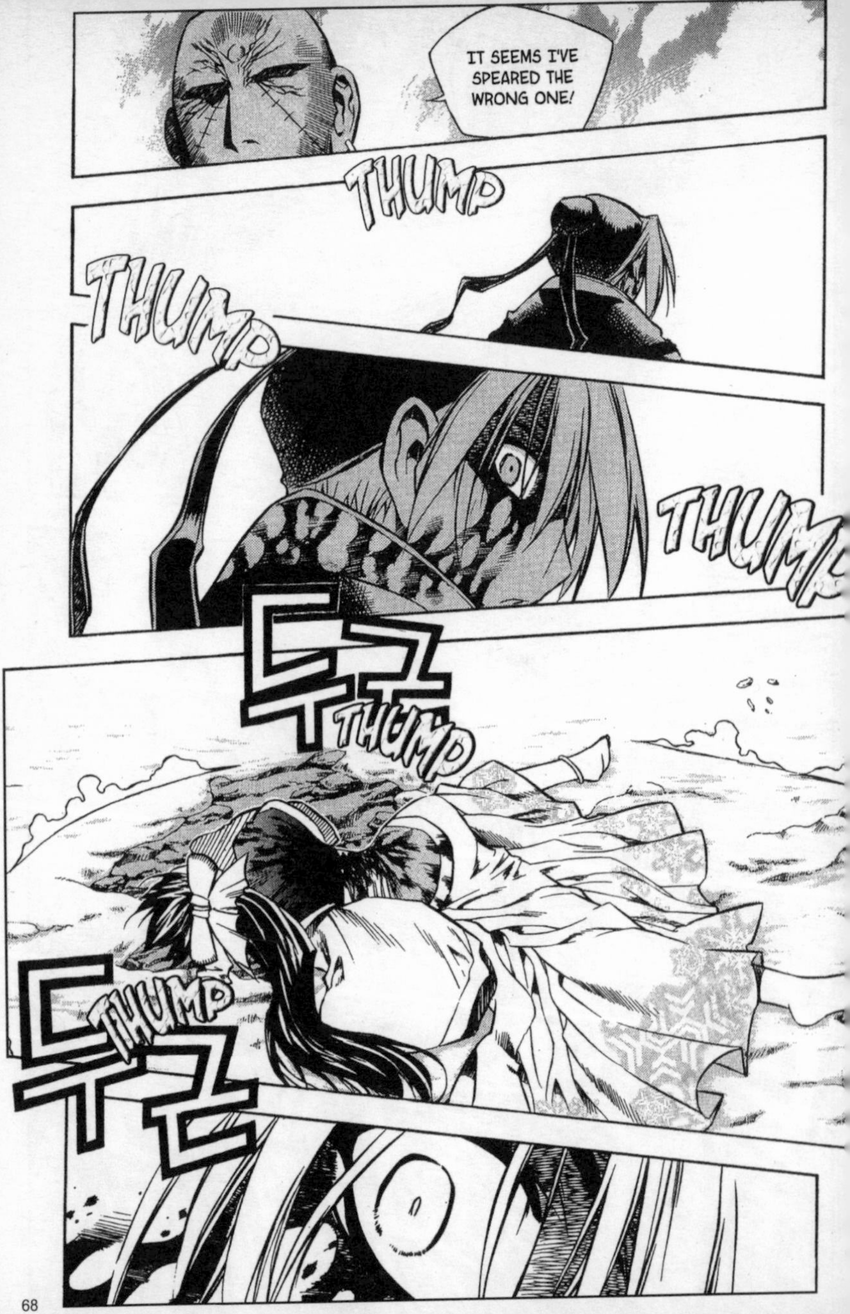
IT SEEMS I'VE SPEARED THE WRONG ONE!
THUMP
THUMP
THUMP
THUMP
THUMP

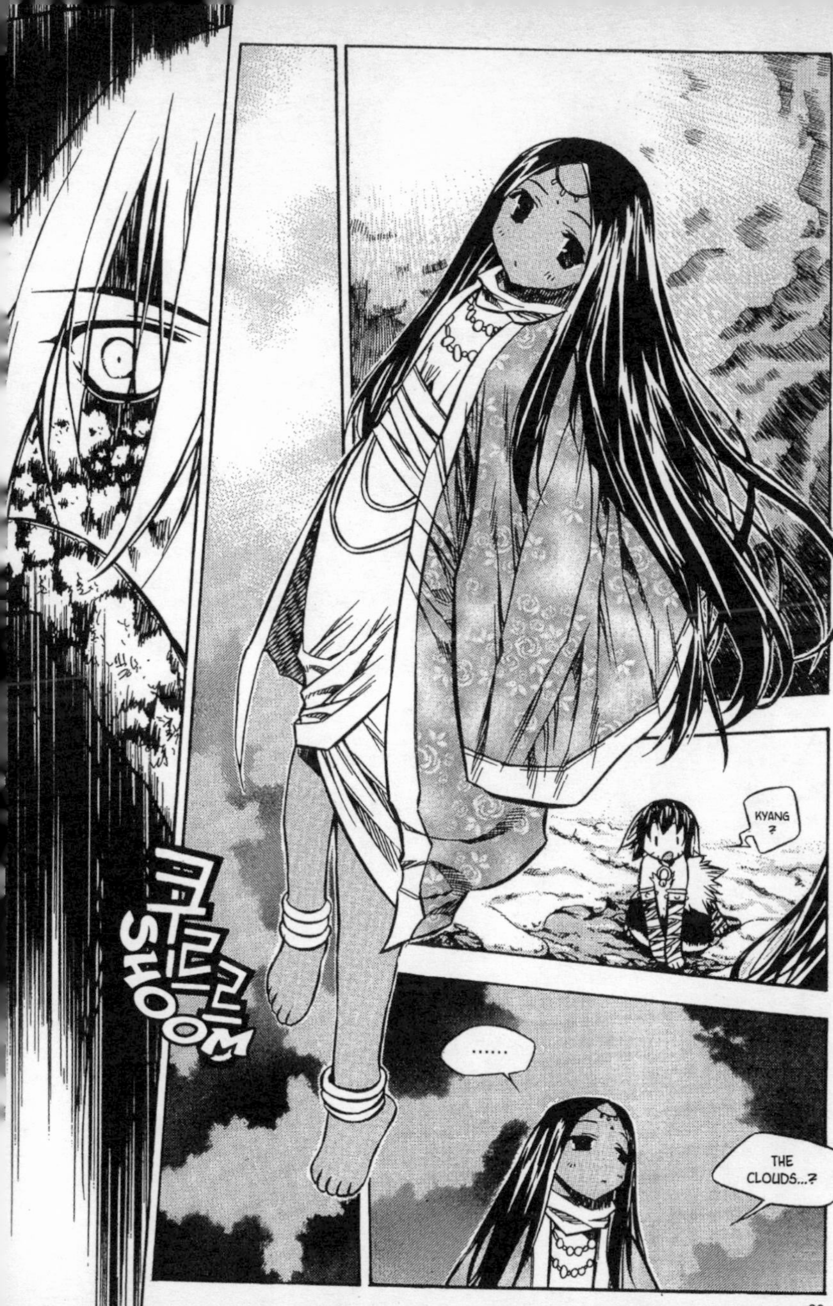
SHOOM
KYANG?
....
THE CLOUDS...?

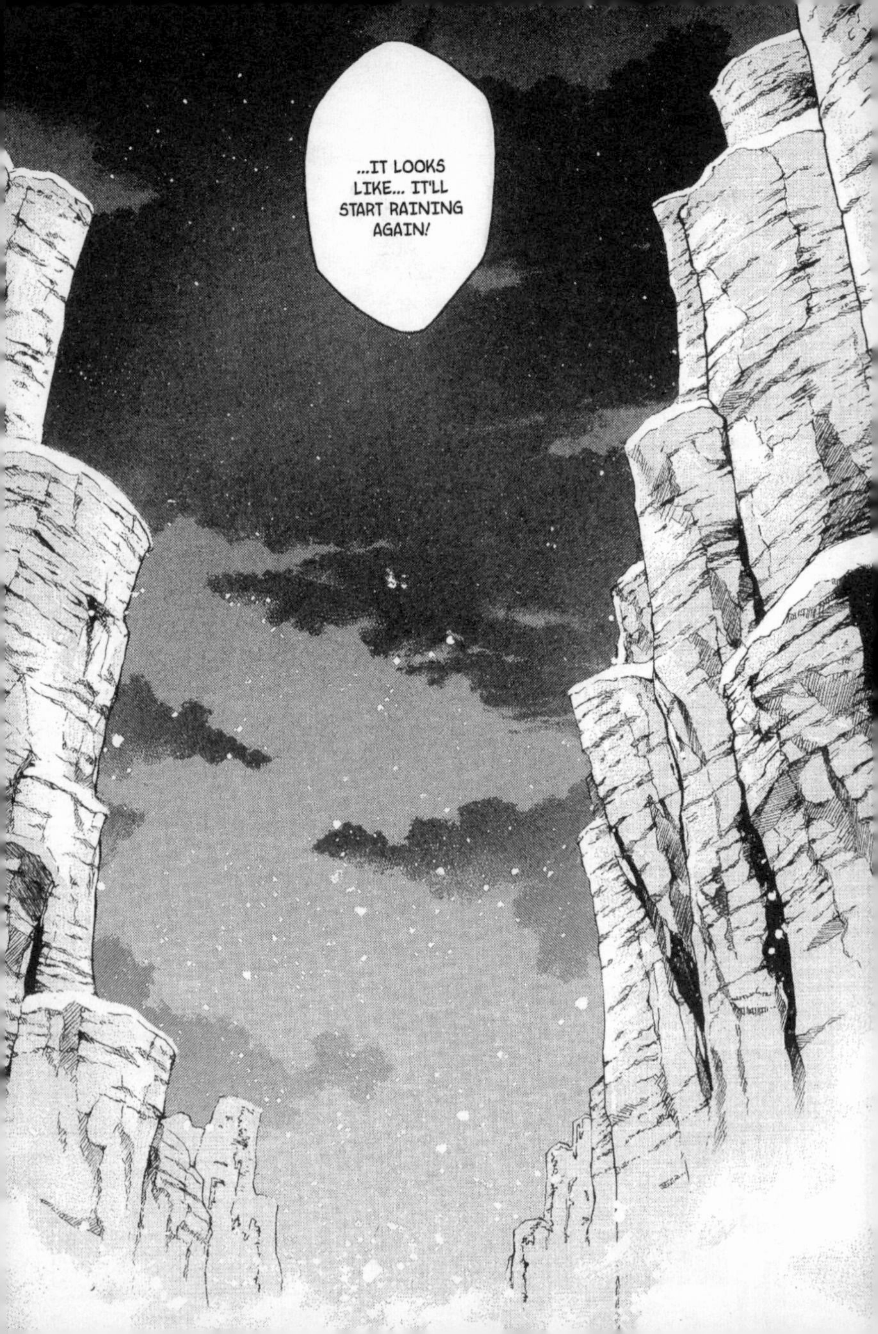
...IT LOOKS LIKE... IT'LL START RAINING AGAIN!

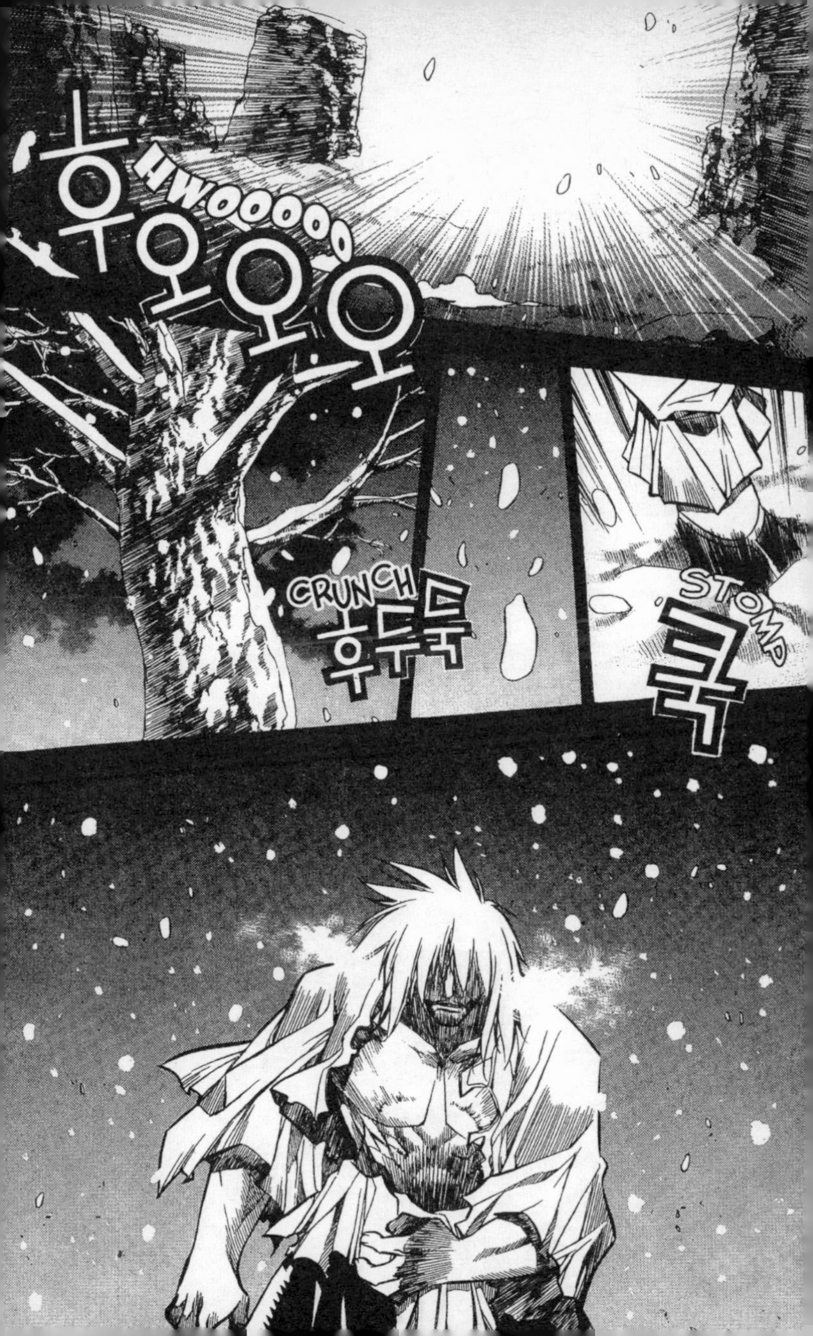

HWOOOOO
CRUNCH
STOMP

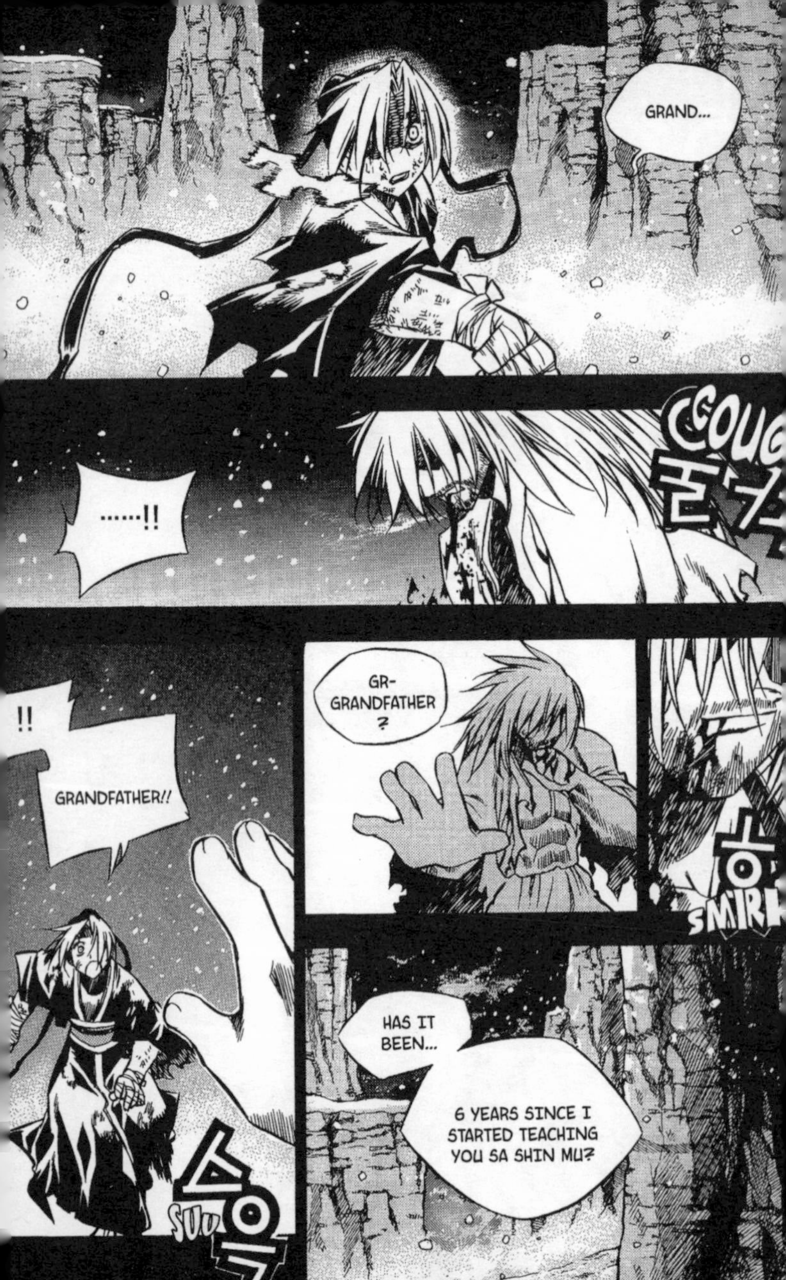
GRAND...
......!!
COUG
!!
GRANDFATHER!!
SUU
GR-
GRANDFATHER?
SMIR
HAS IT BEEN...
6 YEARS SINCE I STARTED TEACHING YOU SA SHIN MU?

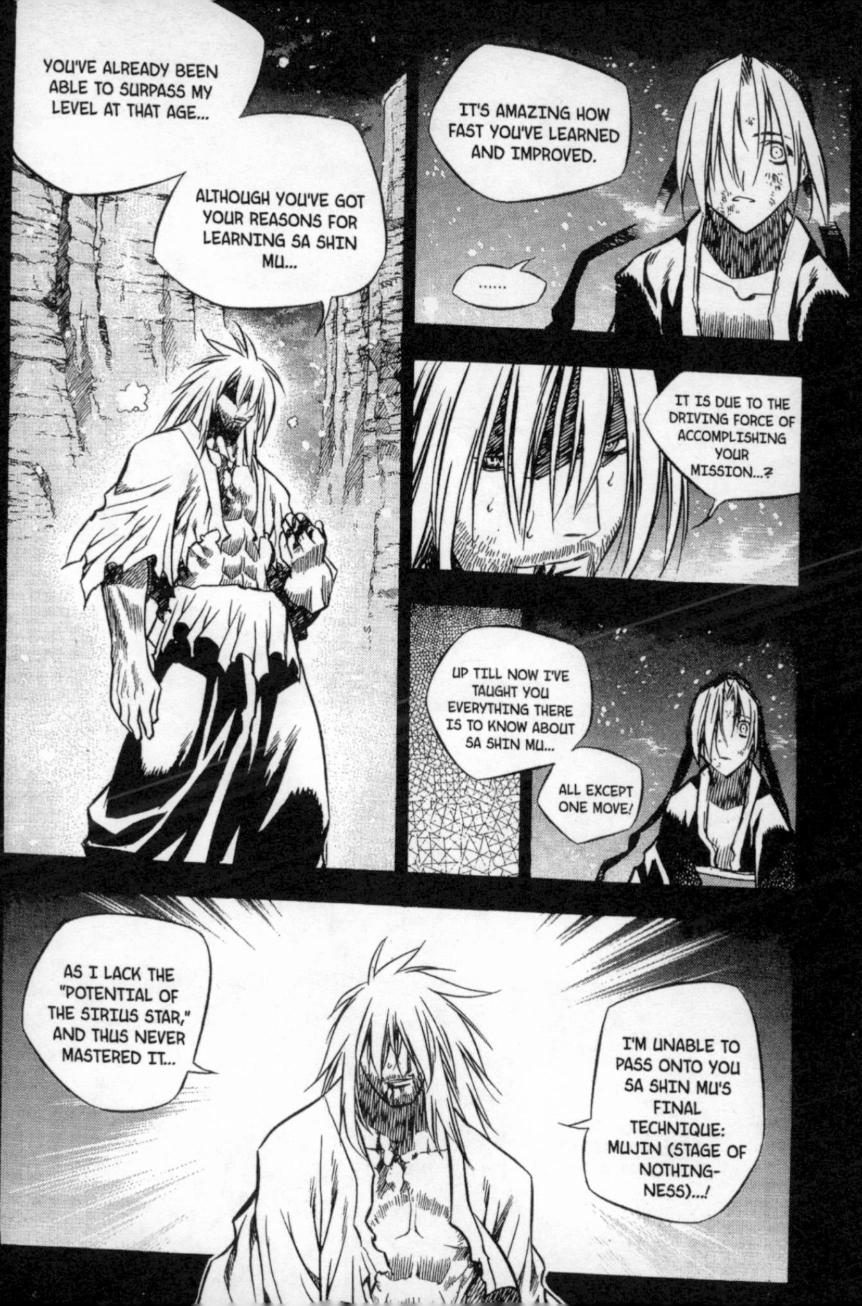
YOU'VE ALREADY BEEN ABLE TO SURPASS MY LEVEL AT THAT AGE...
ALTHOUGH YOU'VE GOT YOUR REASONS FOR LEARNING SA SHIN MU...
IT'S AMAZING HOW FAST YOU'VE LEARNED AND IMPROVED.
......
IT IS DUE TO THE DRIVING FORCE OF ACCOMPLISHING YOUR MISSION...?
UP TILL NOW I'VE TAUGHT YOU EVERYTHING THERE IS TO KNOW ABOUT SA SHIN MU...
ALL EXCEPT ONE MOVE!
AS I LACK THE "POTENTIAL OF THE SIRIUS STAR," AND THUS NEVER MASTERED IT...
I'M UNABLE TO PASS ONTO YOU SA SHIN MU'S FINAL TECHNIQUE: MUJIN (STAGE OF NOTHING-NESS)...!

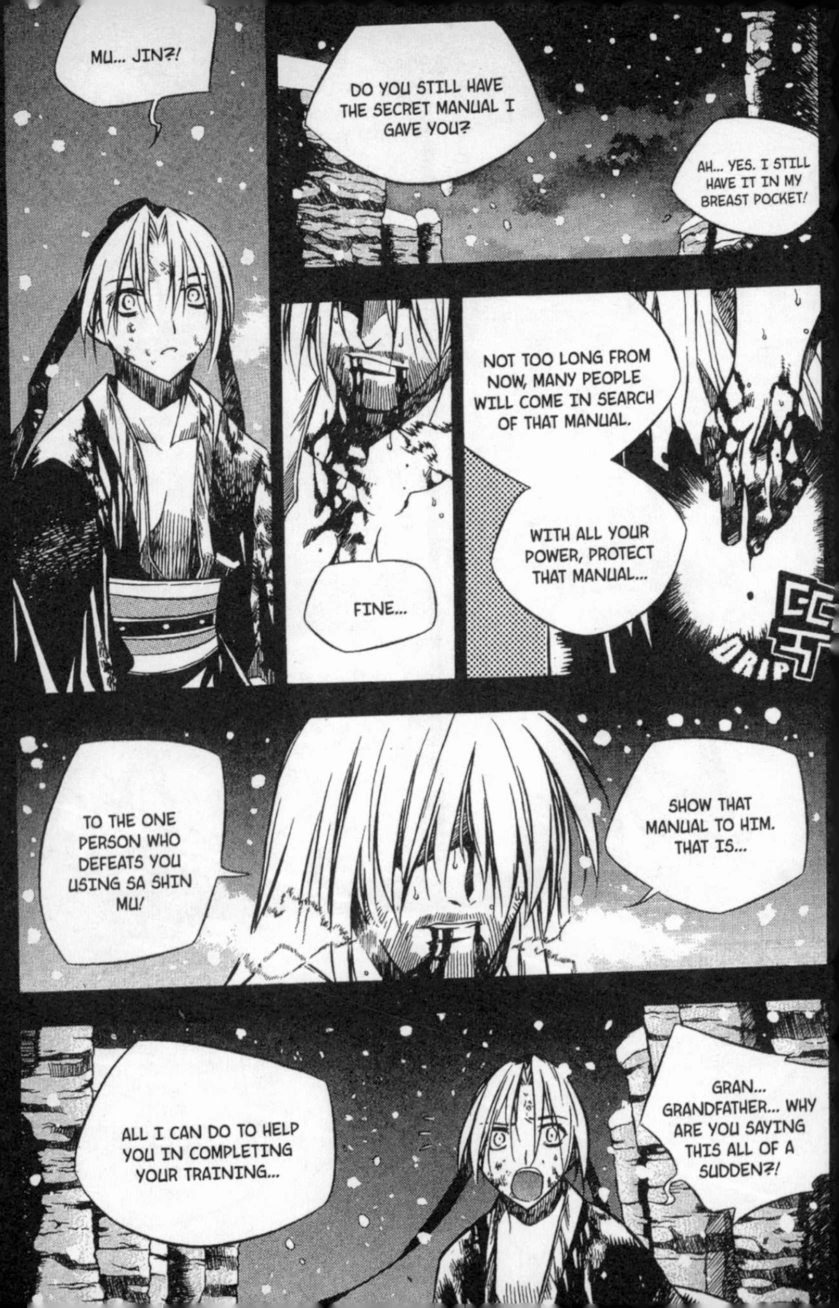
MU... JIN?!
DO YOU STILL HAVE THE SECRET MANUAL I GAVE YOU?
AH... YES. I STILL HAVE IT IN MY BREAST POCKET!
FINE...
NOT TOO LONG FROM NOW, MANY PEOPLE WILL COME IN SEARCH OF THAT MANUAL.
WITH ALL YOUR POWER, PROTECT THAT MANUAL...
DRIP
TO THE ONE PERSON WHO DEFEATS YOU USING SA SHIN MU!
SHOW THAT MANUAL TO HIM. THAT IS...
ALL I CAN DO TO HELP YOU IN COMPLETING YOUR TRAINING...
GRAN... GRANDFATHER... WHY ARE YOU SAYING THIS ALL OF A SUDDEN?!

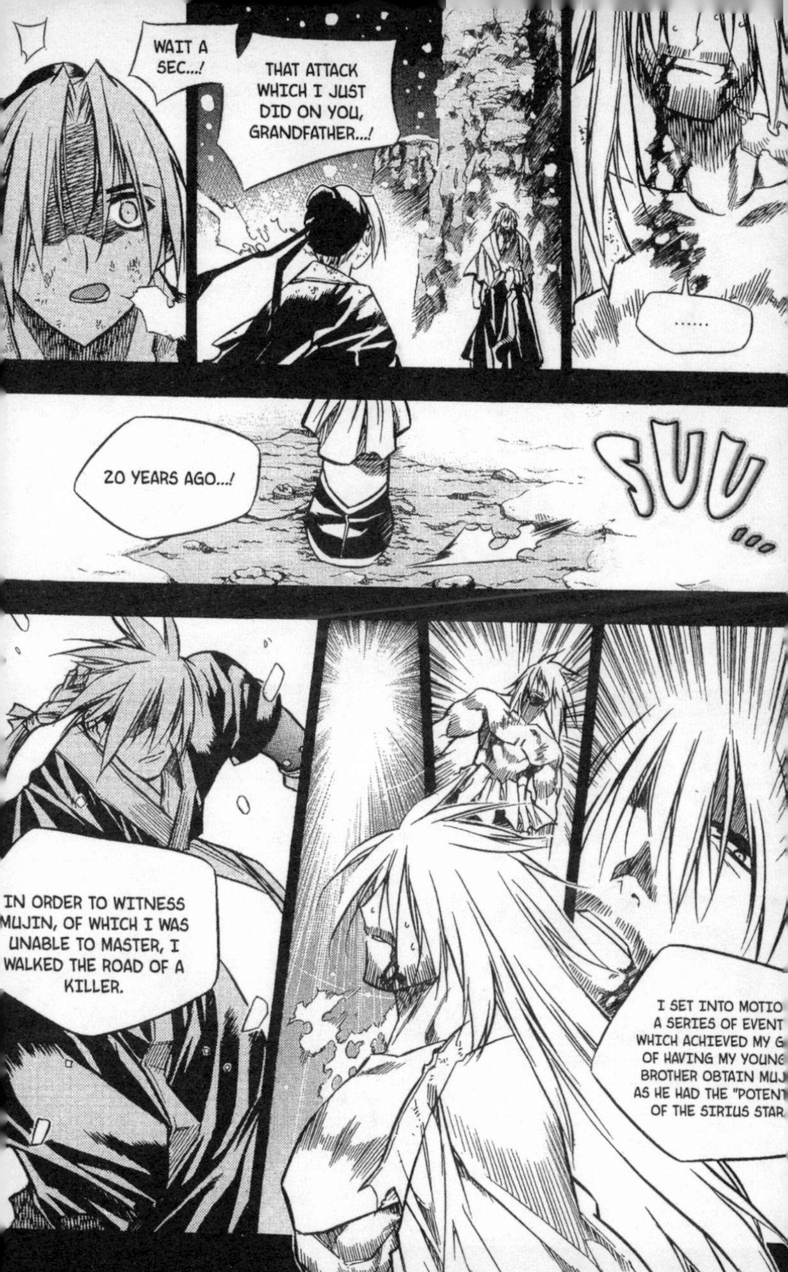

WAIT A SEC...!
THAT ATTACK WHICH I JUST DID ON YOU, GRANDFATHER...!
......
20 YEARS AGO...!
SUU...
IN ORDER TO WITNESS MUJIN, OF WHICH I WAS UNABLE TO MASTER, I WALKED THE ROAD OF A KILLER.
I SET INTO MOTIO A SERIES OF EVENT WHICH ACHIEVED MY G OF HAVING MY YOUNG BROTHER OBTAIN MUJ AS HE HAD THE "POTENT OF THE SIRIUS STAR

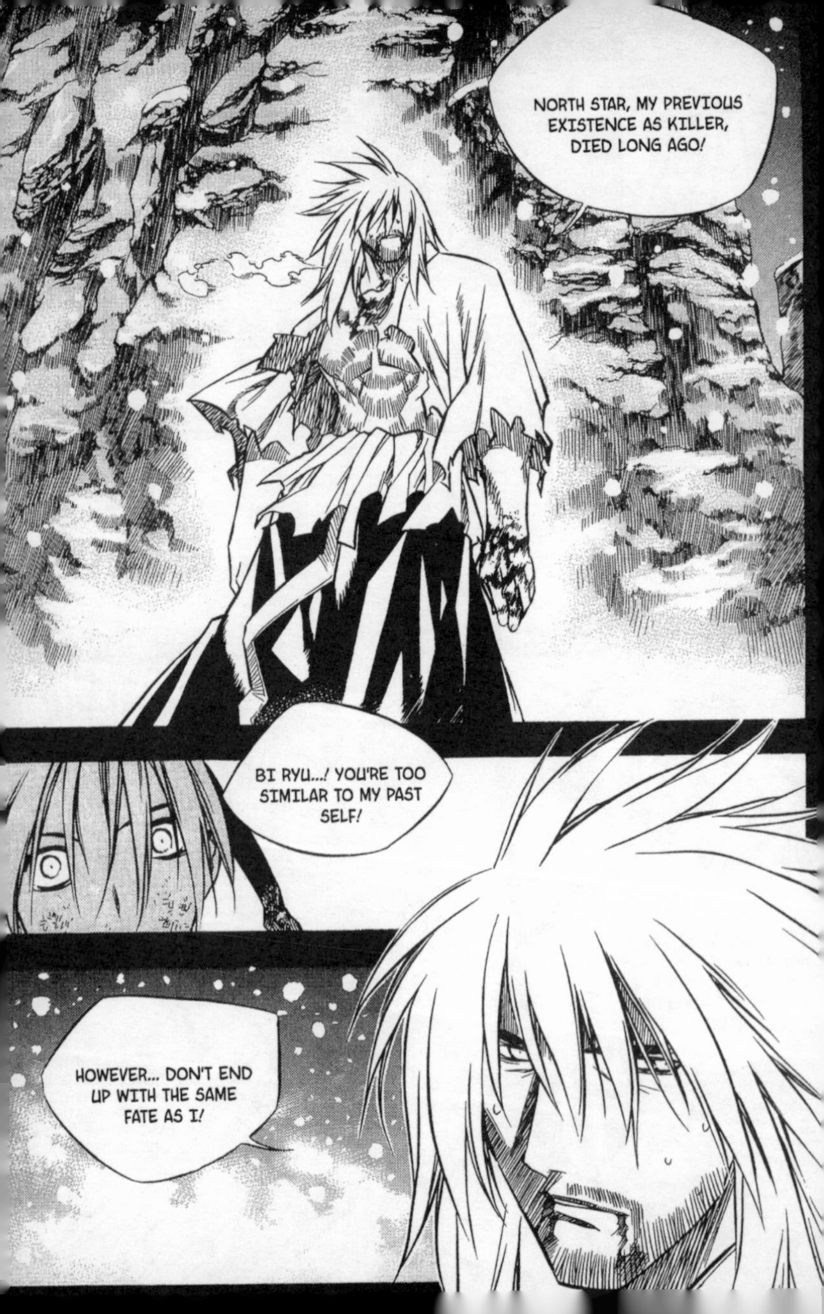
NORTH STAR, MY PREVIOUS EXISTENCE AS KILLER, DIED LONG AGO!
BI RYU...! YOU'RE TOO SIMILAR TO MY PAST SELF!
HOWEVER... DON'T END UP WITH THE SAME FATE AS I!

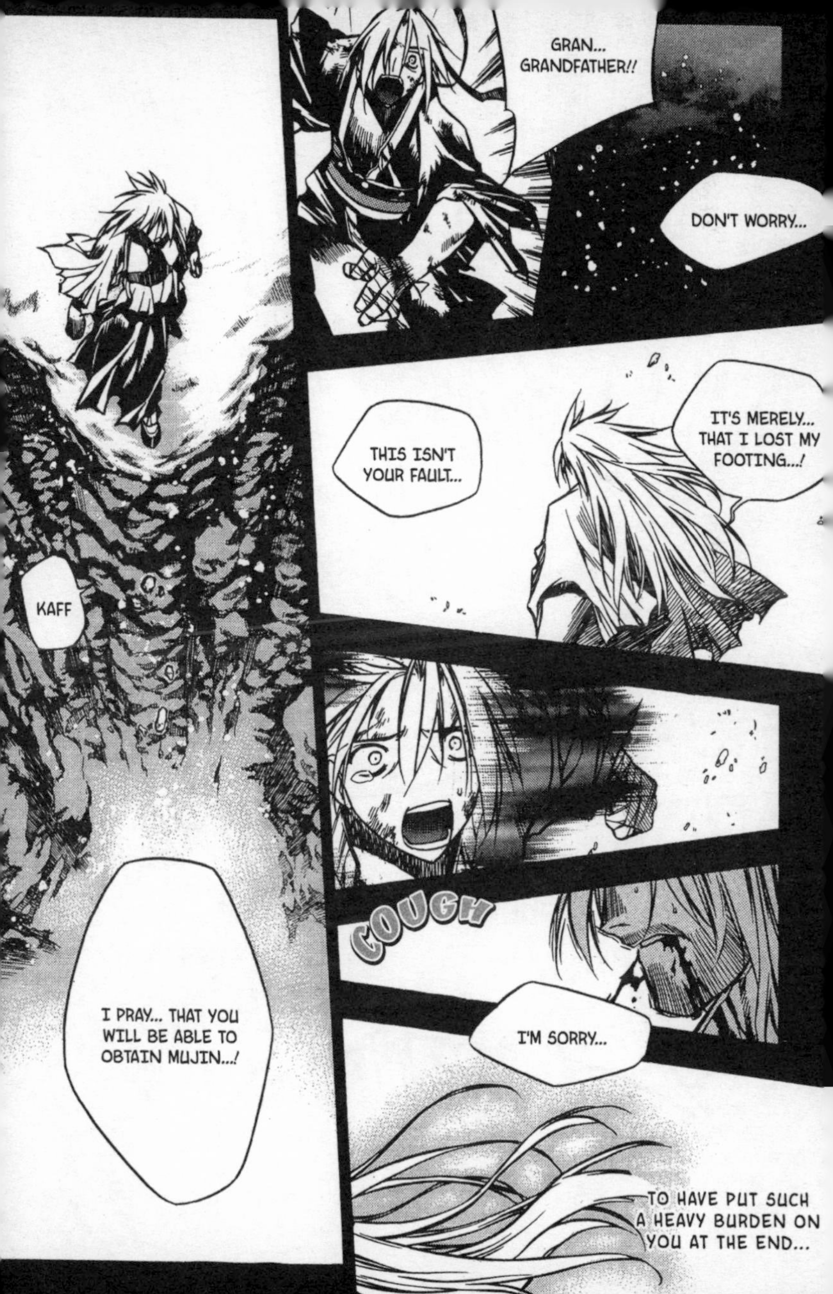
GRAN... GRANDFATHER!!
DON'T WORRY...
THIS ISN'T YOUR FAULT...
IT'S MERELY... THAT I LOST MY FOOTING...!
COUGH
I'M SORRY...
TO HAVE PUT SUCH A HEAVY BURDEN ON YOU AT THE END...
KAFF
I PRAY... THAT YOU WILL BE ABLE TO OBTAIN MUJIN...!

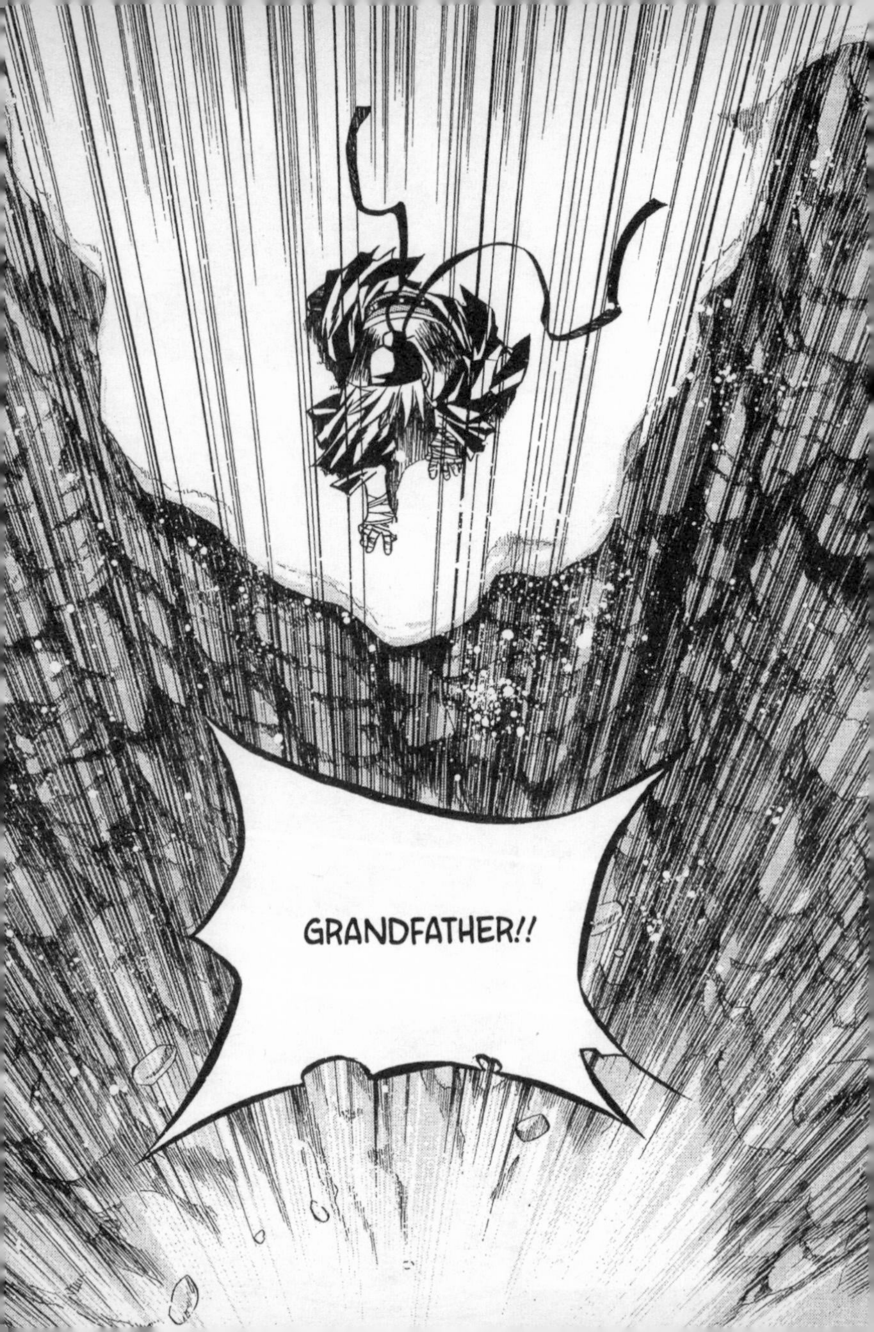
GRANDFATHER!!

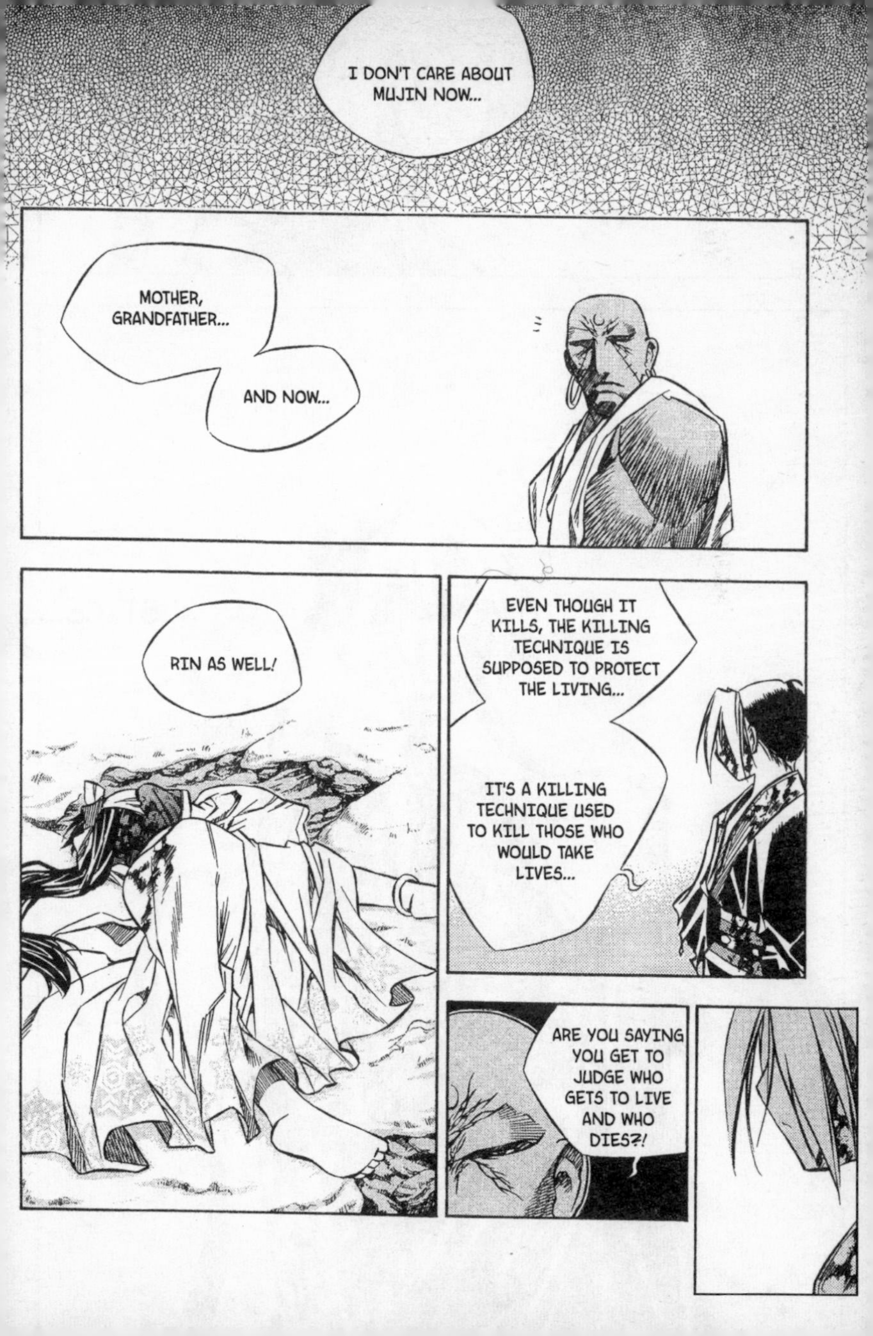
I DON'T CARE ABOUT MUJIN NOW...
MOTHER, GRANDFATHER...
AND NOW...
RIN AS WELL!
EVEN THOUGH IT KILLS, THE KILLING TECHNIQUE IS SUPPOSED TO PROTECT THE LIVING...
IT'S A KILLING TECHNIQUE USED TO KILL THOSE WHO WOULD TAKE LIVES...
ARE YOU SAYING YOU GET TO JUDGE WHO GETS TO LIVE AND WHO DIES?!

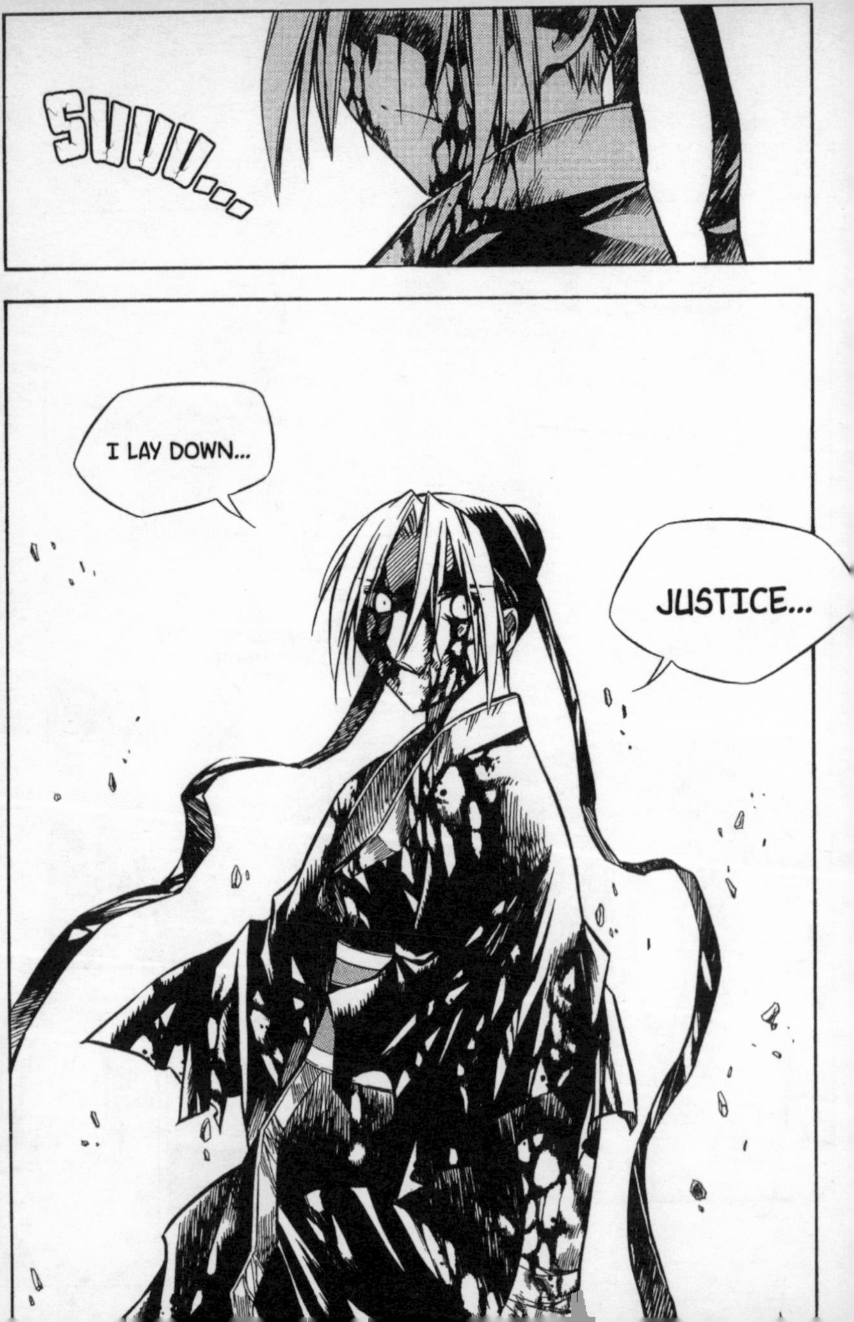
SUUU...
I LAY DOWN...
JUSTICE...

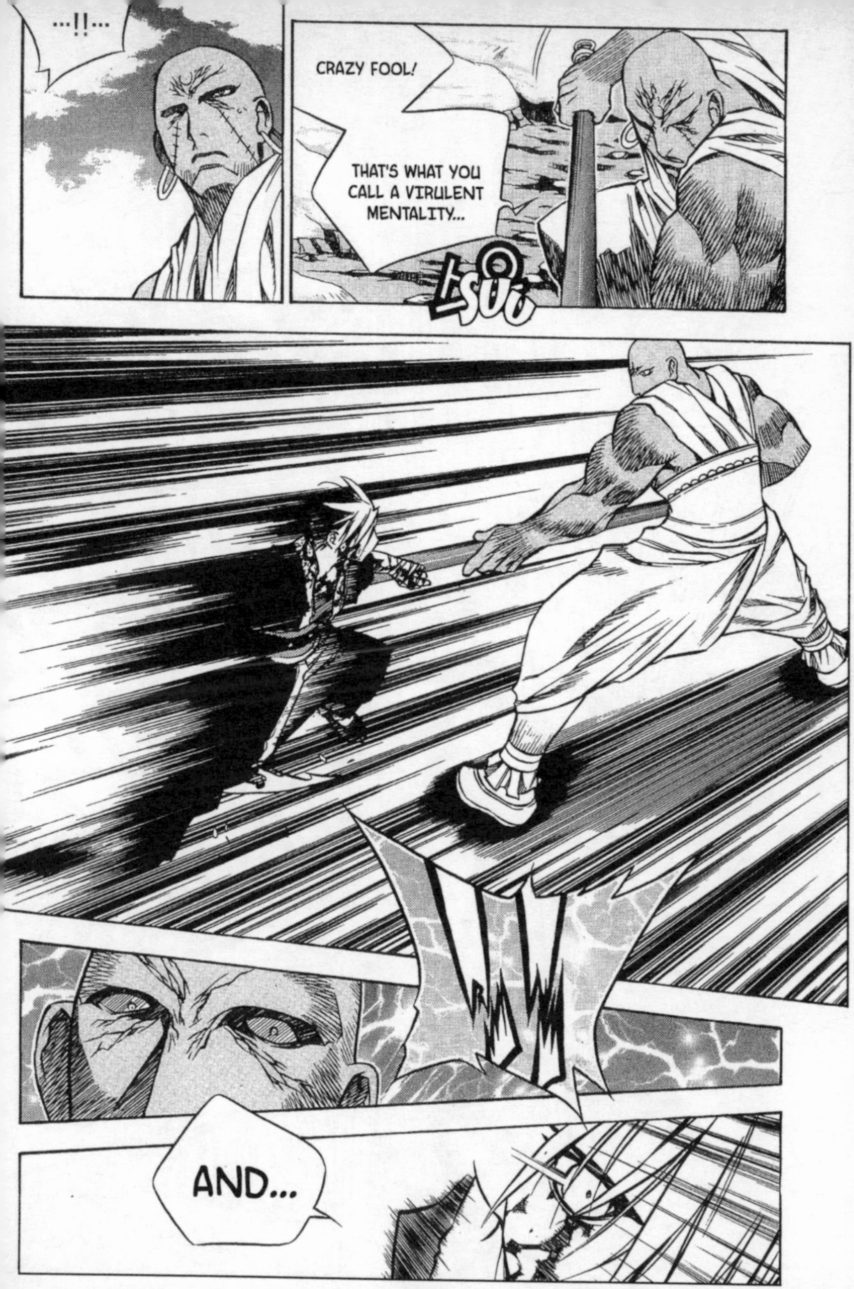
...!!...
CRAZY FOOL!
THAT'S WHAT YOU CALL A VIRULENT MENTALITY...
tsuu
AND...

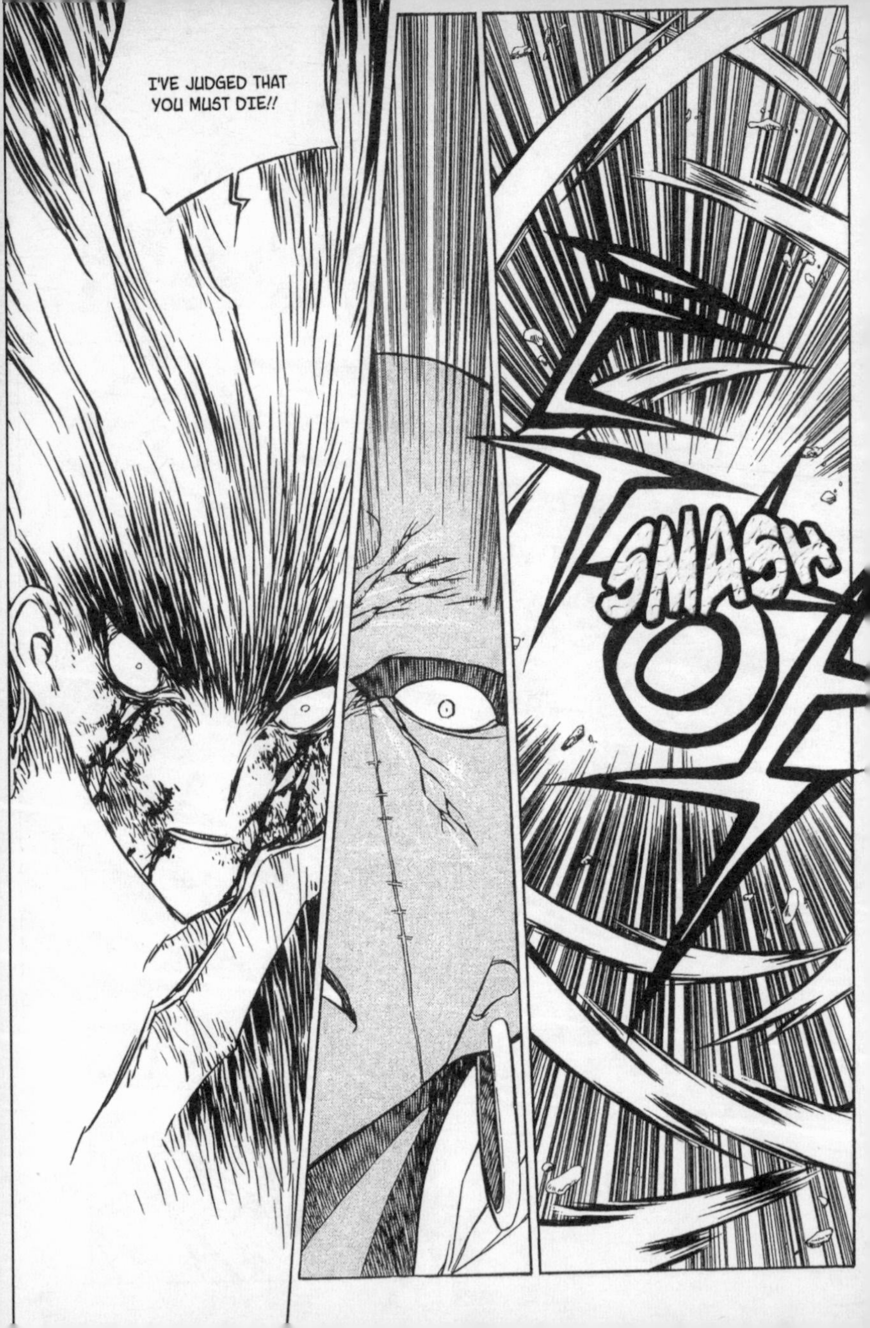
I'VE JUDGED THAT YOU MUST DIE!!
SMASH

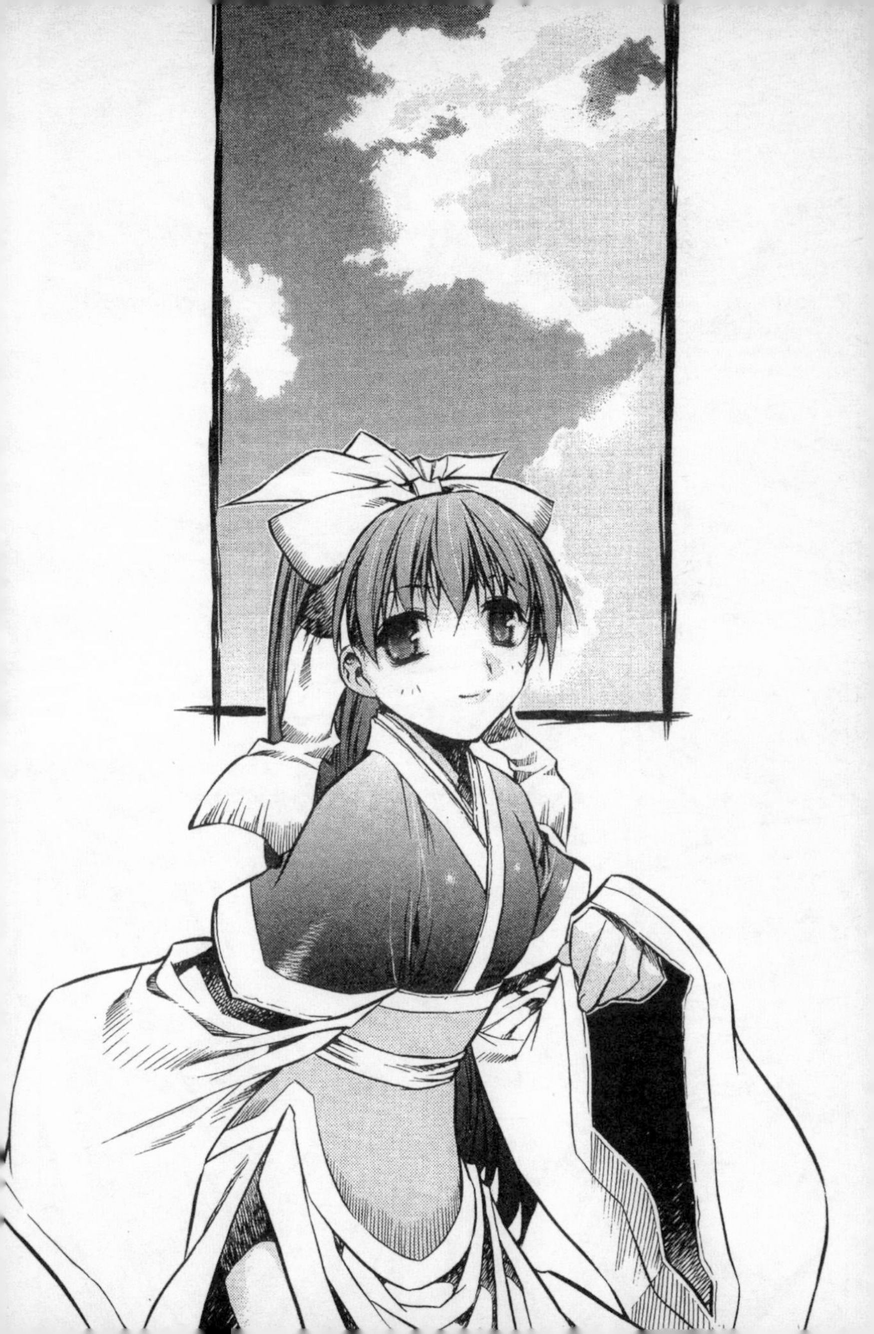

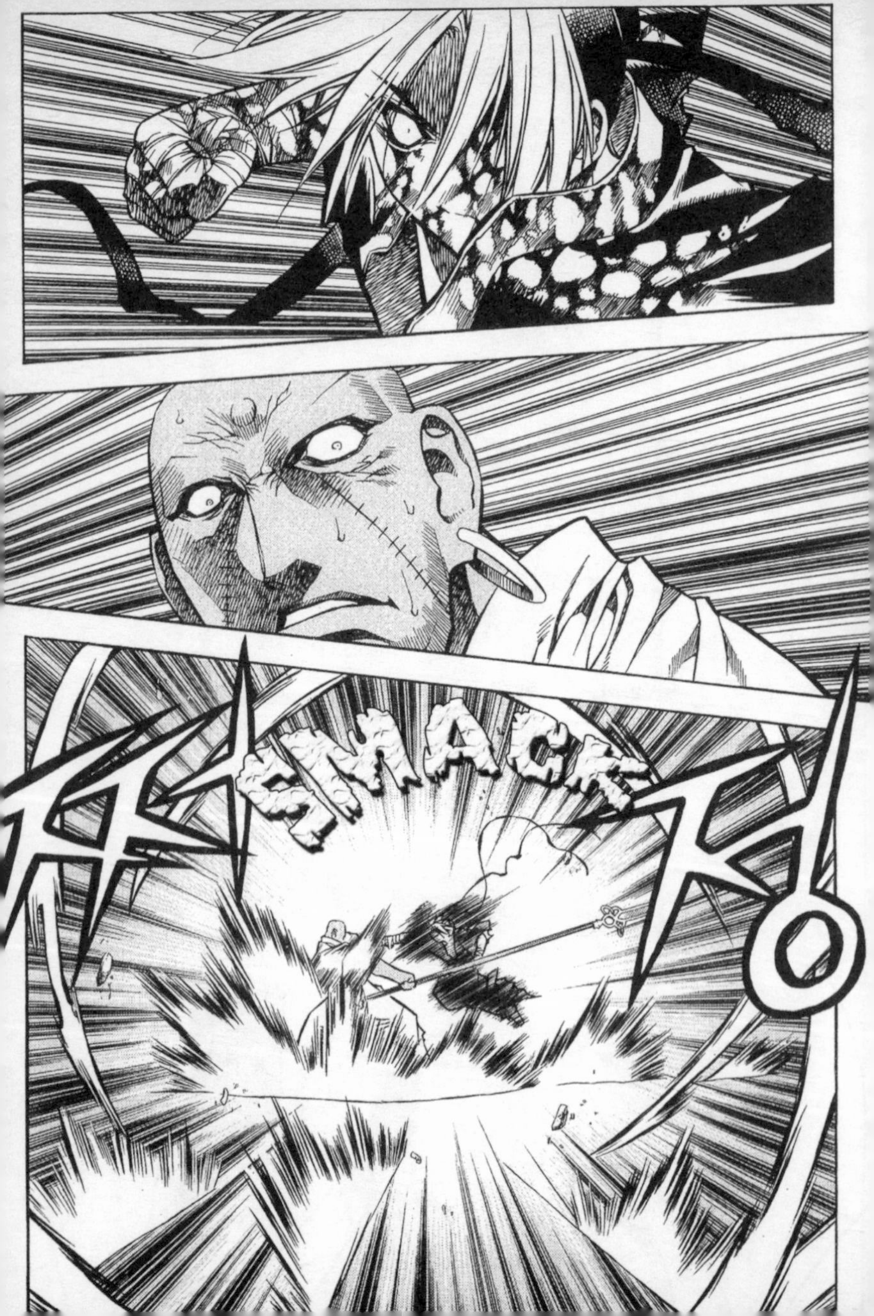
SMACK

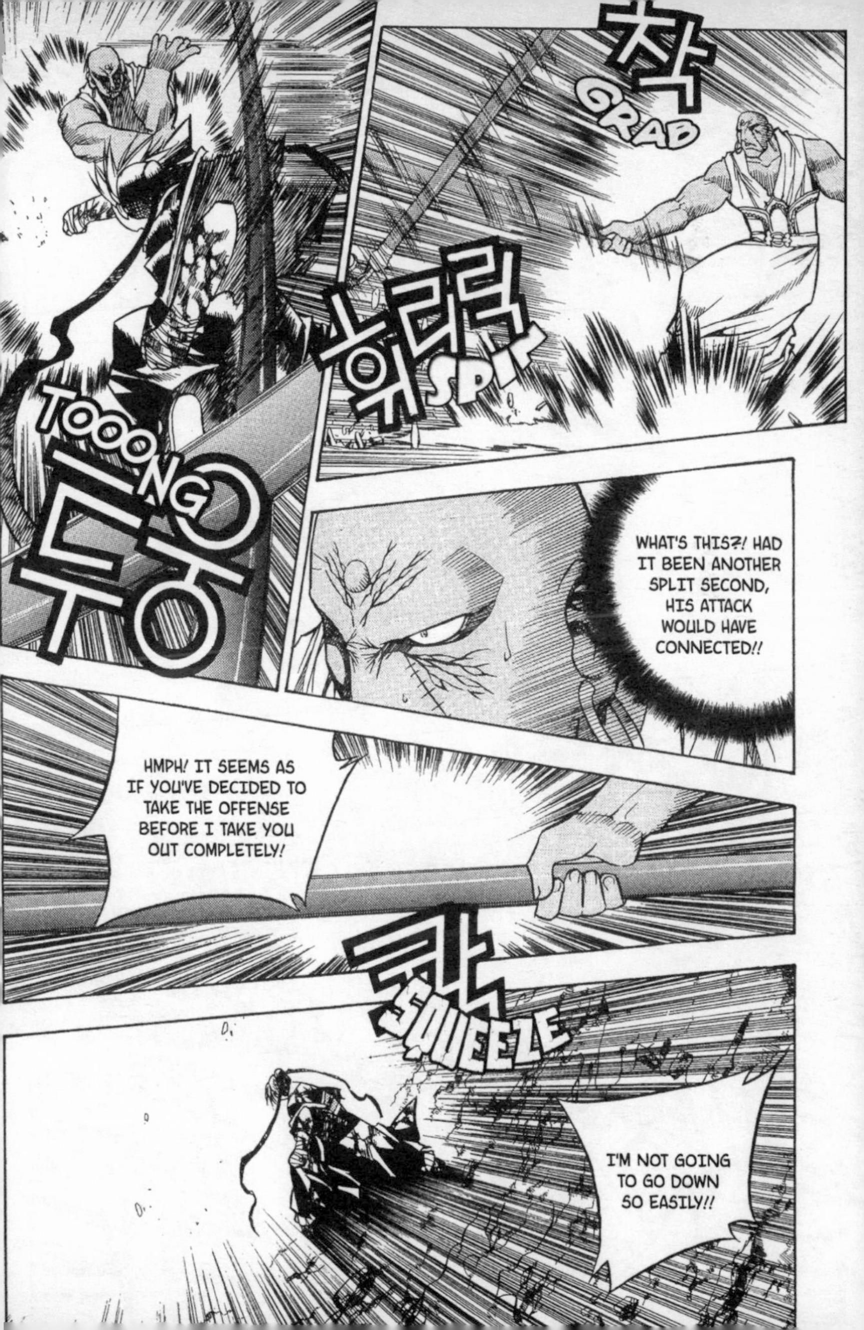
TOOONG
착
GRAB
SPIT
WHAT'S THIS?! HAD IT BEEN ANOTHER SPLIT SECOND, HIS ATTACK WOULD HAVE CONNECTED!!
HMPH! IT SEEMS AS IF YOU'VE DECIDED TO TAKE THE OFFENSE BEFORE I TAKE YOU OUT COMPLETELY!
SQUEEZE
I'M NOT GOING TO GO DOWN SO EASILY!!

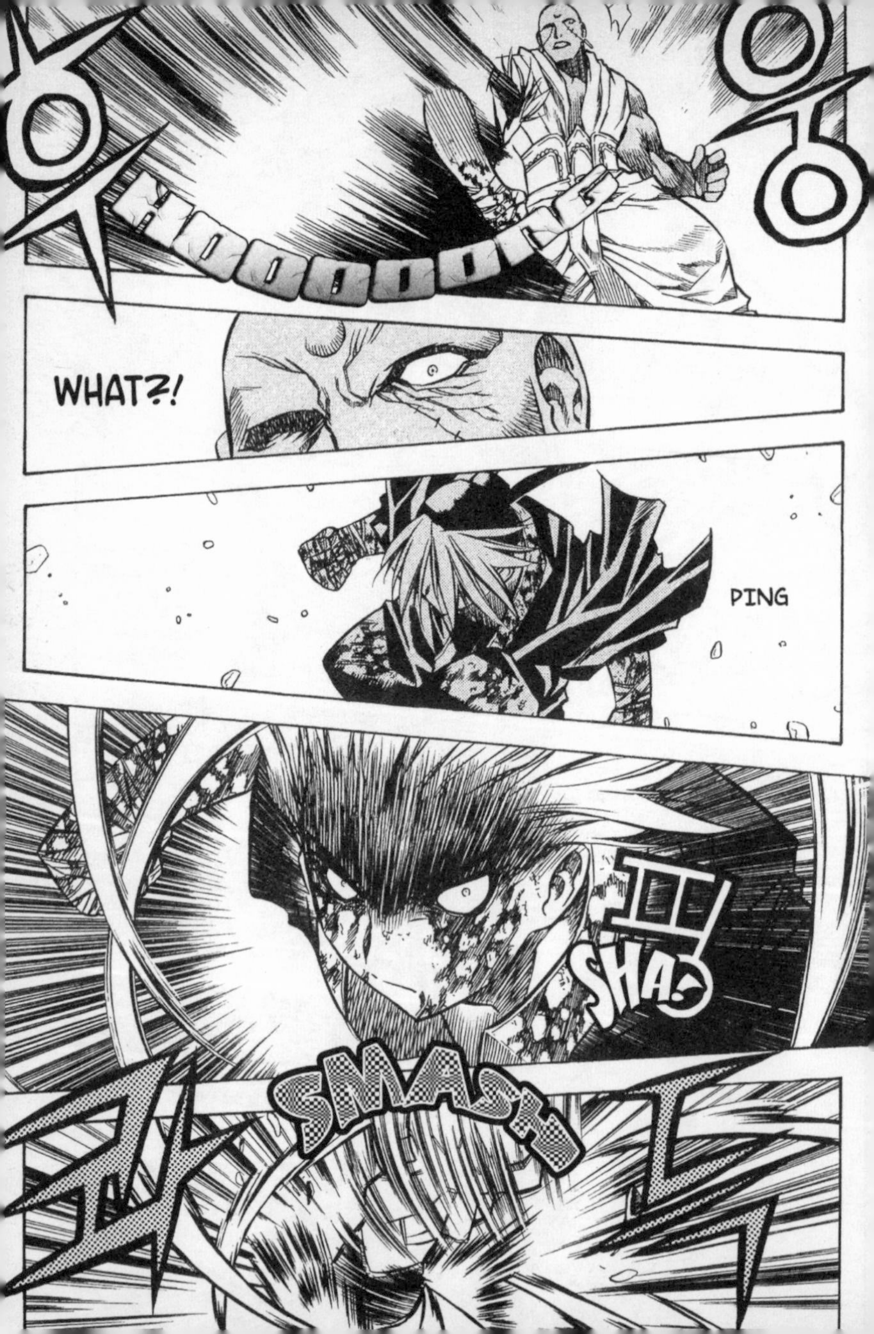
WHAT?!
PING
SHA!
SMASH

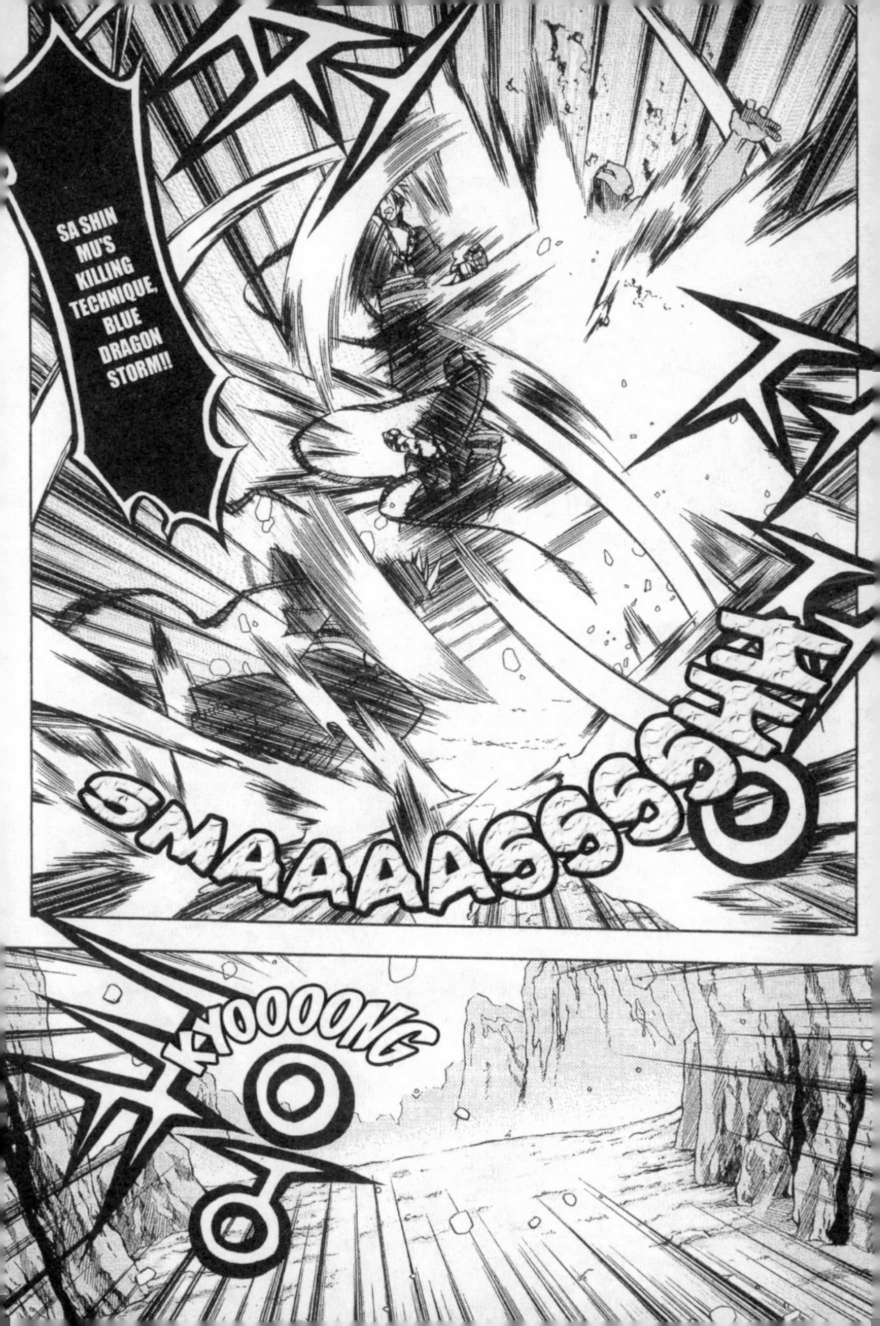
SA SHIN MU'S KILLING TECHNIQUE, BLUE DRAGON STORM!!
SMAAAASSSH
KYOOOONG

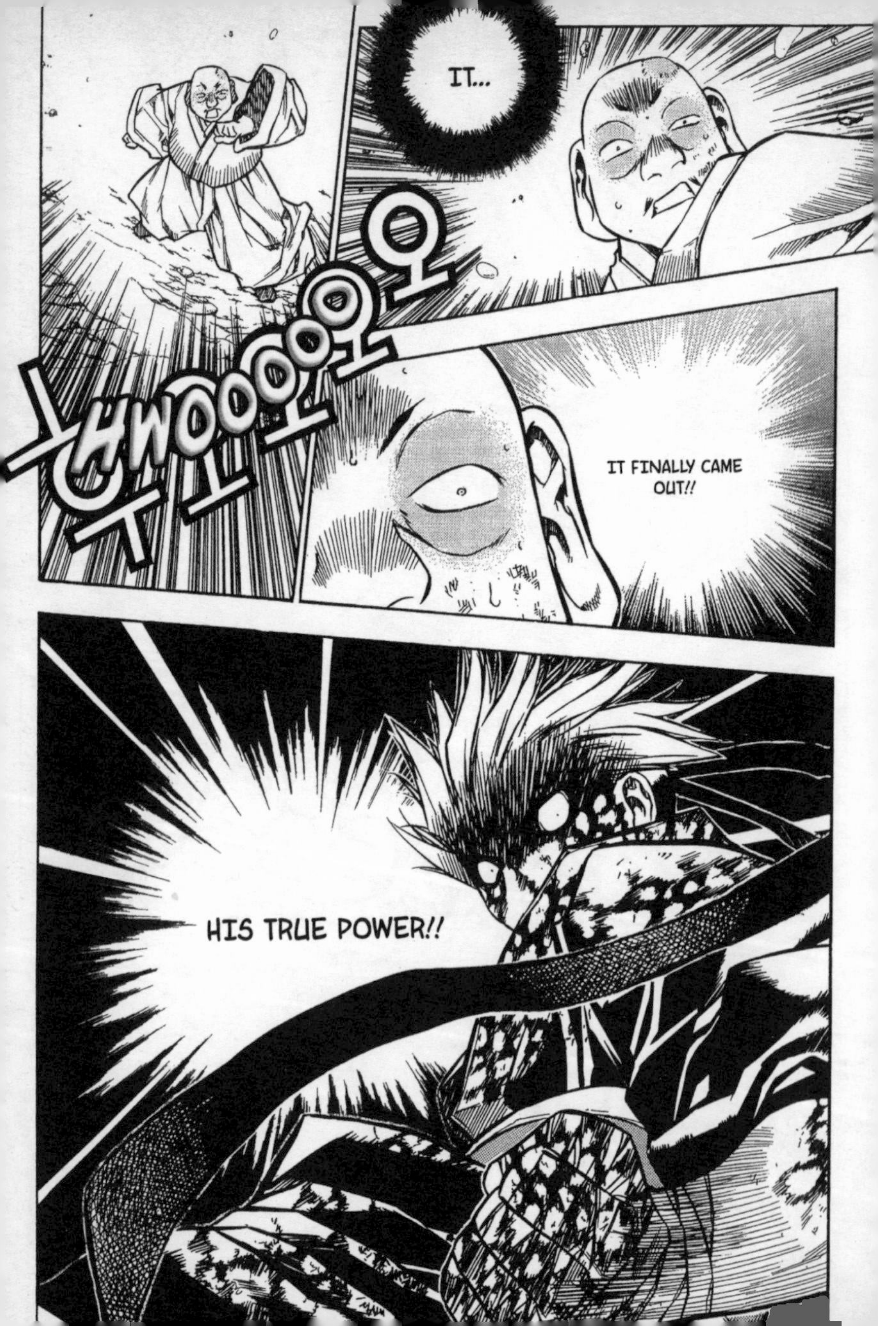
IT...
HWOOOOO
IT FINALLY CAME OUT!!
HIS TRUE POWER!!

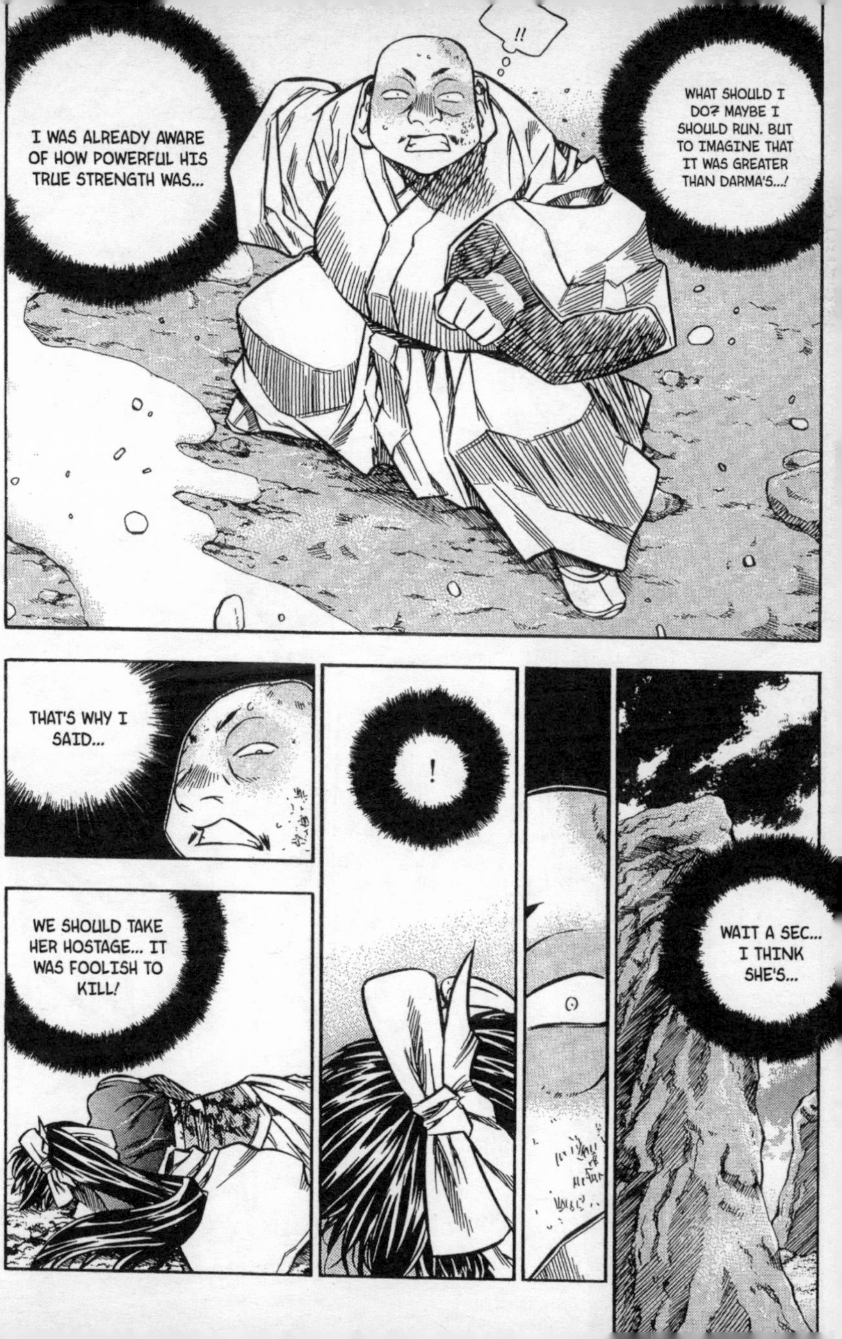
!!
I WAS ALREADY AWARE OF HOW POWERFUL HIS TRUE STRENGTH WAS...
WHAT SHOULD I DO? MAYBE I SHOULD RUN. BUT TO IMAGINE THAT IT WAS GREATER THAN DARMA'S...!
THAT'S WHY I SAID...
WE SHOULD TAKE HER HOSTAGE... IT WAS FOOLISH TO KILL!
!
WAIT A SEC... I THINK SHE'S...

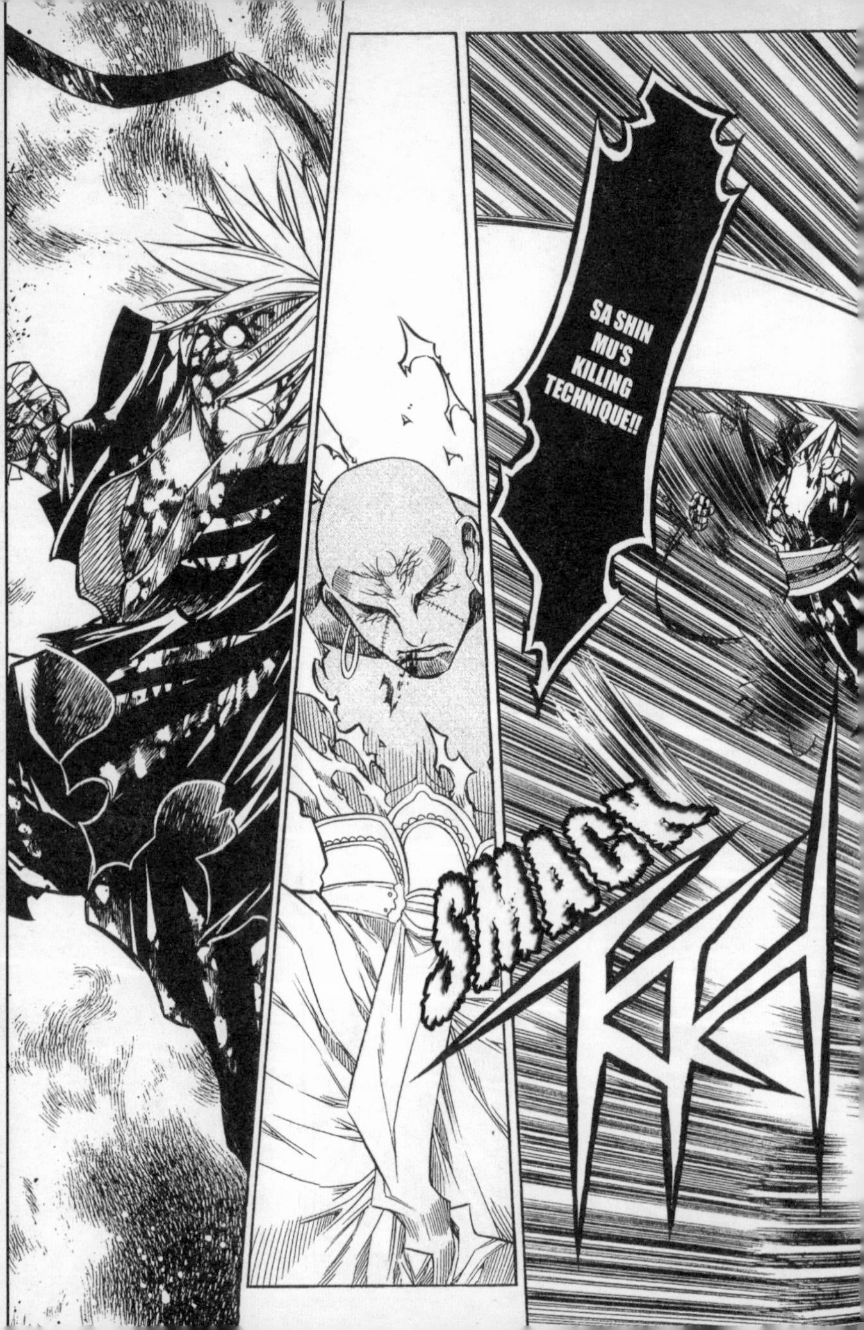
SA SHIN MU'S KILLING TECHNIQUE!!
SMACK

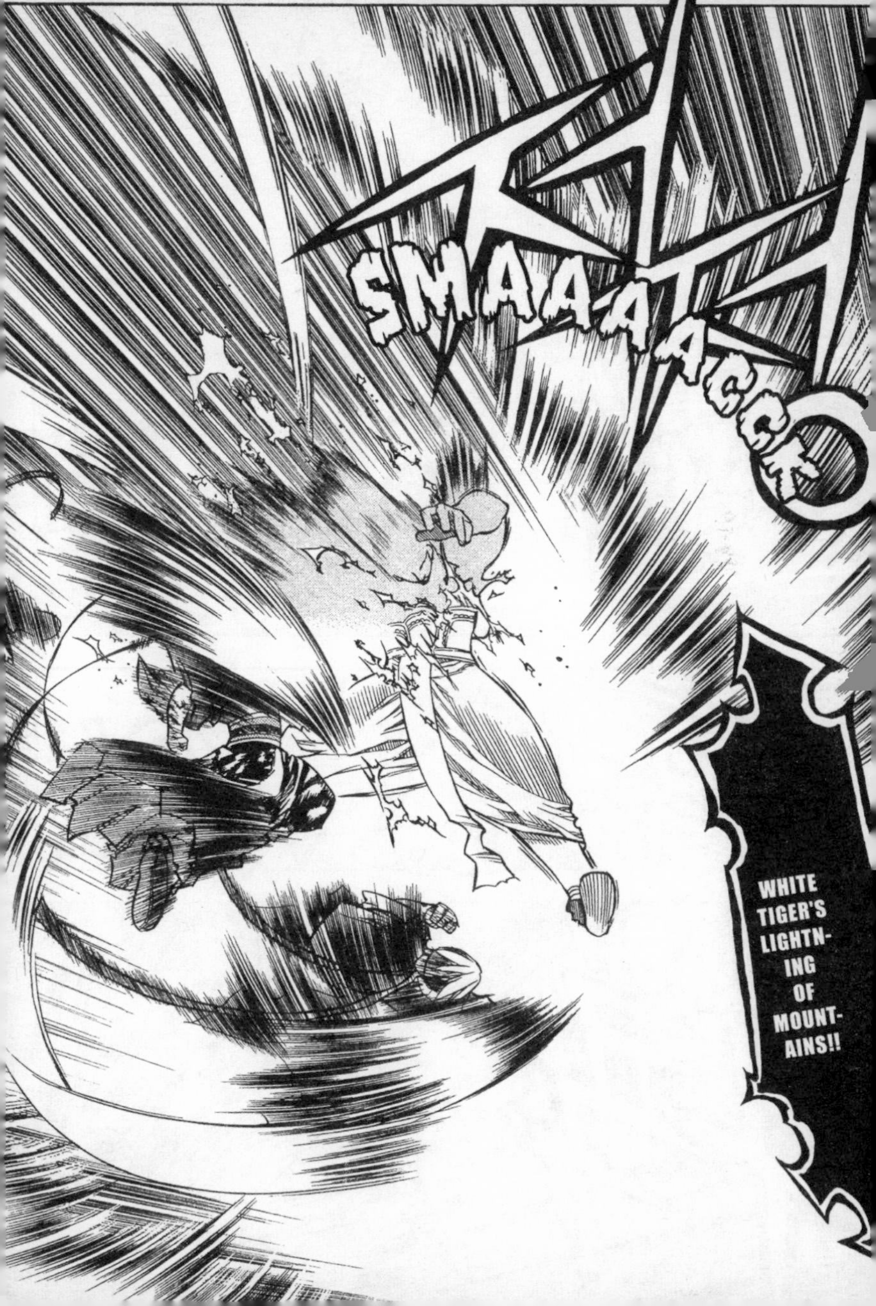
SMAAAACCK
WHITE TIGER'S LIGHTN-ING OF MOUNT-AINS!!

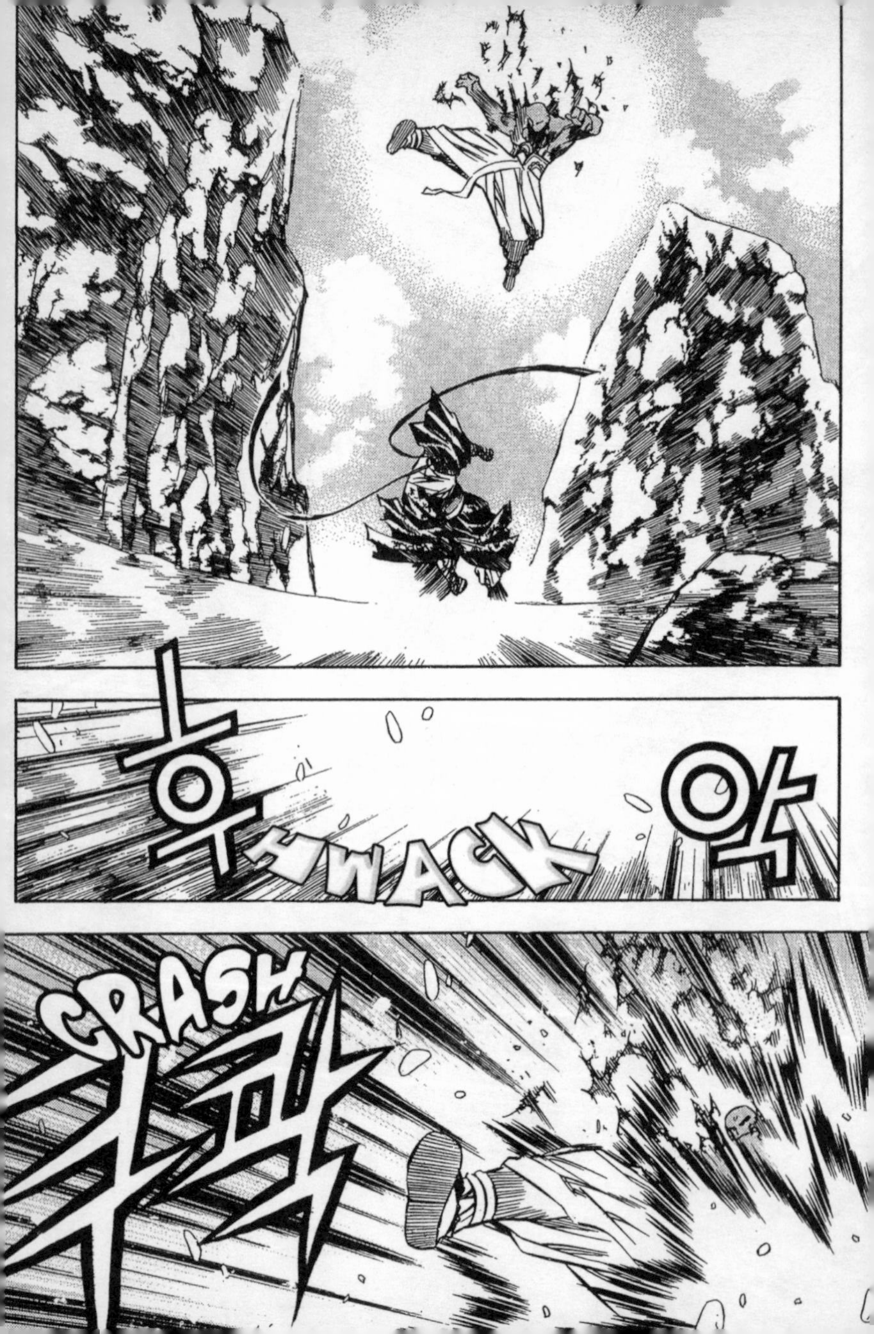
WHACK
CRASH

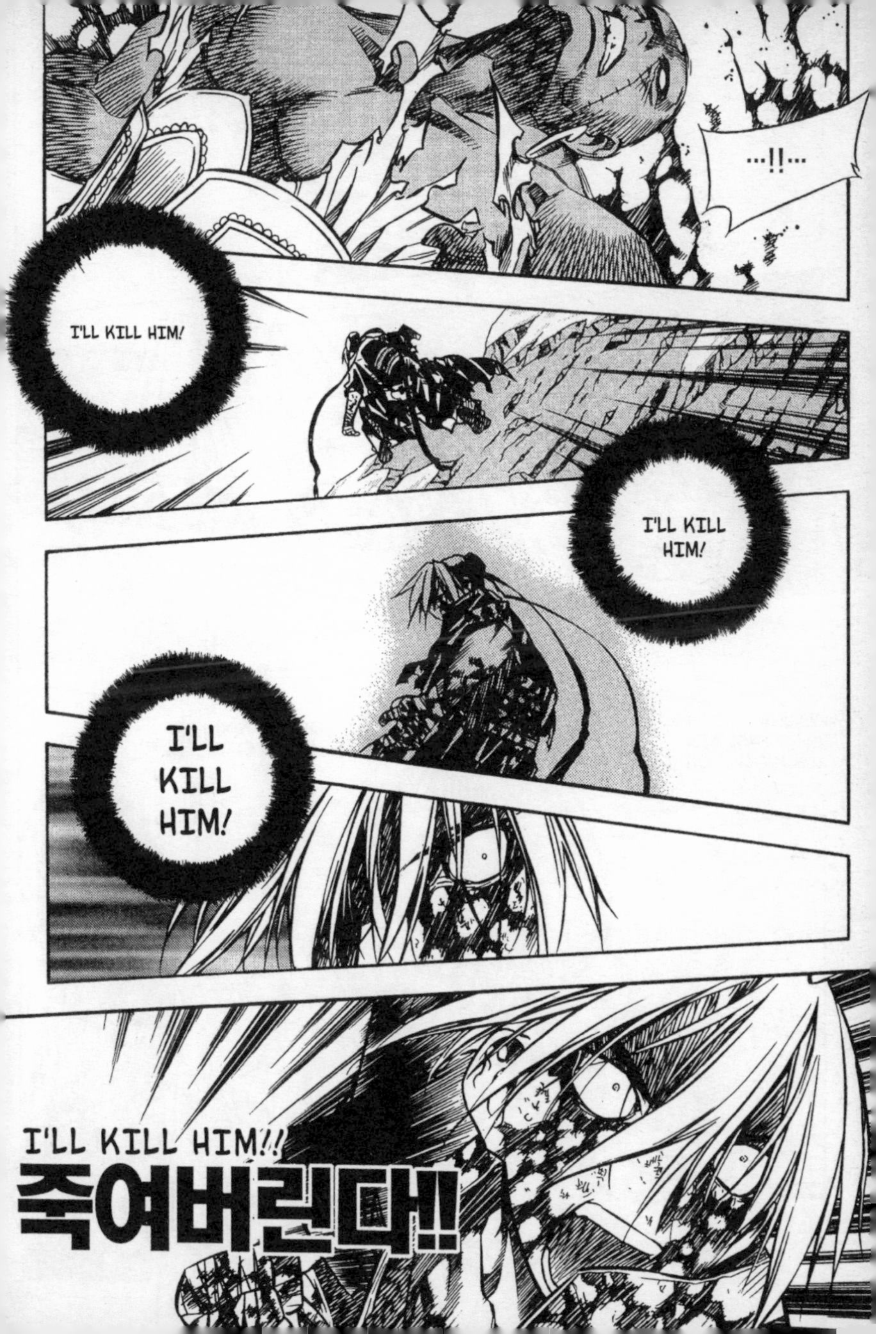
...!!...
I'LL KILL HIM!
I'LL KILL HIM!
I'LL KILL HIM!
I'LL KILL HIM!!
죽여버린다!!

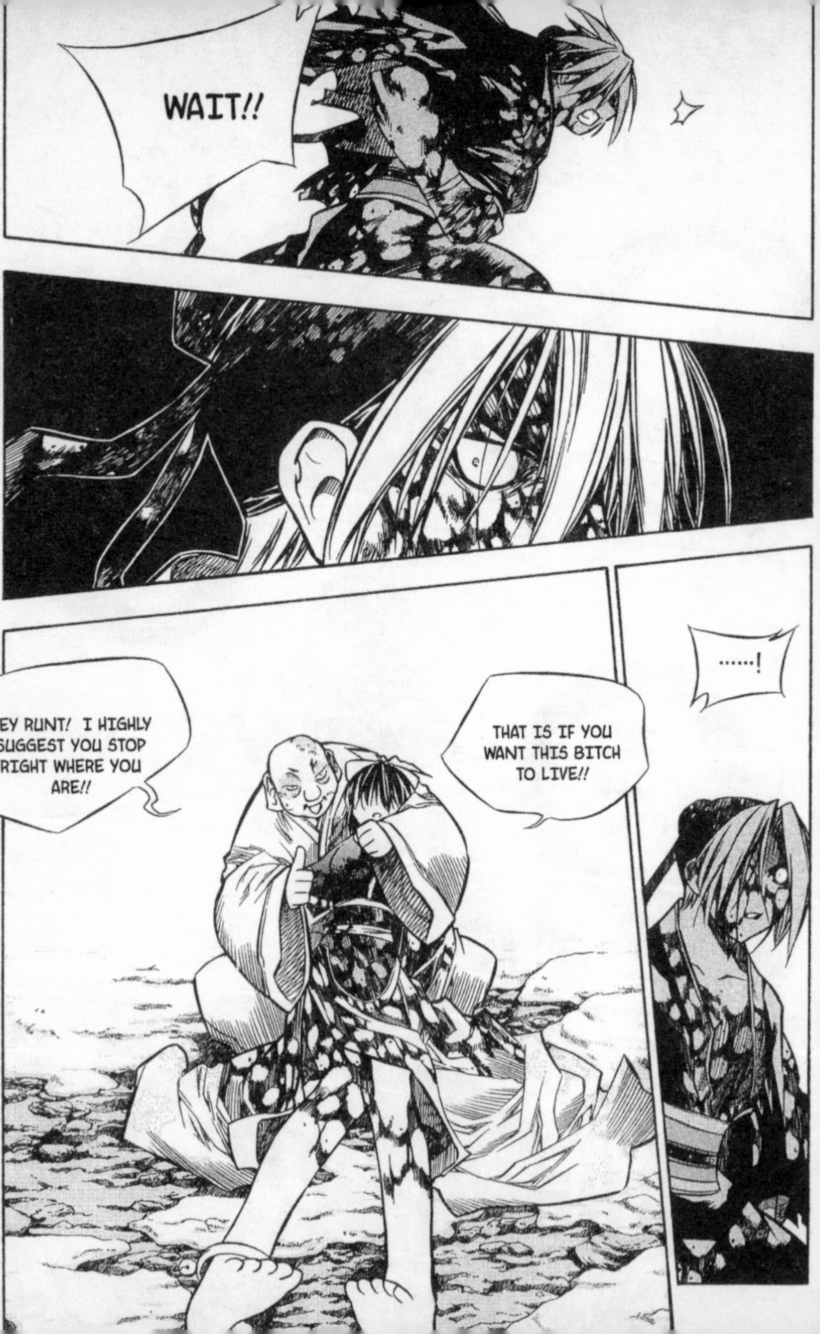
WAIT!!
HEY RUNT! I HIGHLY SUGGEST YOU STOP RIGHT WHERE YOU ARE!!
THAT IS IF YOU WANT THIS BITCH TO LIVE!!
......!

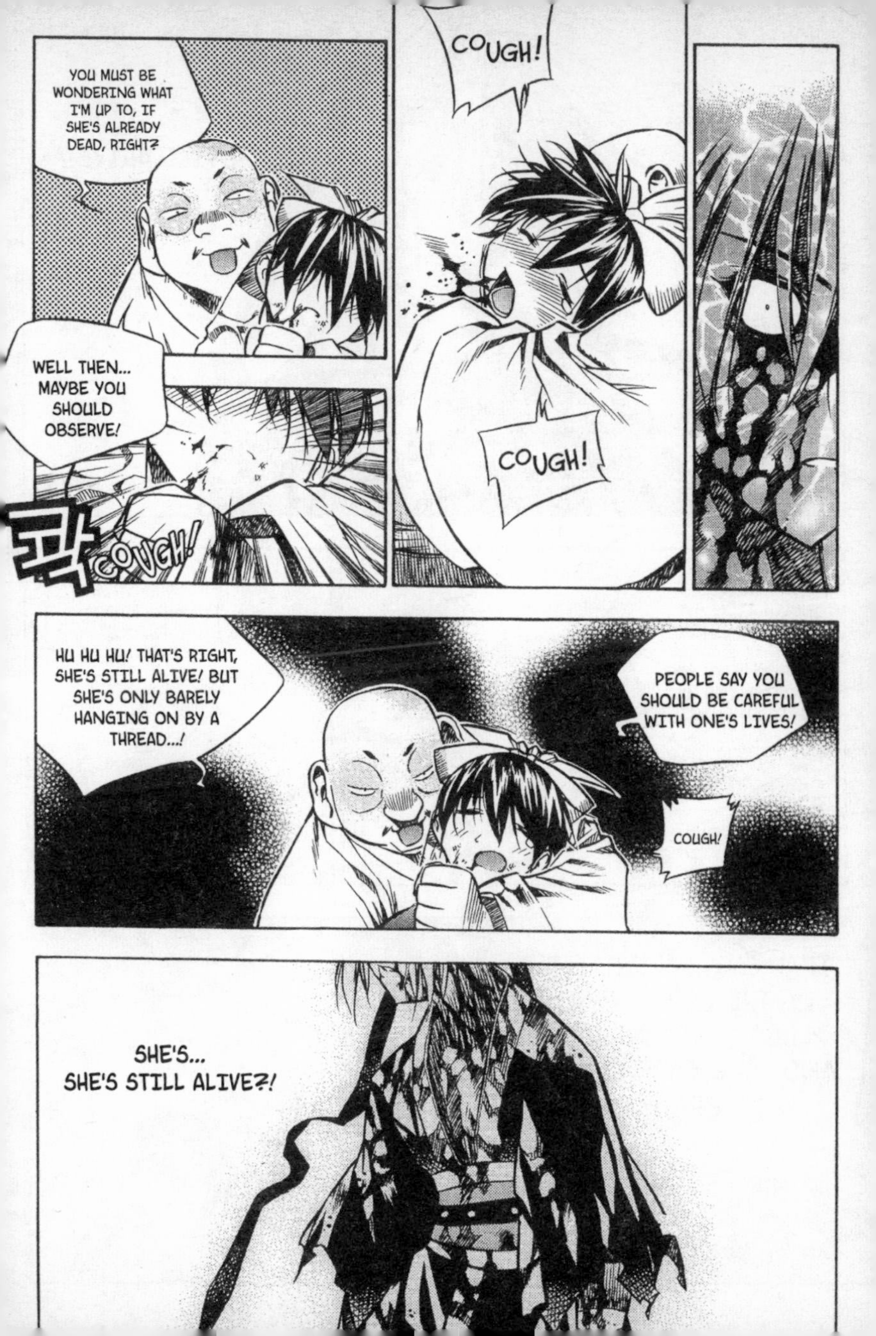
YOU MUST BE WONDERING WHAT I'M UP TO, IF SHE'S ALREADY DEAD, RIGHT?
WELL THEN... MAYBE YOU SHOULD OBSERVE!
COUGH!
COUGH!
COUGH!
HU HU HU! THAT'S RIGHT, SHE'S STILL ALIVE! BUT SHE'S ONLY BARELY HANGING ON BY A THREAD...!
PEOPLE SAY YOU SHOULD BE CAREFUL WITH ONE'S LIVES!
COUGH!
SHE'S... SHE'S STILL ALIVE?!

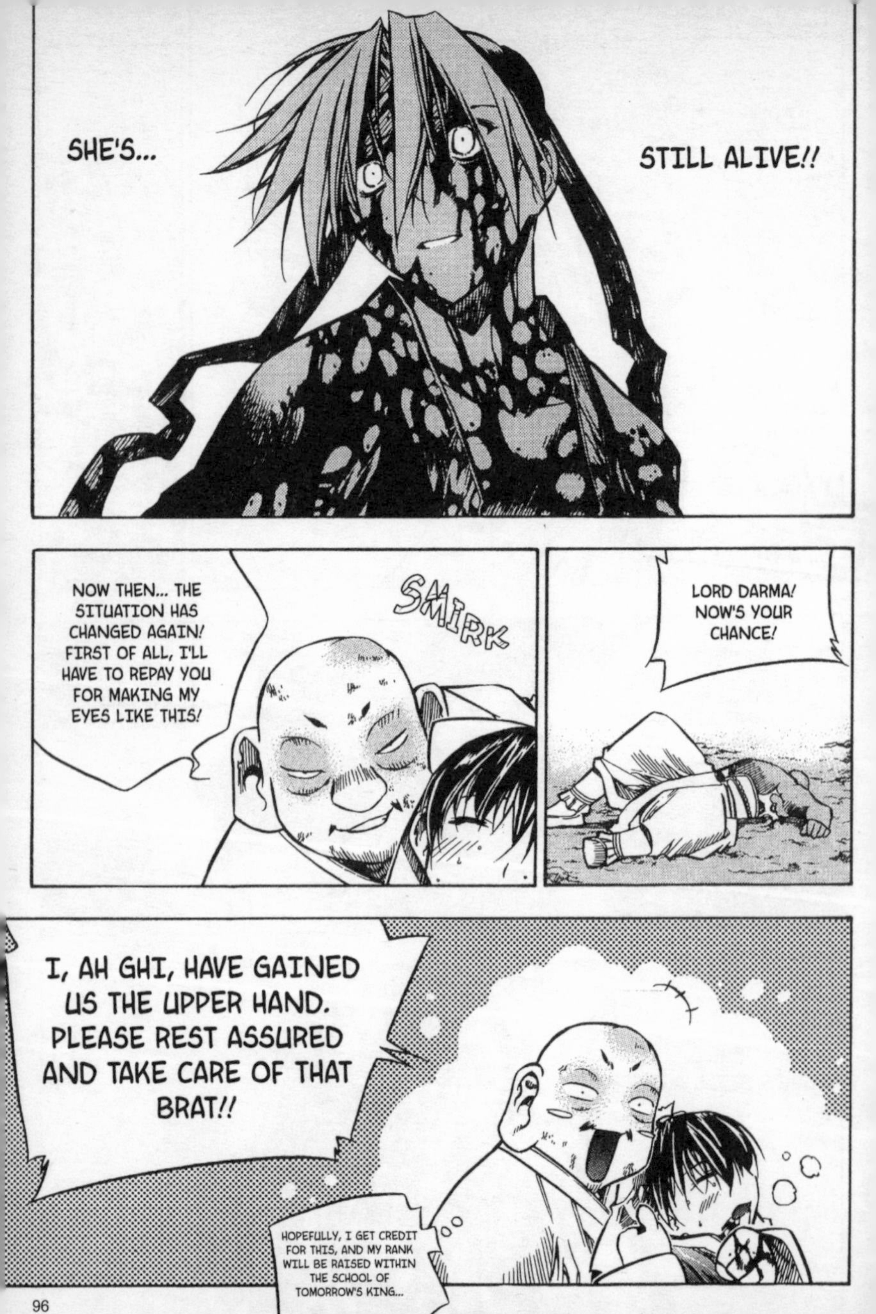
SHE'S...
STILL ALIVE!!
NOW THEN... THE SITUATION HAS CHANGED AGAIN! FIRST OF ALL, I'LL HAVE TO REPAY YOU FOR MAKING MY EYES LIKE THIS!
SMIRK
LORD DARMA! NOW'S YOUR CHANCE!
I, AH GHI, HAVE GAINED US THE UPPER HAND. PLEASE REST ASSURED AND TAKE CARE OF THAT BRAT!!
HOPEFULLY, I GET CREDIT FOR THIS, AND MY RANK WILL BE RAISED WITHIN THE SCHOOL OF TOMORROW'S KING...

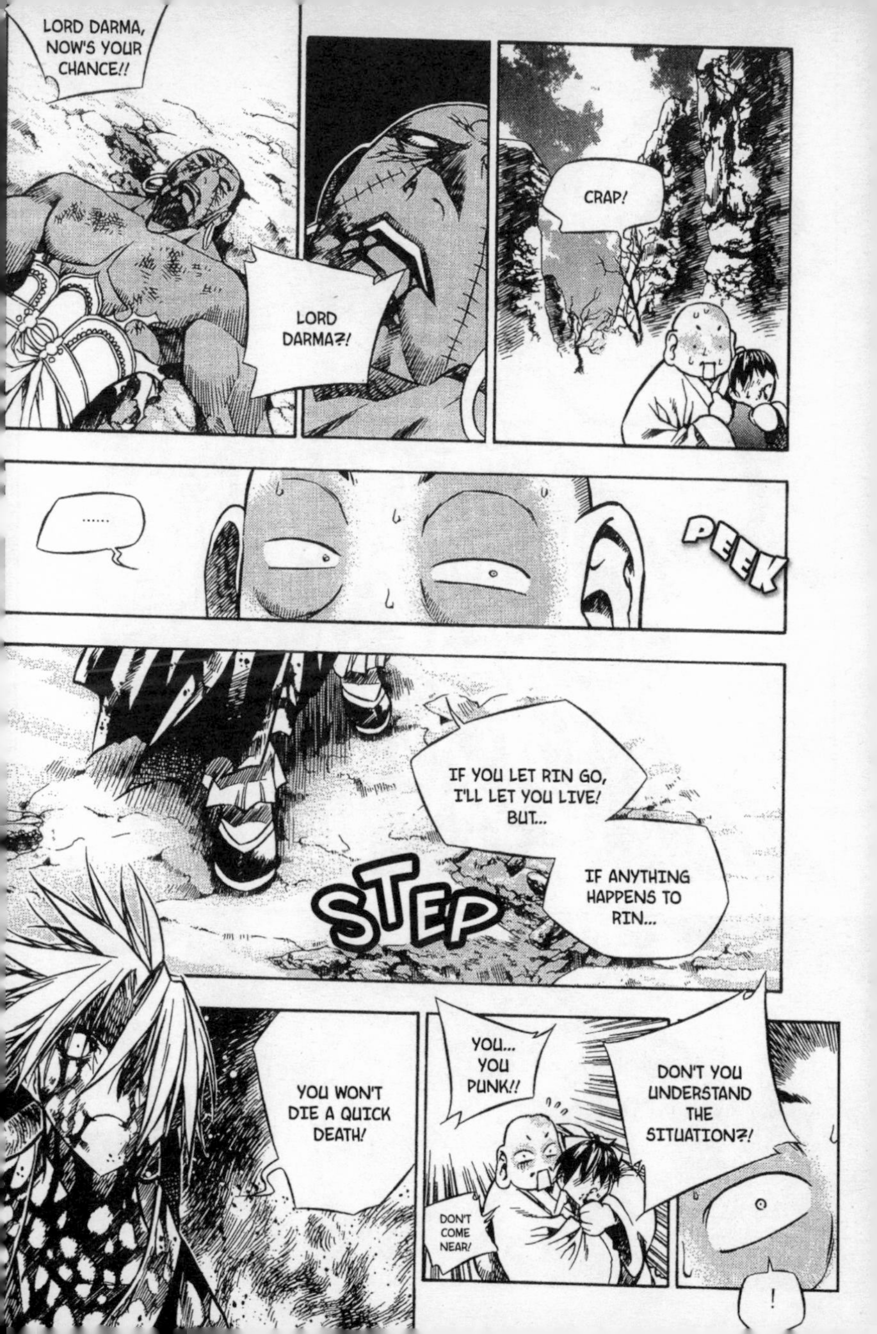
CRAP!
LORD DARMA?!
LORD DARMA, NOW'S YOUR CHANCE!!
PEEK
......
IF YOU LET RIN GO, I'LL LET YOU LIVE! BUT...
IF ANYTHING HAPPENS TO RIN...
STEP
YOU WON'T DIE A QUICK DEATH!
!
DON'T YOU UNDERSTAND THE SITUATION?!
YOU... YOU PUNK!!
DON'T COME NEAR!

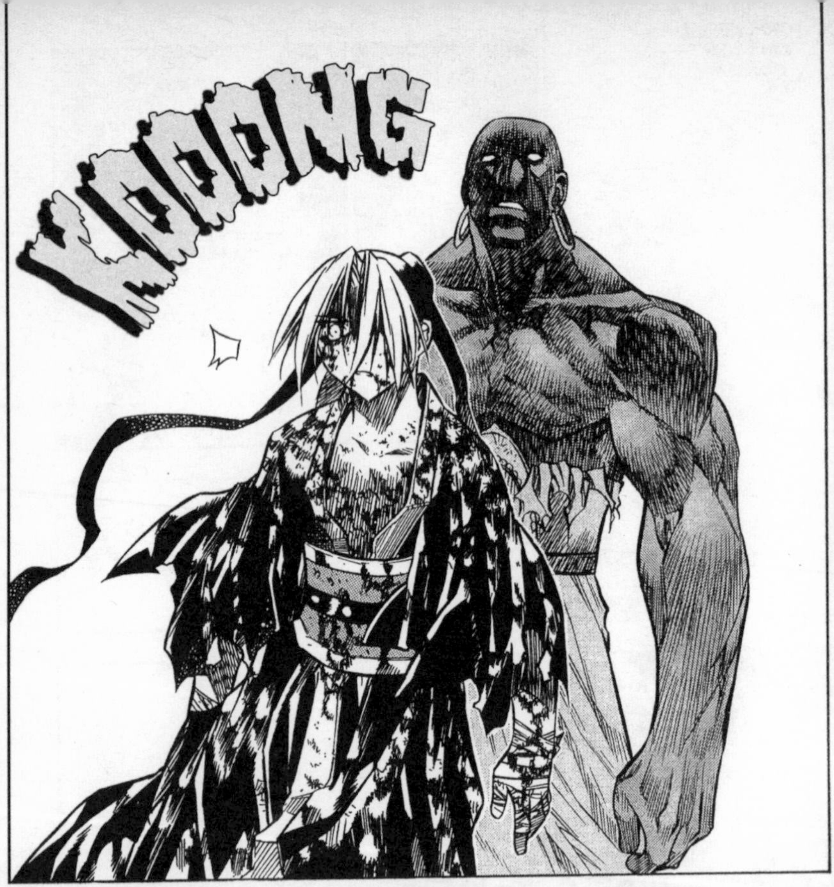
KDDDNG

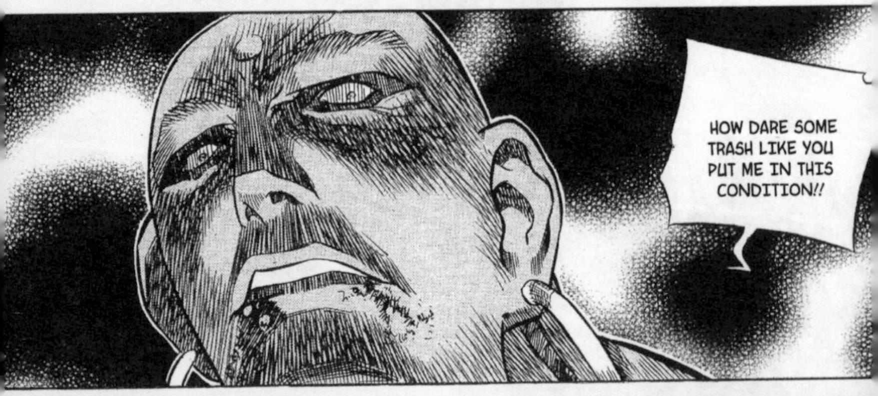
HOW DARE SOME TRASH LIKE YOU PUT ME IN THIS CONDITION!!

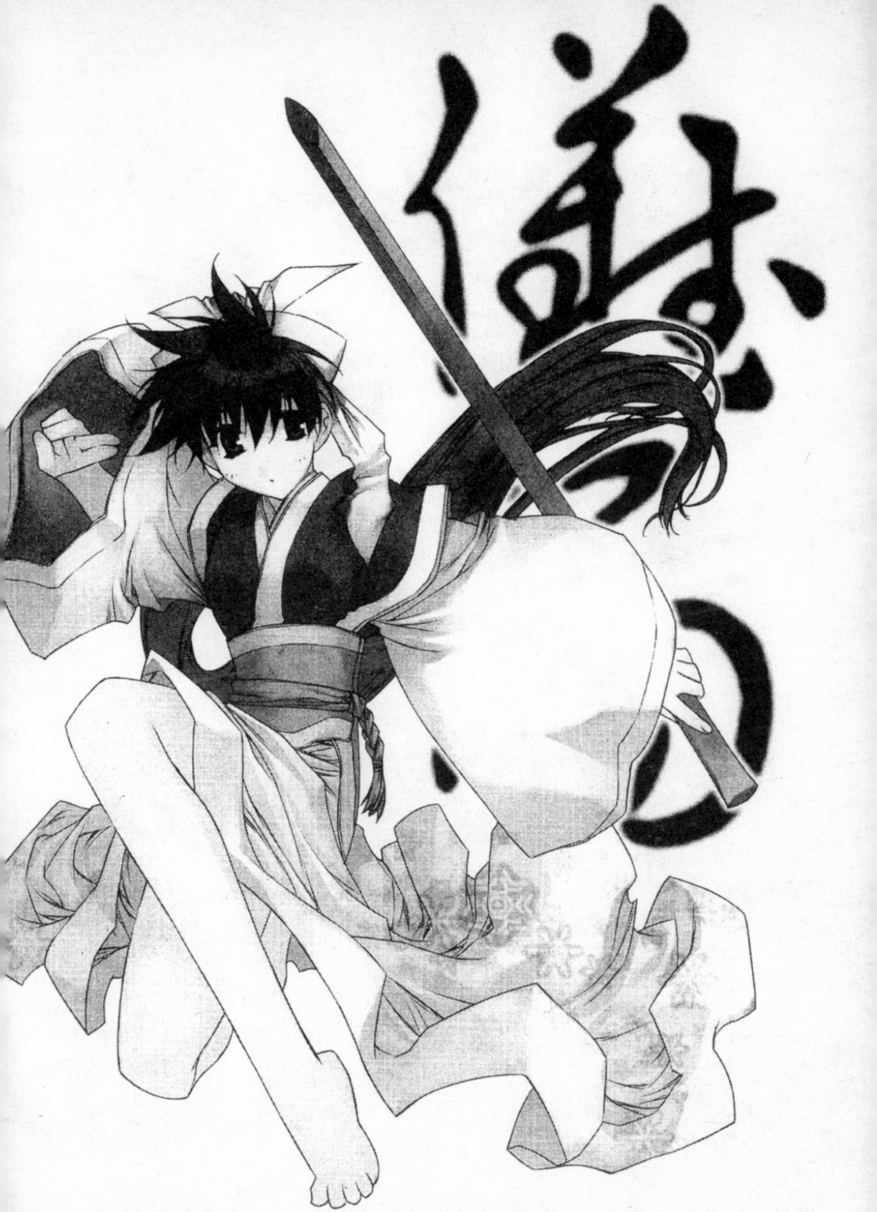

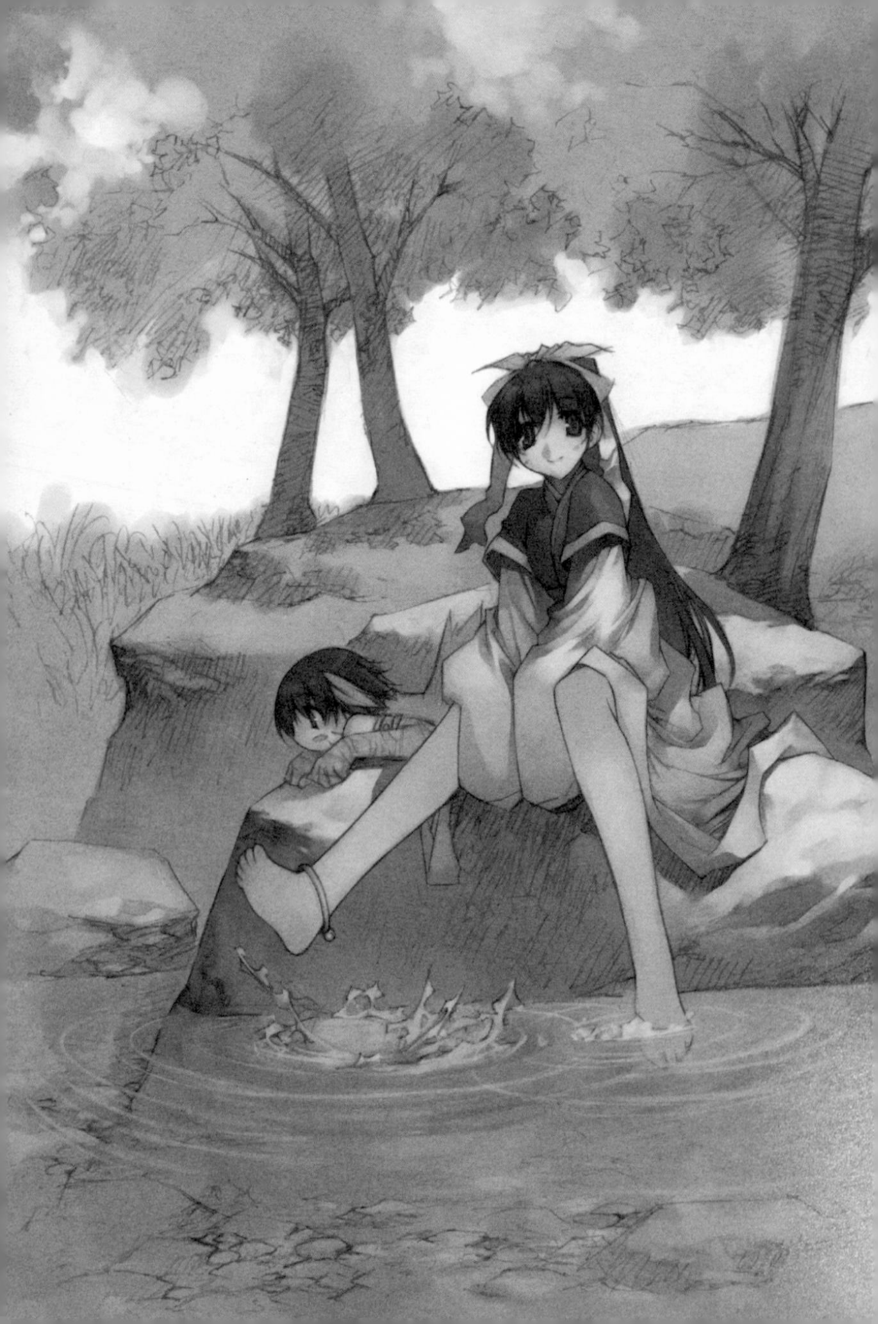

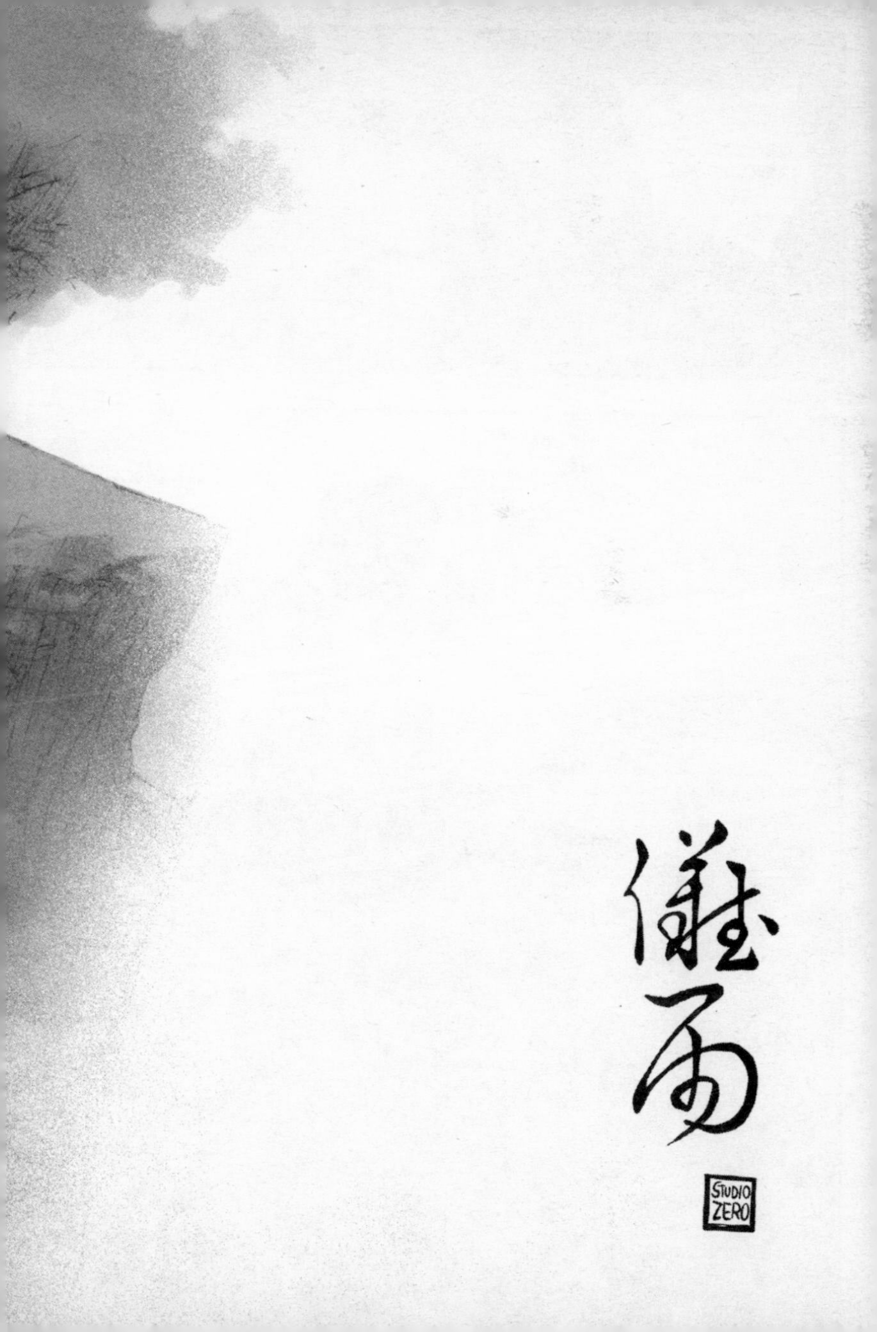
STUDIO ZERO

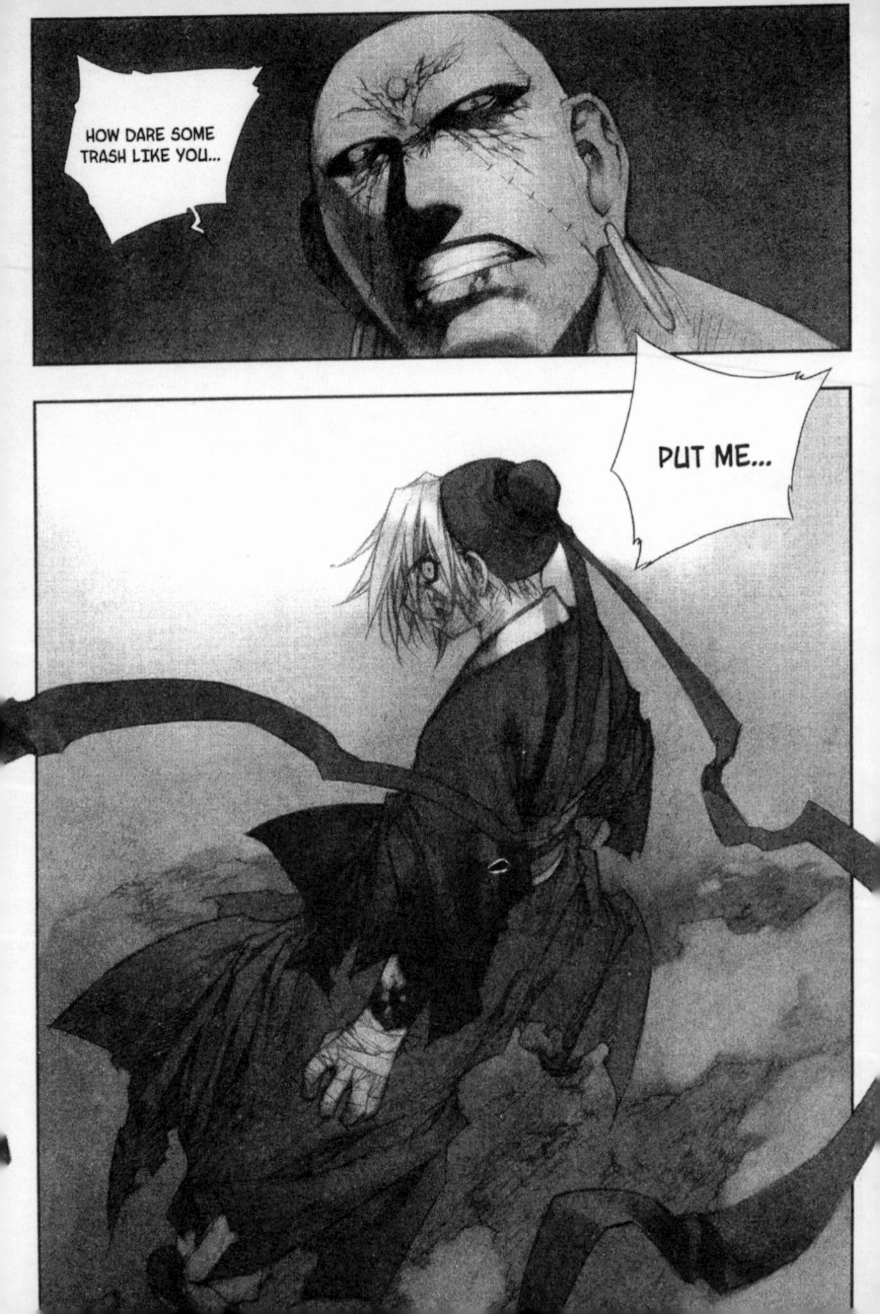
HOW DARE SOME TRASH LIKE YOU...
PUT ME...

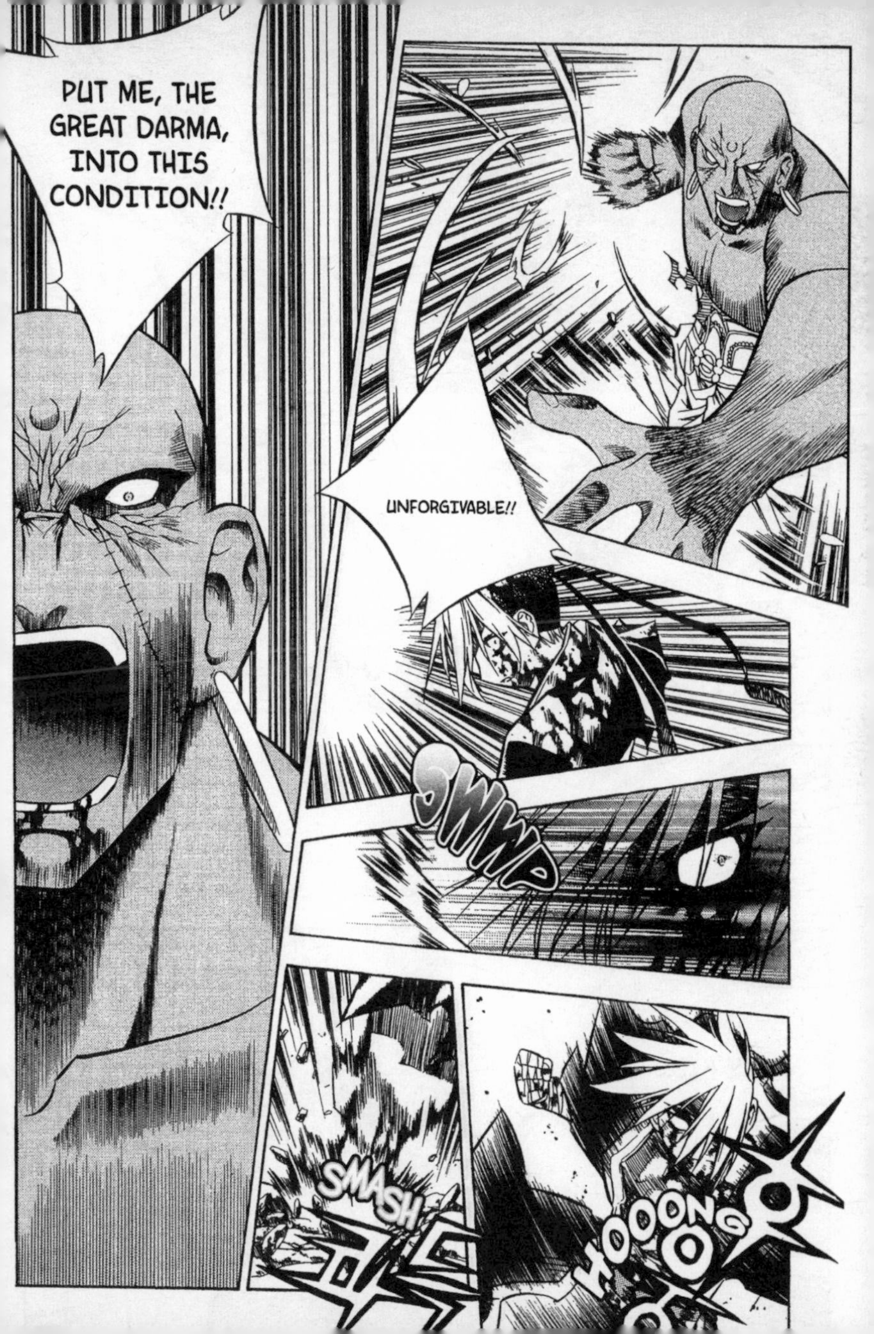
PUT ME, THE GREAT DARMA, INTO THIS CONDITION!!
UNFORGIVABLE!!
SWWP
SMASH
HOOONG

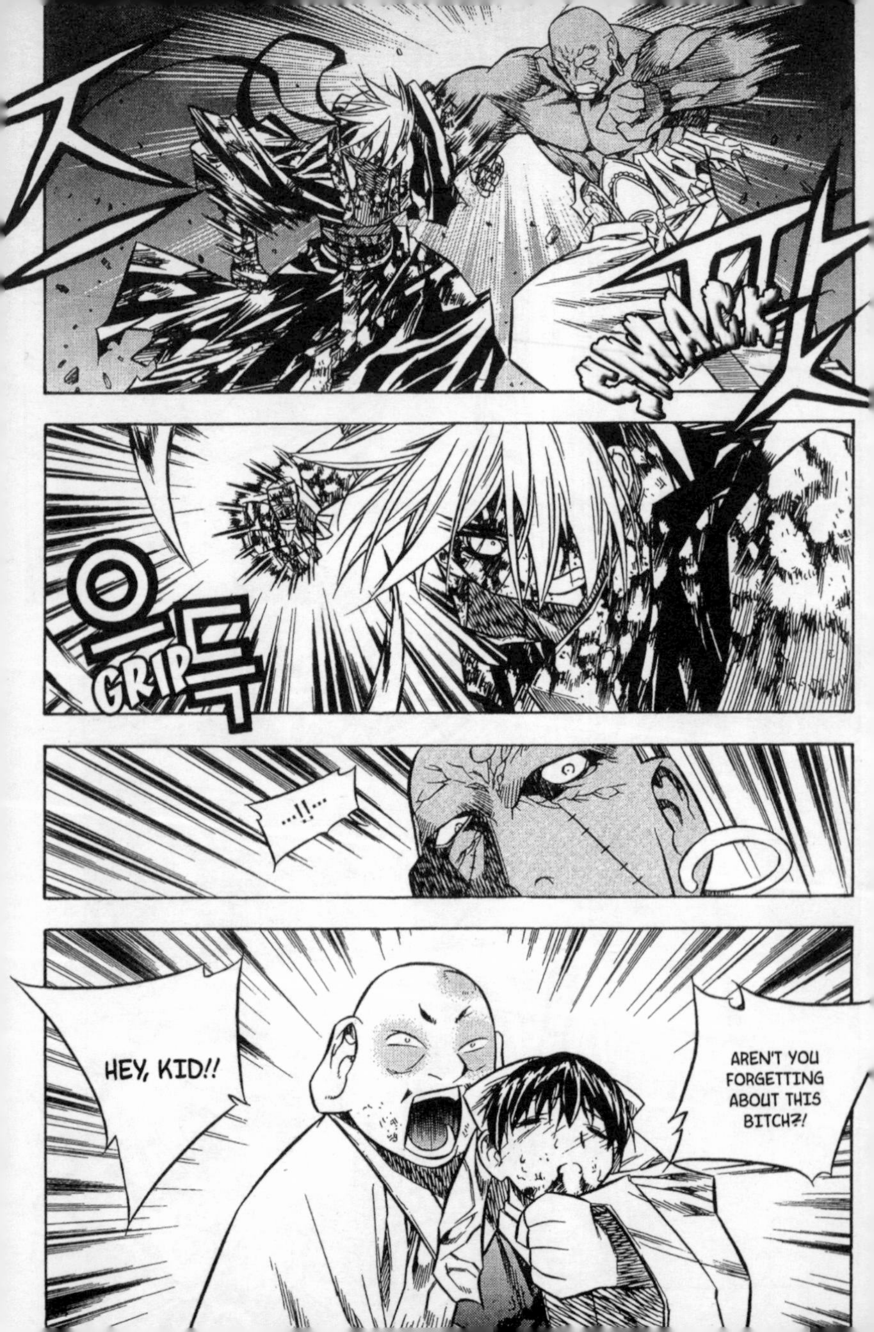

SMACK
GRIP
...!!...
HEY, KID!!
AREN'T YOU FORGETTING ABOUT THIS BITCH?!

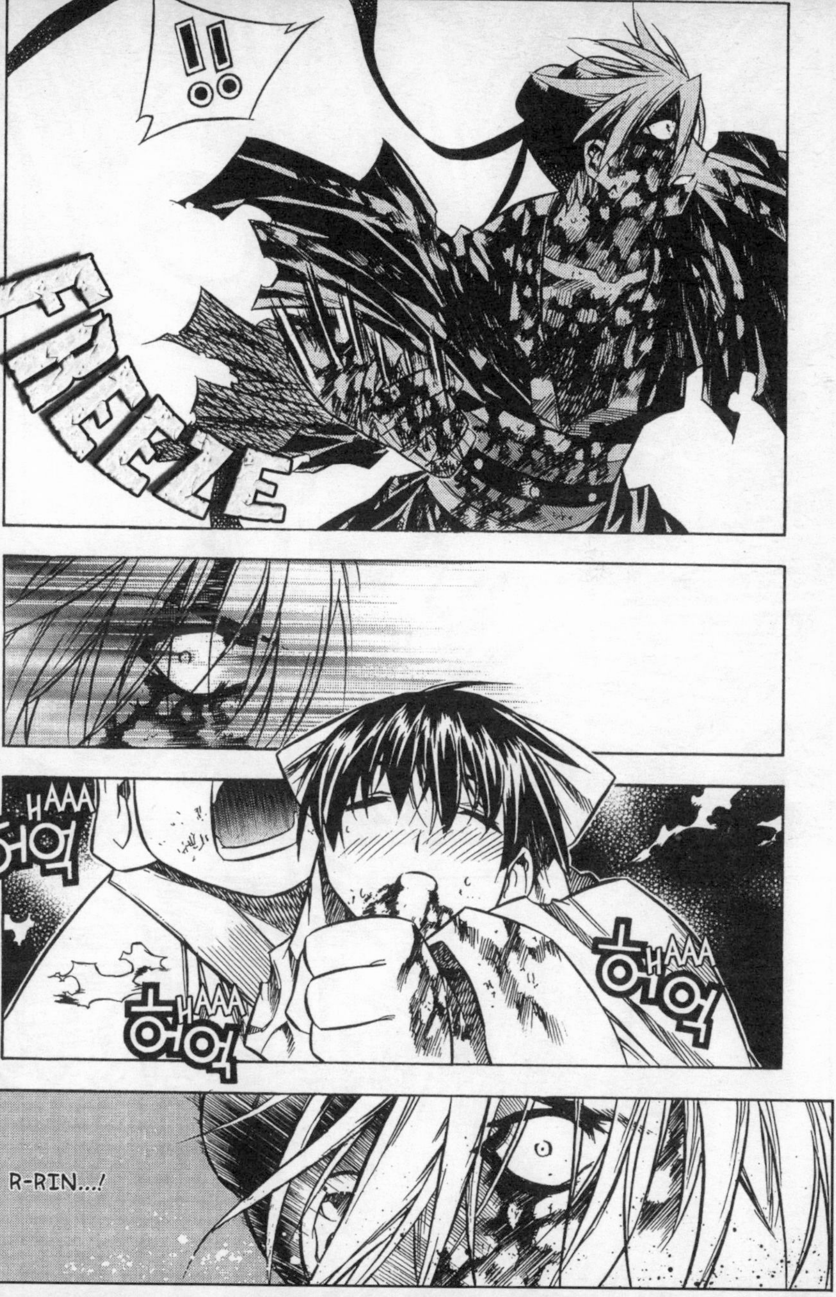
!!
FREEZE
허억 HAAA
허억 HAAA
허억 HAAA
R-RIN...!

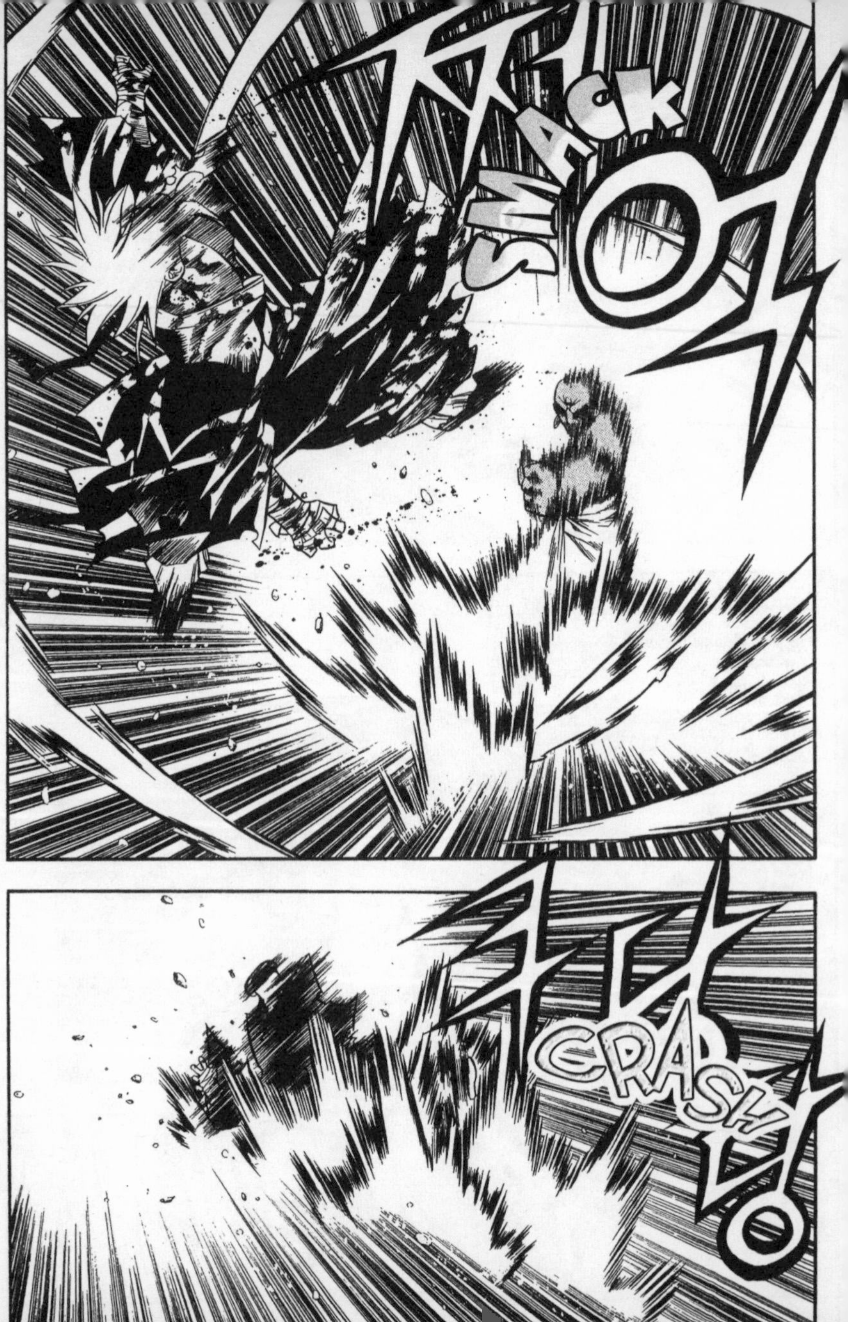
SMACK
CRASH

KKKKK!

ALRIGHT...! IT WAS PRETTY CLOSE BUT NOW WE HAVE THAT RUNT UNDER CONTROL!

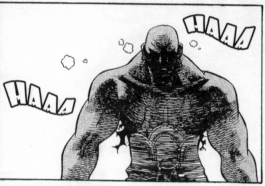

HAAA

HAAA

I WAS ORIGINALLY THINKING ABOUT JUST INCAPACITATING YOU...

COUGH

...!!

BUT I'VE CHANGED MY MIND!!

SA SHIN MU IS TOO DANGEROUS TO TAME! YOU'LL BECOME TOO MUCH OF A RISK FOR THE SCHOOL OF TOMORROW'S KING!!

SUUUU

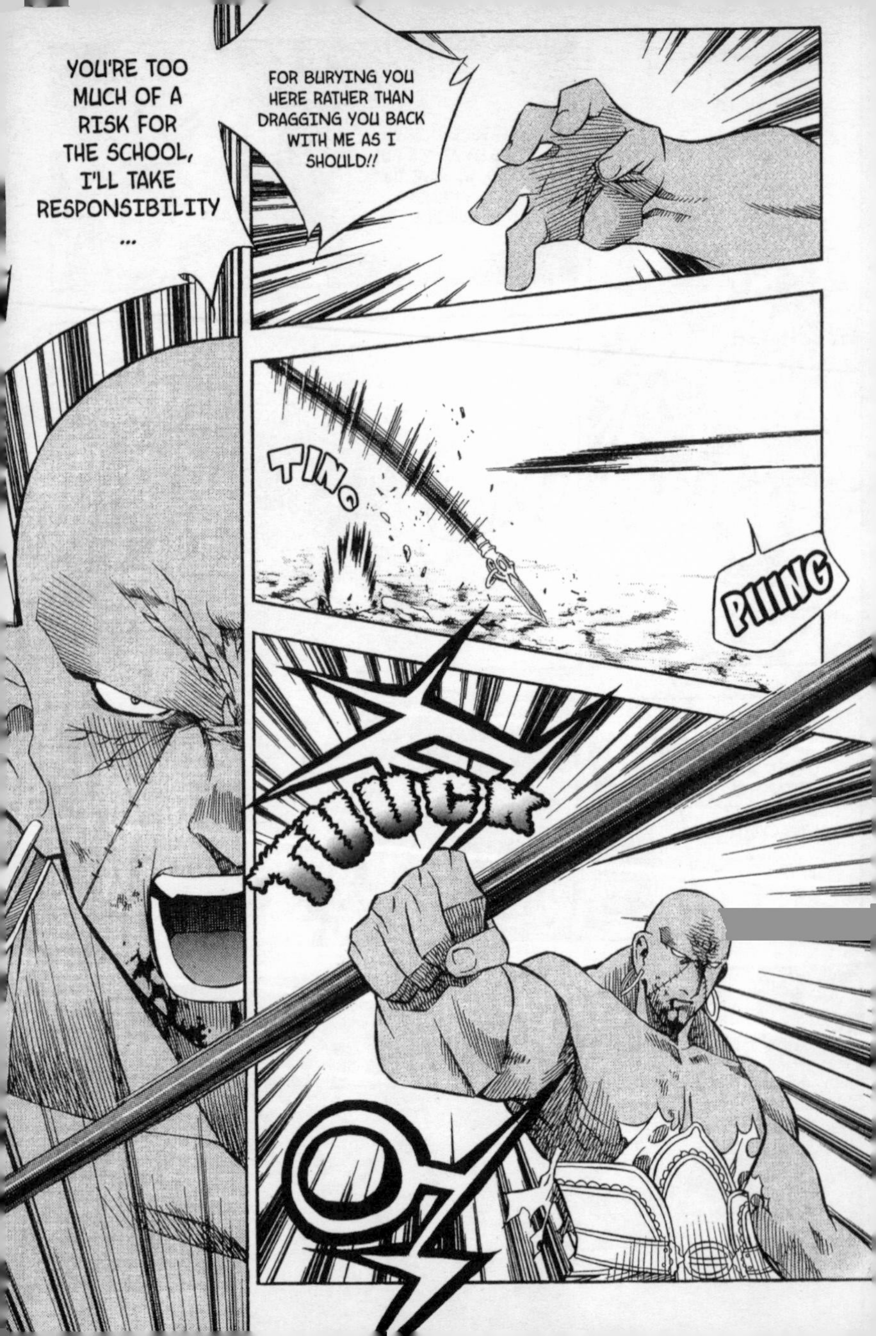
FOR BURYING YOU HERE RATHER THAN DRAGGING YOU BACK WITH ME AS I SHOULD!!
YOU'RE TOO MUCH OF A RISK FOR THE SCHOOL, I'LL TAKE RESPONSIBILITY ...
TING
PIIING
THUCK

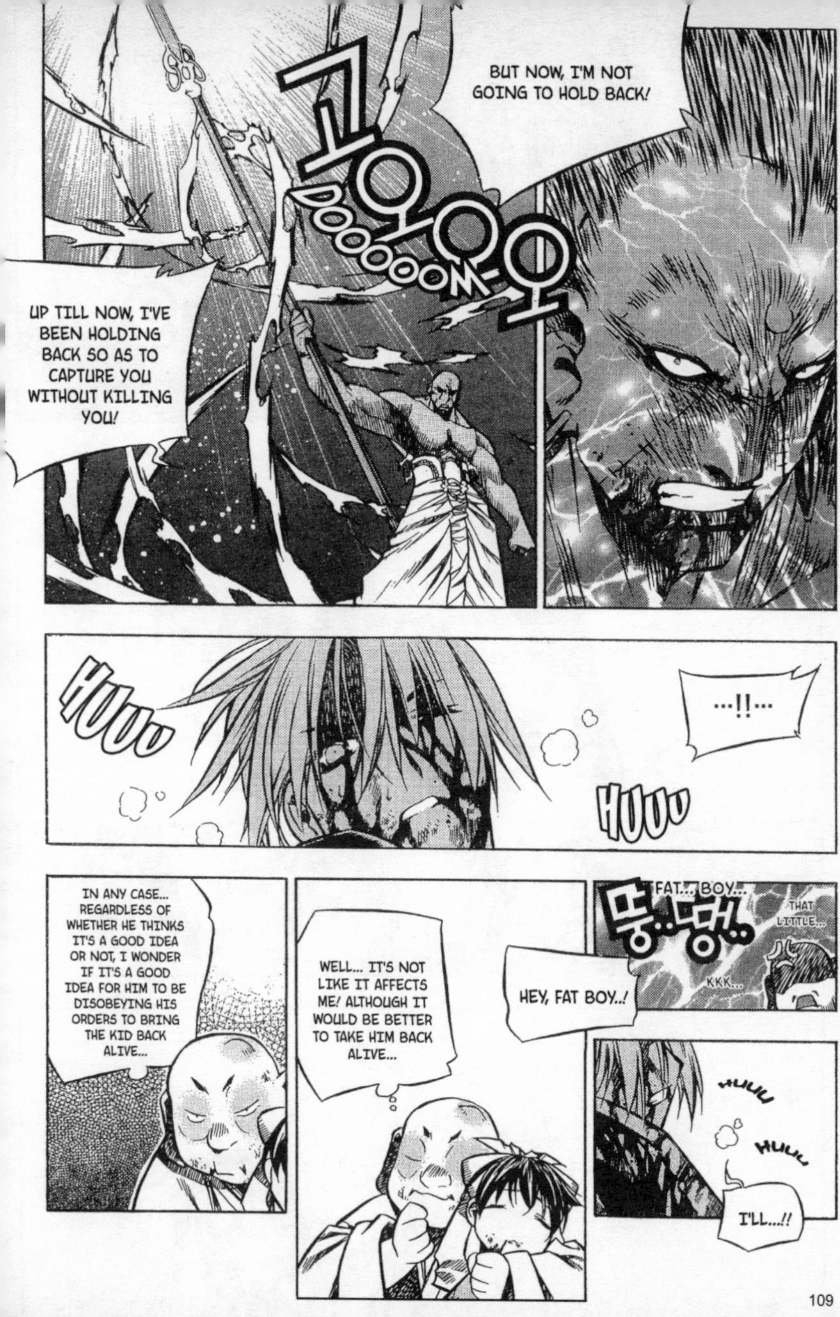
UP TILL NOW, I'VE BEEN HOLDING BACK SO AS TO CAPTURE YOU WITHOUT KILLING YOU!
DOOOOOOM-
BUT NOW, I'M NOT GOING TO HOLD BACK!
HUUU
...!!...
HUUU
IN ANY CASE... REGARDLESS OF WHETHER HE THINKS IT'S A GOOD IDEA OR NOT, I WONDER IF IT'S A GOOD IDEA FOR HIM TO BE DISOBEYING HIS ORDERS TO BRING THE KID BACK ALIVE...
WELL... IT'S NOT LIKE IT AFFECTS ME! ALTHOUGH IT WOULD BE BETTER TO TAKE HIM BACK ALIVE...
HEY, FAT BOY..!
뚱..땡..
FAT... BOY...
THAT LITTLE...
KKK...
HUUU
HUUU
I'LL...!!

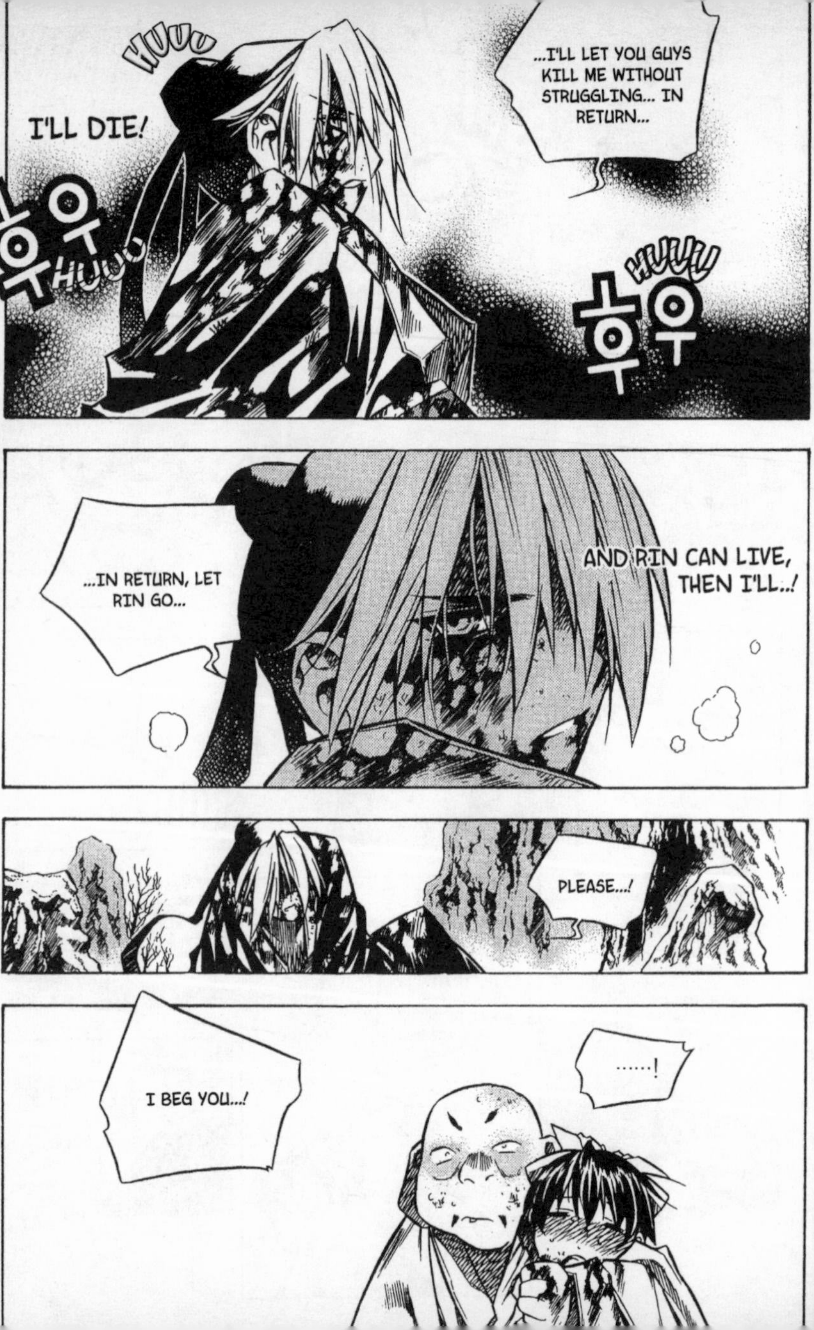
HUUU
I'LL DIE!
...I'LL LET YOU GUYS KILL ME WITHOUT STRUGGLING... IN RETURN...
HUUU
HUUU
흐우
...IN RETURN, LET RIN GO...
AND RIN CAN LIVE, THEN I'LL..!
PLEASE...!
I BEG YOU...!
......!

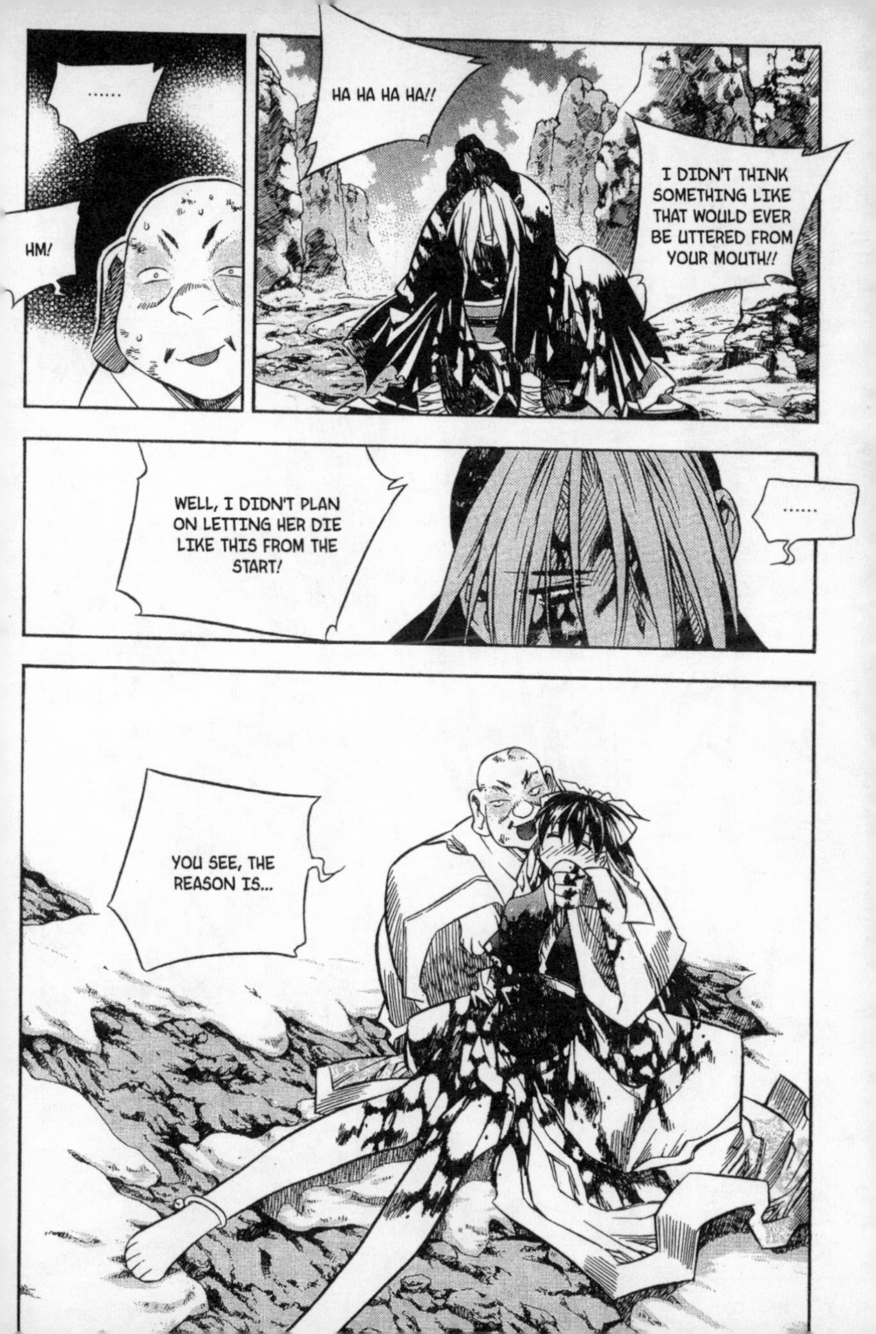

HA HA HA HA!!
I DIDN'T THINK SOMETHING LIKE THAT WOULD EVER BE UTTERED FROM YOUR MOUTH!!
......
HM!
......
WELL, I DIDN'T PLAN ON LETTING HER DIE LIKE THIS FROM THE START!
YOU SEE, THE REASON IS...

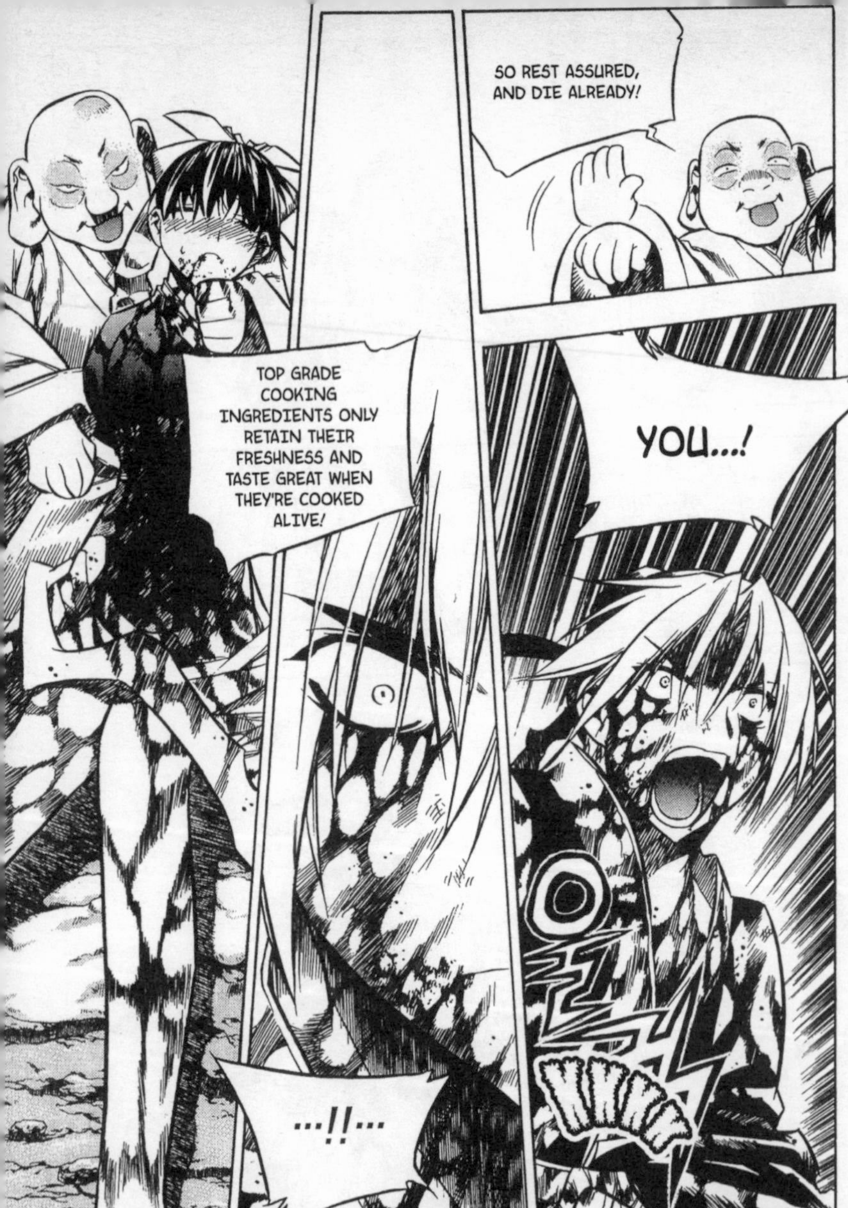
TOP GRADE COOKING INGREDIENTS ONLY RETAIN THEIR FRESHNESS AND TASTE GREAT WHEN THEY'RE COOKED ALIVE!
SO REST ASSURED, AND DIE ALREADY!
YOU...!
...!!...

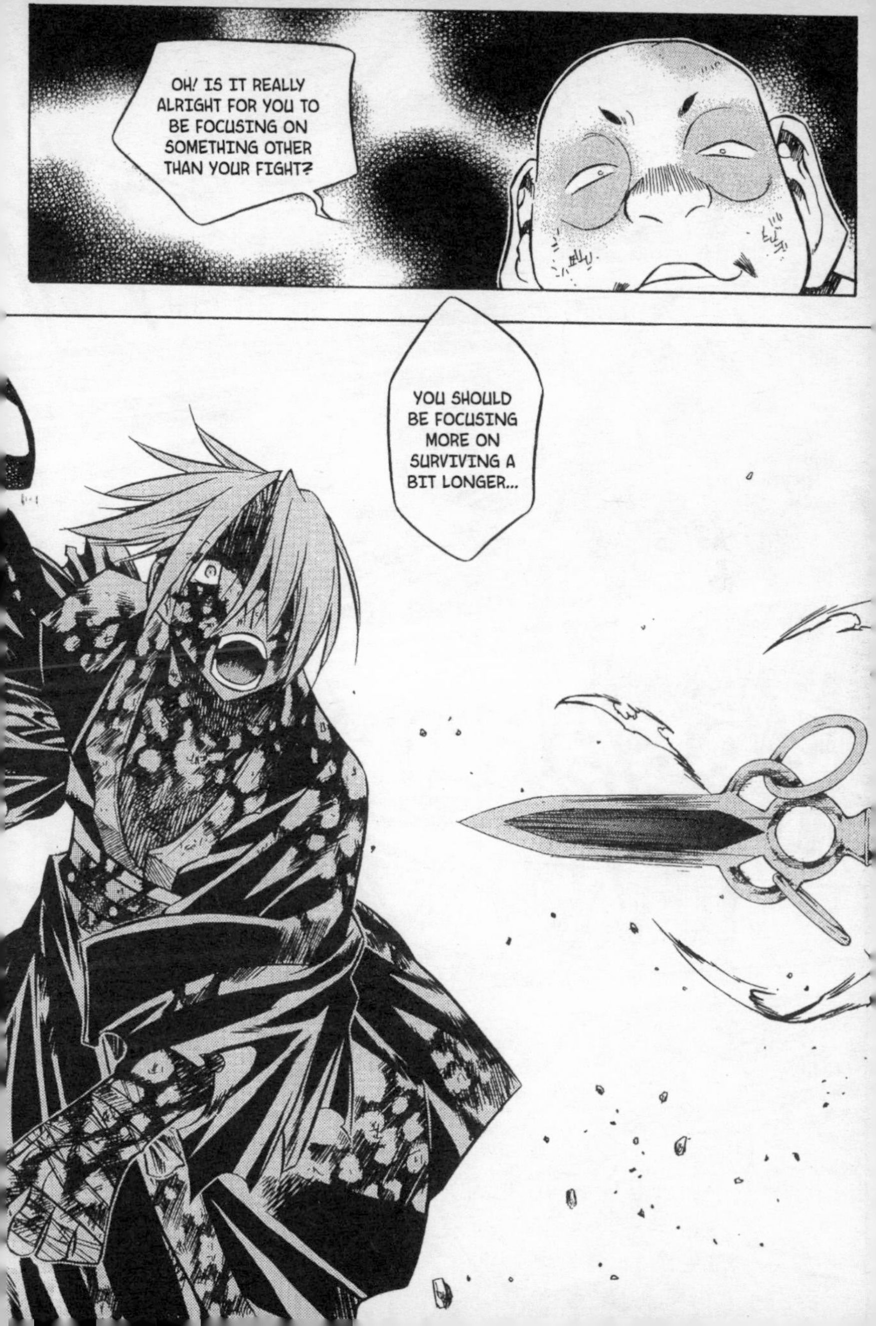
OH! IS IT REALLY ALRIGHT FOR YOU TO BE FOCUSING ON SOMETHING OTHER THAN YOUR FIGHT?
YOU SHOULD BE FOCUSING MORE ON SURVIVING A BIT LONGER...

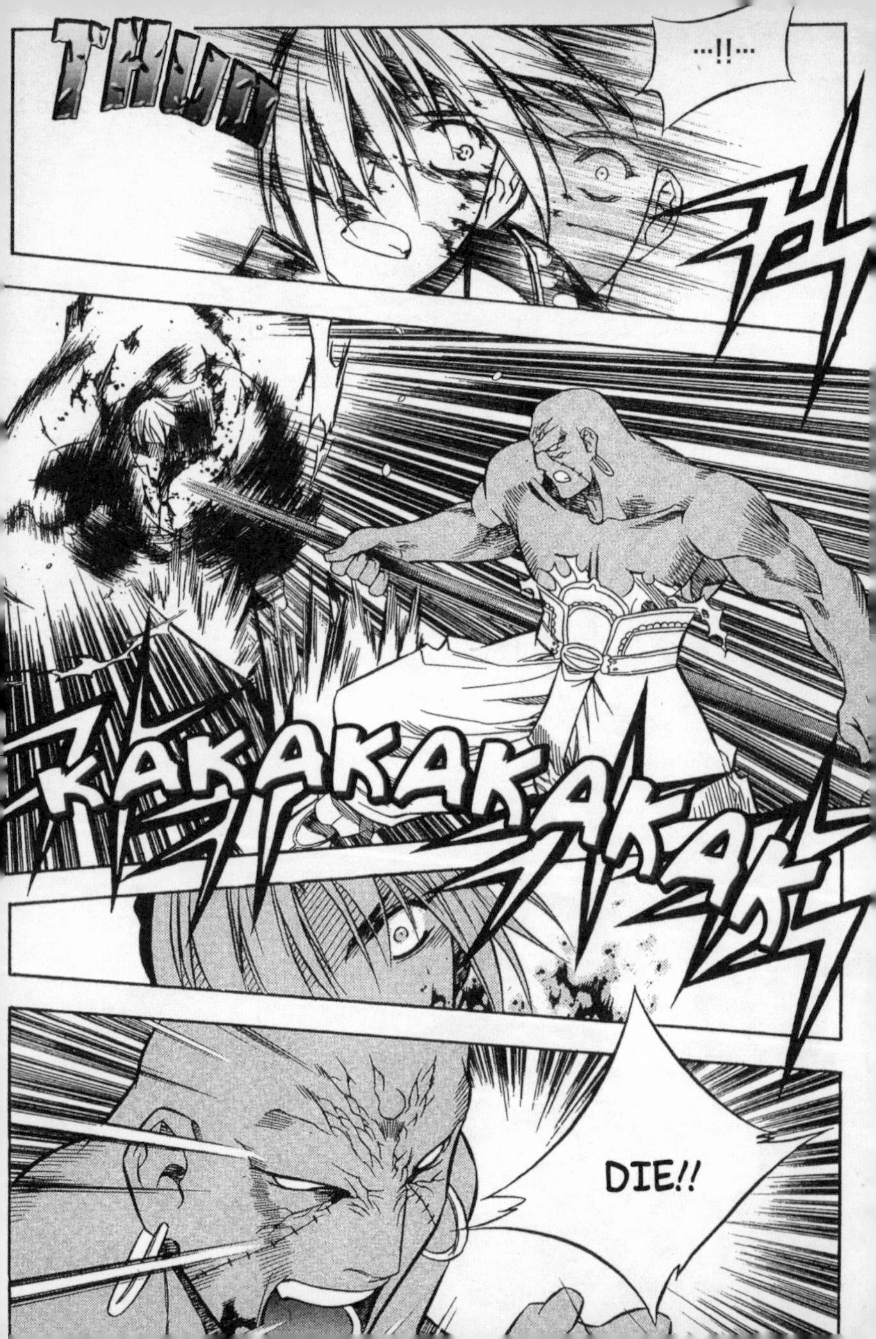
THUD
...!!...
ZZT
KAKAKAKAKAKAKAK
DIE!!

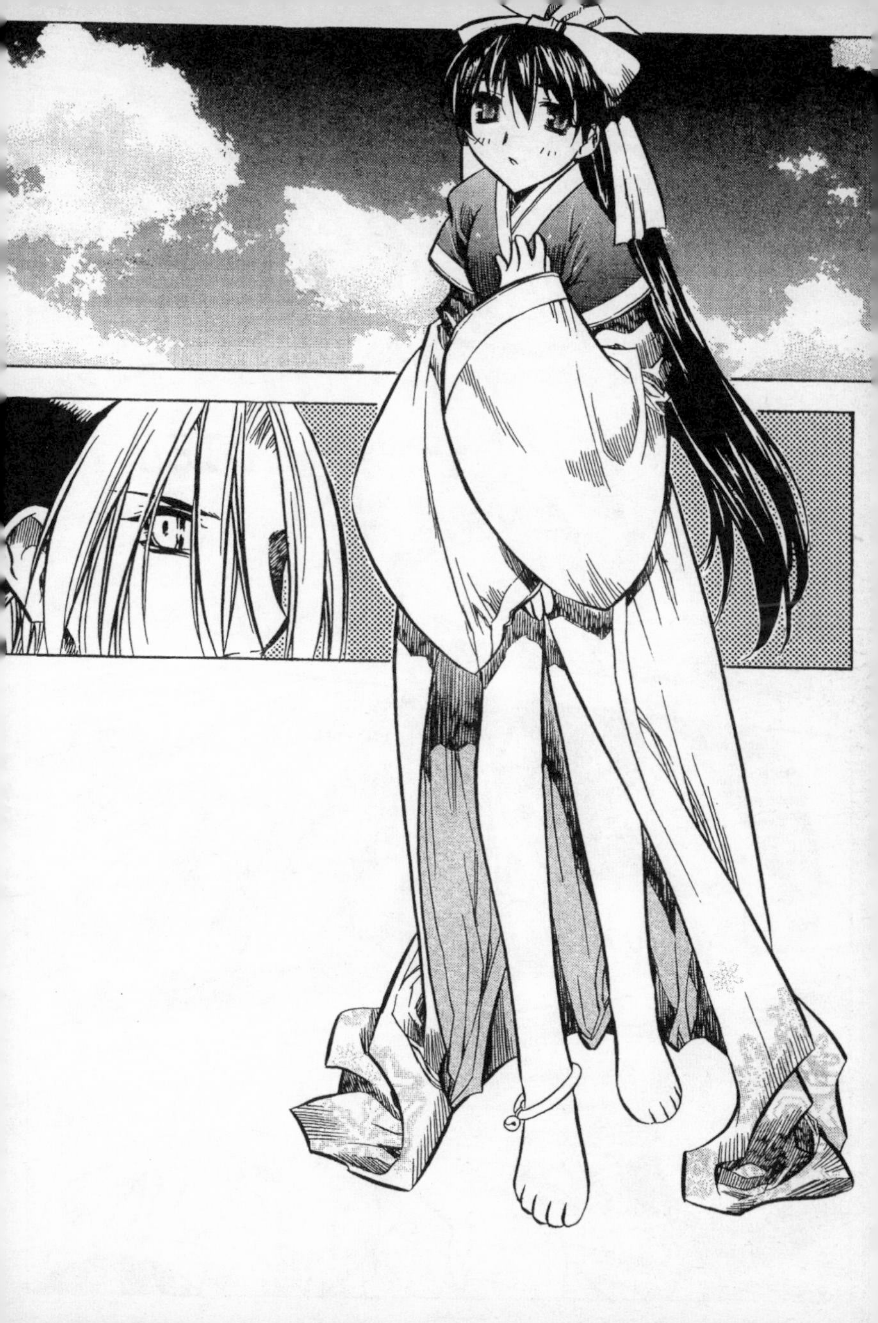

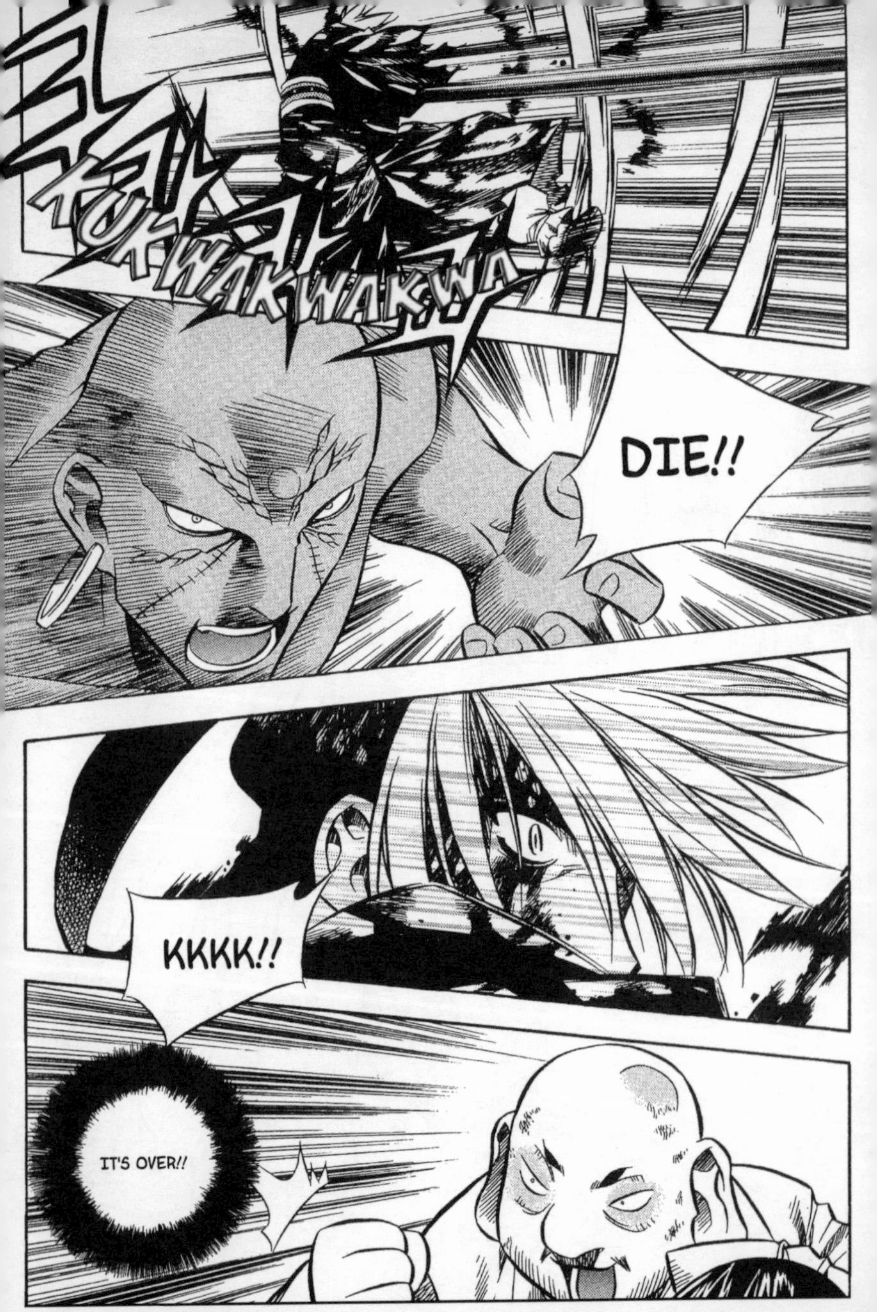
KUKWAKWAKWAKWA
DIE!!
KKKK!!
IT'S OVER!!

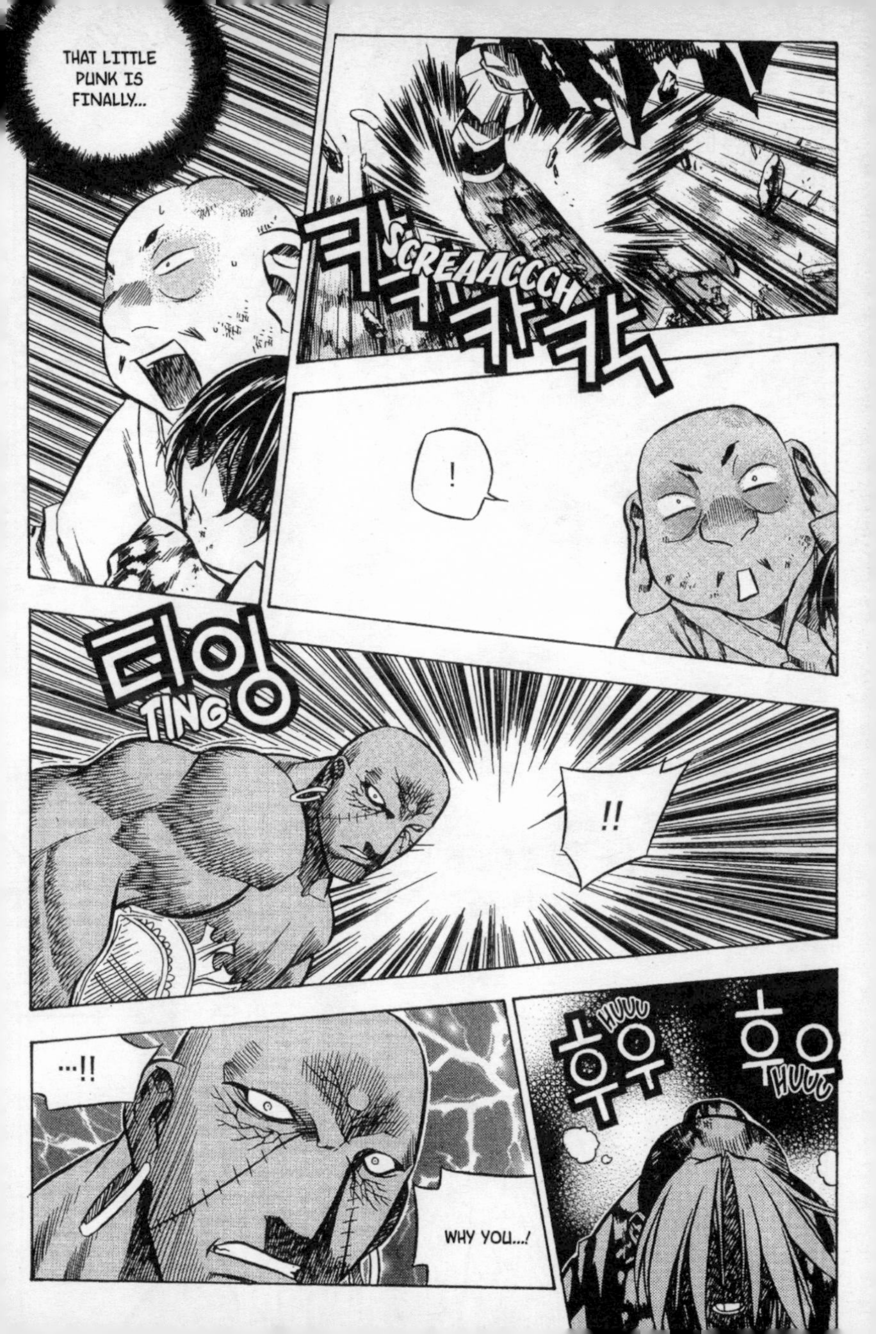

THAT LITTLE PUNK IS FINALLY...
SCREAACCCH
!
TING
!!
...!!
WHY YOU...!
HUUU
HUUU

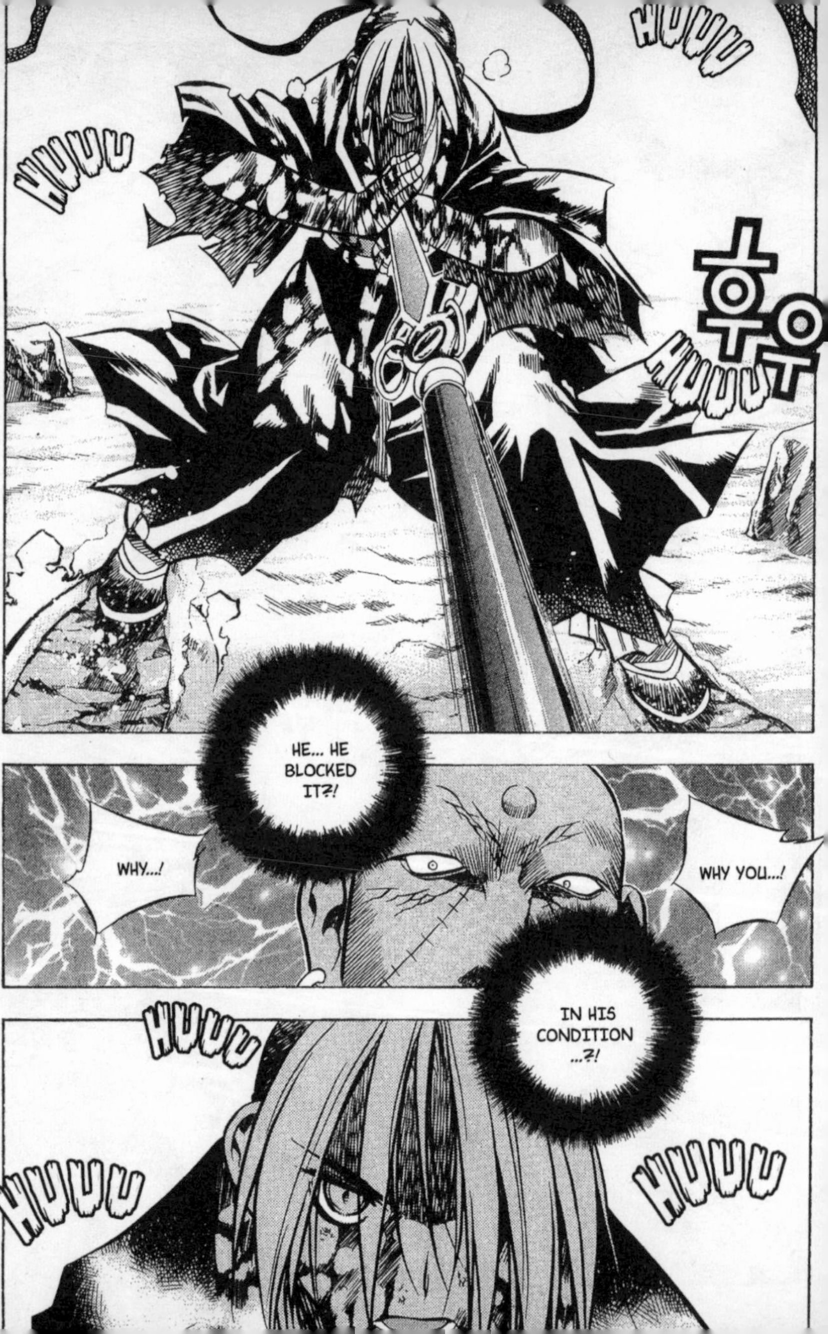
HUUUU
HUUUU
후우
HUUUUT
HE... HE BLOCKED IT?!
WHY...!
WHY YOU...!
IN HIS CONDITION ...?!
HUUUU
HUUUU
HUUUU

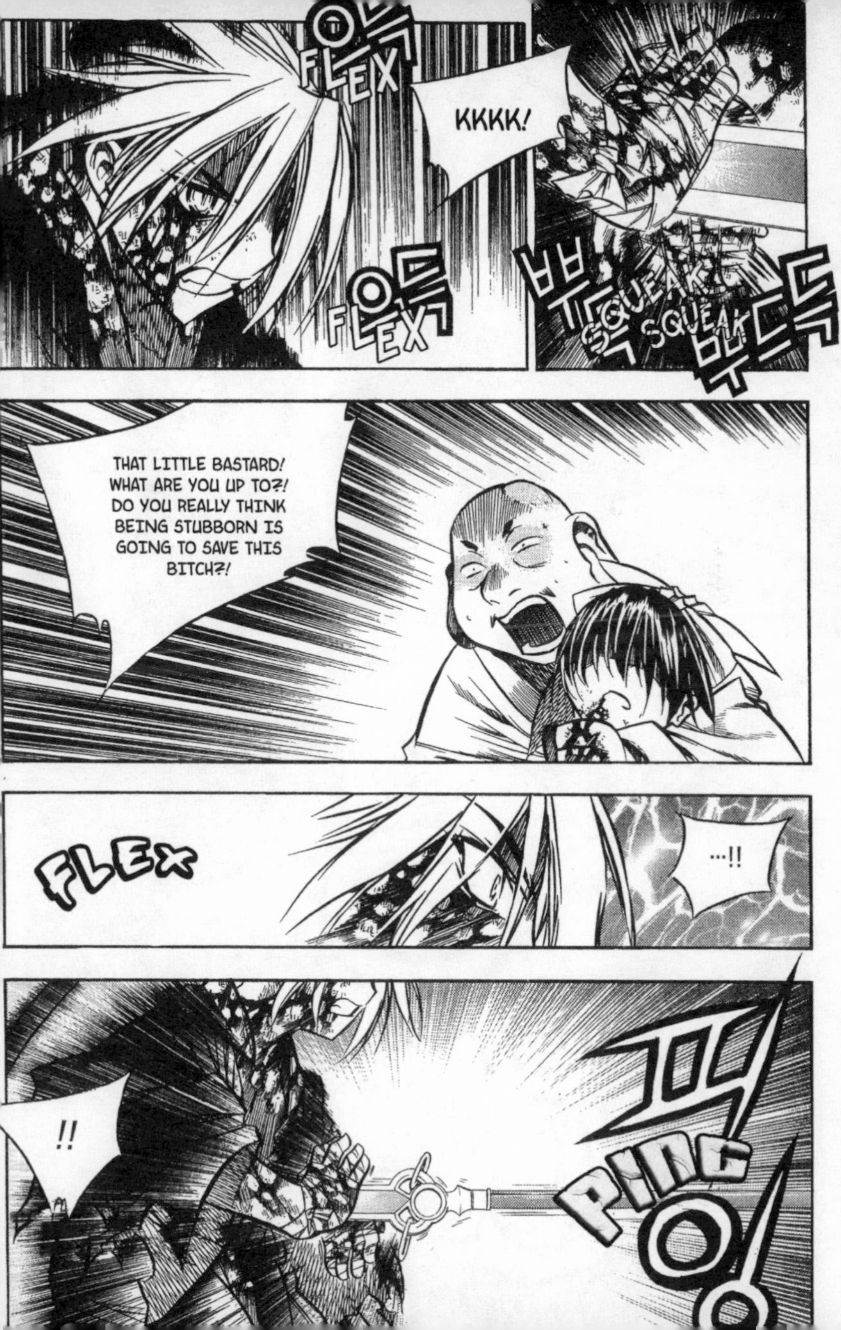
KKKK!
FLEX
FLEX
SQUEAK
SQUEAK
THAT LITTLE BASTARD! WHAT ARE YOU UP TO?! DO YOU REALLY THINK BEING STUBBORN IS GOING TO SAVE THIS BITCH?!
...!!
FLEX
PING
!!

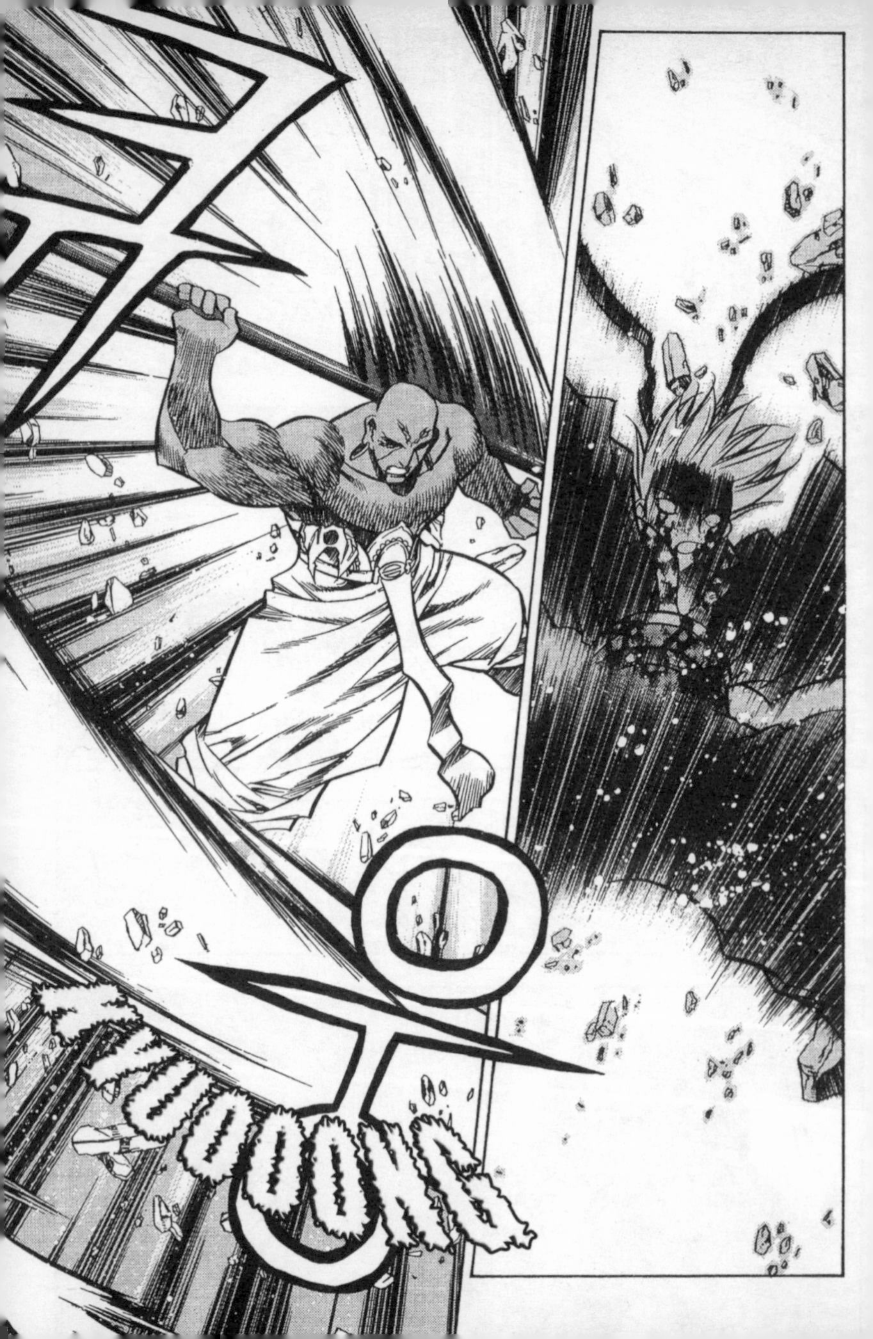

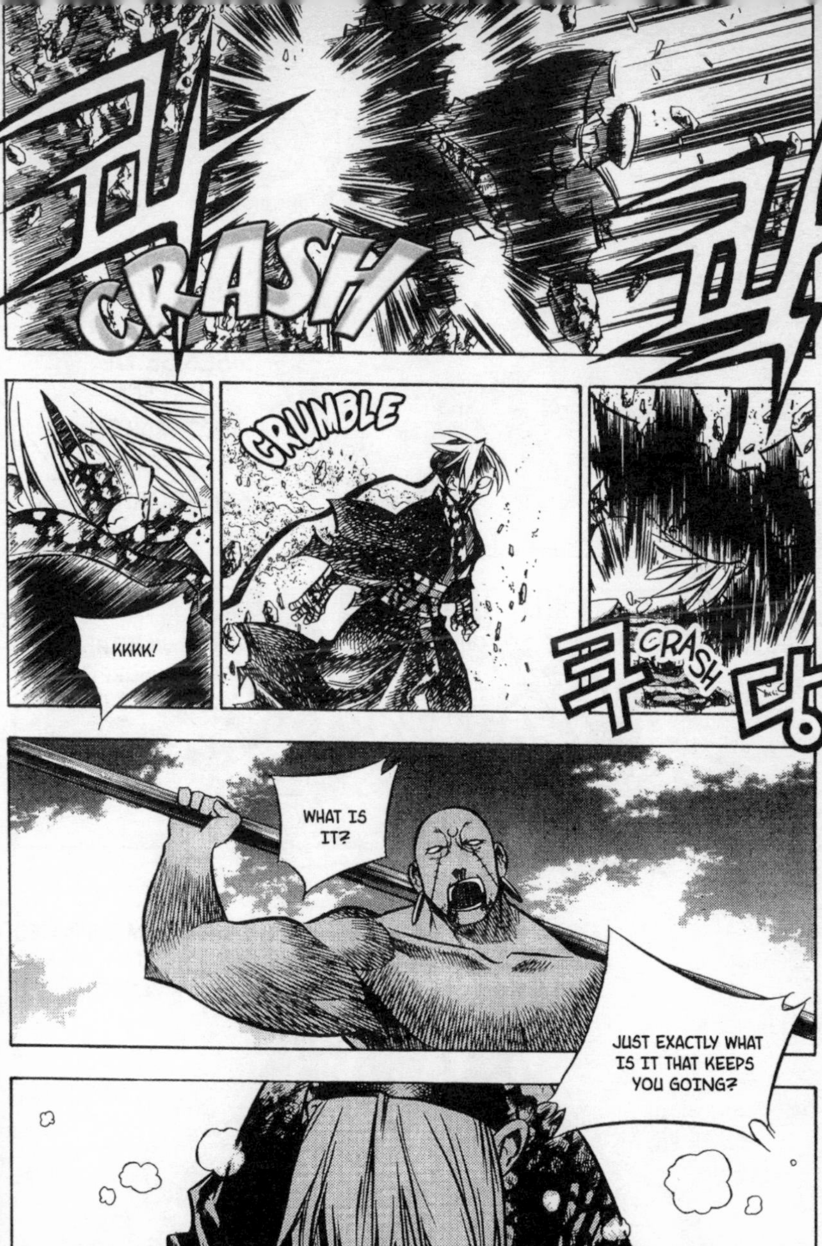
CRASH
CRUMBLE
KKKK!
CRASH
WHAT IS IT?
JUST EXACTLY WHAT IS IT THAT KEEPS YOU GOING?

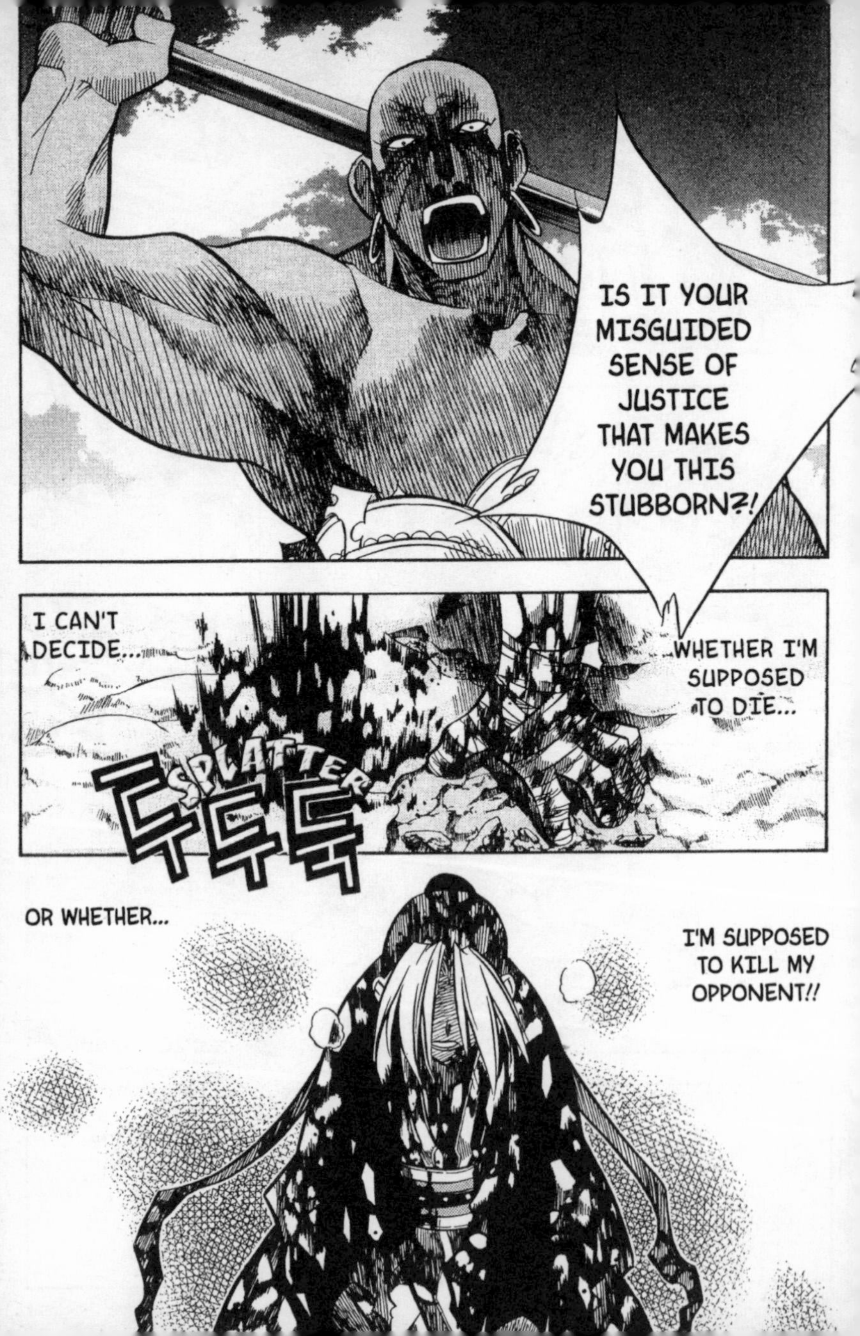
IS IT YOUR MISGUIDED SENSE OF JUSTICE THAT MAKES YOU THIS STUBBORN?!
I CAN'T DECIDE...
...WHETHER I'M SUPPOSED TO DIE...
SPLATTER
OR WHETHER...
I'M SUPPOSED TO KILL MY OPPONENT!!

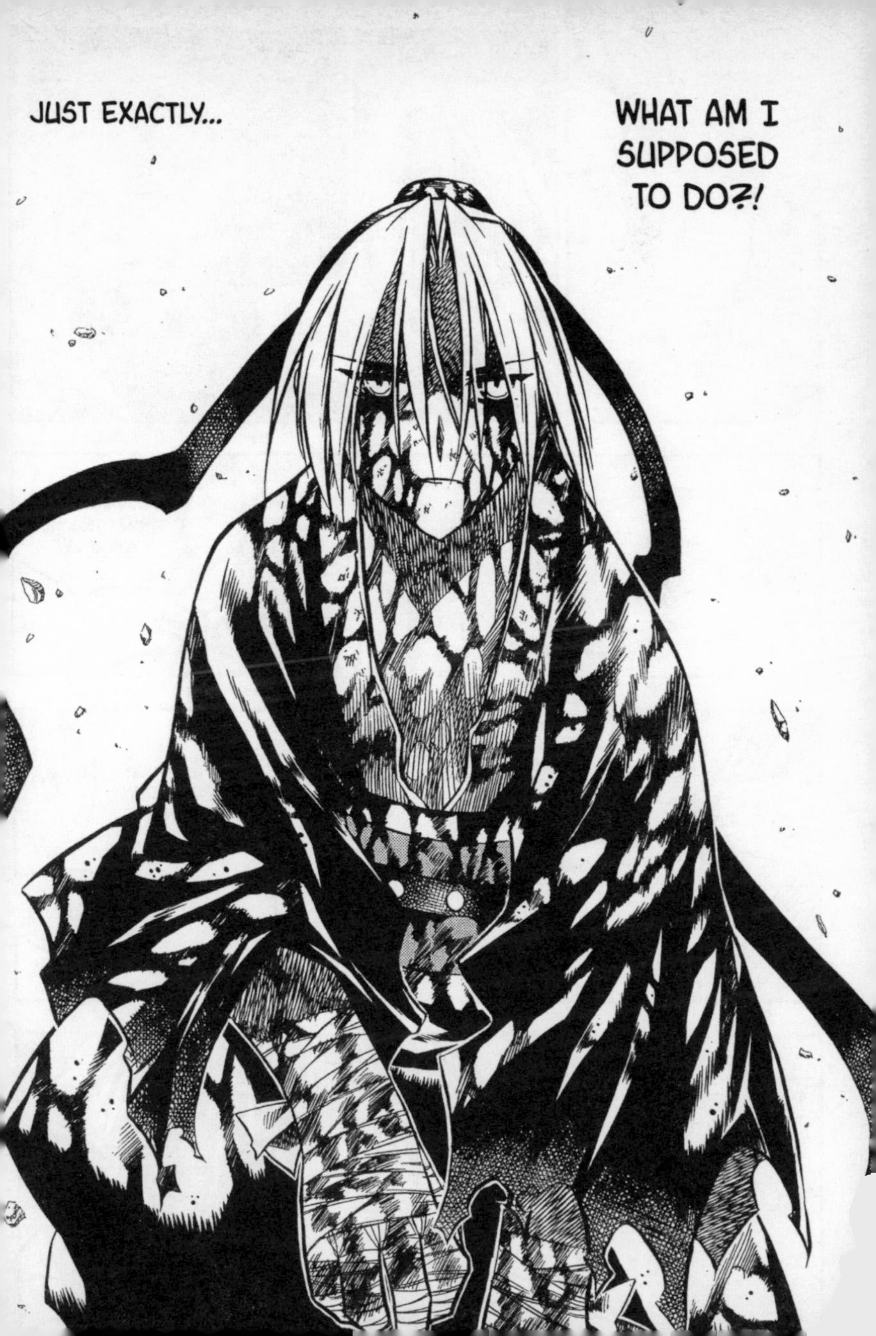
JUST EXACTLY...
WHAT AM I SUPPOSED TO DO?!

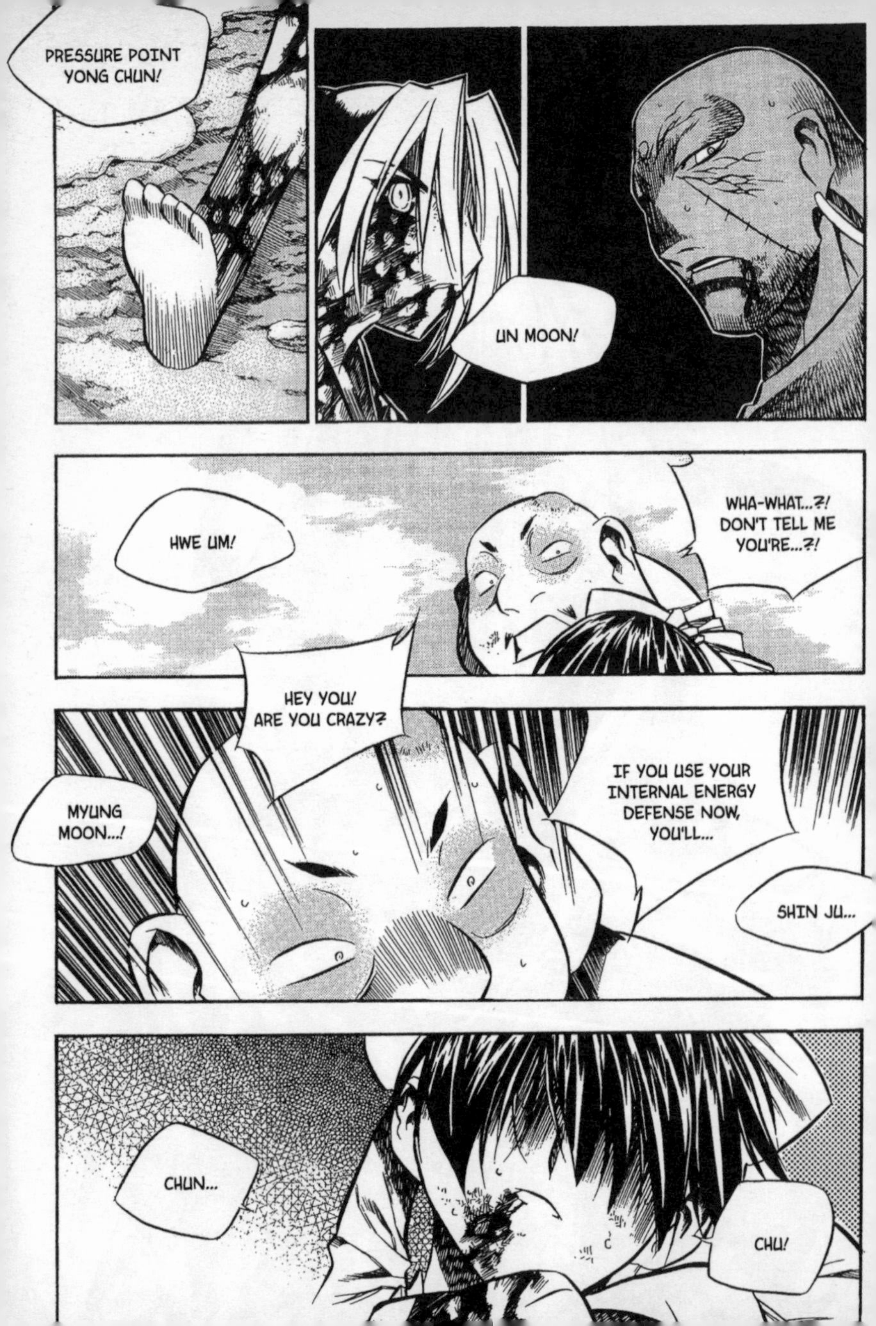
PRESSURE POINT YONG CHUN!
UN MOON!
WHA-WHAT...?! DON'T TELL ME YOU'RE...?!
HWE UM!
HEY YOU! ARE YOU CRAZY?
IF YOU USE YOUR INTERNAL ENERGY DEFENSE NOW, YOU'LL...
MYUNG MOON...!
SHIN JU...
CHUN...
CHU!

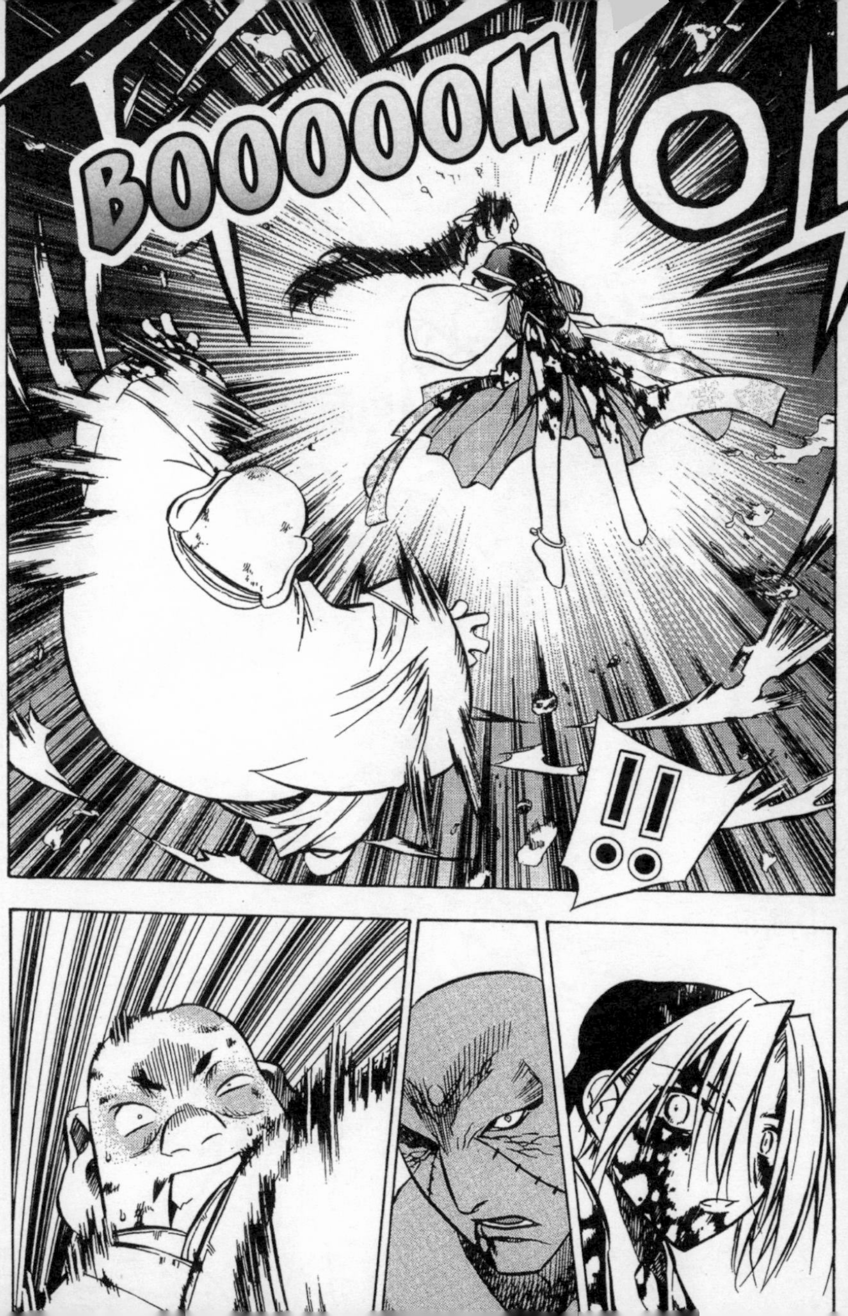
BOOOOOM
!!

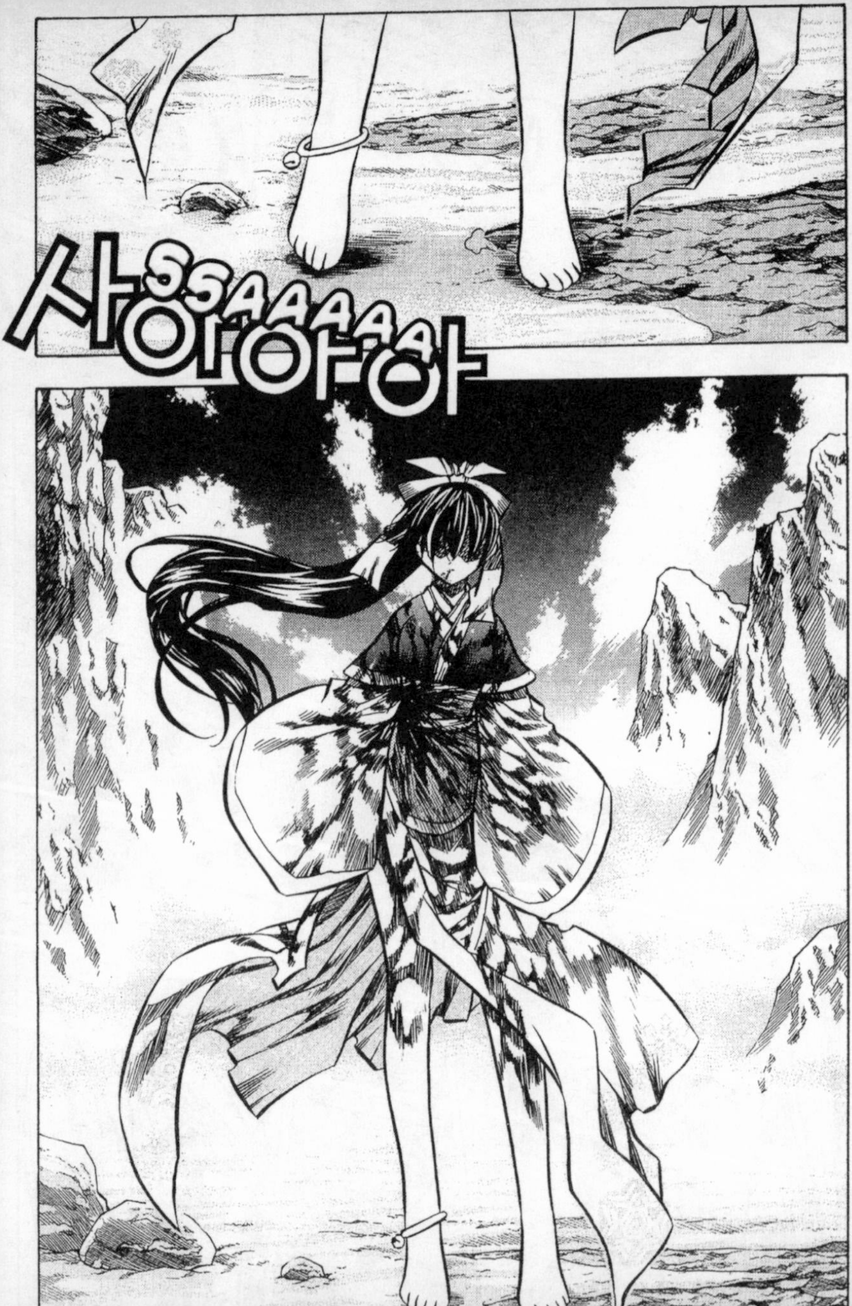
SSAAAAAA!

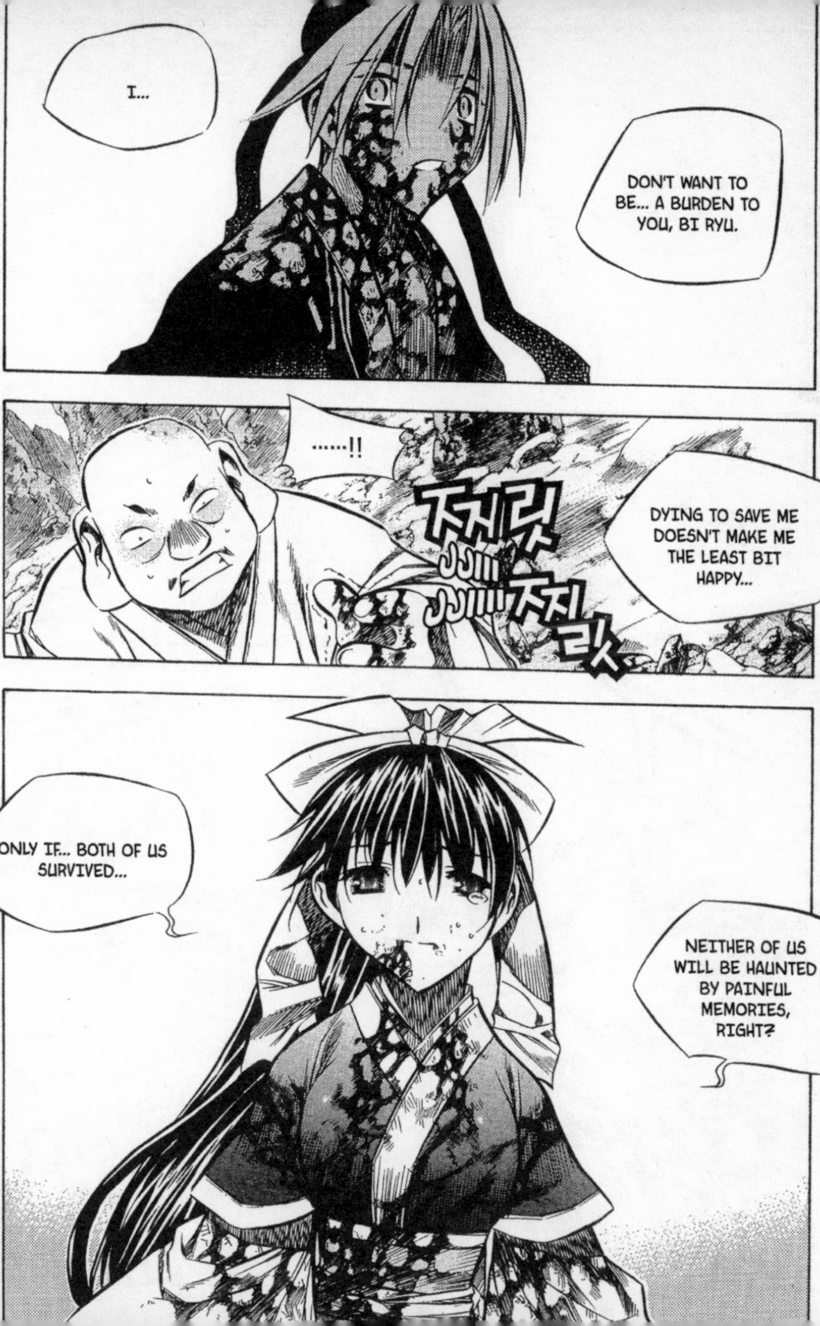
I...
DON'T WANT TO BE... A BURDEN TO YOU, BI RYU.
......!!
DYING TO SAVE ME DOESN'T MAKE ME THE LEAST BIT HAPPY...
ONLY IF... BOTH OF US SURVIVED...
NEITHER OF US WILL BE HAUNTED BY PAINFUL MEMORIES, RIGHT?

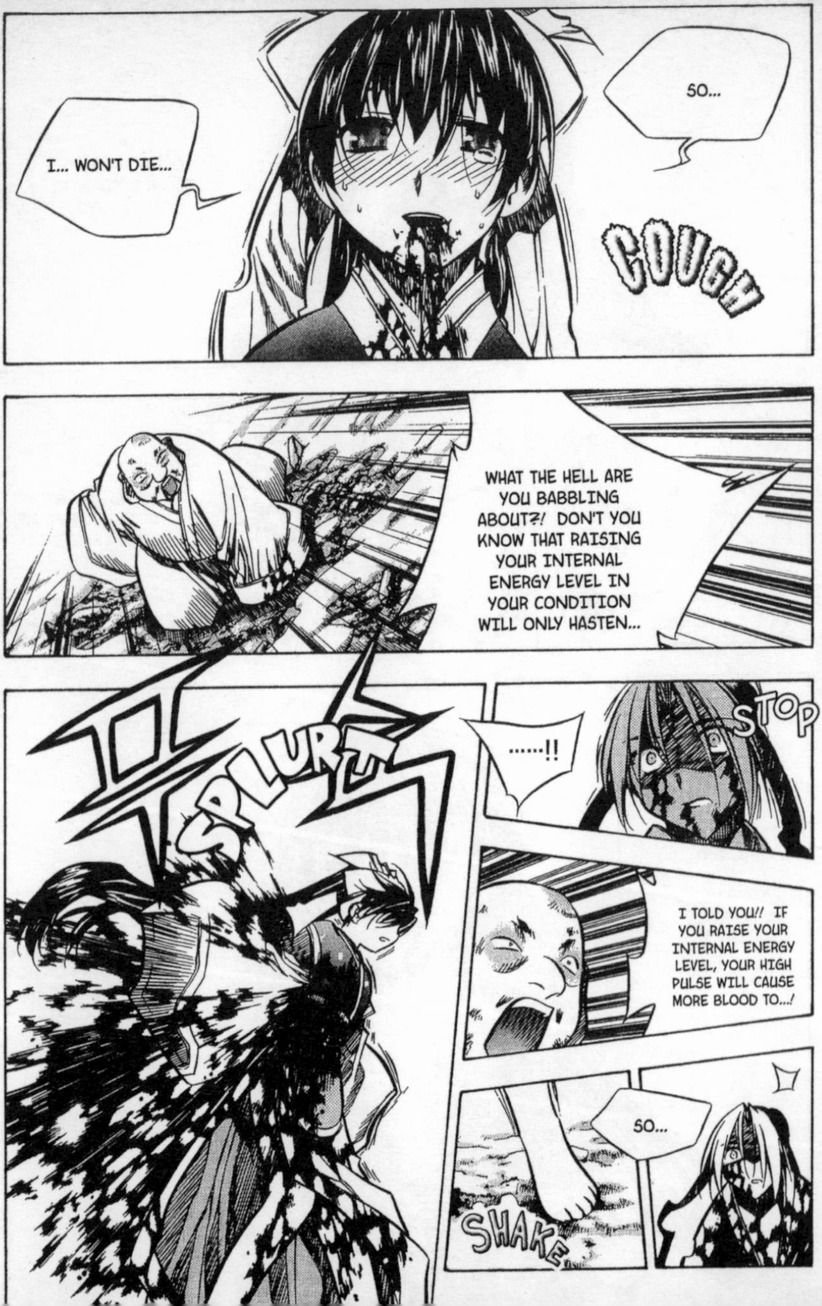
SO...
I... WON'T DIE...
COUGH
WHAT THE HELL ARE YOU BABBLING ABOUT?! DON'T YOU KNOW THAT RAISING YOUR INTERNAL ENERGY LEVEL IN YOUR CONDITION WILL ONLY HASTEN...
STOP
......!!
SPLURT
I TOLD YOU!! IF YOU RAISE YOUR INTERNAL ENERGY LEVEL, YOUR HIGH PULSE WILL CAUSE MORE BLOOD TO...!
SO...
SHAKE

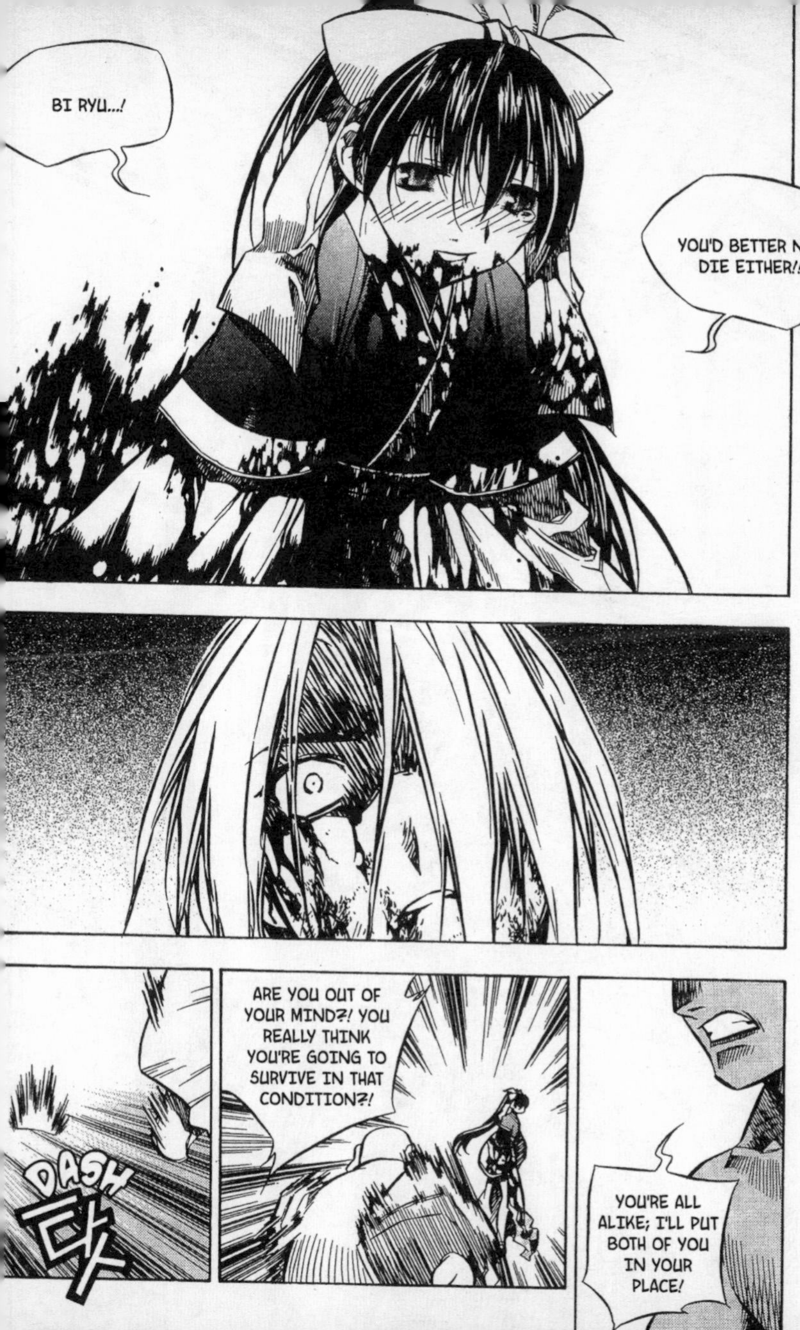
YOU'D BETTER NOT DIE EITHER!!
BI RYU...!
YOU'RE ALL ALIKE; I'LL PUT BOTH OF YOU IN YOUR PLACE!
ARE YOU OUT OF YOUR MIND?! YOU REALLY THINK YOU'RE GOING TO SURVIVE IN THAT CONDITION?!
DASH

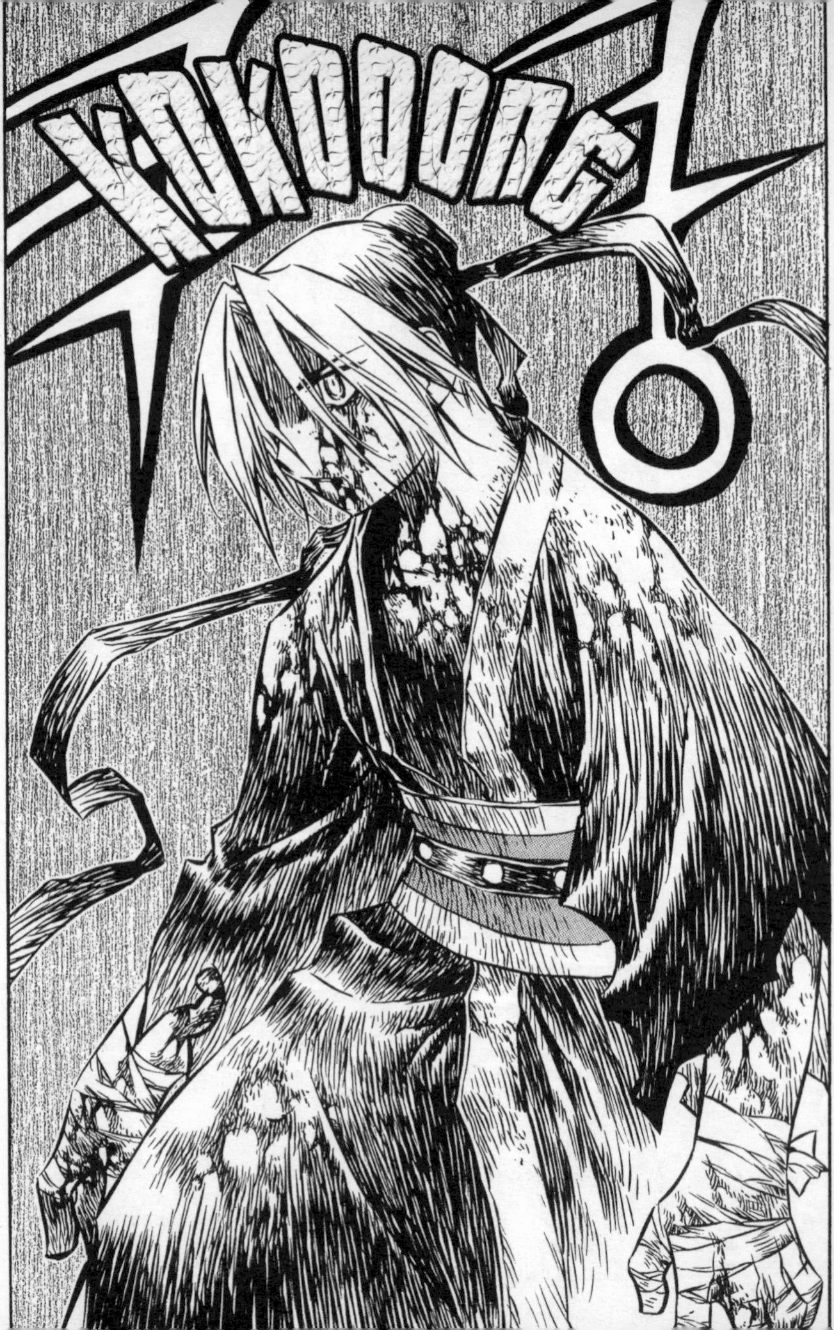

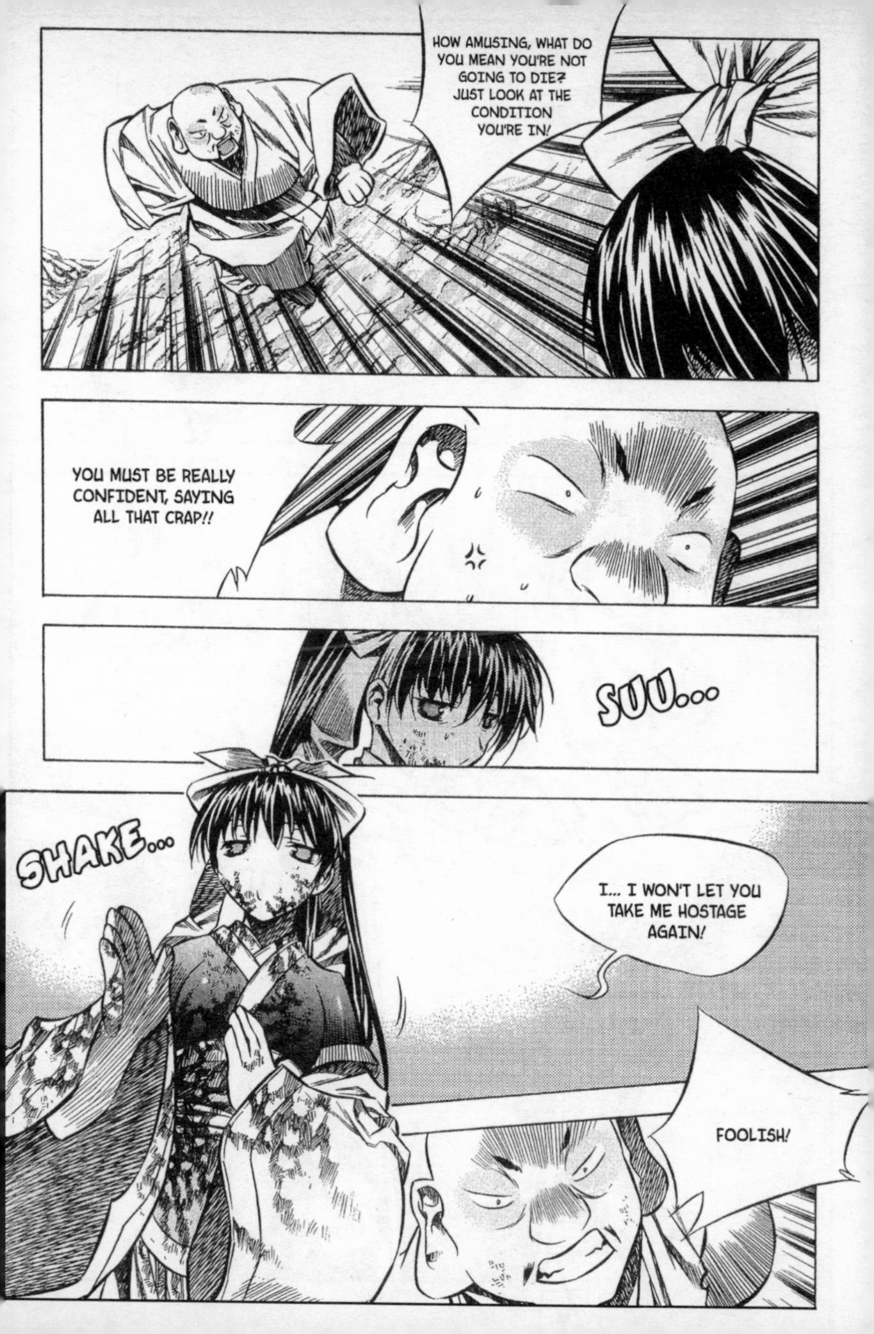
HOW AMUSING, WHAT DO YOU MEAN YOU'RE NOT GOING TO DIE? JUST LOOK AT THE CONDITION YOU'RE IN!
YOU MUST BE REALLY CONFIDENT, SAYING ALL THAT CRAP!!
SUU...
SHAKE...
I... I WON'T LET YOU TAKE ME HOSTAGE AGAIN!
FOOLISH!

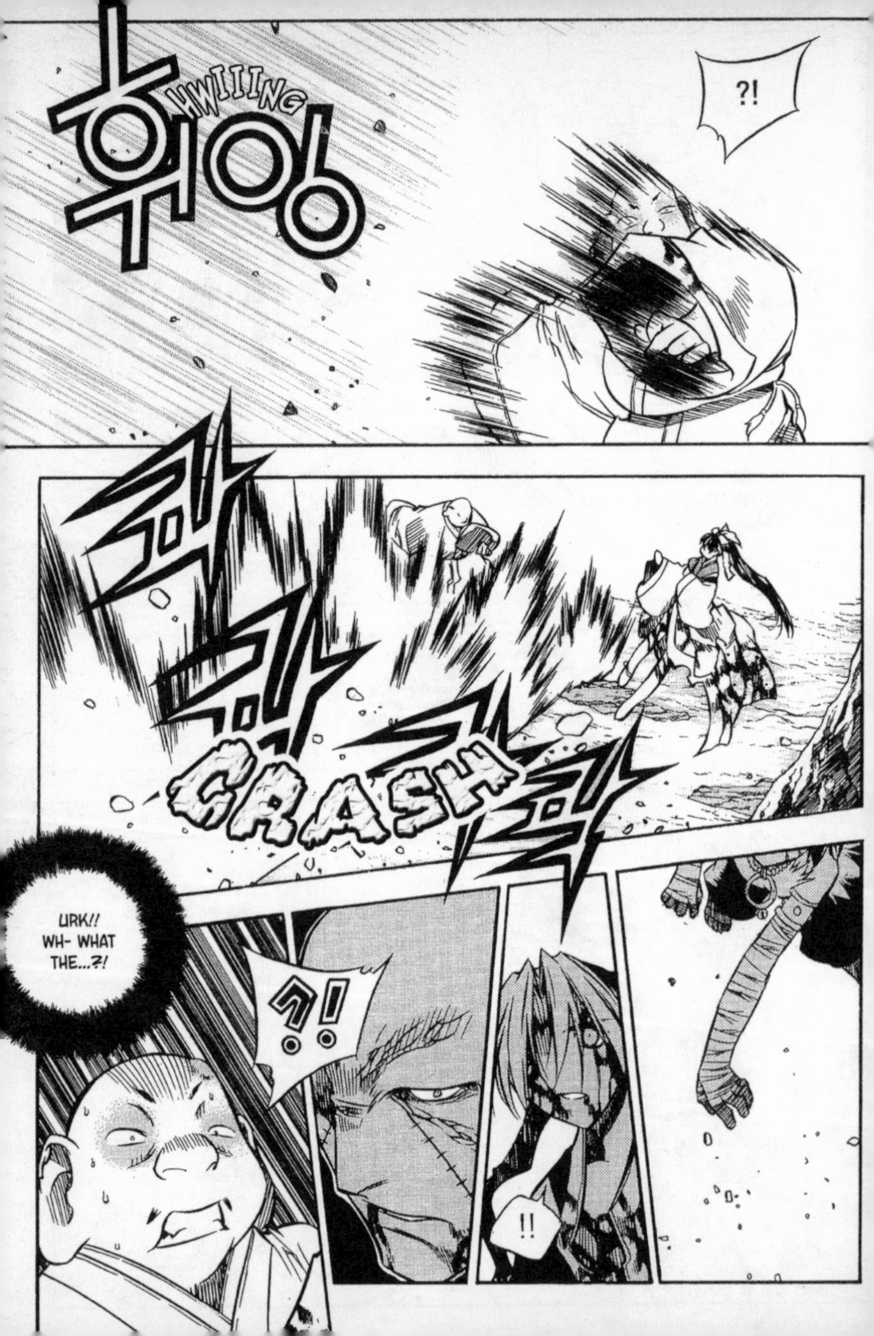
HWIIING
?!
CRASH
URK!! WH- WHAT THE...?!
?!
!!

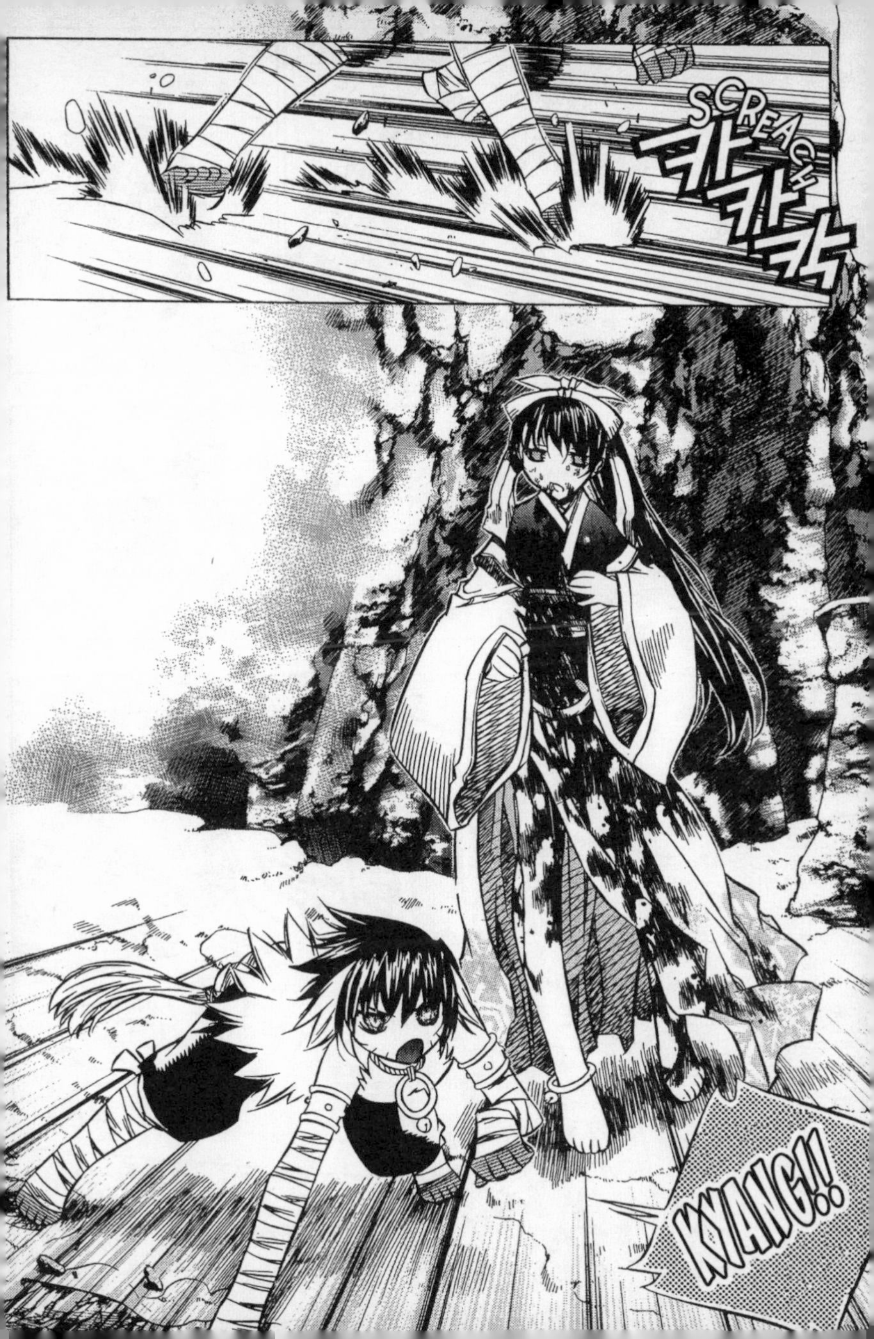
SCREACH
ヲトヲトヲち
KYANG!!

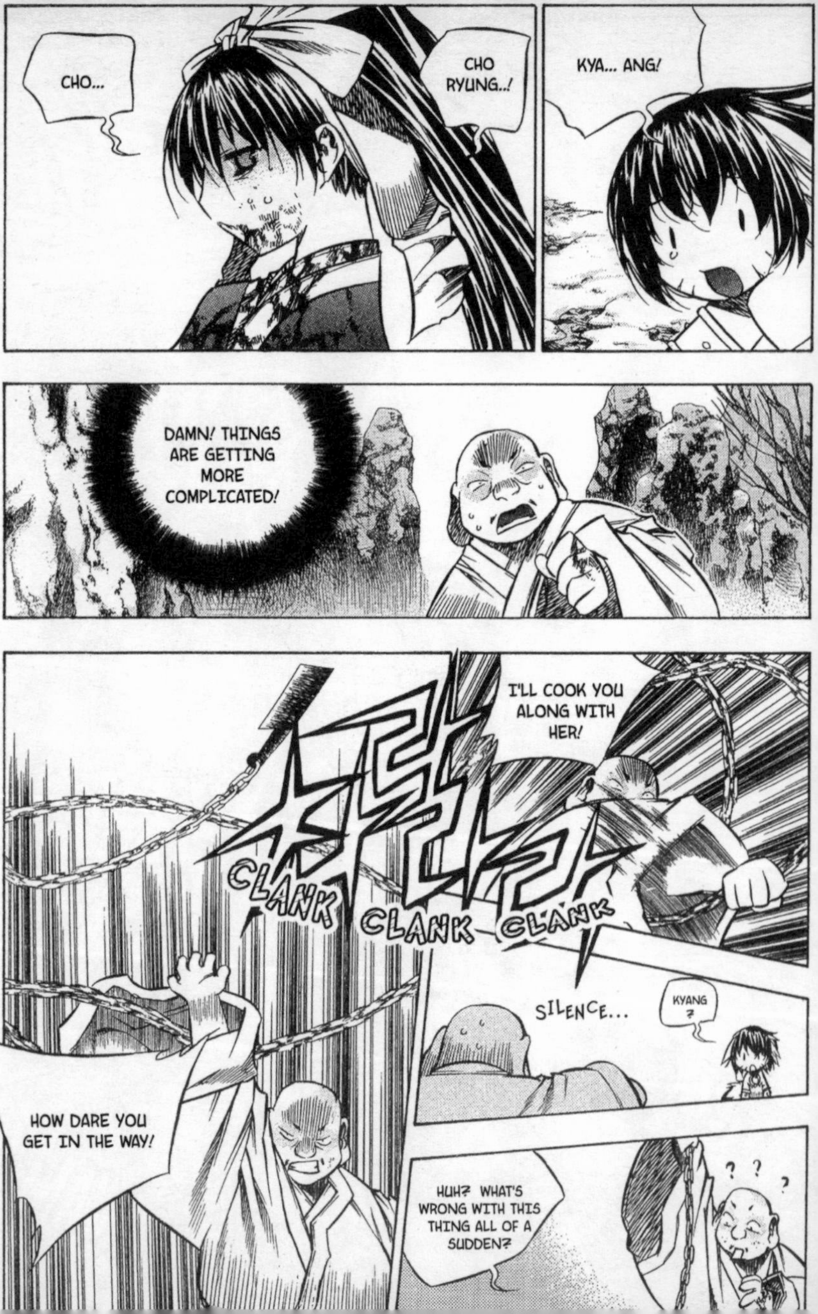

CHO...
CHO RYUNG..!
KYA... ANG!
DAMN! THINGS ARE GETTING MORE COMPLICATED!
HOW DARE YOU GET IN THE WAY!
I'LL COOK YOU ALONG WITH HER!
CLANK CLANK CLANK
SILENCE...
KYANG ?
HUH? WHAT'S WRONG WITH THIS THING ALL OF A SUDDEN?
? ? ?

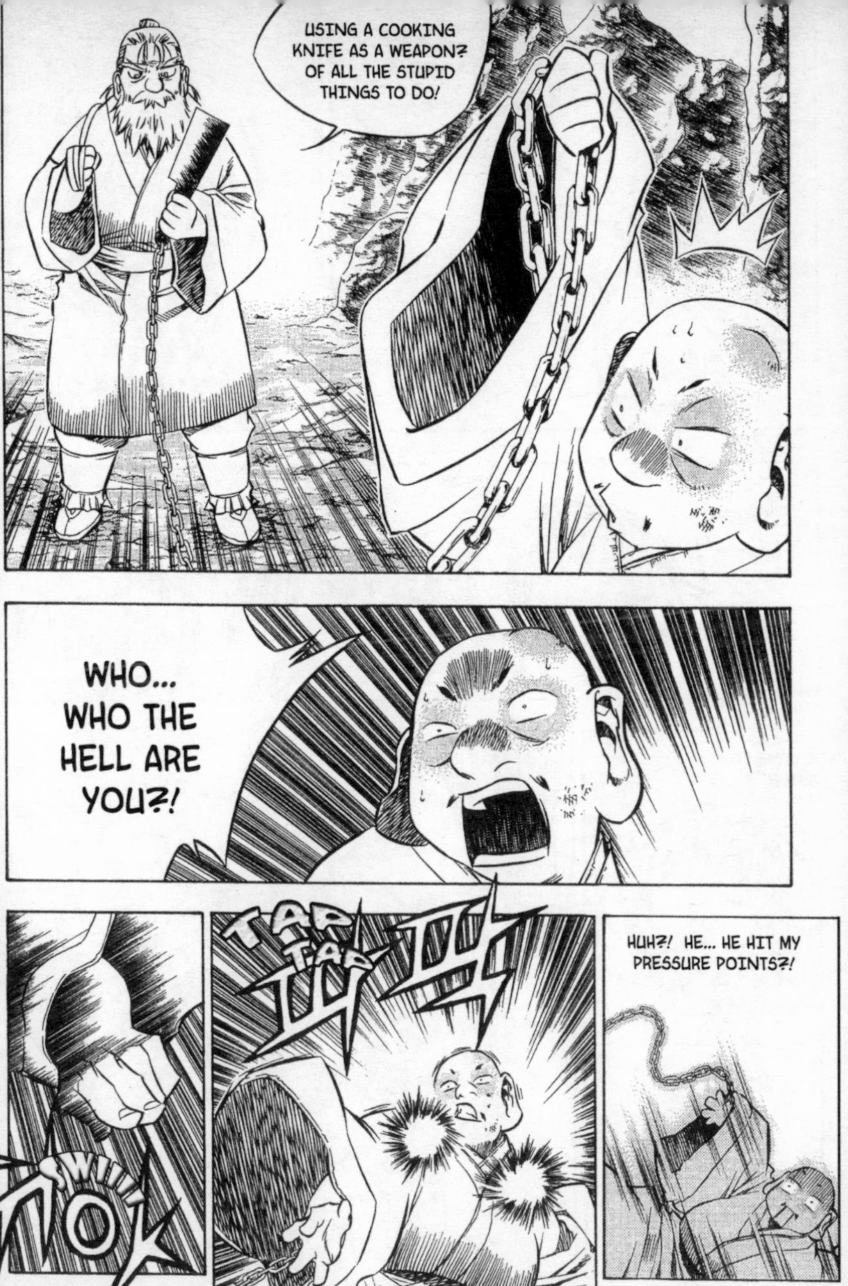
USING A COOKING KNIFE AS A WEAPON?
OF ALL THE STUPID THINGS TO DO!
WHO... WHO THE HELL ARE YOU?!
TAP TAP
HUH?! HE... HE HIT MY PRESSURE POINTS?!

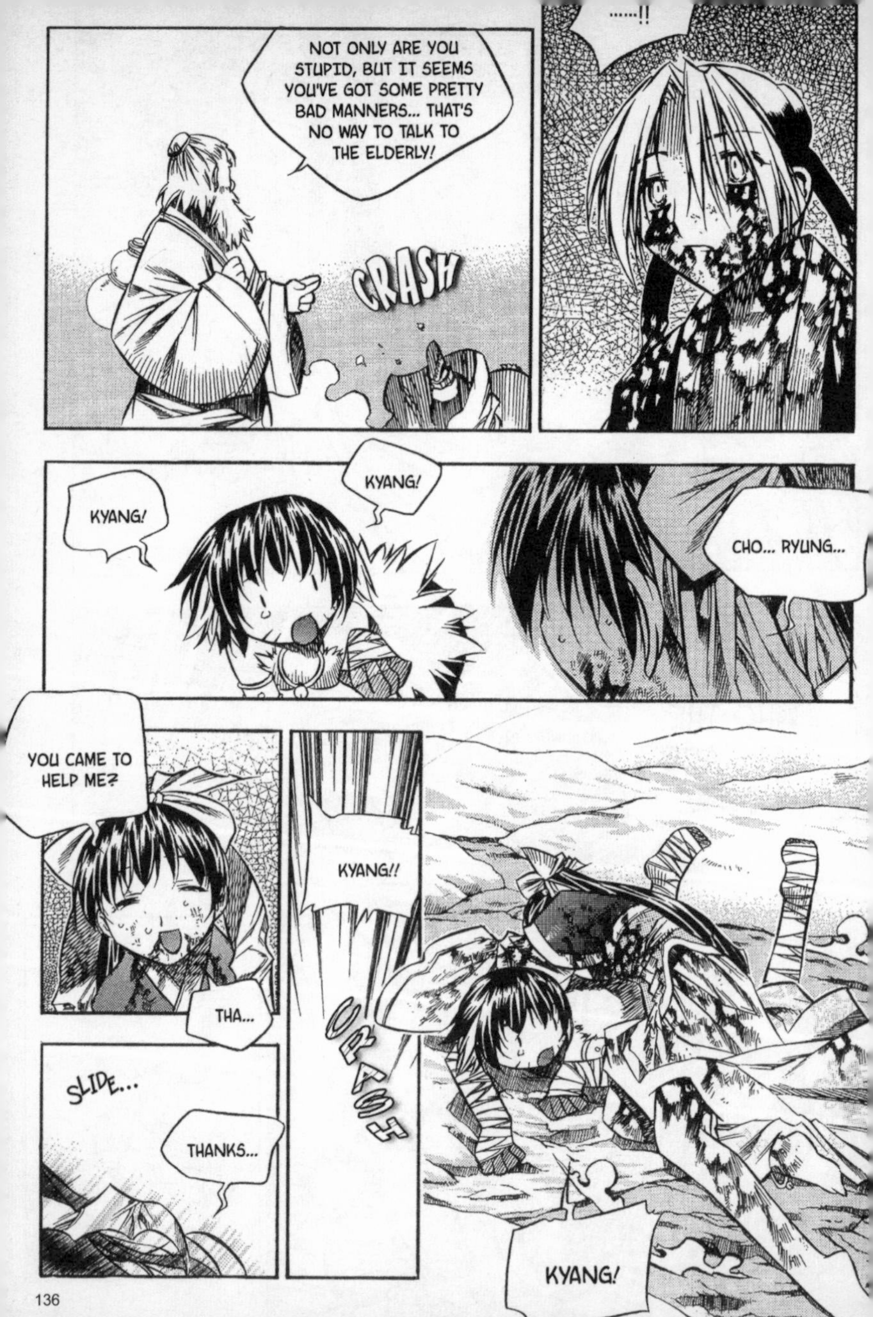
NOT ONLY ARE YOU STUPID, BUT IT SEEMS YOU'VE GOT SOME PRETTY BAD MANNERS... THAT'S NO WAY TO TALK TO THE ELDERLY!
CRASH
......!!
KYANG!
KYANG!
CHO... RYUNG...
YOU CAME TO HELP ME?
THA...
SLIDE...
THANKS...
KYANG!!
CRASH
KYANG!

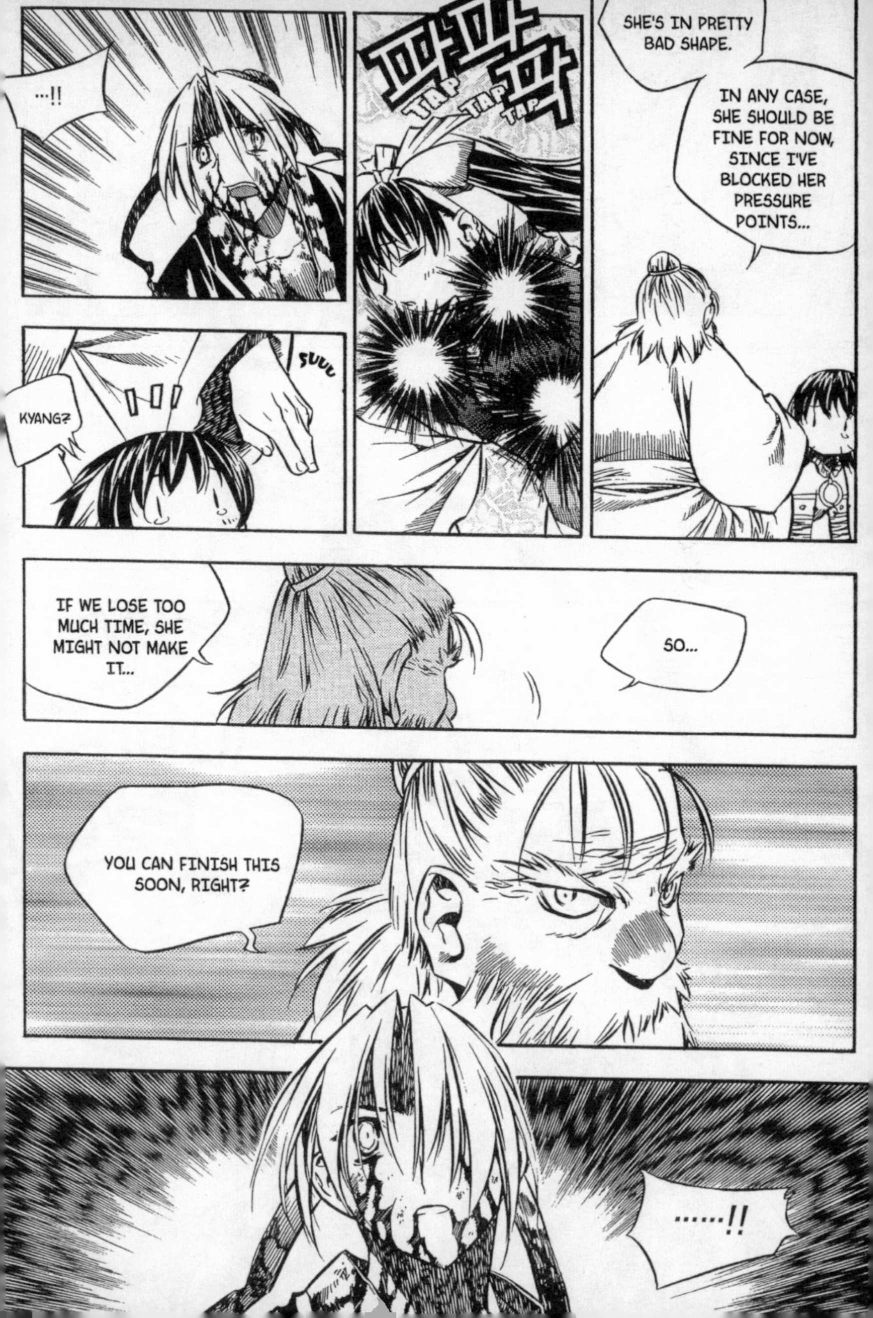
...!!
KYANG?
SUUU
TAP TAP TAP
SHE'S IN PRETTY BAD SHAPE.
IN ANY CASE, SHE SHOULD BE FINE FOR NOW, SINCE I'VE BLOCKED HER PRESSURE POINTS...
IF WE LOSE TOO MUCH TIME, SHE MIGHT NOT MAKE IT...
SO...
YOU CAN FINISH THIS SOON, RIGHT?
......!!

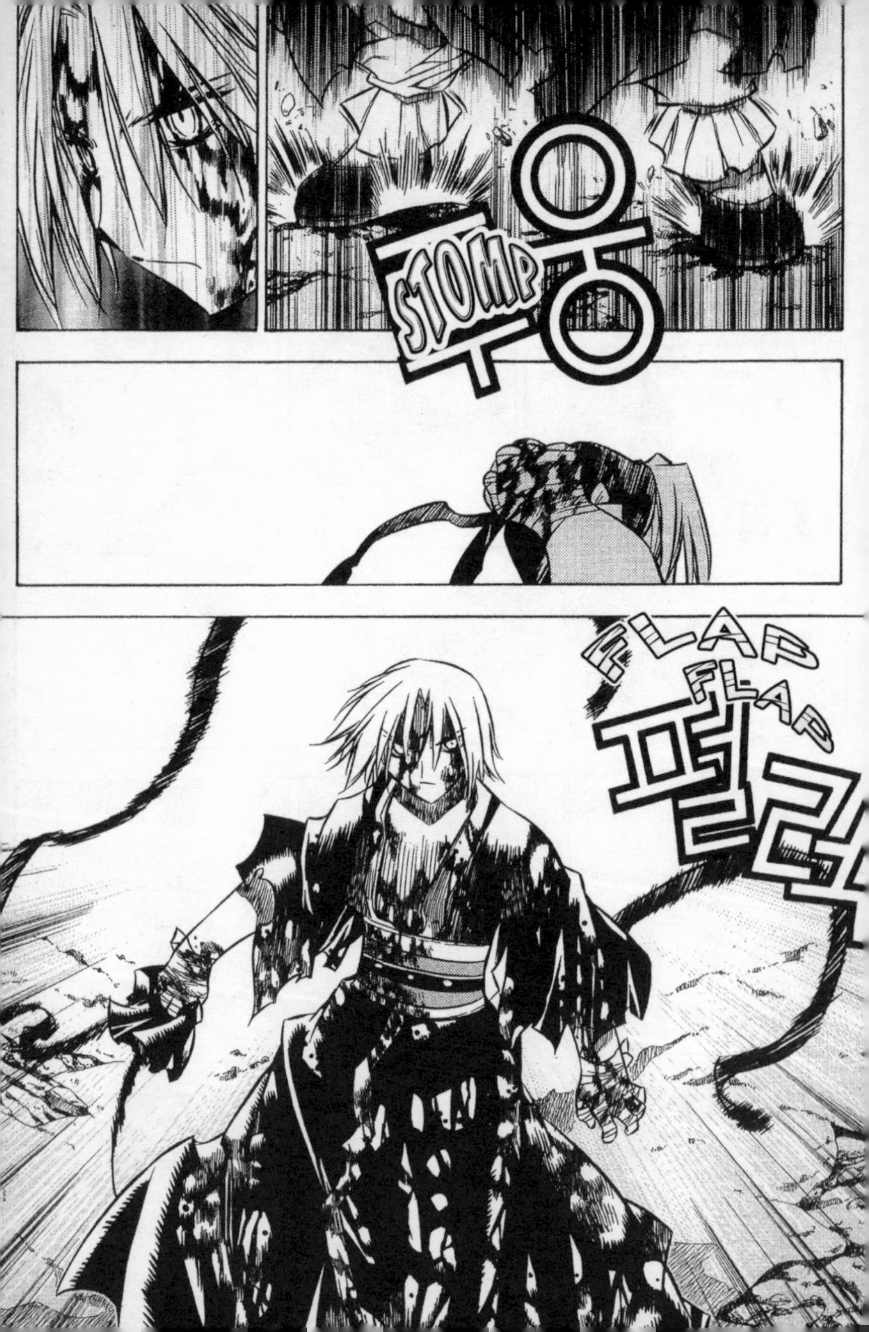
STOMP
FLAP
FLAP

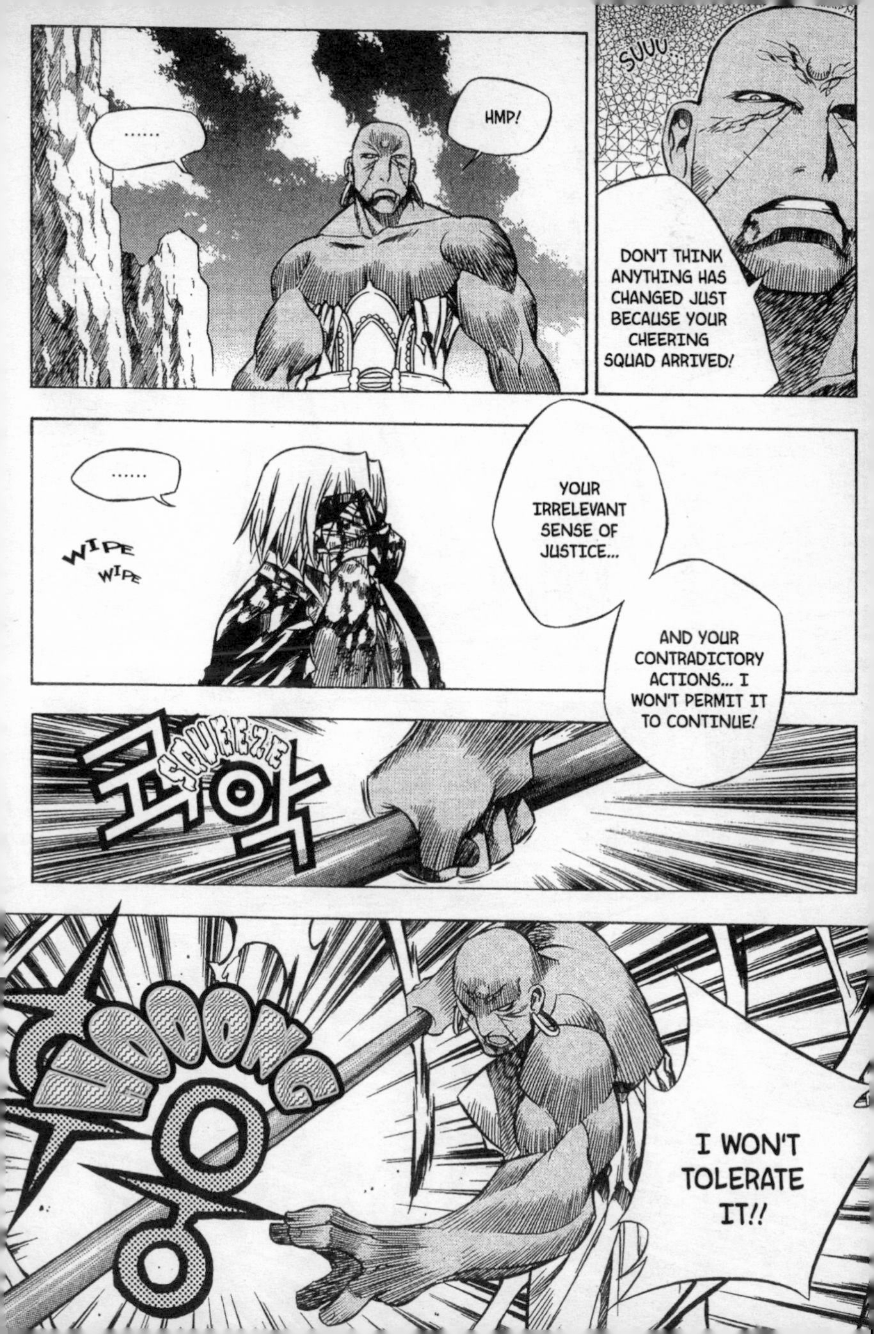

SUUU...
DON'T THINK ANYTHING HAS CHANGED JUST BECAUSE YOUR CHEERING SQUAD ARRIVED!
HMP!
......
YOUR IRRELEVANT SENSE OF JUSTICE...
......
WIPE WIPE
AND YOUR CONTRADICTORY ACTIONS... I WON'T PERMIT IT TO CONTINUE!
SQUEEZE
I WON'T TOLERATE IT!!

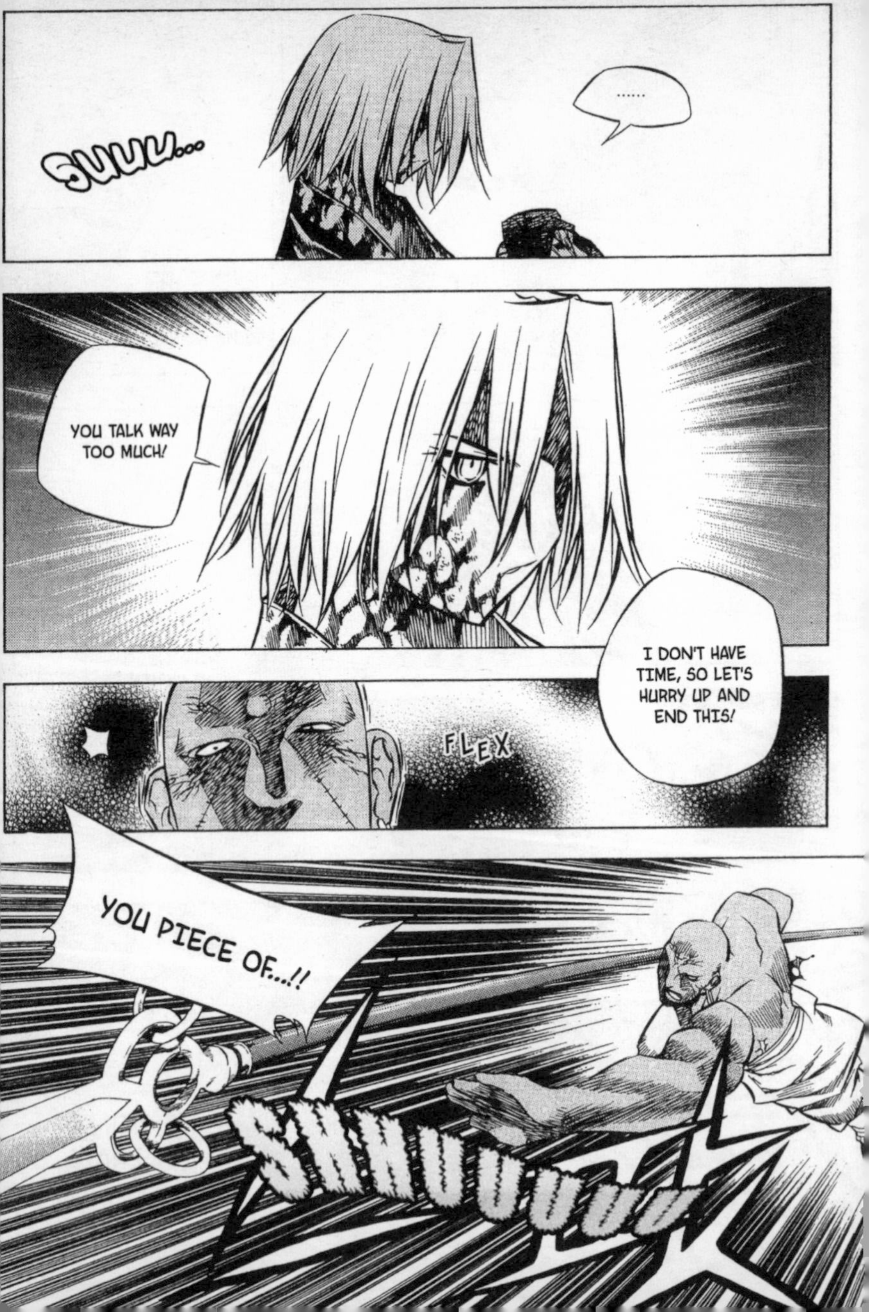
......
SUUU...
YOU TALK WAY TOO MUCH!
I DON'T HAVE TIME, SO LET'S HURRY UP AND END THIS!
FLEX
YOU PIECE OF...!!

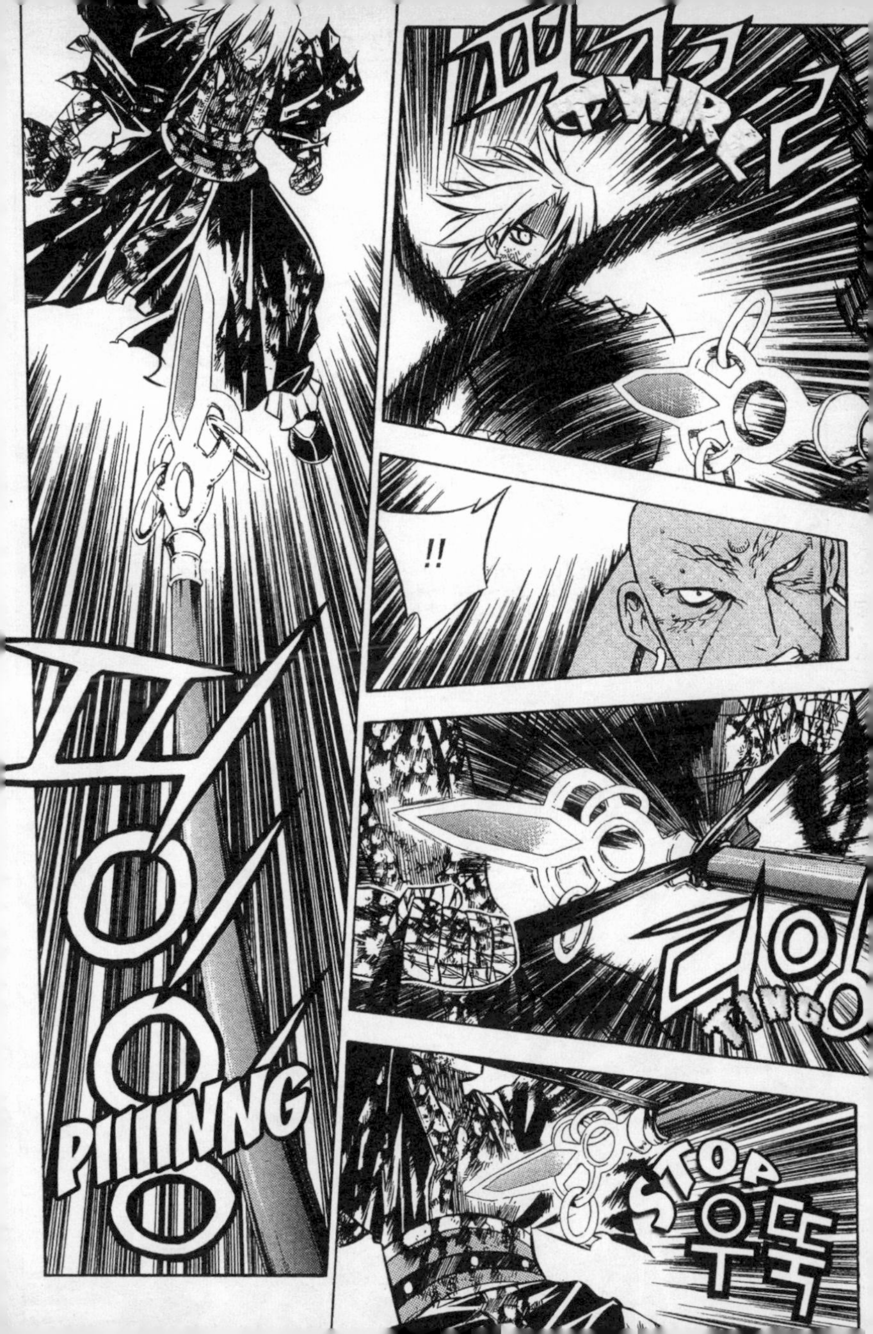

WIRR
!!
TING
STOP
PIIIINNG

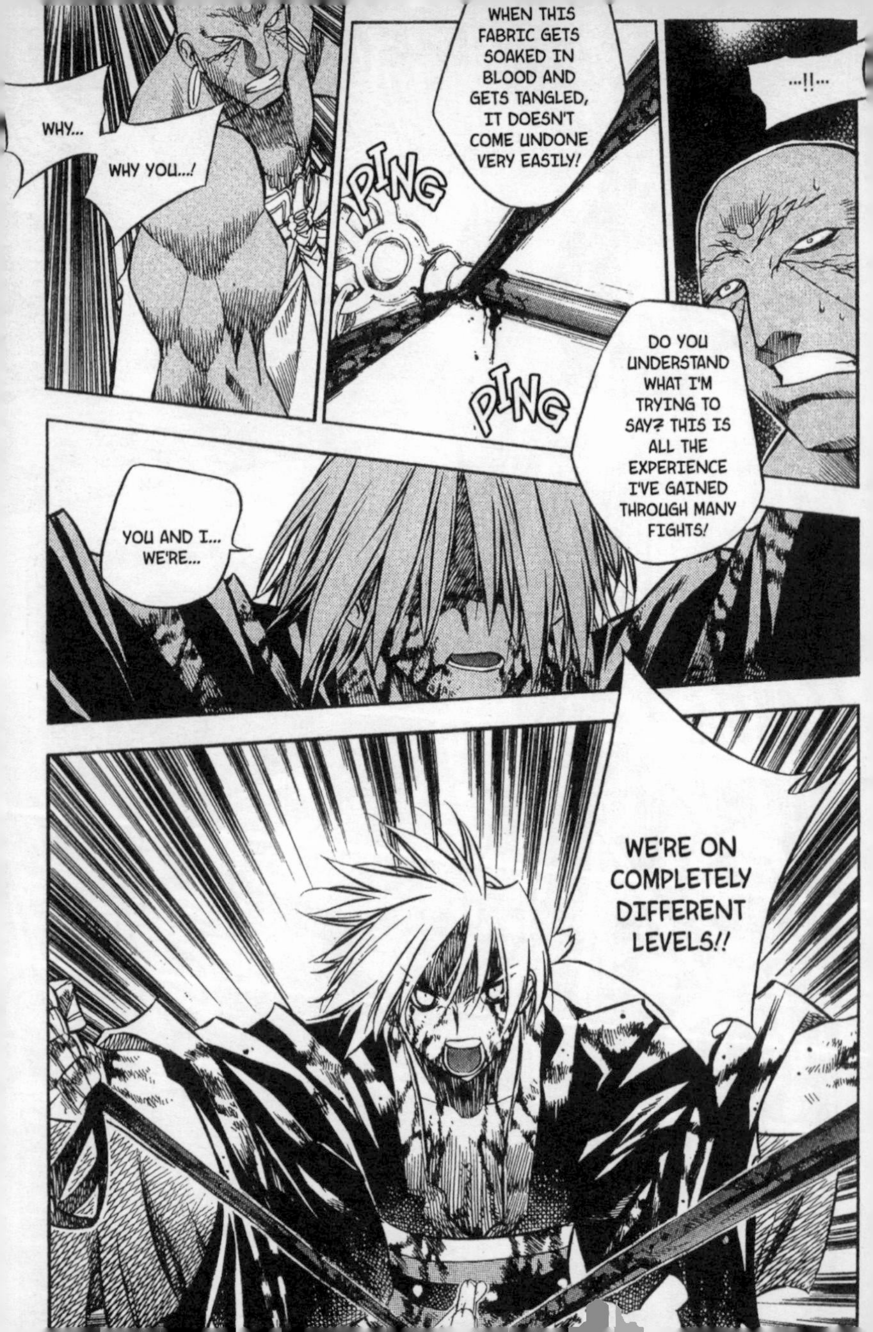
WHY...
WHY YOU...!
WHEN THIS FABRIC GETS SOAKED IN BLOOD AND GETS TANGLED, IT DOESN'T COME UNDONE VERY EASILY!
PING
PING
...!!...
DO YOU UNDERSTAND WHAT I'M TRYING TO SAY? THIS IS ALL THE EXPERIENCE I'VE GAINED THROUGH MANY FIGHTS!
YOU AND I... WE'RE...
WE'RE ON COMPLETELY DIFFERENT LEVELS!!

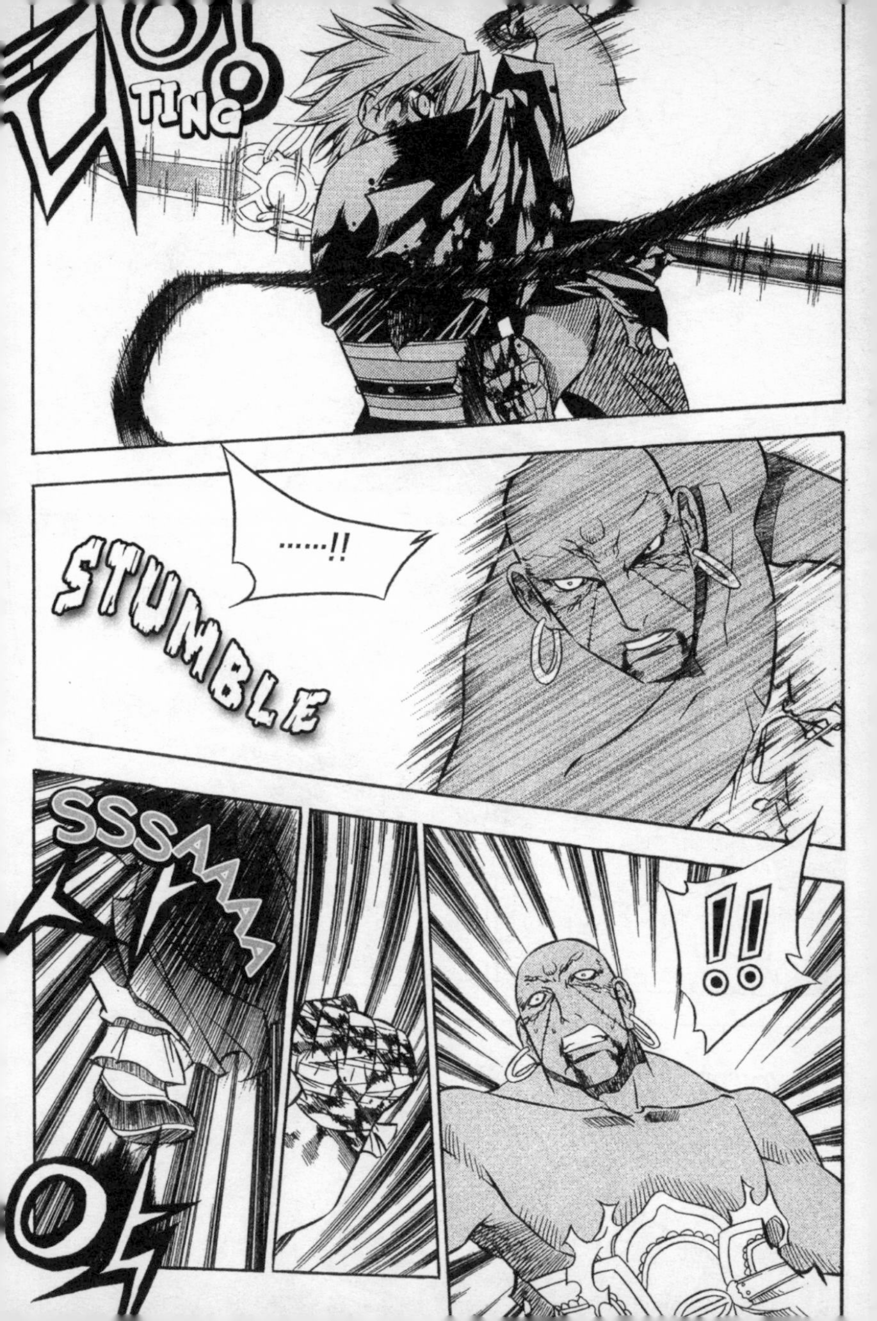
TING
......!!
STUMBLE
SSSAAAAA
!!

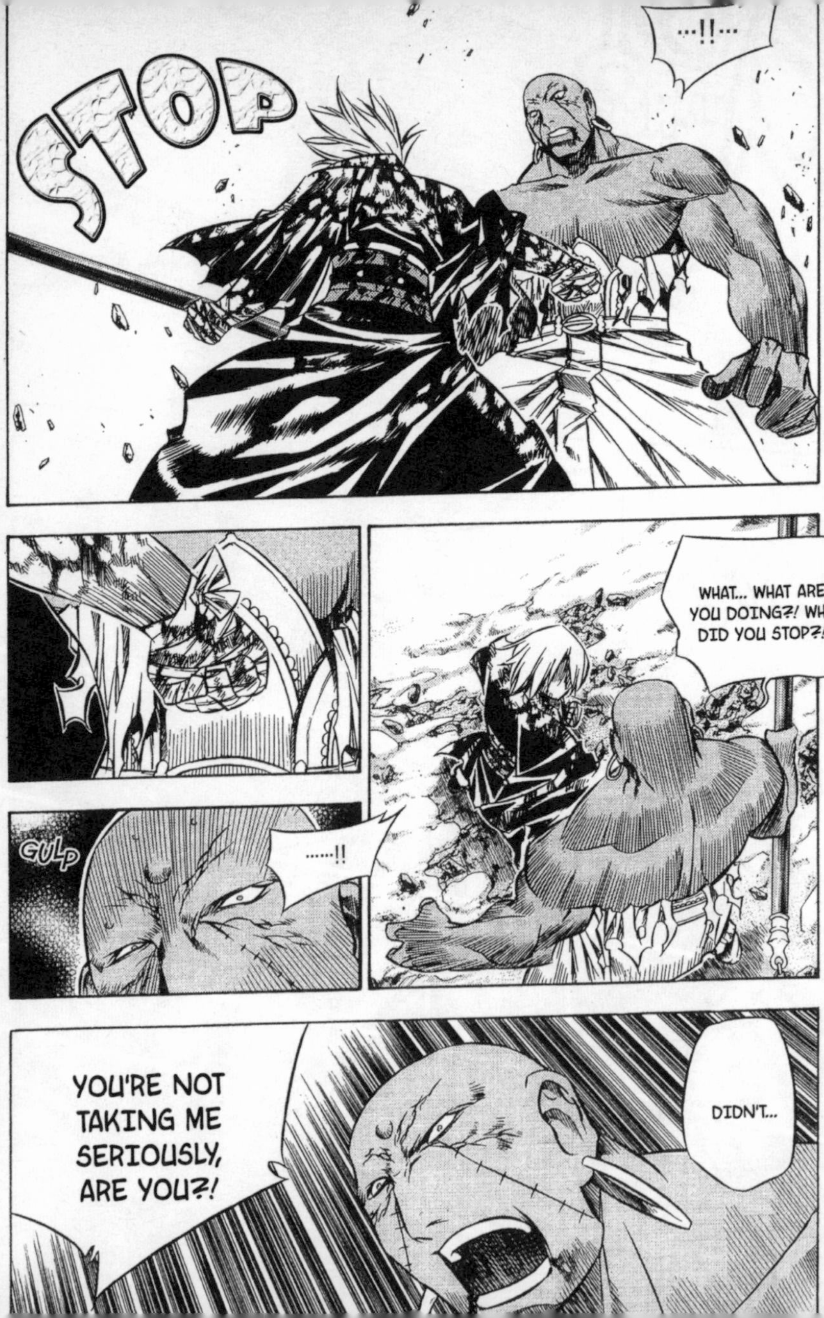
...!!...
STOP
WHAT... WHAT ARE YOU DOING?! WHY DID YOU STOP?!
GULP
......!!
DIDN'T...
YOU'RE NOT TAKING ME SERIOUSLY, ARE YOU?!

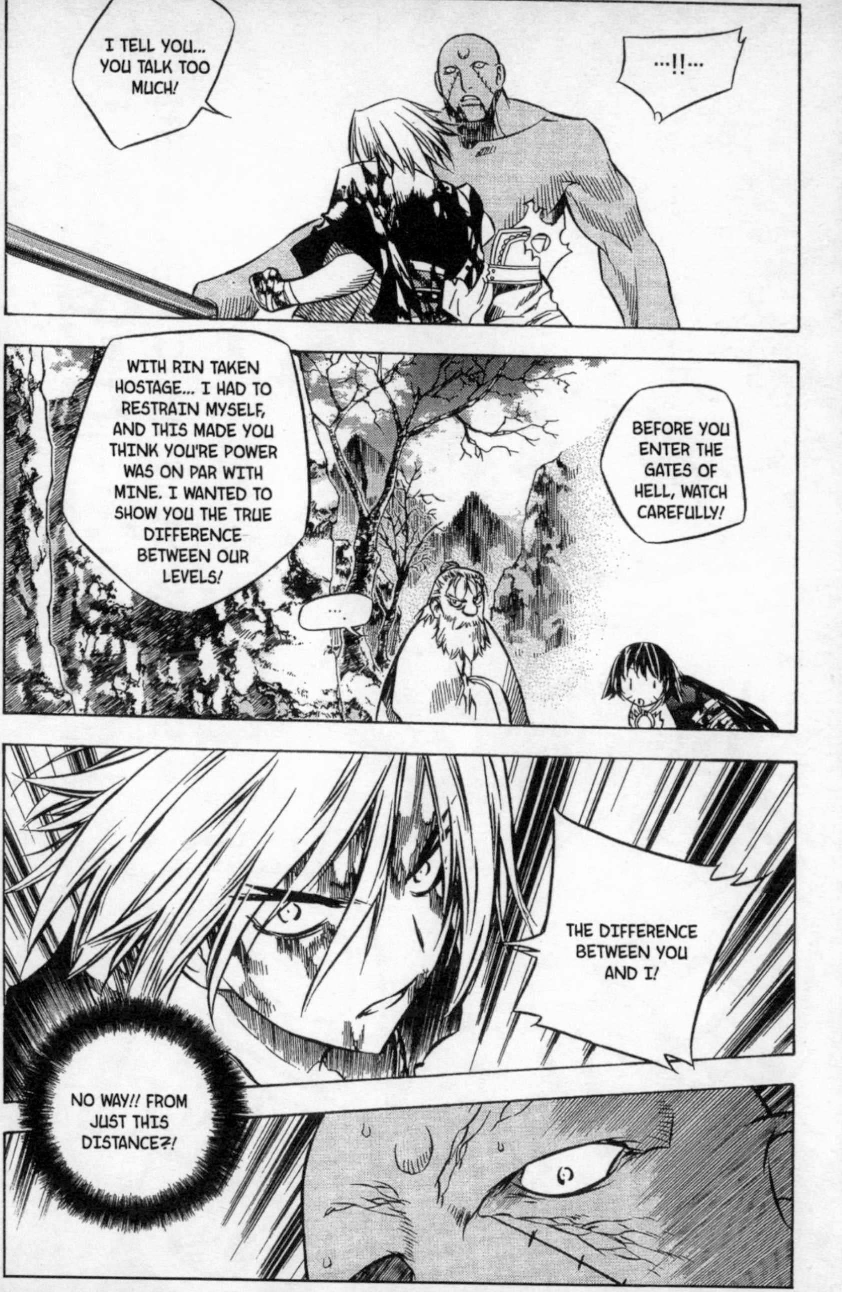
I TELL YOU... YOU TALK TOO MUCH!
...!!...
WITH RIN TAKEN HOSTAGE... I HAD TO RESTRAIN MYSELF, AND THIS MADE YOU THINK YOU'RE POWER WAS ON PAR WITH MINE. I WANTED TO SHOW YOU THE TRUE DIFFERENCE BETWEEN OUR LEVELS!
BEFORE YOU ENTER THE GATES OF HELL, WATCH CAREFULLY!
...
THE DIFFERENCE BETWEEN YOU AND I!
NO WAY!! FROM JUST THIS DISTANCE?!

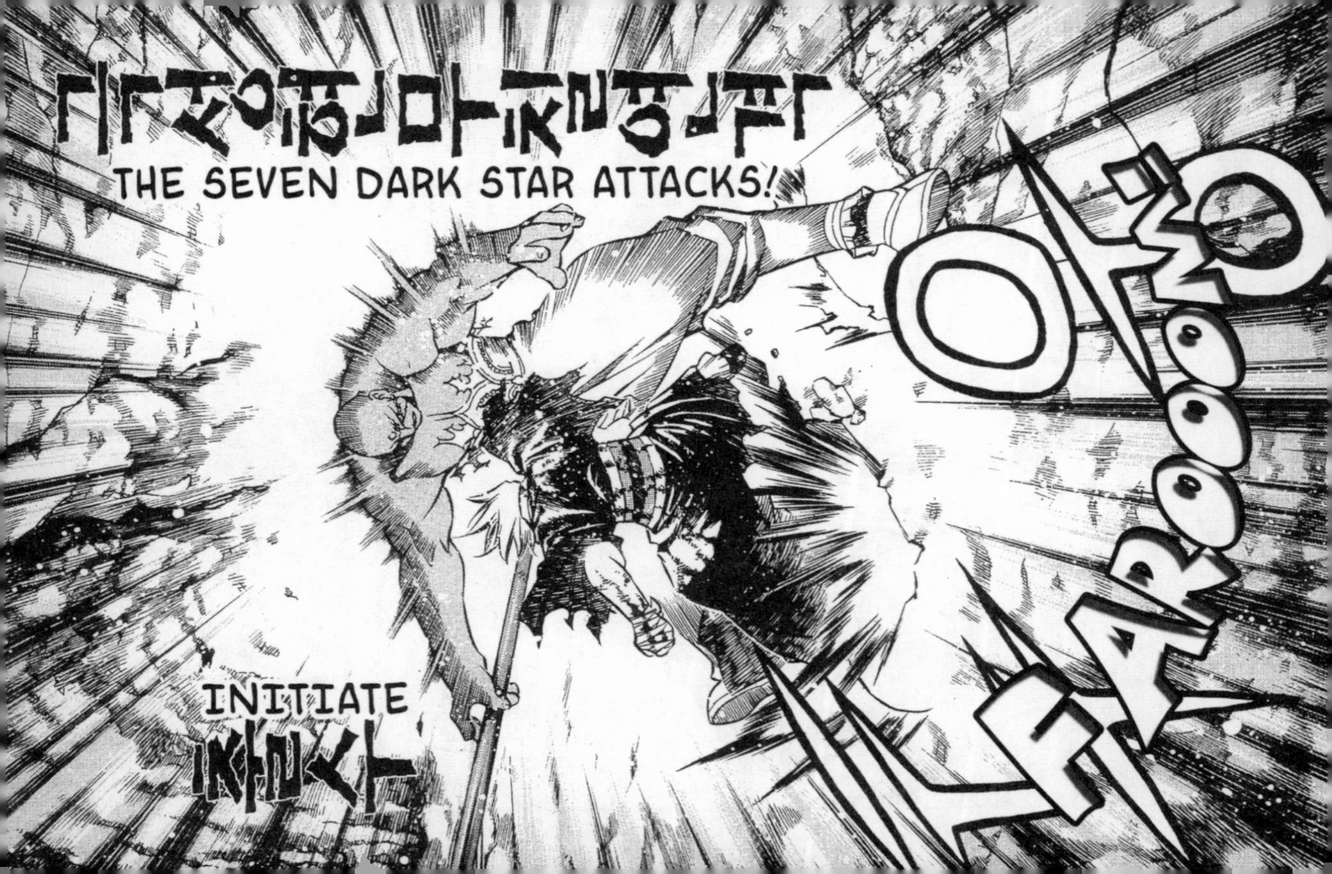
극성현무칠여격
THE SEVEN DARK STAR ATTACKS!
INITIATE
출수
FAROOOOOM!

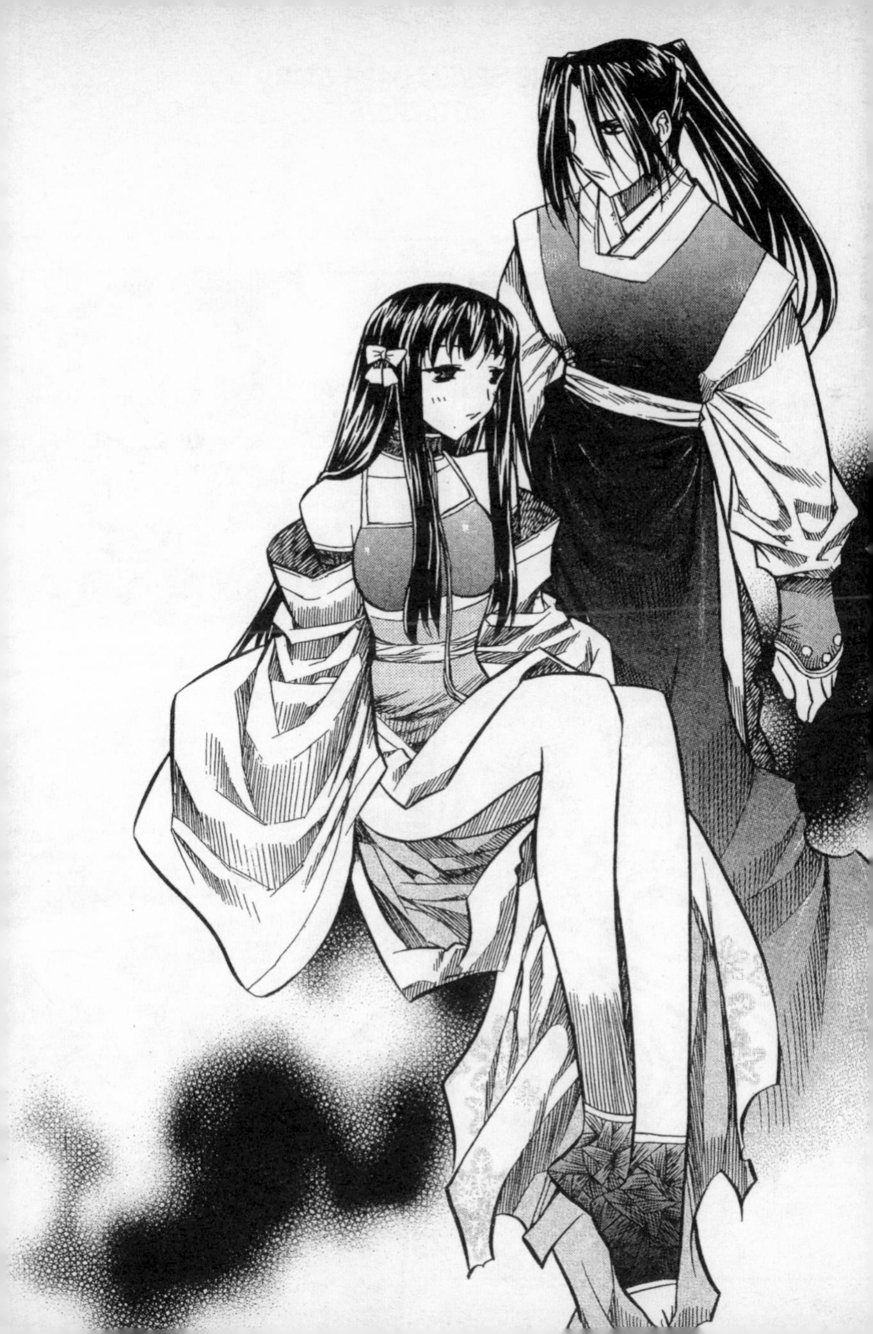

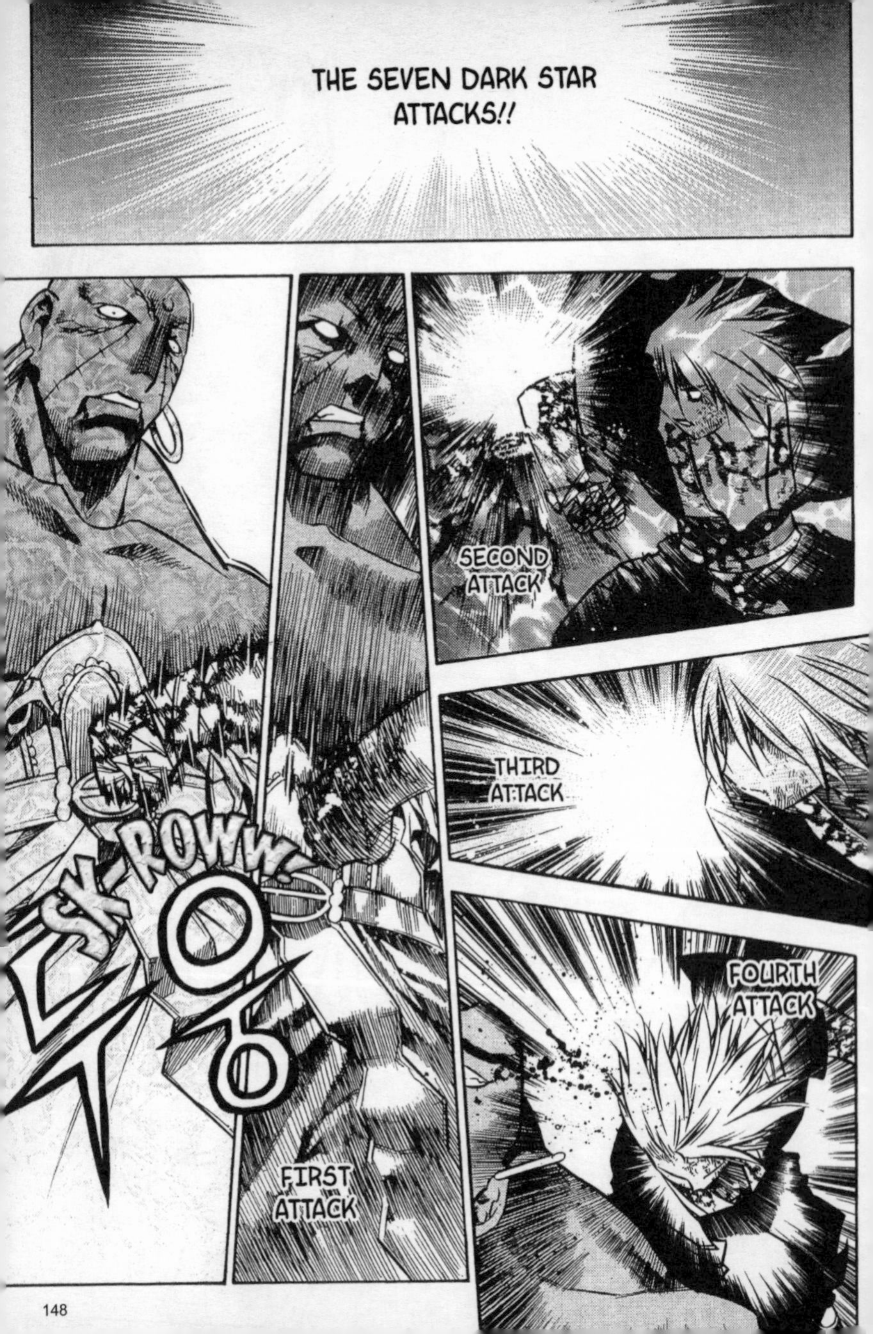
THE SEVEN DARK STAR ATTACKS!!
SK-ROWW
FIRST ATTACK
SECOND ATTACK
THIRD ATTACK
FOURTH ATTACK

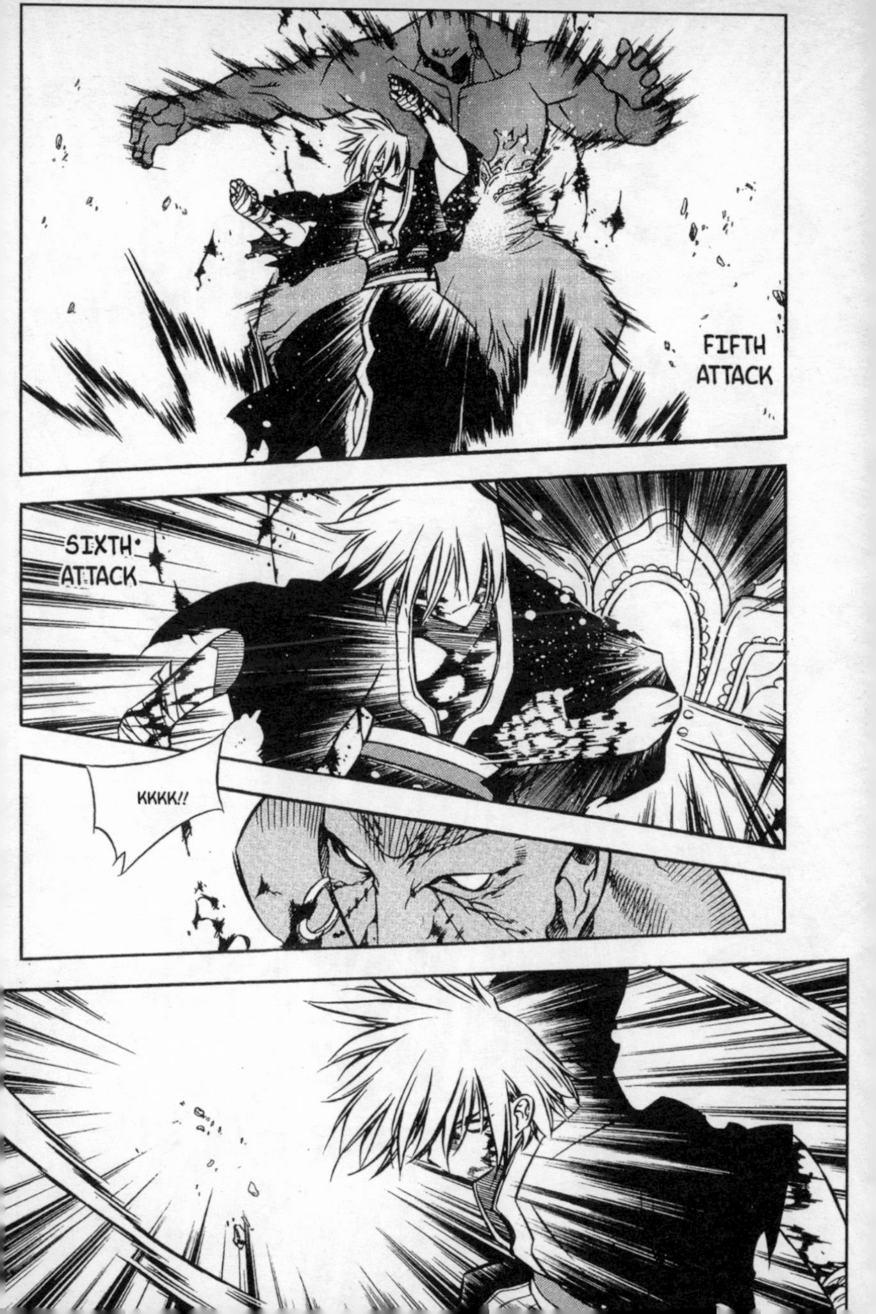
FIFTH ATTACK
SIXTH ATTACK
KKKK!!

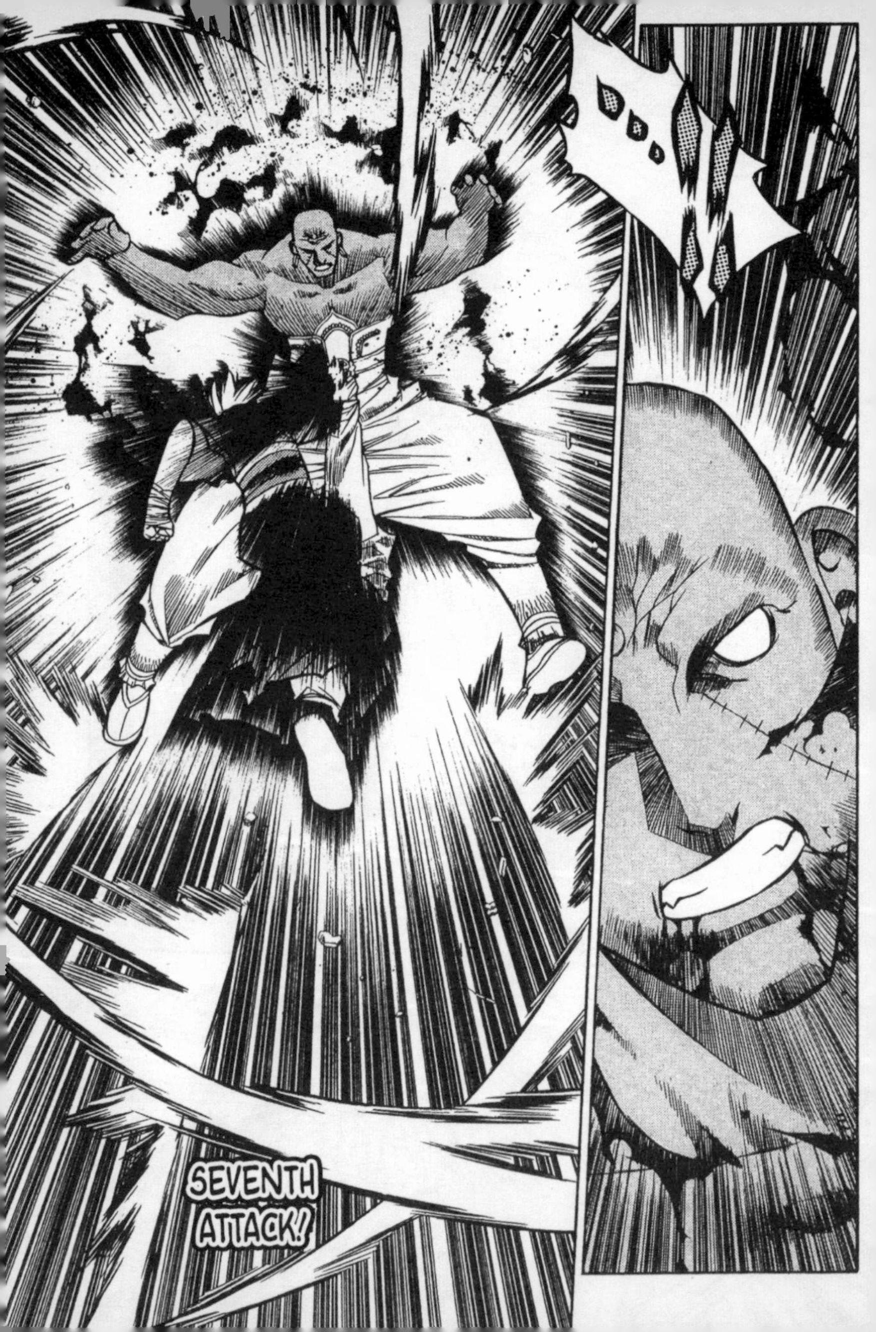
SEVENTH
ATTACK!

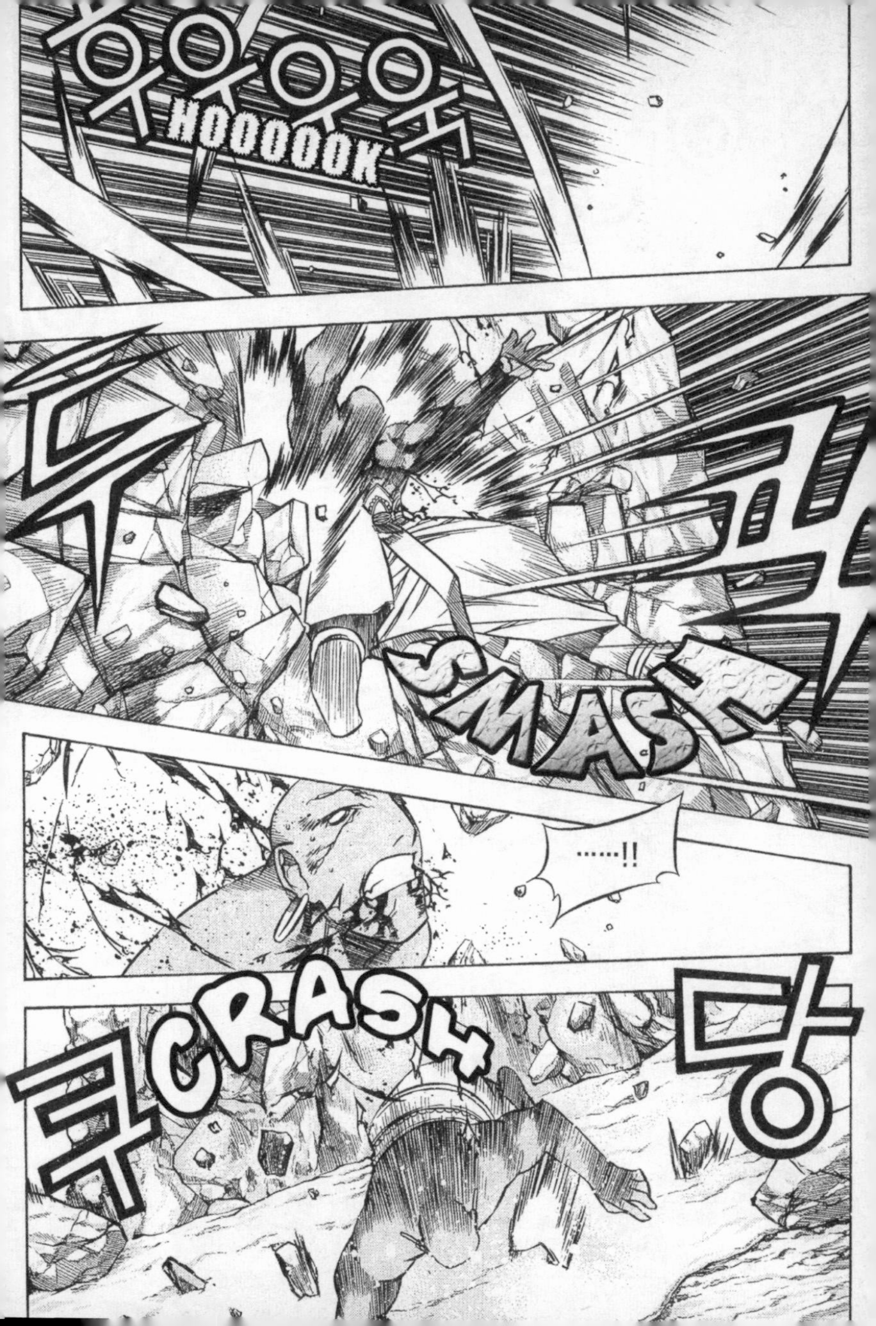
HOOOOOK
SMASH
......!!
CRASH

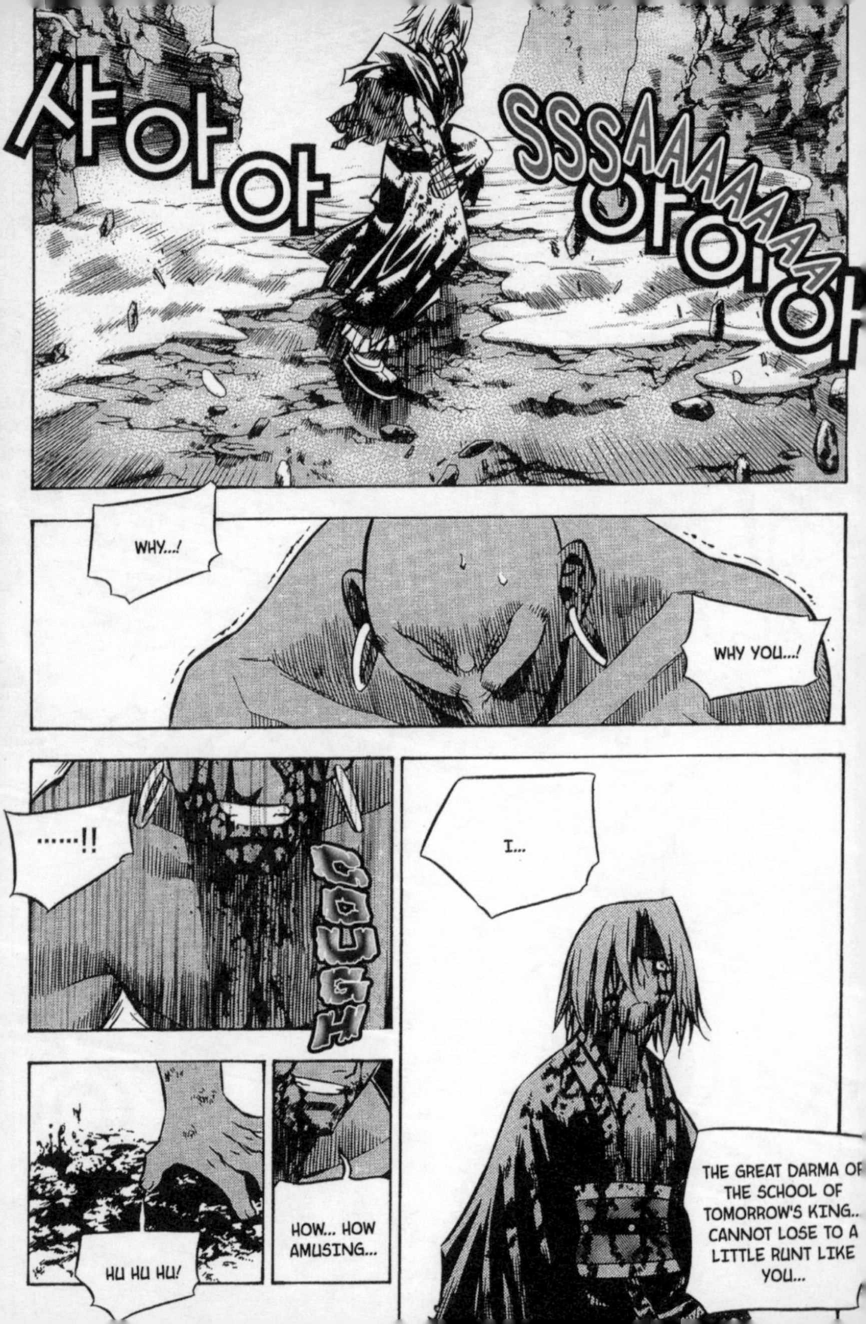
샤아아
SSSAAAAAAAA
아아아
WHY...!
WHY YOU...!
......!!
COUGH
I...
HU HU HU!
HOW... HOW AMUSING...
THE GREAT DARMA OF THE SCHOOL OF TOMORROW'S KING... CANNOT LOSE TO A LITTLE RUNT LIKE YOU...

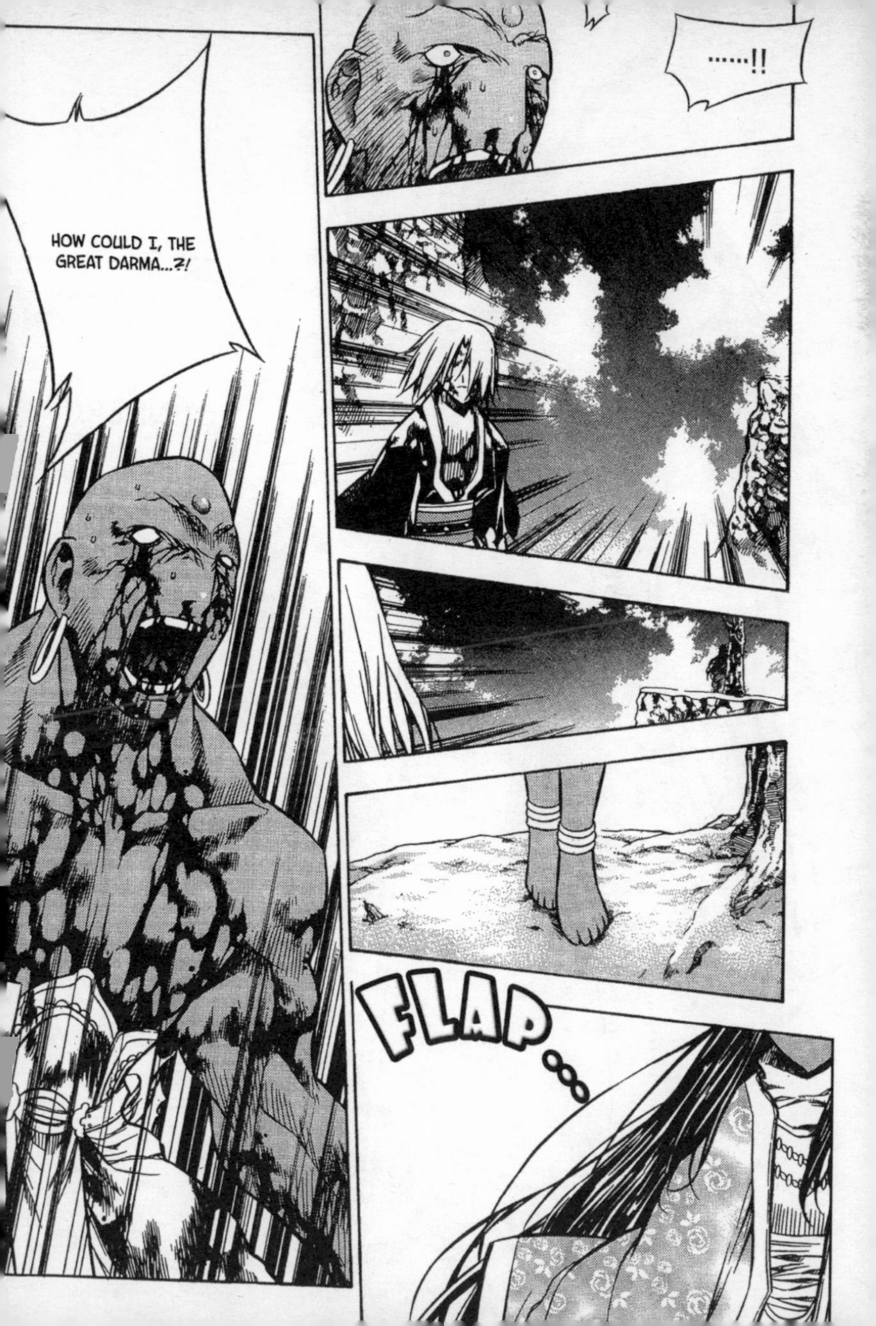

......!!
HOW COULD I, THE GREAT DARMA...?!
FLAP...

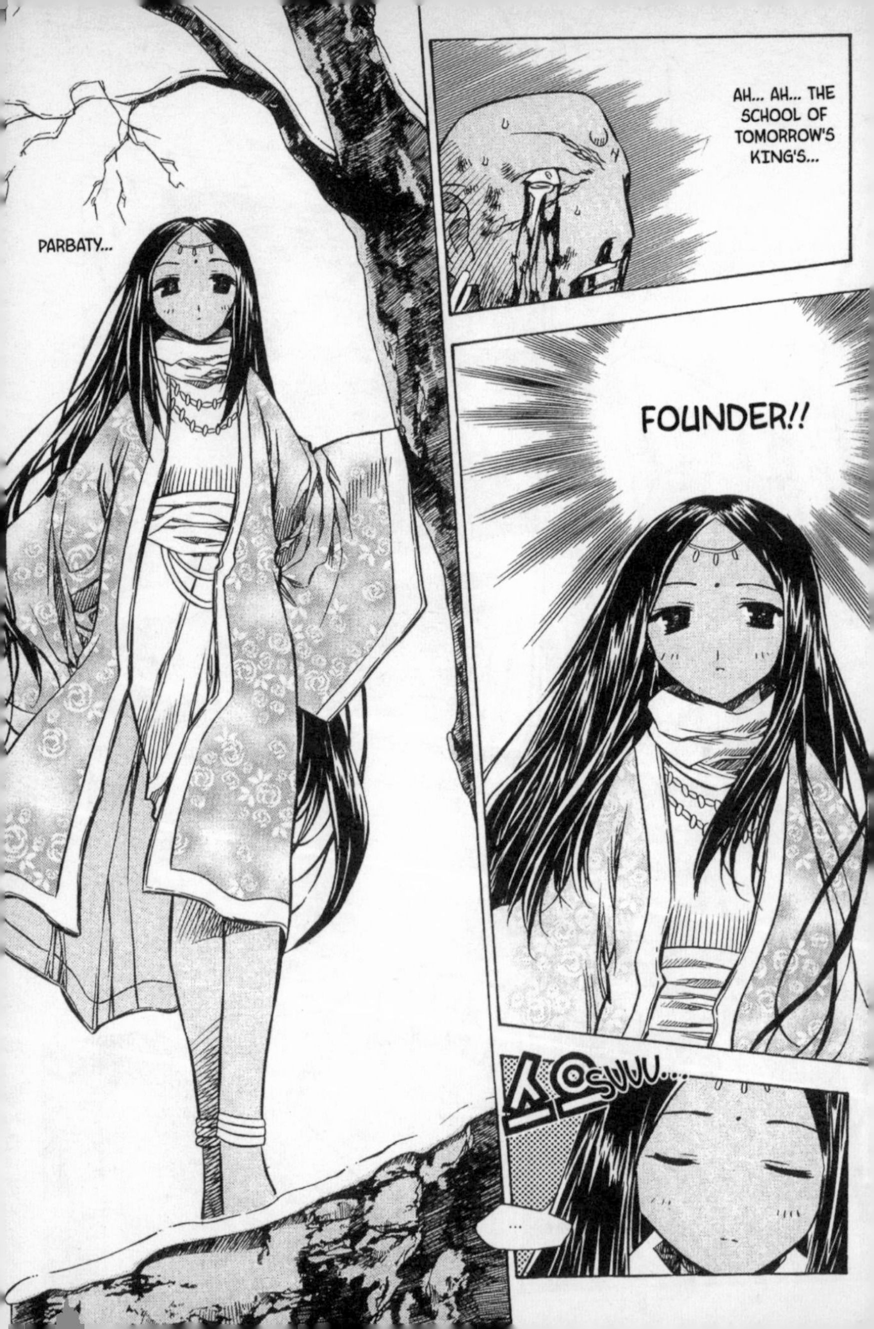
AH... AH... THE SCHOOL OF TOMORROW'S KING'S...
FOUNDER!!
SUUU...
...
PARBATY...

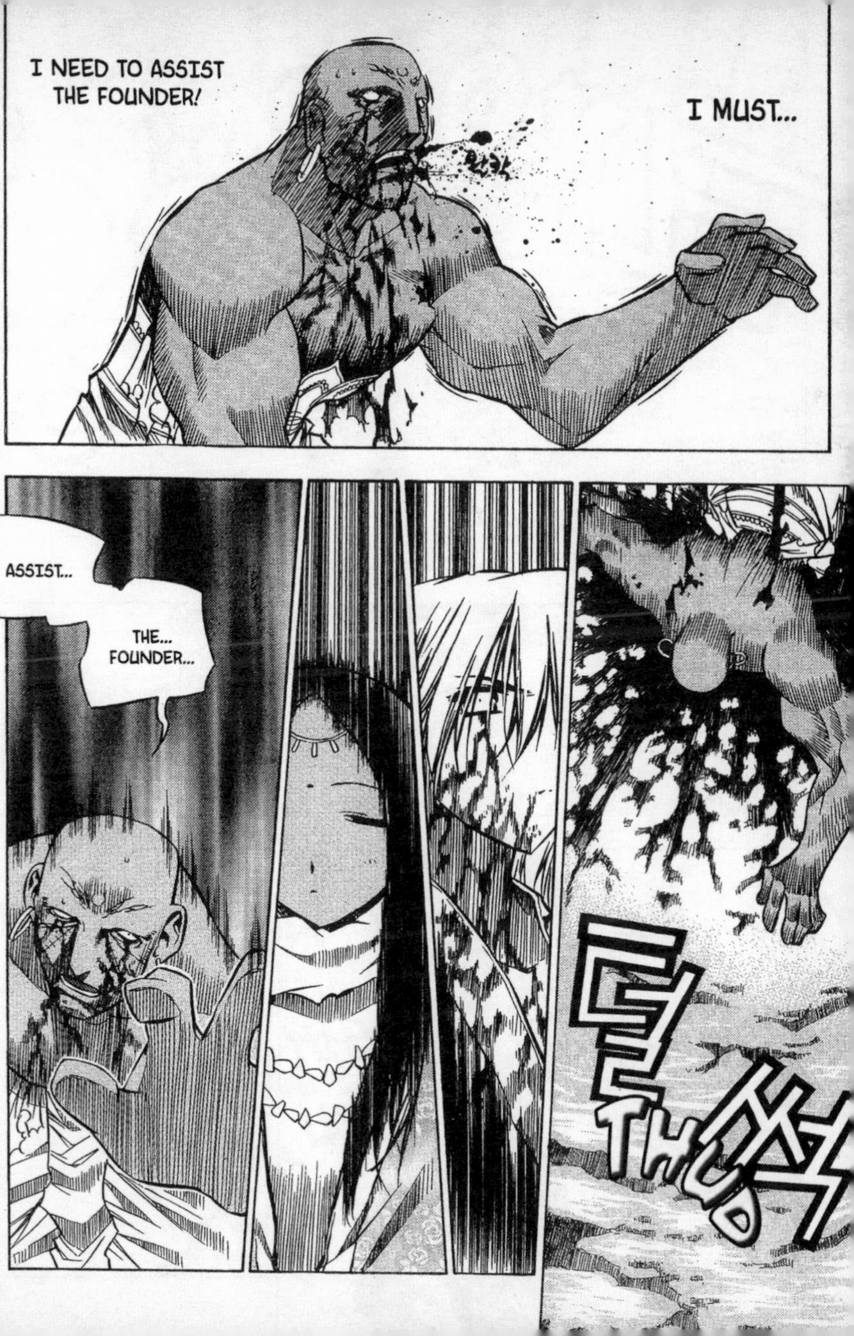
I NEED TO ASSIST THE FOUNDER!
I MUST...
ASSIST...
THE... FOUNDER...
THUD

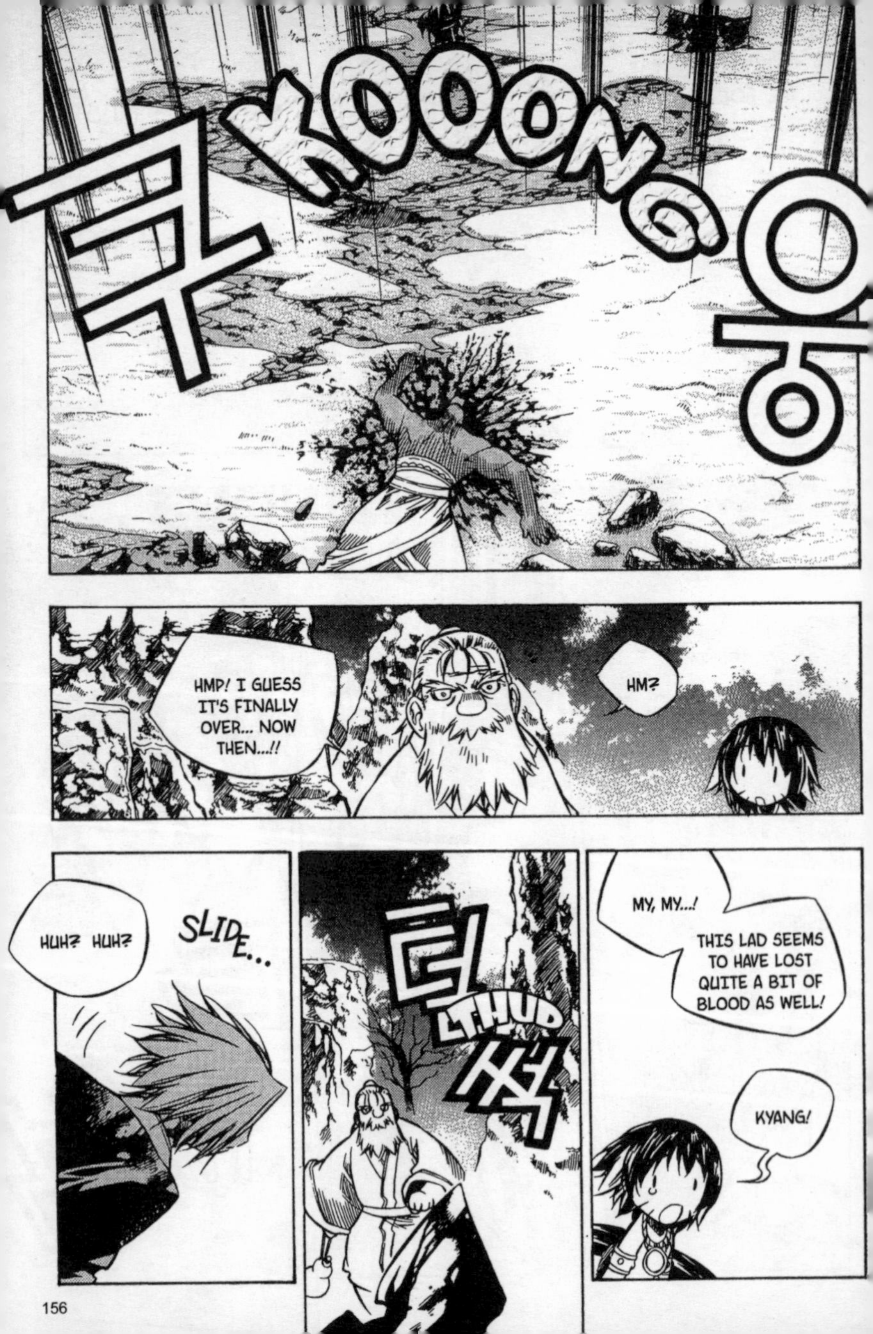
KOOONG
HMP! I GUESS IT'S FINALLY OVER... NOW THEN...!!
HM?
HUH? HUH?
SLIDE...
THUD
MY, MY...!
THIS LAD SEEMS TO HAVE LOST QUITE A BIT OF BLOOD AS WELL!
KYANG!

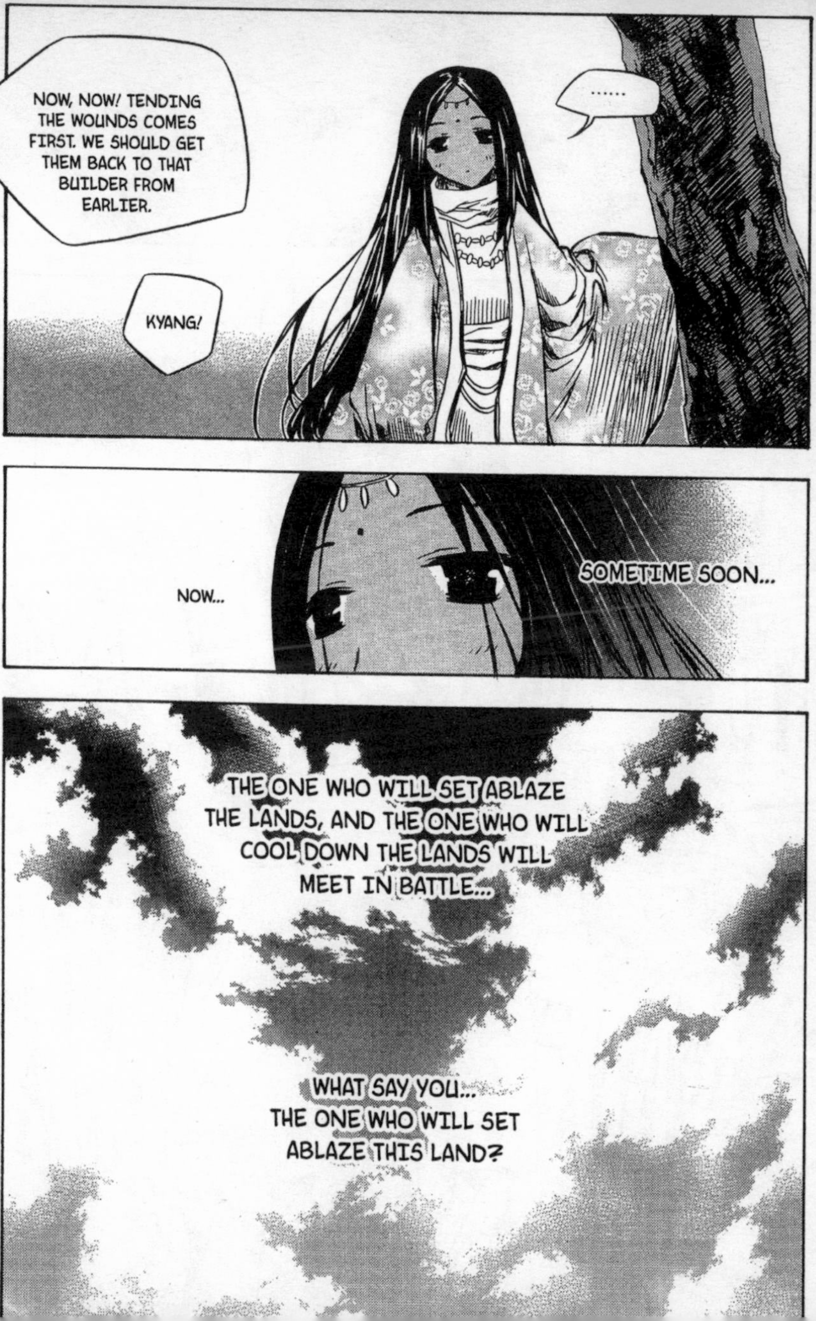

......
NOW, NOW! TENDING THE WOUNDS COMES FIRST. WE SHOULD GET THEM BACK TO THAT BUILDER FROM EARLIER.
KYANG!
SOMETIME SOON...
NOW...
THE ONE WHO WILL SET ABLAZE THE LANDS, AND THE ONE WHO WILL COOL DOWN THE LANDS WILL MEET IN BATTLE...
WHAT SAY YOU... THE ONE WHO WILL SET ABLAZE THIS LAND?

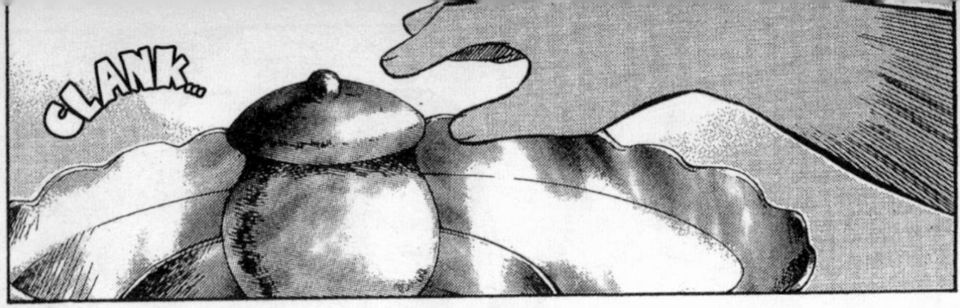
CLANK...

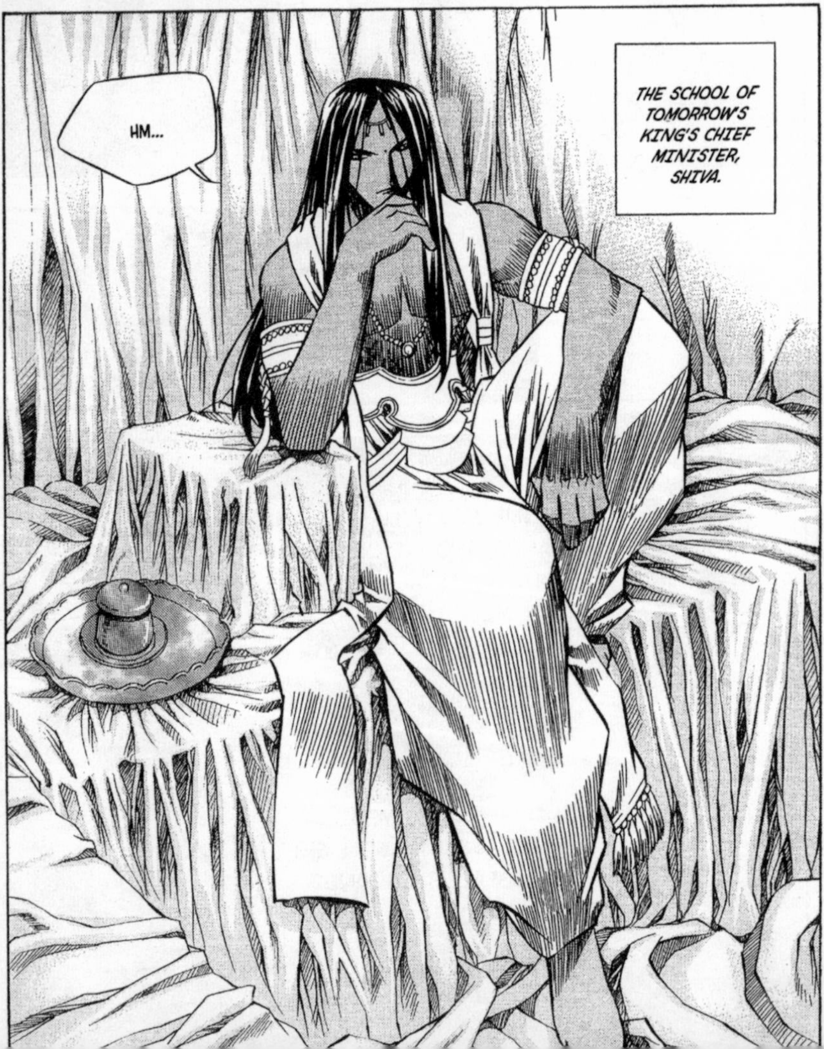
THE SCHOOL OF TOMORROW'S KING'S CHIEF MINISTER, SHIVA.
HM...

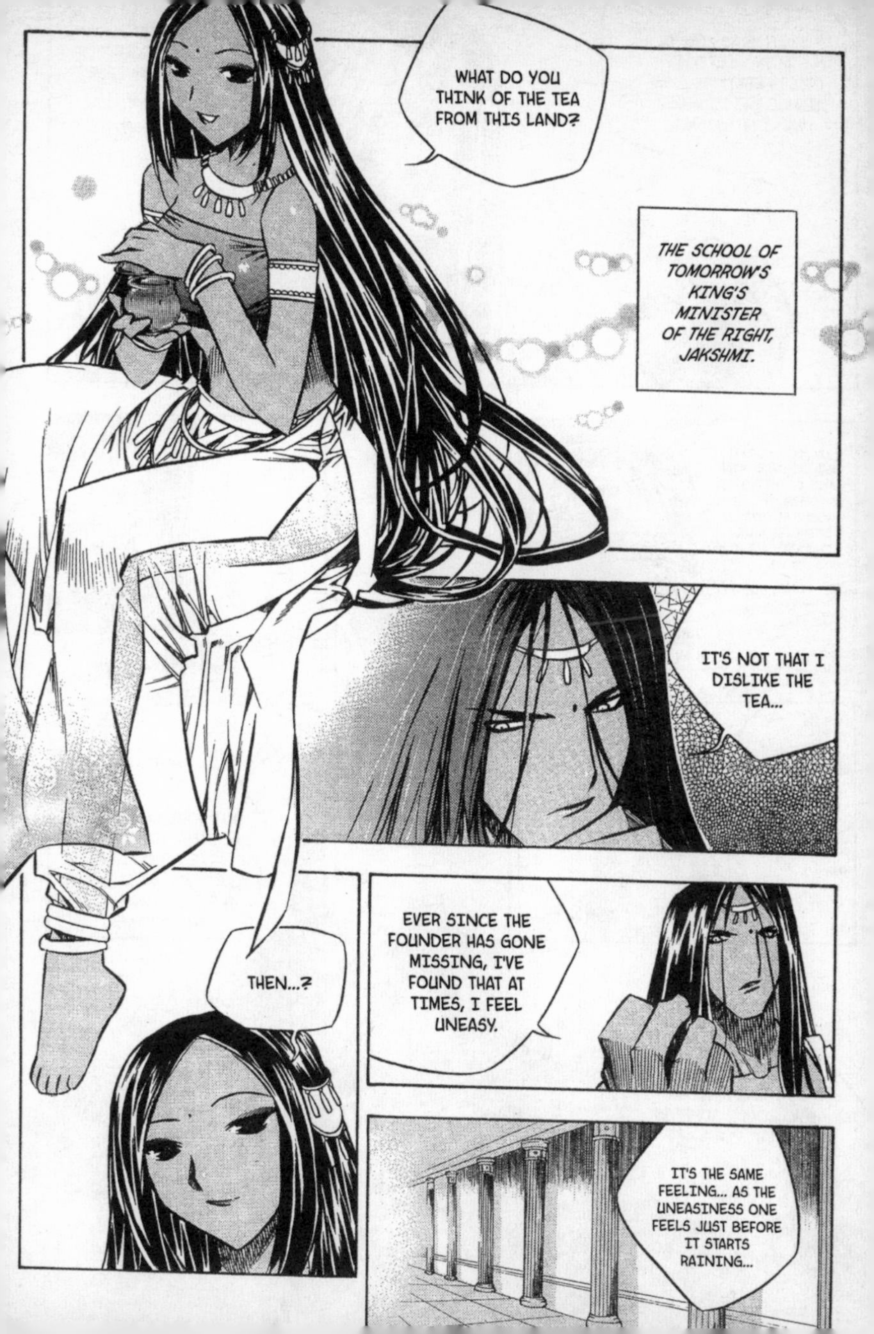
WHAT DO YOU THINK OF THE TEA FROM THIS LAND?
THE SCHOOL OF TOMORROW'S KING'S MINISTER OF THE RIGHT, JAKSHMI.
IT'S NOT THAT I DISLIKE THE TEA...
THEN...?
EVER SINCE THE FOUNDER HAS GONE MISSING, I'VE FOUND THAT AT TIMES, I FEEL UNEASY.
IT'S THE SAME FEELING... AS THE UNEASINESS ONE FEELS JUST BEFORE IT STARTS RAINING...

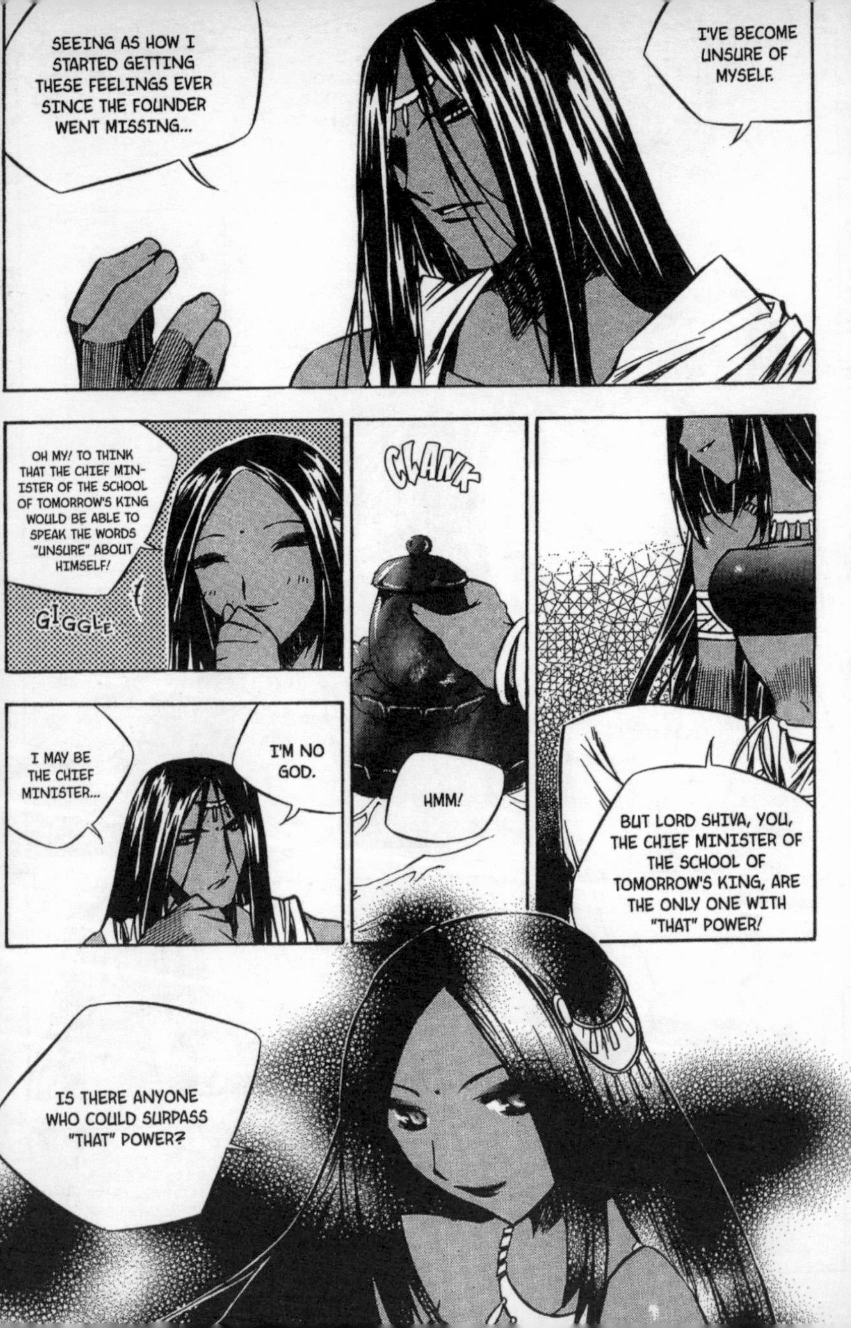
I'VE BECOME UNSURE OF MYSELF.
SEEING AS HOW I STARTED GETTING THESE FEELINGS EVER SINCE THE FOUNDER WENT MISSING...
CLANK
OH MY! TO THINK THAT THE CHIEF MINISTER OF THE SCHOOL OF TOMORROW'S KING WOULD BE ABLE TO SPEAK THE WORDS "UNSURE" ABOUT HIMSELF!
GIGGLE
I'M NO GOD.
I MAY BE THE CHIEF MINISTER...
HMM!
BUT LORD SHIVA, YOU, THE CHIEF MINISTER OF THE SCHOOL OF TOMORROW'S KING, ARE THE ONLY ONE WITH "THAT" POWER!
IS THERE ANYONE WHO COULD SURPASS "THAT" POWER?

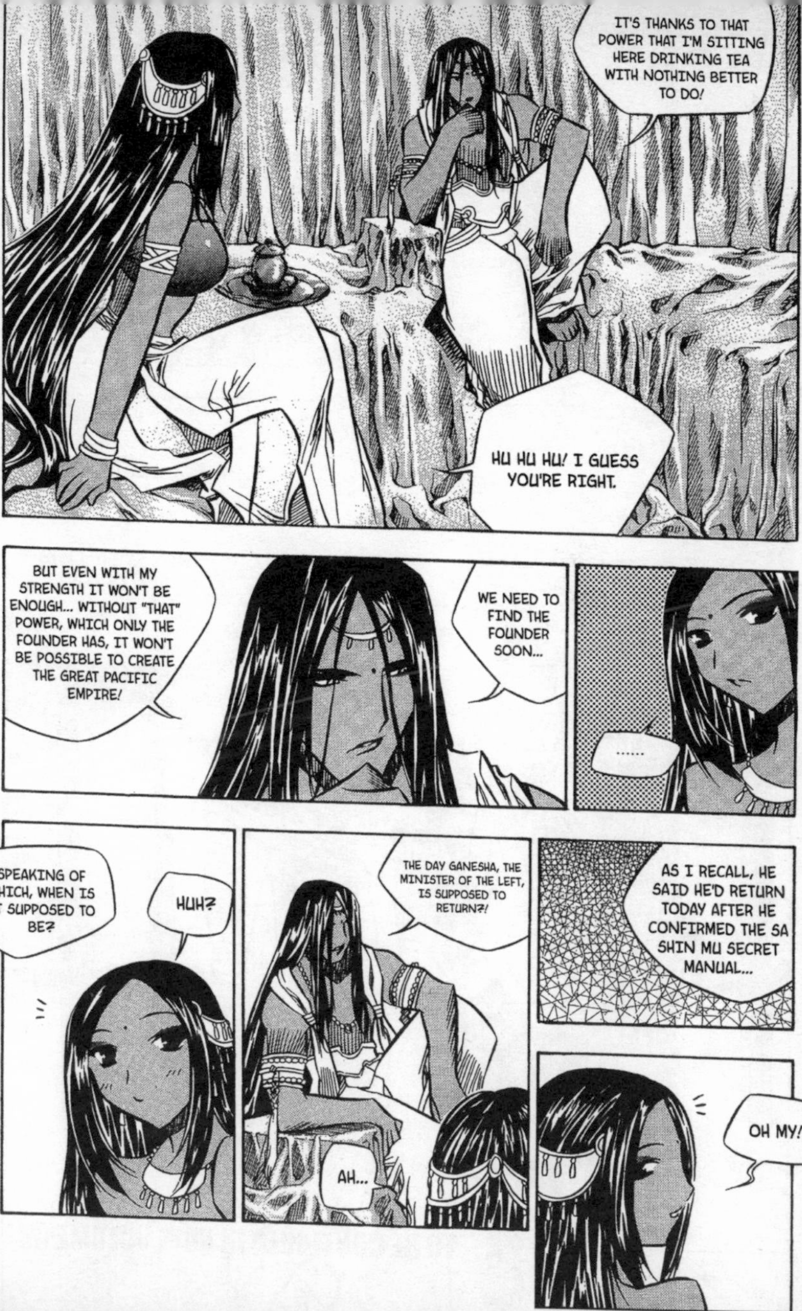
IT'S THANKS TO THAT POWER THAT I'M SITTING HERE DRINKING TEA WITH NOTHING BETTER TO DO!
HU HU HU! I GUESS YOU'RE RIGHT.
BUT EVEN WITH MY STRENGTH IT WON'T BE ENOUGH... WITHOUT "THAT" POWER, WHICH ONLY THE FOUNDER HAS, IT WON'T BE POSSIBLE TO CREATE THE GREAT PACIFIC EMPIRE!
WE NEED TO FIND THE FOUNDER SOON...
......
SPEAKING OF WHICH, WHEN IS IT SUPPOSED TO BE?
HUH?
THE DAY GANESHA, THE MINISTER OF THE LEFT, IS SUPPOSED TO RETURN?!
AS I RECALL, HE SAID HE'D RETURN TODAY AFTER HE CONFIRMED THE SA SHIN MU SECRET MANUAL...
AH...
OH MY!

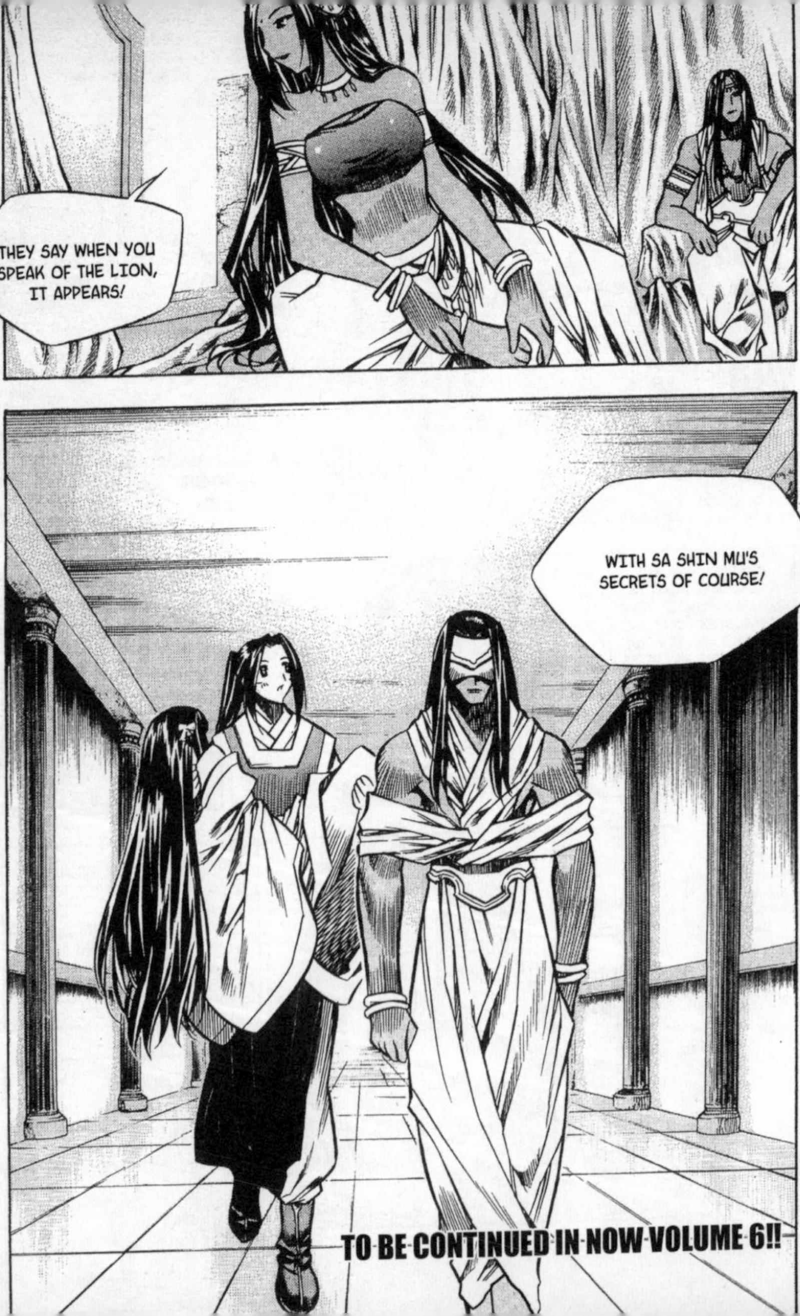
THEY SAY WHEN YOU SPEAK OF THE LION, IT APPEARS!
WITH SA SHIN MU'S SECRETS OF COURSE!
TO BE CONTINUED IN NOW VOLUME 6!!

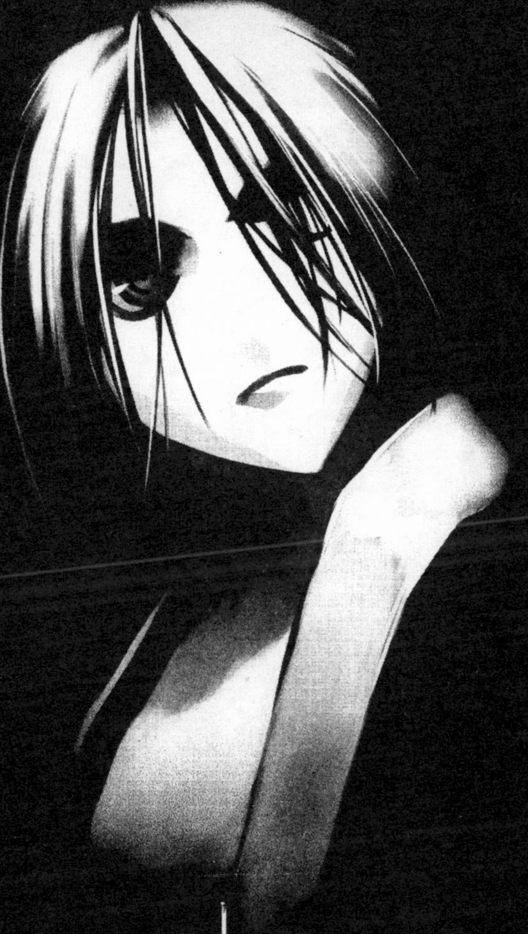

NOW

CHARACTER INTRODUCTIONS

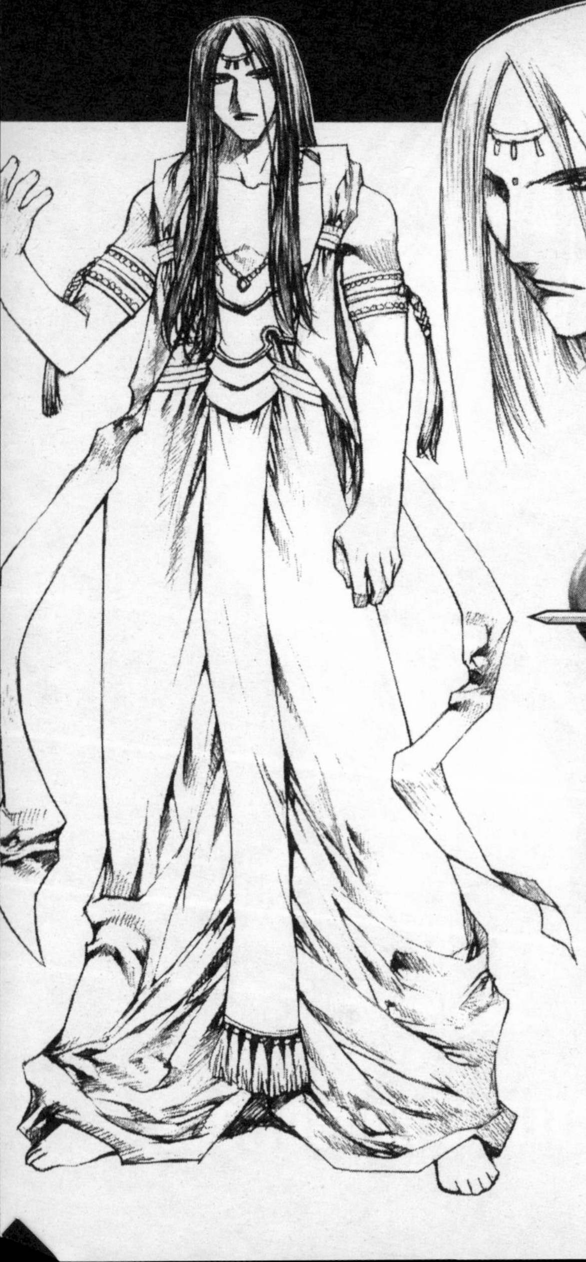

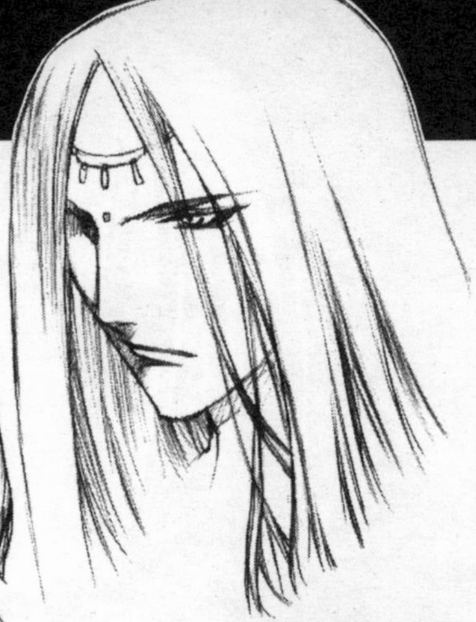

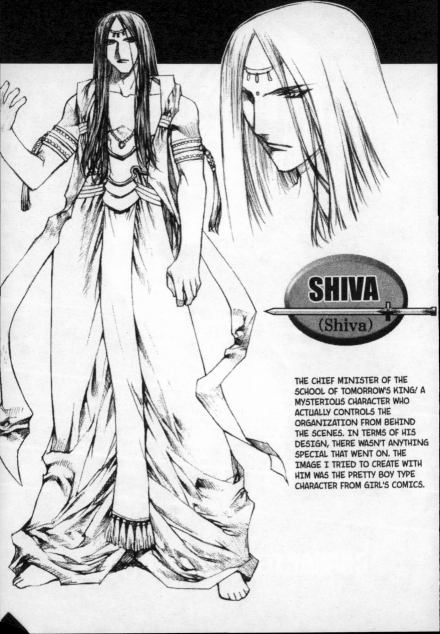

SHIVA
(Shiva)

THE CHIEF MINISTER OF THE SCHOOL OF TOMORROW'S KING! A MYSTERIOUS CHARACTER WHO ACTUALLY CONTROLS THE ORGANIZATION FROM BEHIND THE SCENES. IN TERMS OF HIS DESIGN, THERE WASN'T ANYTHING SPECIAL THAT WENT ON. THE IMAGE I TRIED TO CREATE WITH HIM WAS THE PRETTY BOY TYPE CHARACTER FROM GIRL'S COMICS.

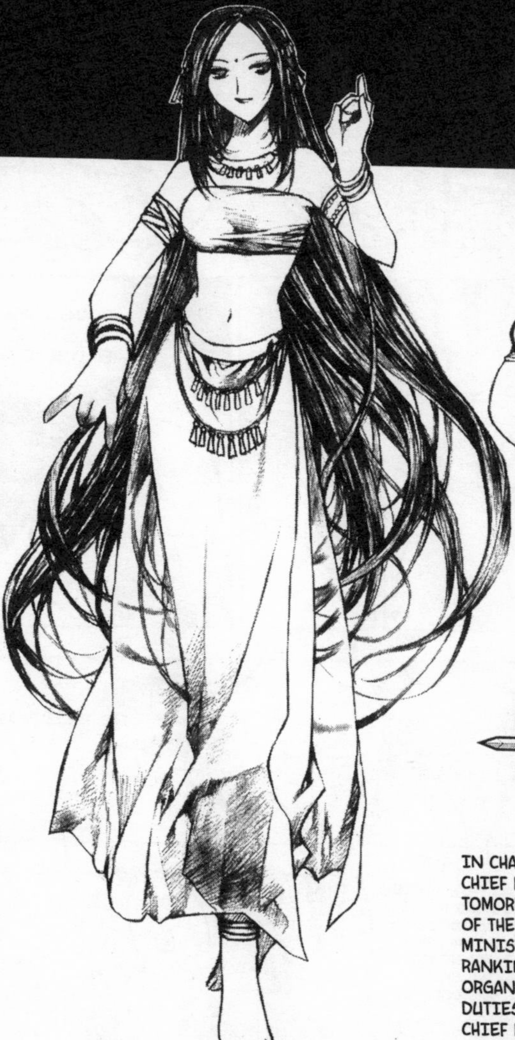

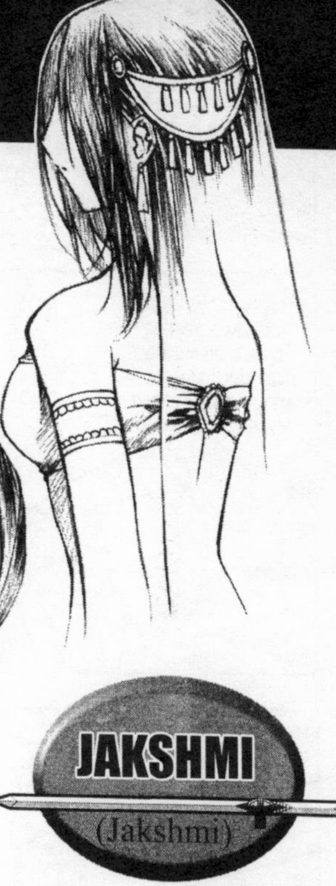

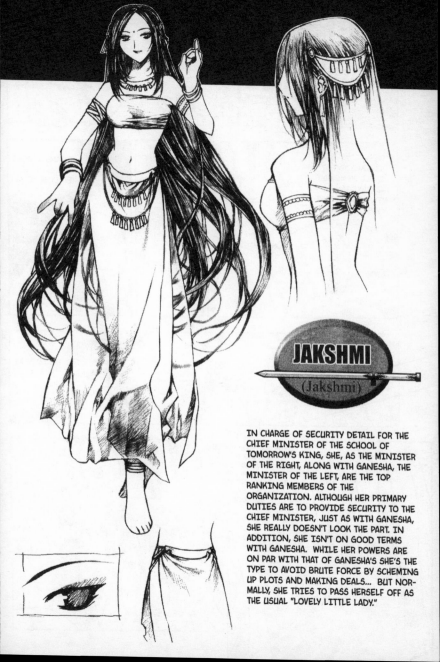

JAKSHMI

(Jakshmi)

IN CHARGE OF SECURITY DETAIL FOR THE CHIEF MINISTER OF THE SCHOOL OF TOMORROW'S KING, SHE, AS THE MINISTER OF THE RIGHT, ALONG WITH GANESHA, THE MINISTER OF THE LEFT, ARE THE TOP RANKING MEMBERS OF THE ORGANIZATION. ALTHOUGH HER PRIMARY DUTIES ARE TO PROVIDE SECURITY TO THE CHIEF MINISTER, JUST AS WITH GANESHA, SHE REALLY DOESN'T LOOK THE PART. IN ADDITION, SHE ISN'T ON GOOD TERMS WITH GANESHA. WHILE HER POWERS ARE ON PAR WITH THAT OF GANESHA'S SHE'S THE TYPE TO AVOID BRUTE FORCE BY SCHEMING UP PLOTS AND MAKING DEALS... BUT NORMALLY, SHE TRIES TO PASS HERSELF OFF AS THE USUAL "LOVELY LITTLE LADY."

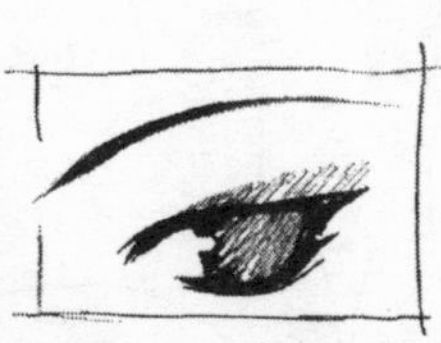

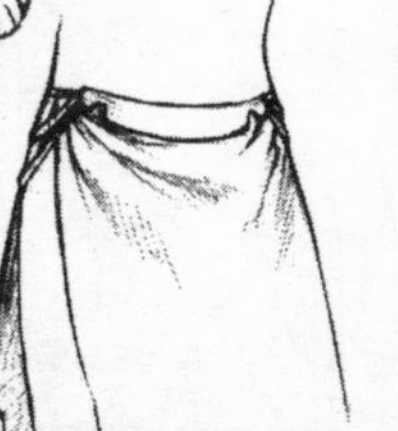

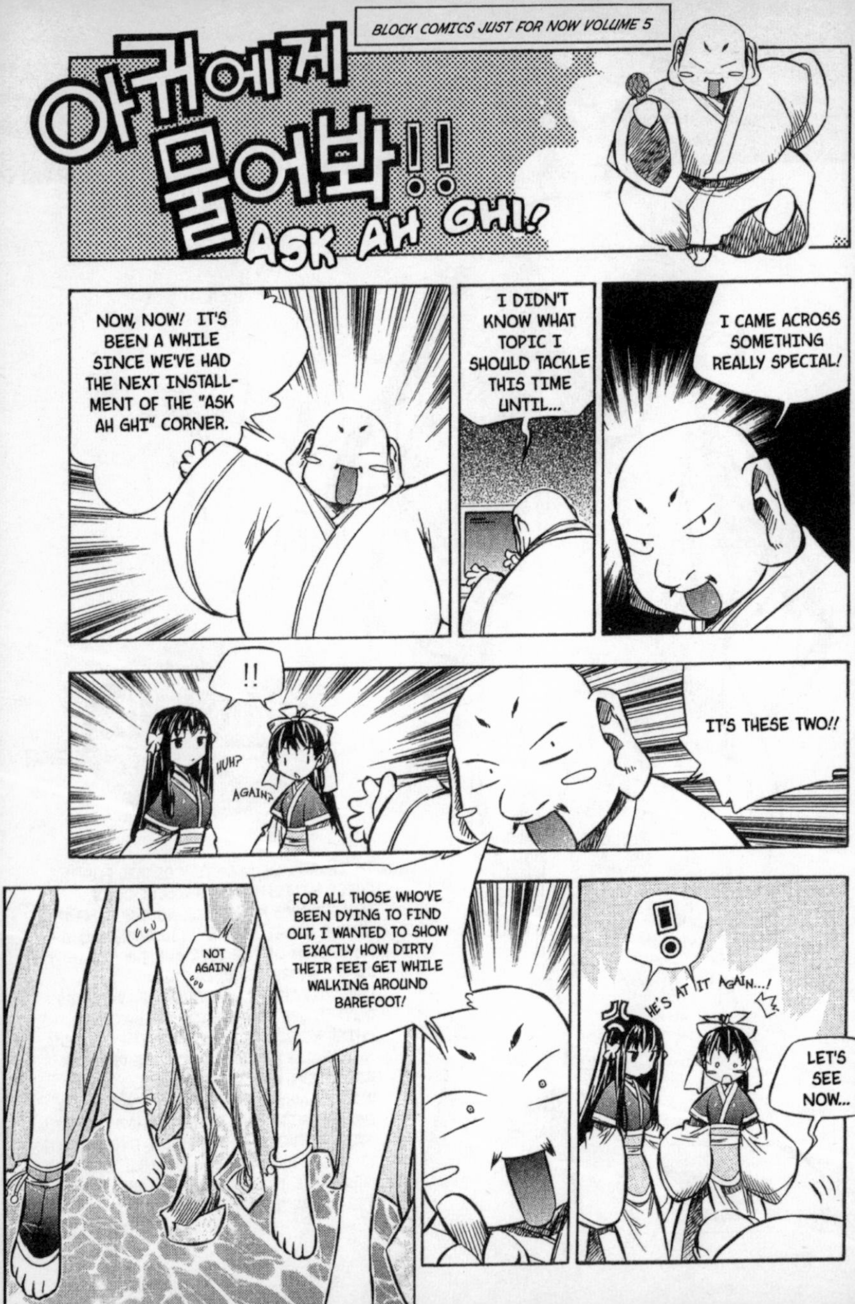
BLOCK COMICS JUST FOR NOW VOLUME 5
아귀에게 물어봐!!
ASK AH GHI!
NOW, NOW! IT'S BEEN A WHILE SINCE WE'VE HAD THE NEXT INSTALL-MENT OF THE "ASK AH GHI" CORNER.
I DIDN'T KNOW WHAT TOPIC I SHOULD TACKLE THIS TIME UNTIL...
I CAME ACROSS SOMETHING REALLY SPECIAL!
!!
HUH?
AGAIN?
IT'S THESE TWO!!
NOT AGAIN!
FOR ALL THOSE WHO'VE BEEN DYING TO FIND OUT, I WANTED TO SHOW EXACTLY HOW DIRTY THEIR FEET GET WHILE WALKING AROUND BAREFOOT!
!
HE'S AT IT AGAIN...!
LET'S SEE NOW...

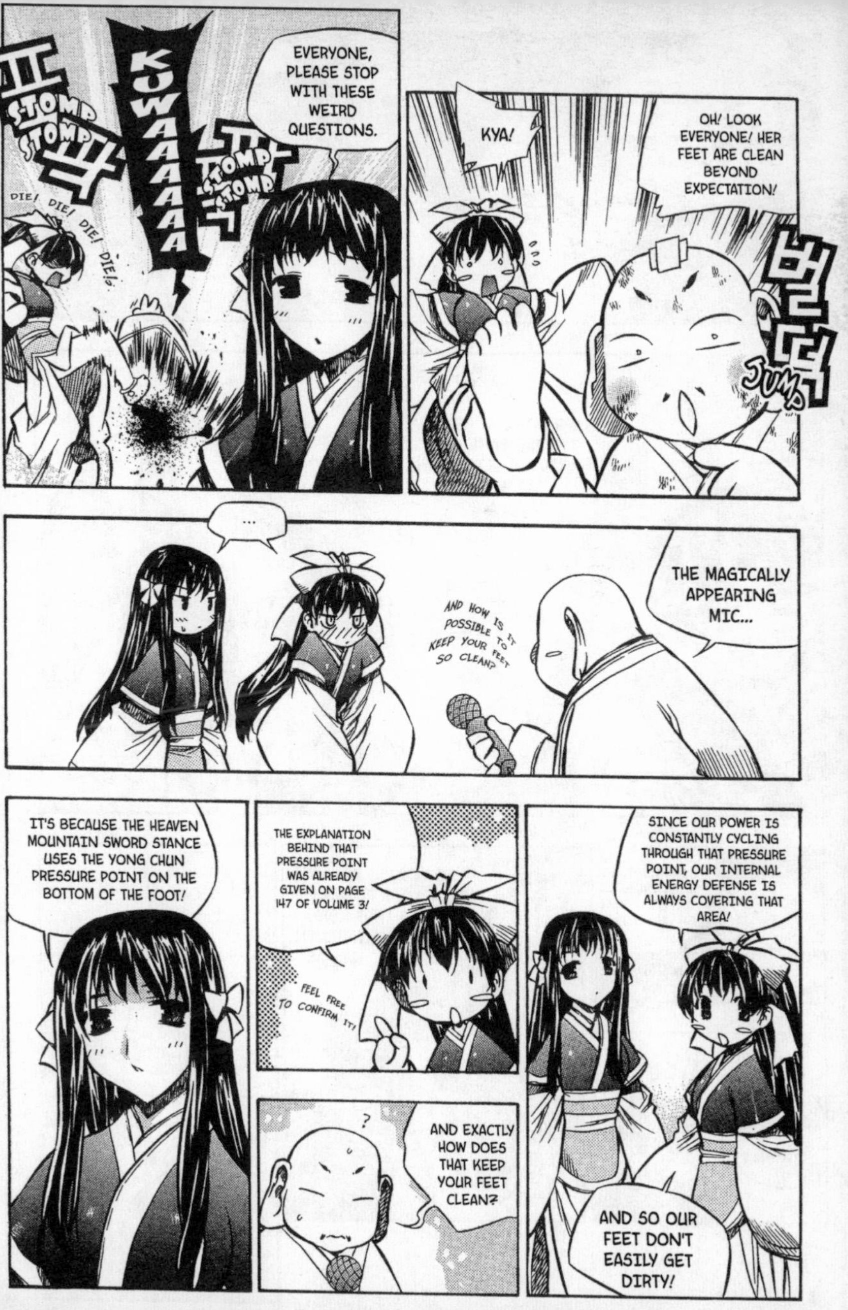
STOMP STOMP
KUWAAAAAA
STOMP STOMP
DIE! DIE! DIE! DIE!
EVERYONE, PLEASE STOP WITH THESE WEIRD QUESTIONS.
KYA!
OH! LOOK EVERYONE! HER FEET ARE CLEAN BEYOND EXPECTATION!
벌떡
JUMP
...
THE MAGICALLY APPEARING MIC...
AND HOW IS IT POSSIBLE TO KEEP YOUR FEET SO CLEAN?
IT'S BECAUSE THE HEAVEN MOUNTAIN SWORD STANCE USES THE YONG CHUN PRESSURE POINT ON THE BOTTOM OF THE FOOT!
THE EXPLANATION BEHIND THAT PRESSURE POINT WAS ALREADY GIVEN ON PAGE 147 OF VOLUME 3!
FEEL FREE TO CONFIRM IT!
?
AND EXACTLY HOW DOES THAT KEEP YOUR FEET CLEAN?
SINCE OUR POWER IS CONSTANTLY CYCLING THROUGH THAT PRESSURE POINT, OUR INTERNAL ENERGY DEFENSE IS ALWAYS COVERING THAT AREA!
AND SO OUR FEET DON'T EASILY GET DIRTY!

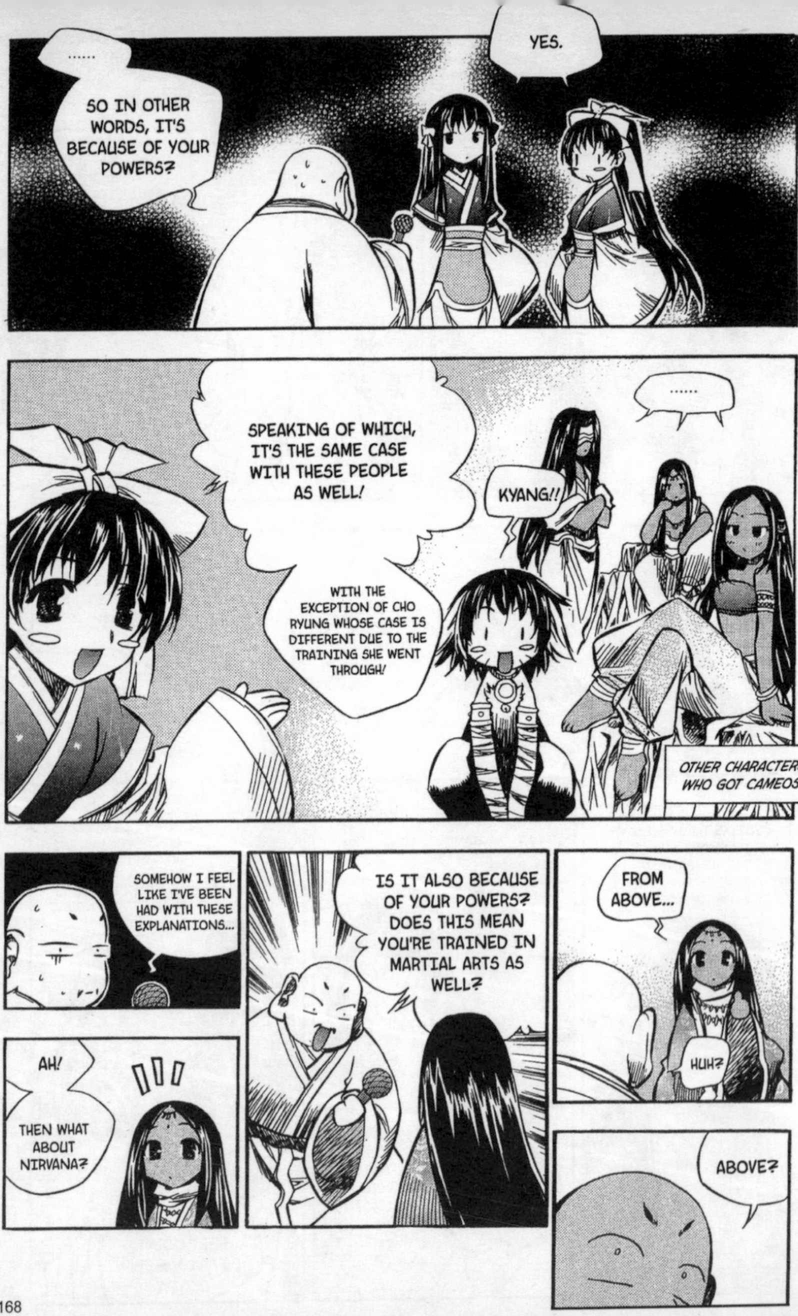
......
SO IN OTHER WORDS, IT'S BECAUSE OF YOUR POWERS?
YES.
SPEAKING OF WHICH, IT'S THE SAME CASE WITH THESE PEOPLE AS WELL!
WITH THE EXCEPTION OF CHO RYUNG WHOSE CASE IS DIFFERENT DUE TO THE TRAINING SHE WENT THROUGH!
KYANG!!
......
OTHER CHARACTERS WHO GOT CAMEOS.
SOMEHOW I FEEL LIKE I'VE BEEN HAD WITH THESE EXPLANATIONS...
AH!
THEN WHAT ABOUT NIRVANA?
IS IT ALSO BECAUSE OF YOUR POWERS? DOES THIS MEAN YOU'RE TRAINED IN MARTIAL ARTS AS WELL?
FROM ABOVE...
HUH?
ABOVE?

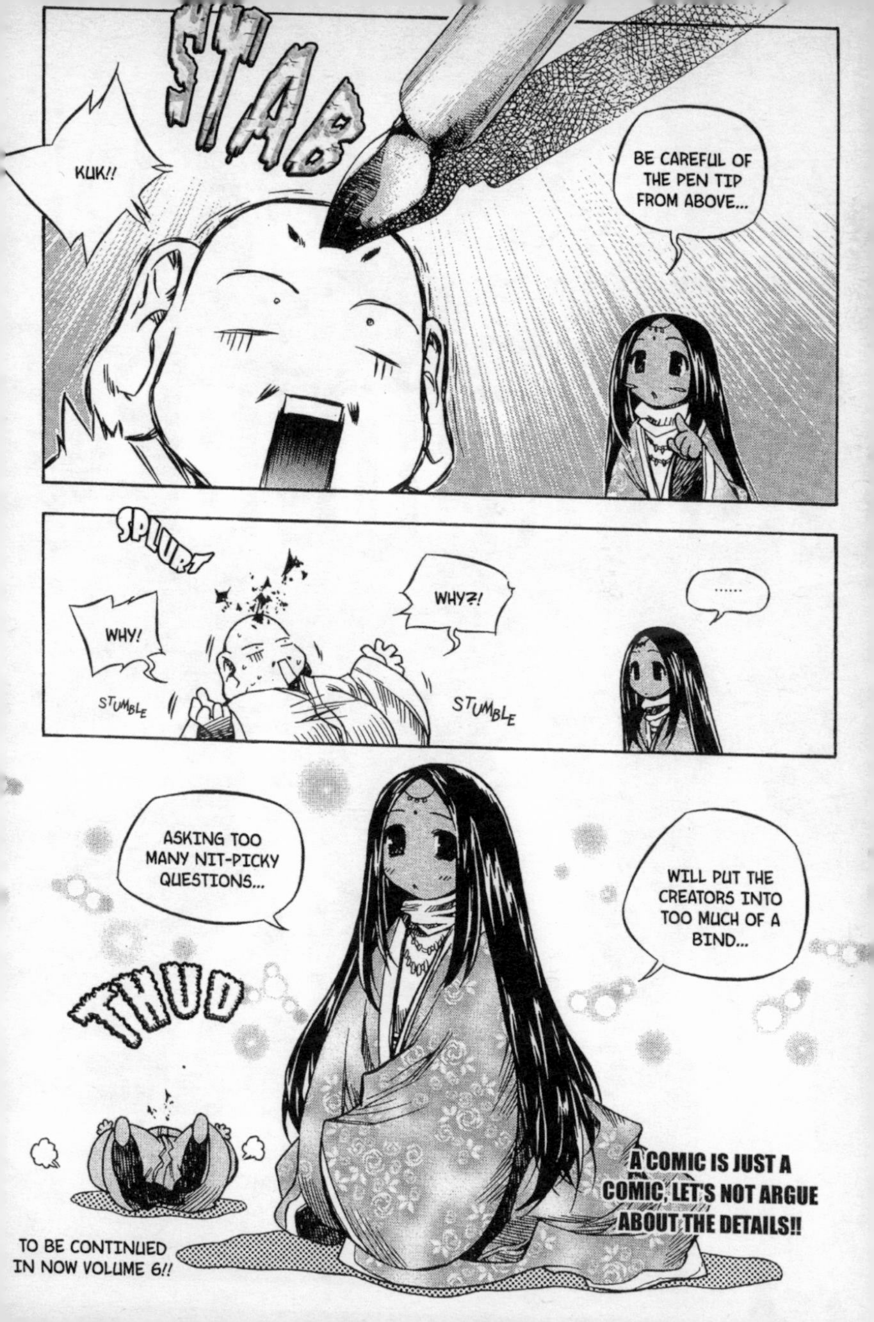
STAB
KUK!!
BE CAREFUL OF THE PEN TIP FROM ABOVE...
SPLURT
WHY?!
WHY!
......
STUMBLE
STUMBLE
ASKING TOO MANY NIT-PICKY QUESTIONS...
WILL PUT THE CREATORS INTO TOO MUCH OF A BIND...
THUD
A COMIC IS JUST A COMIC, LET'S NOT ARGUE ABOUT THE DETAILS!!
TO BE CONTINUED IN NOW VOLUME 6!!

まにいロ～ド
MANIAC ROAD

SHINSUKE KURIHASHI

©SHINSUKE KURIHASHI

Maniac Road is a story about a run down electronics store, located in the backstreets of Akihabara Japan. On its last leg, three sisters the store owners hire the resourceful Takezou. With a stroke of genius, Takezou, refashions the store into the perfect shopping ground for otaku. Business begins to boom and the adventure is on, as the sisters meet some of the strangest characters of the growing Japanese manga/anime scene. With its finger directly on the pulse of the modern-day otaku, this hip comedy will thrust you into the eclectic world of Japanese pop culture. Are you a maniac for anime and manga? Then jump on the road--the true otaku breaks for no one!

DARK EDGE

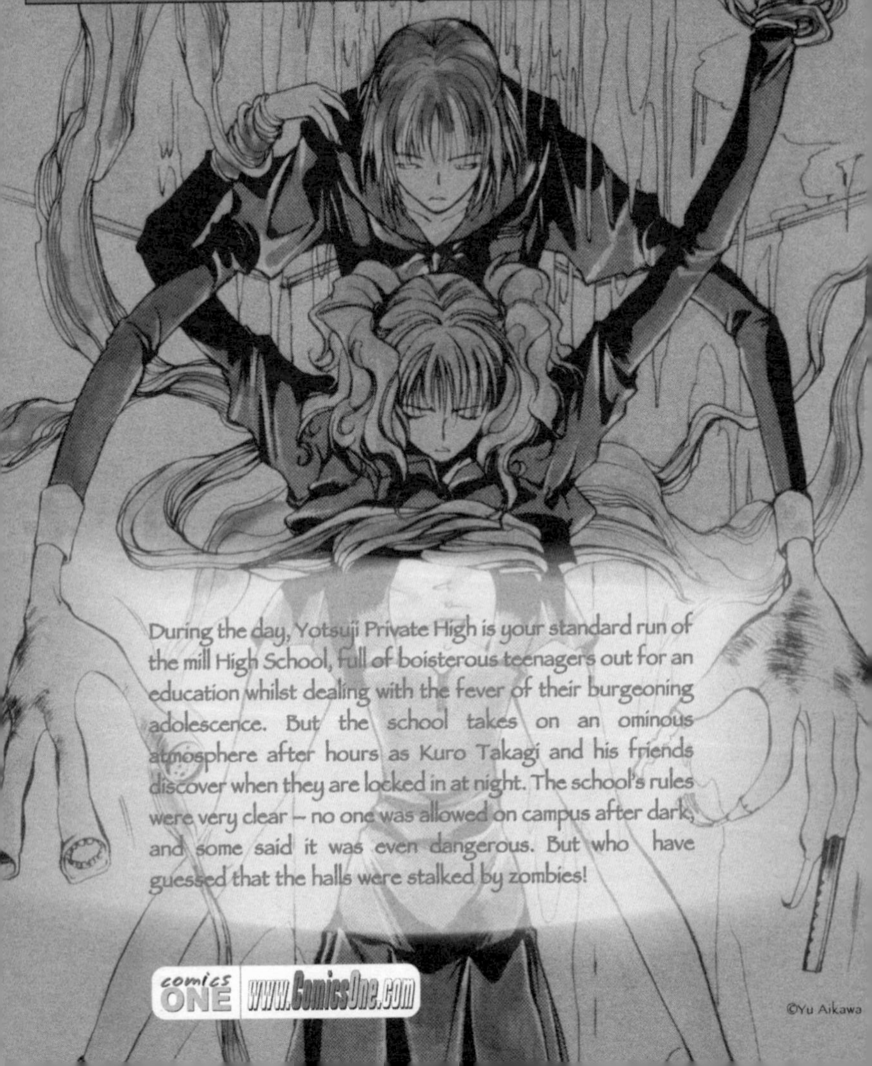
During the day, Yotsuji Private High is your standard run of the mill High School, full of boisterous teenagers out for an education whilst dealing with the fever of their burgeoning adolescence. But the school takes on an ominous atmosphere after hours as Kuro Takagi and his friends discover when they are locked in at night. The school's rules were very clear – no one was allowed on campus after dark, and some said it was even dangerous. But who have guessed that the halls were stalked by zombies!
comics ONE
www.ComicsOne.com
©Yu Aikawa

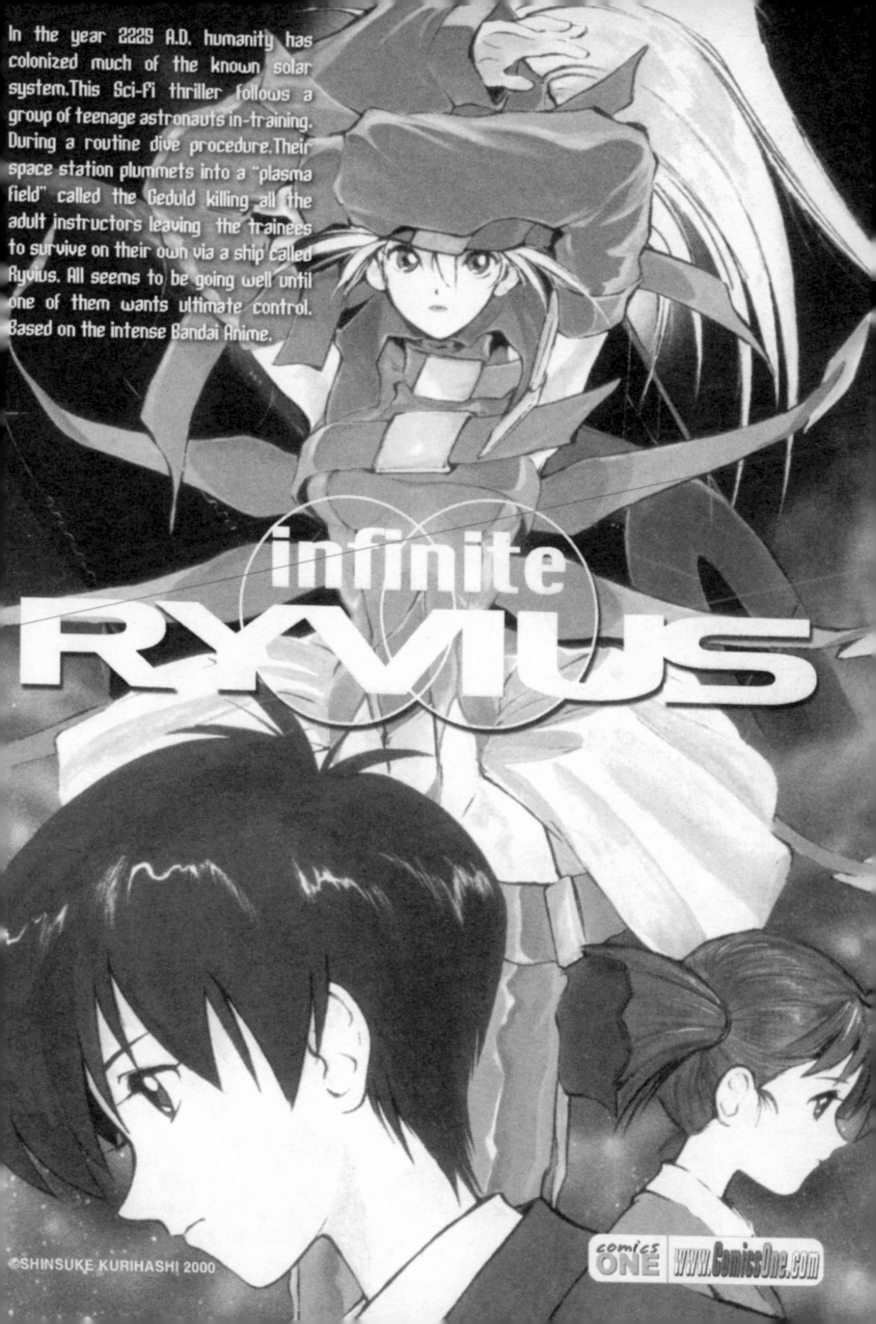
In the year 2225 A.D. humanity has colonized much of the known solar system.This Sci-fi thriller follows a group of teenage astronauts in-training. During a routine dive procedure.Their space station plummets into a "plasma field" called the Geduld killing all the adult instructors leaving the trainees to survive on their own via a ship called Ryvius. All seems to be going well until one of them wants ultimate control. Based on the intense Bandai Anime.
infinite
RYVIUS
©SHINSUKE KURIHASHI 2000
comics ONE
www.ComicsOne.com

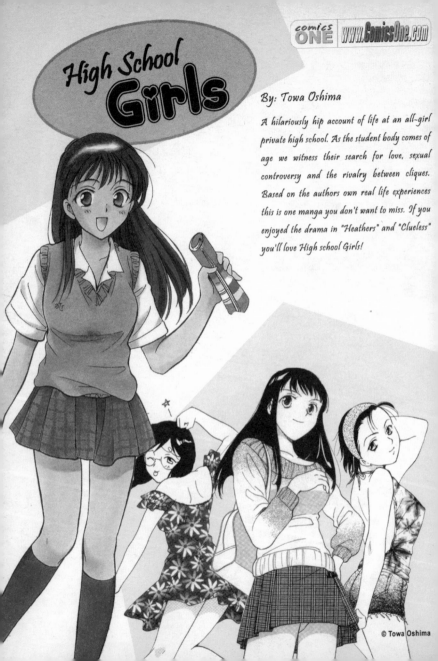

High School Girls

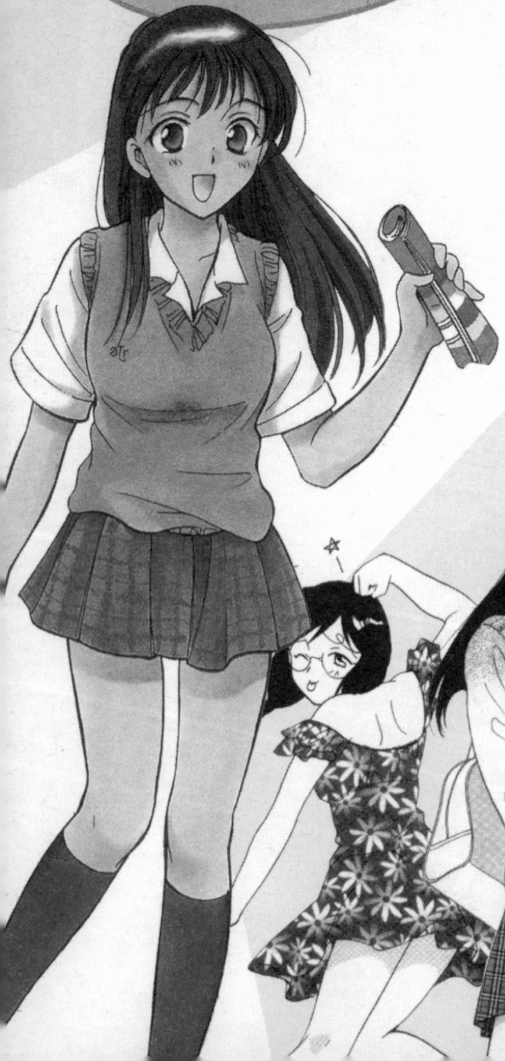

By: Towa Oshima

A hilariously hip account of life at an all-girl private high school. As the student body comes of age we witness their search for love, sexual controversy and the rivalry between cliques. Based on the authors own real life experiences this is one manga you don't want to miss. If you enjoyed the drama in "Heathers" and "Clueless" you'll love High school Girls!

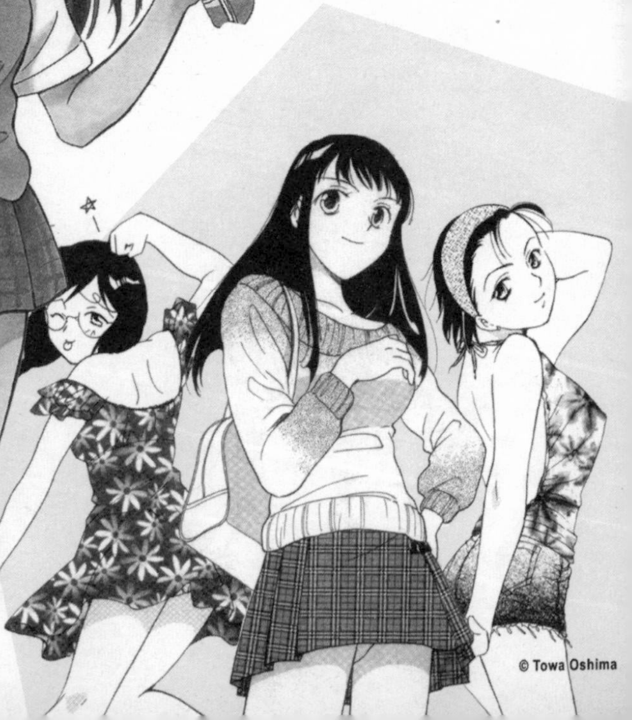

TOP SPEED
UNDERGROUND

MOST OF THE FOUR KINGS HAVE SINCE FALLEN
FROM GRACE, AND NOW THE STREETS ARE RULED
BY THE 13 GHOSTS! BUT WHEN A LEGENDARY
RACING GOD COMES OUT OF RETIREMENT TO
RECRUIT SOME NEW TALENT, THE DIE IS CAST, AND
THE WHEEL IS SET IN MOTION FOR SOME MAJOR
COMPETIOTION WITH THE 13 TO RULE THE STREET
OF ASIA! SO IT COMES THAT THE CHILDREN OF
RASCING ICONS TIEN REN AND ICHIRO SAKAZAKI
STEP FORWARD TO PROVE THEIR WORTH AS
CHAMPIONS! BUT WILL THE HEIRS TO STREET
THUNDER RECEIVE THEIR CROWNS, OR WILL
PREVIOUS KINGS FUMA AND THEIR SEER INTERVENE
WITH A PLAN OF THEIR OWN?

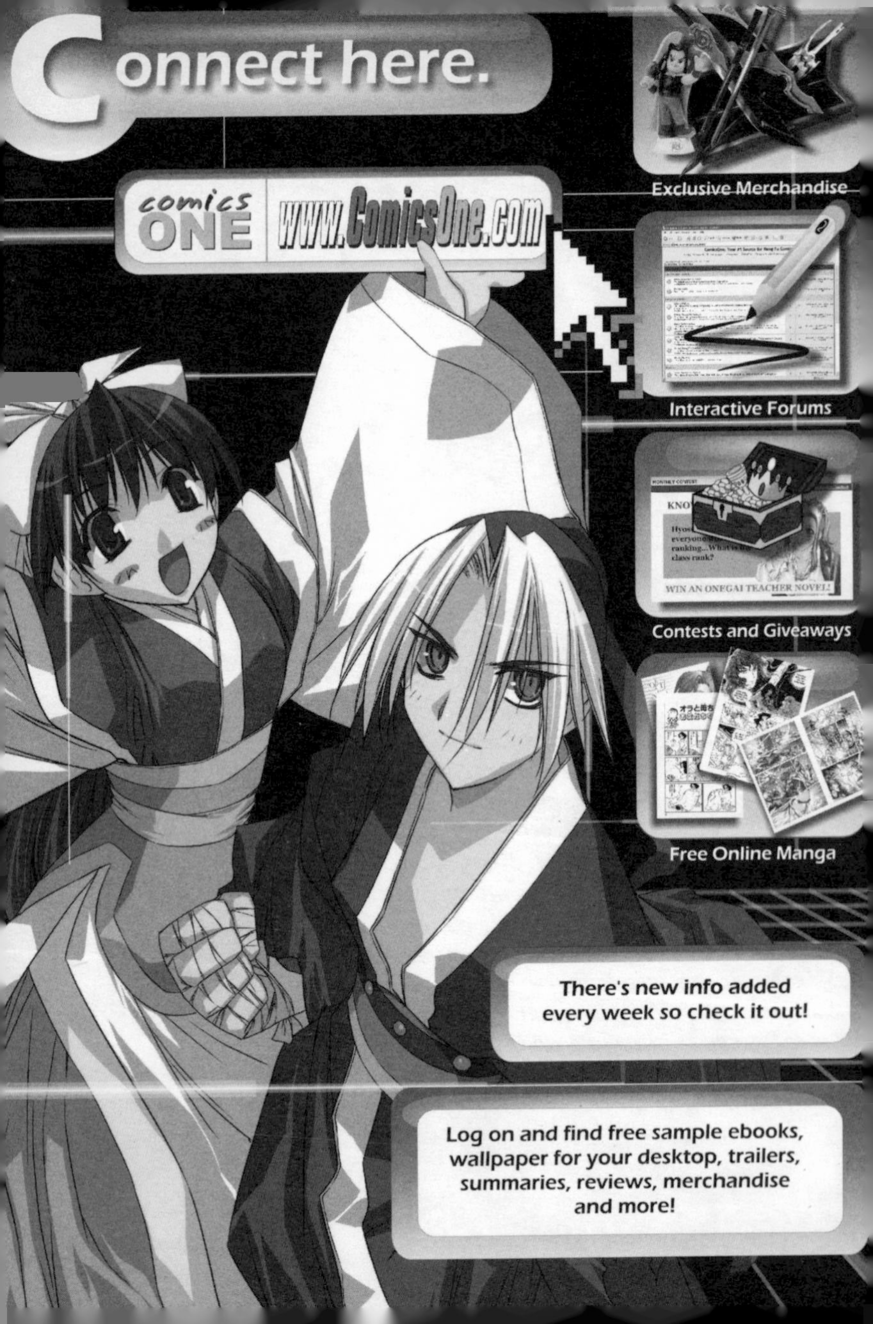